Chibi Vampire

Airmail

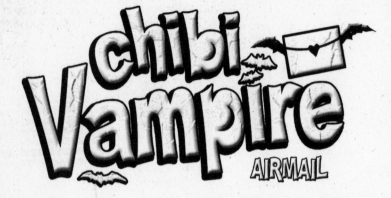

Created by
Yuna Kagesaki

TOKYOPOP®

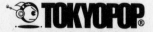

HAMBURG // LONDON // LOS ANGELES // TOKYO

Chibi Vampire Airmail
Created by Yuna Kagesaki

Translation - Katherine Schilling
English Adaptation - Katherine Schilling
Copy Editor - Joseph Heller
Retouch and Lettering - Star Print Brokers
Production Artist - Rui Kyo
Graphic Designer - Al-Insan Lashley

Editor - Cindy Suzuki
Print Production Manager - Lucas Rivera
Managing Editor - Vy Nguyen
Senior Designer - Louis Csontos
Art Director - Al-Insan Lashley
Director of Sales and Manufacturing - Allyson De Simone
Associate Publisher - Marco F. Pavia
President and C.O.O. - John Parker
C.E.O. and Chief Creative Officer - Stu Levy

A **TOKYOPOP** Manga

TOKYOPOP and are trademarks or registered trademarks of TOKYOPOP Inc.

TOKYOPOP Inc.
5900 Wilshire Blvd. Suite 2000
Los Angeles, CA 90036

E-mail: info@TOKYOPOP.com
Come visit us online at www.TOKYOPOP.com

KARIN airmail KAGESAKI YUNA TANPENSHU
© 2009 YUNA KAGESAKI First published in Japan in
2009 by FUJIMISHOBO CO., LTD., Tokyo. English translation
rights arranged with KADOKAWA SHOTEN Publishing Co.,
Ltd., Tokyo through TUTTLE-MORI AGENCY, INC., Tokyo.
English text copyright © 2010 TOKYOPOP Inc.

ISBN: 978-1-4278-2551-3

First TOKYOPOP printing: September 2010
10 9 8 7 6 5 4 3 2 1
Printed in the USA

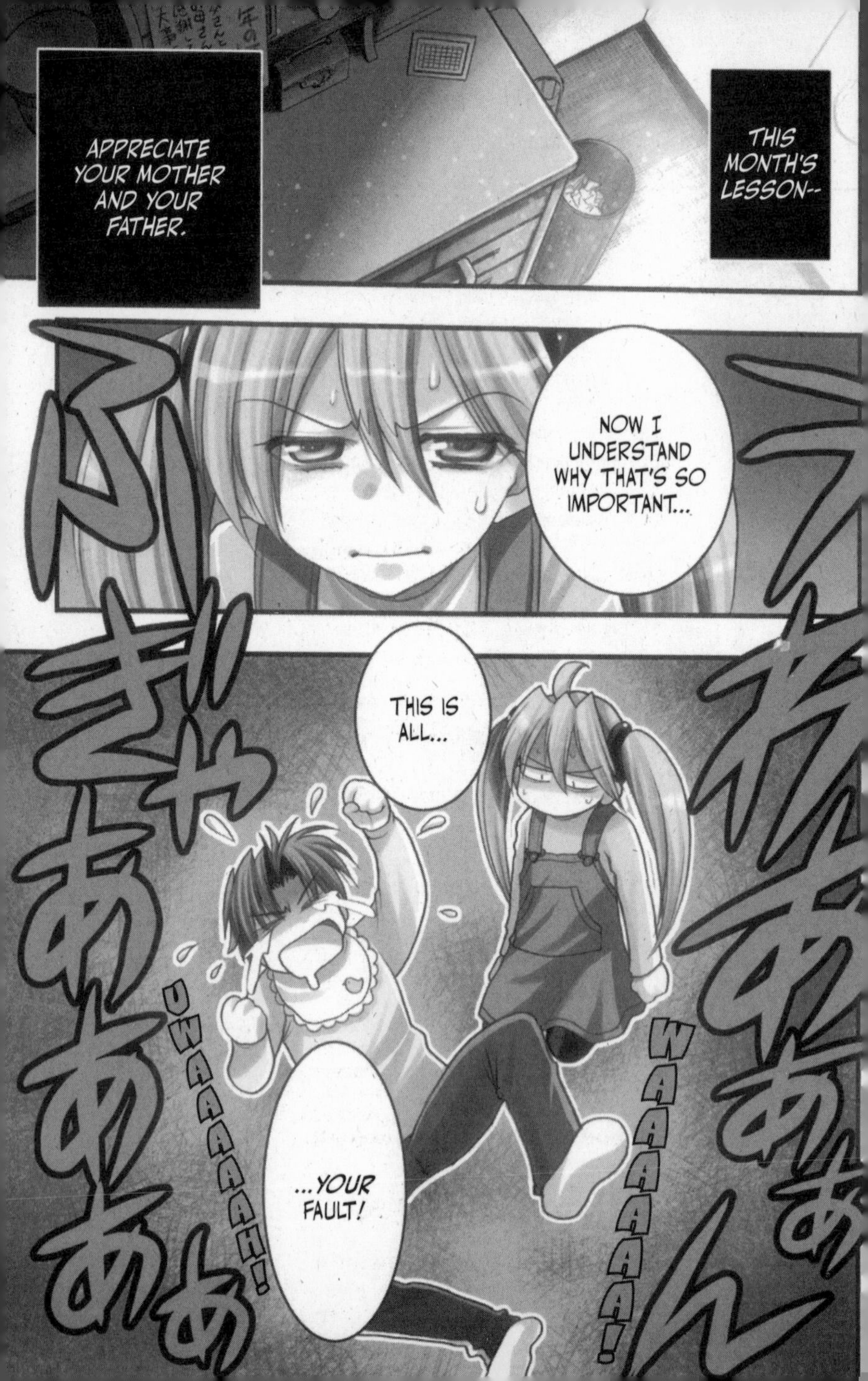
THIS MONTH'S LESSON--
APPRECIATE YOUR MOTHER AND YOUR FATHER.
NOW I UNDERSTAND WHY THAT'S SO IMPORTANT...
WAAAAAAAAAA!
THIS IS ALL...
...YOUR FAULT!
UWAAAAAAAAH!

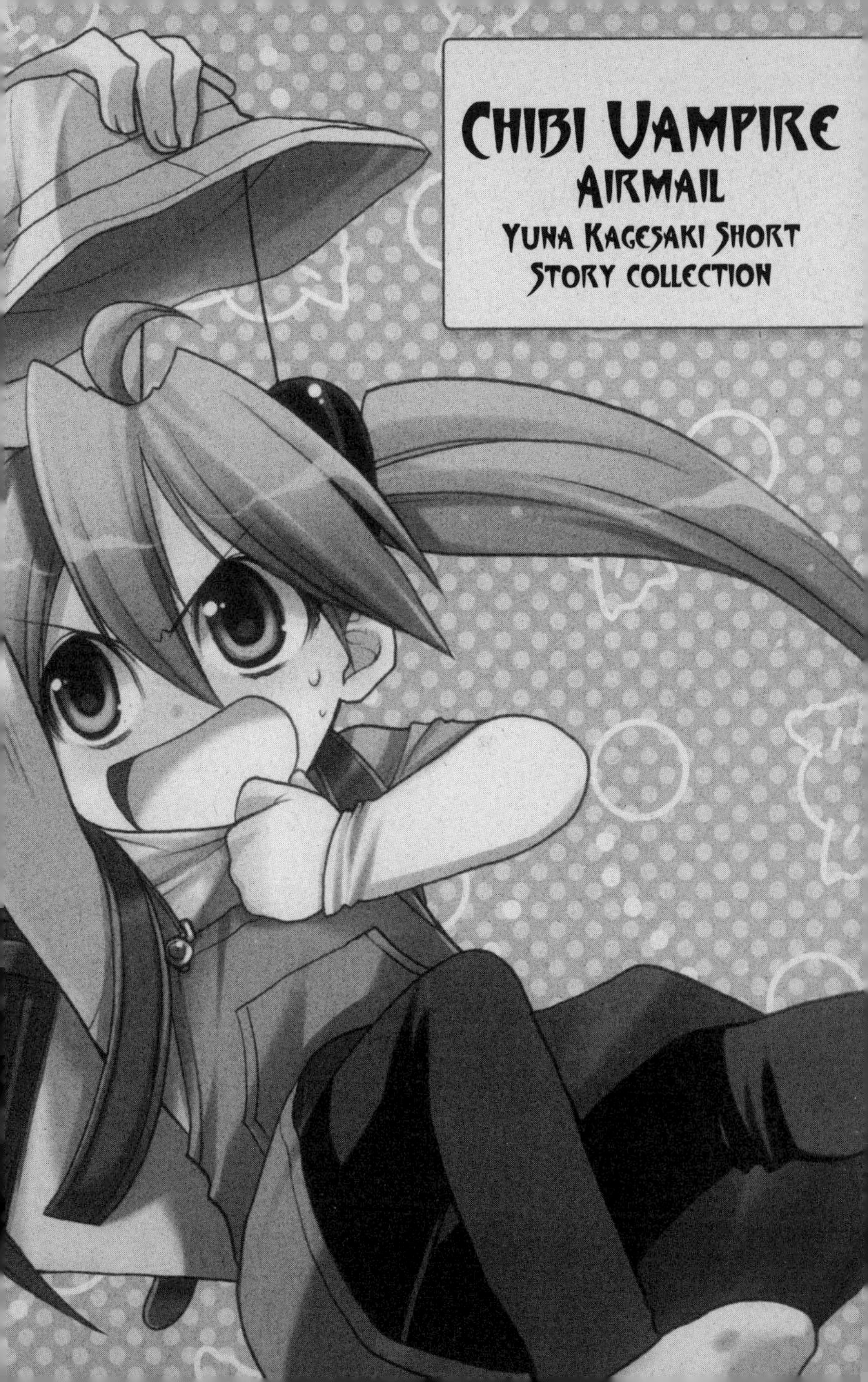
CHIBI VAMPIRE
AIRMAIL
YUNA KAGESAKI SHORT
STORY COLLECTION

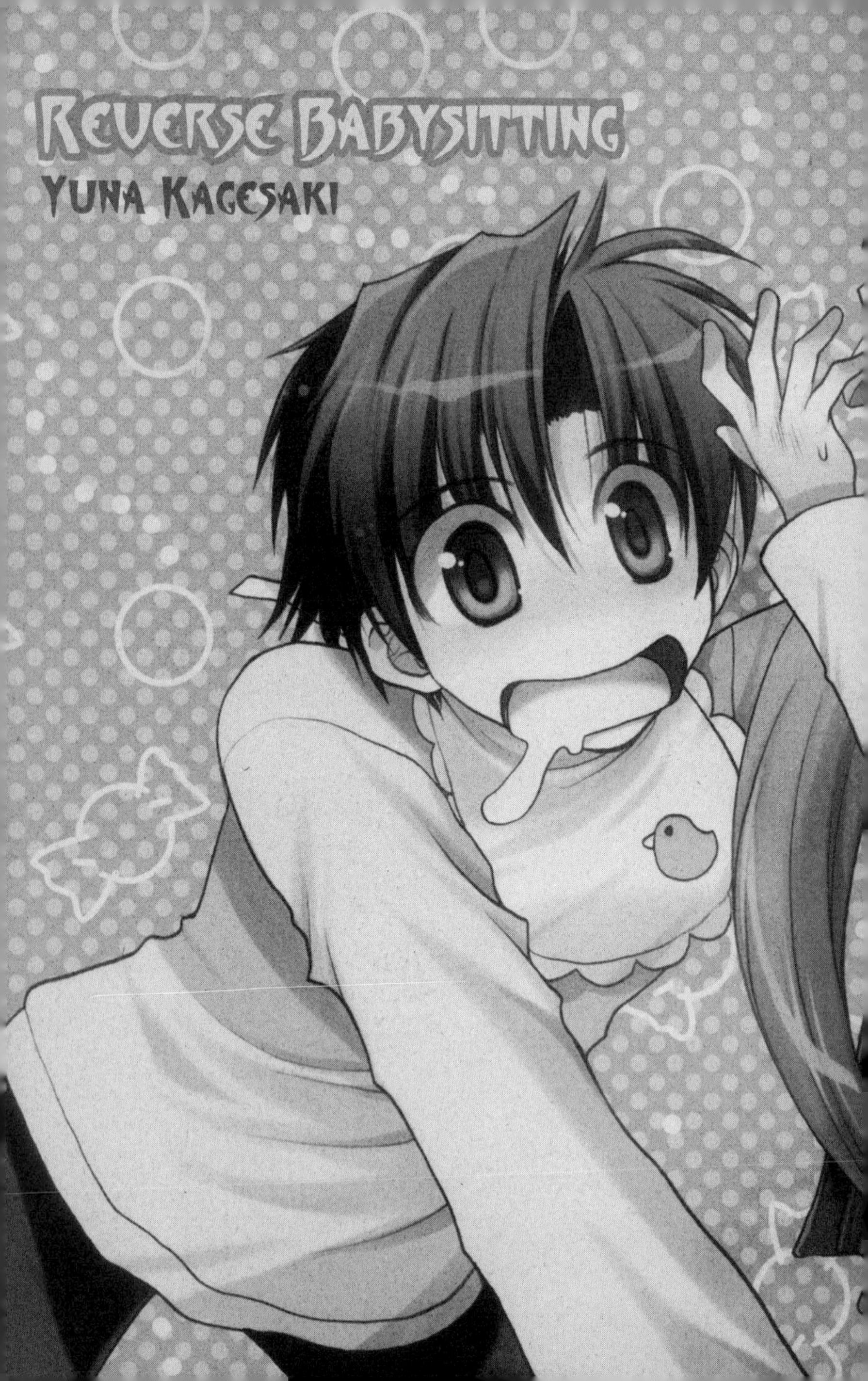
Reverse Babysitting
Yuna Kagesaki

CHIBI VAMPIRE AIRMAIL
YUNA KAGESAKI SHORT STORY COLLECTION

CONTENTS

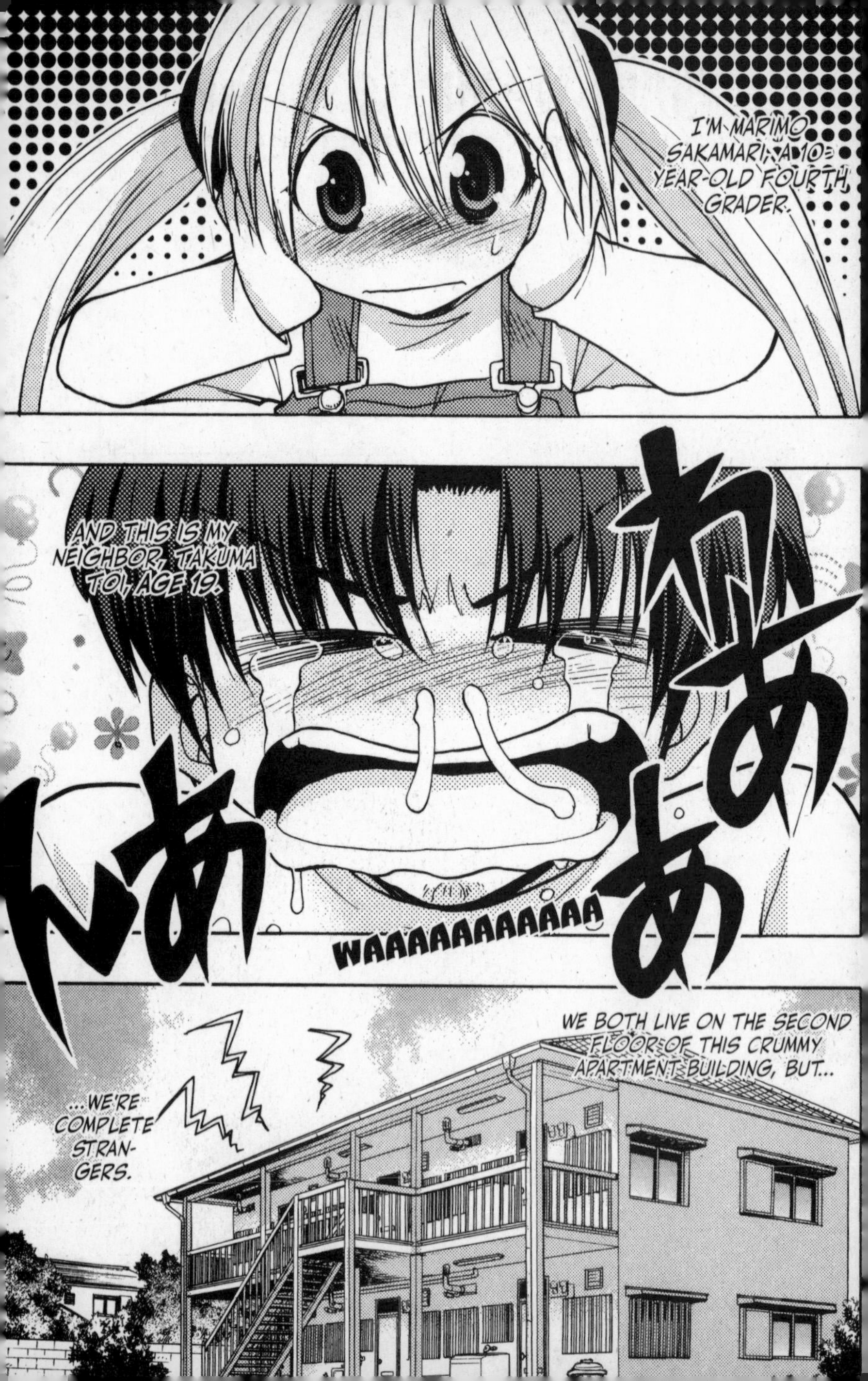
I'M MARIMO SAKAMARI, A 10-YEAR-OLD FOURTH GRADER.
AND THIS IS MY NEIGHBOR, TAKUMA TOI, AGE 19.
わあああ
WAAAAAAAAAA
WE BOTH LIVE ON THE SECOND FLOOR OF THIS CRUMMY APARTMENT BUILDING, BUT...
...WE'RE COMPLETE STRANGERS.

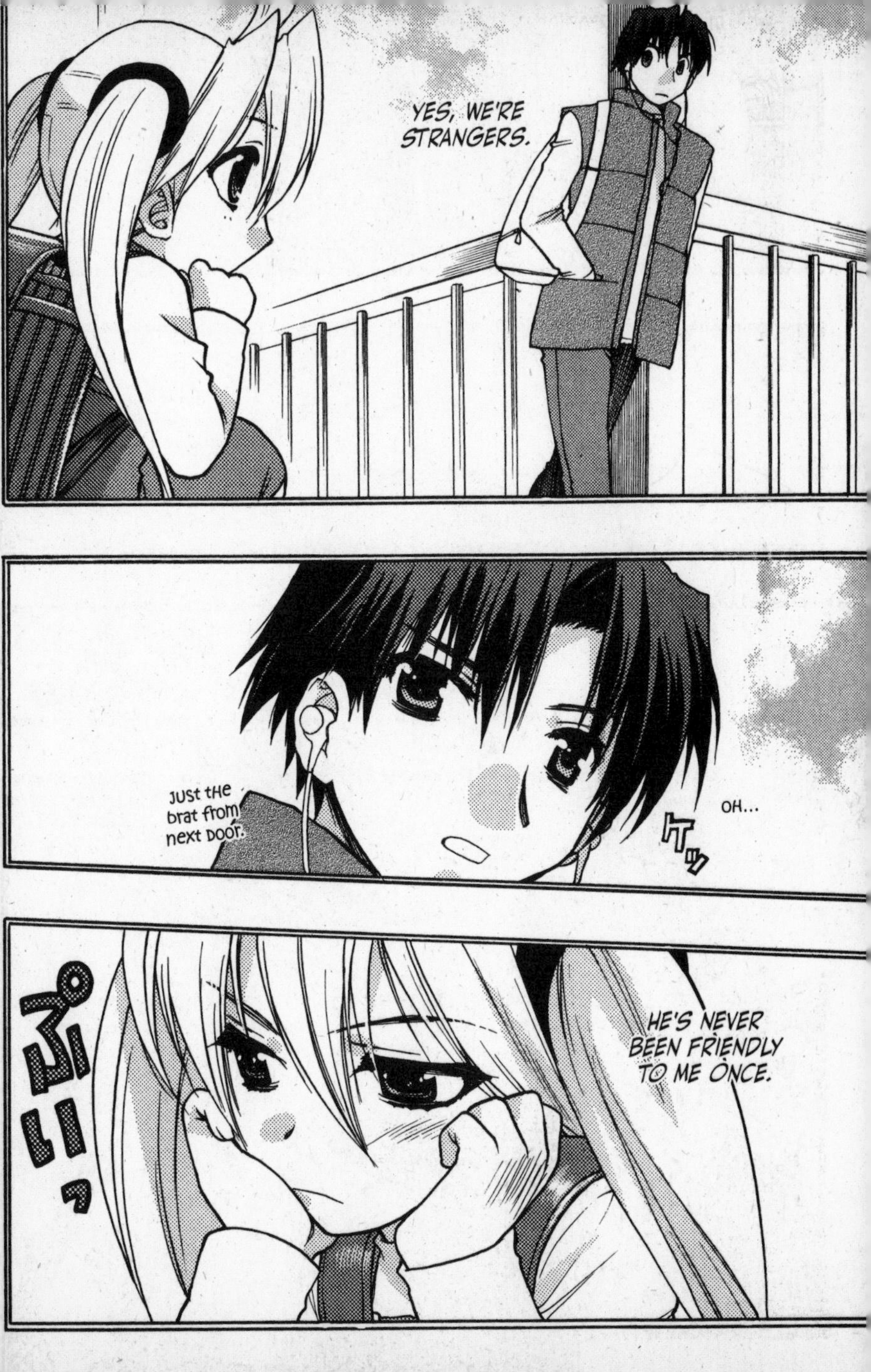
YES, WE'RE STRANGERS.
OH...
ケッ
JUST tHE brat from next Door.
HE'S NEVER BEEN FRIENDLY TO ME ONCE.
ぷいっ

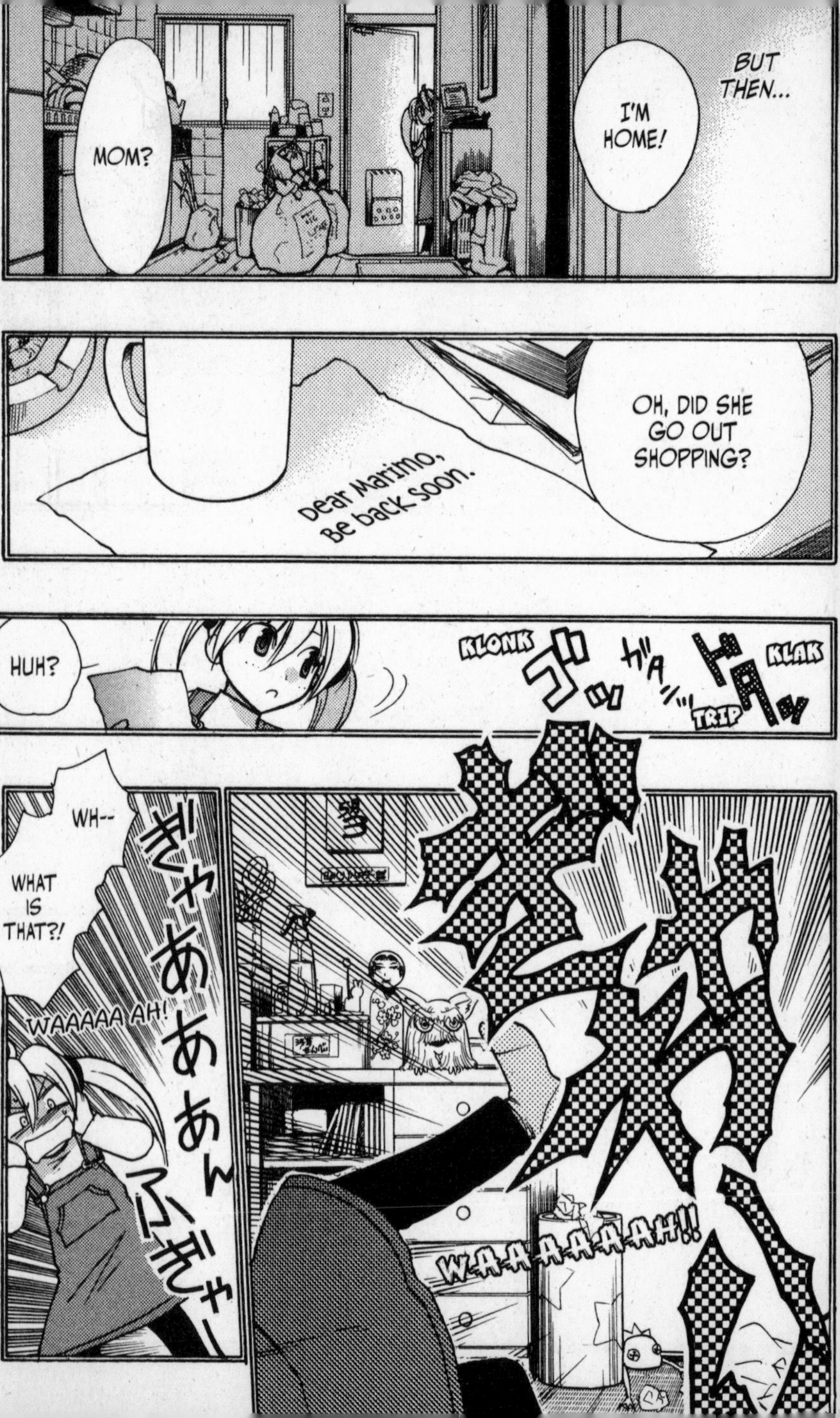

BUT THEN...
I'M HOME!
MOM?
OH, DID SHE GO OUT SHOPPING?
Dear Marimo, Be back soon.
KLAK
TRIP
KLONK
HUH?
WAAAAAAAAH!!
WH--
WHAT IS THAT?!
WAAAAA AH!

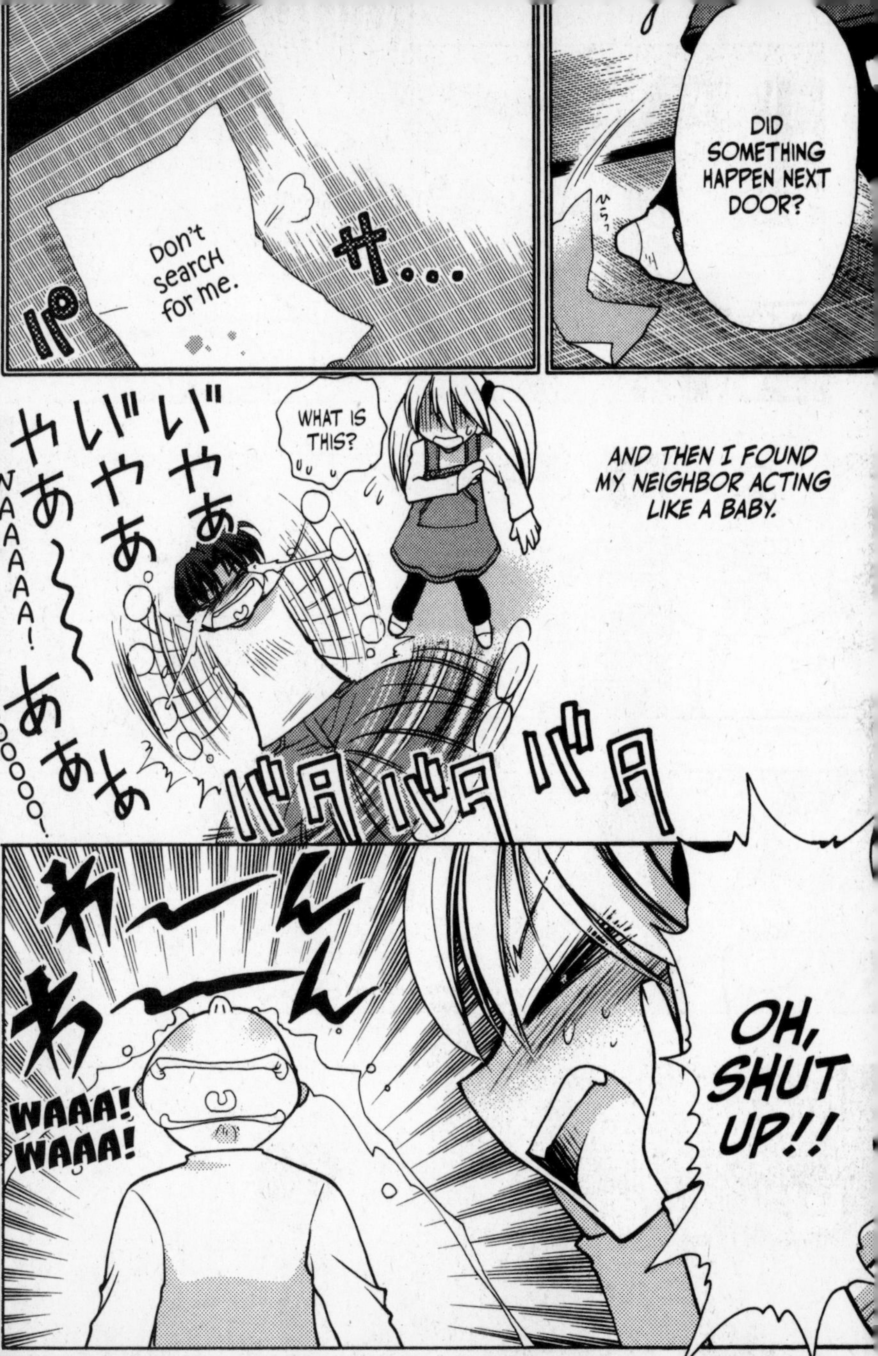
DID SOMETHING HAPPEN NEXT DOOR?
ひらっ
Don't search for me.
パ
サ...
AND THEN I FOUND MY NEIGHBOR ACTING LIKE A BABY.
WHAT IS THIS?
WAAAAAA!
NOOOOOO!
バタバタバタ
OH, SHUT UP!!
わーん
わーん
WAAA! WAAA!

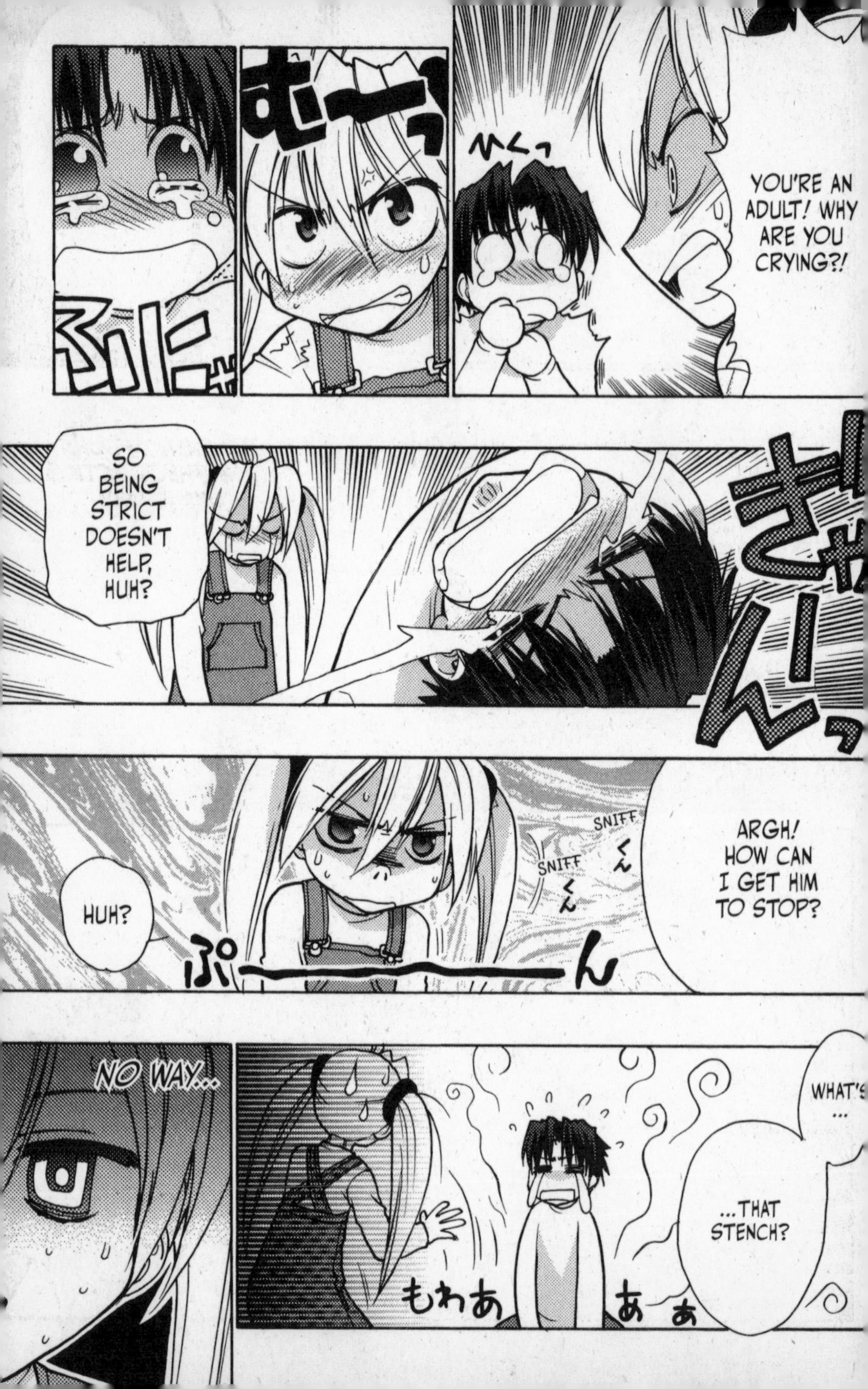

YOU'RE AN ADULT! WHY ARE YOU CRYING?!
ひくっ
むーっ
ふにゃ
きゃーんっ
SO BEING STRICT DOESN'T HELP, HUH?
ARGH! HOW CAN I GET HIM TO STOP?
SNIFF くん
SNIFF くん
ぷーーん
HUH?
WHAT'S ...
...THAT STENCH?
もわあ あぁ
NO WAY...

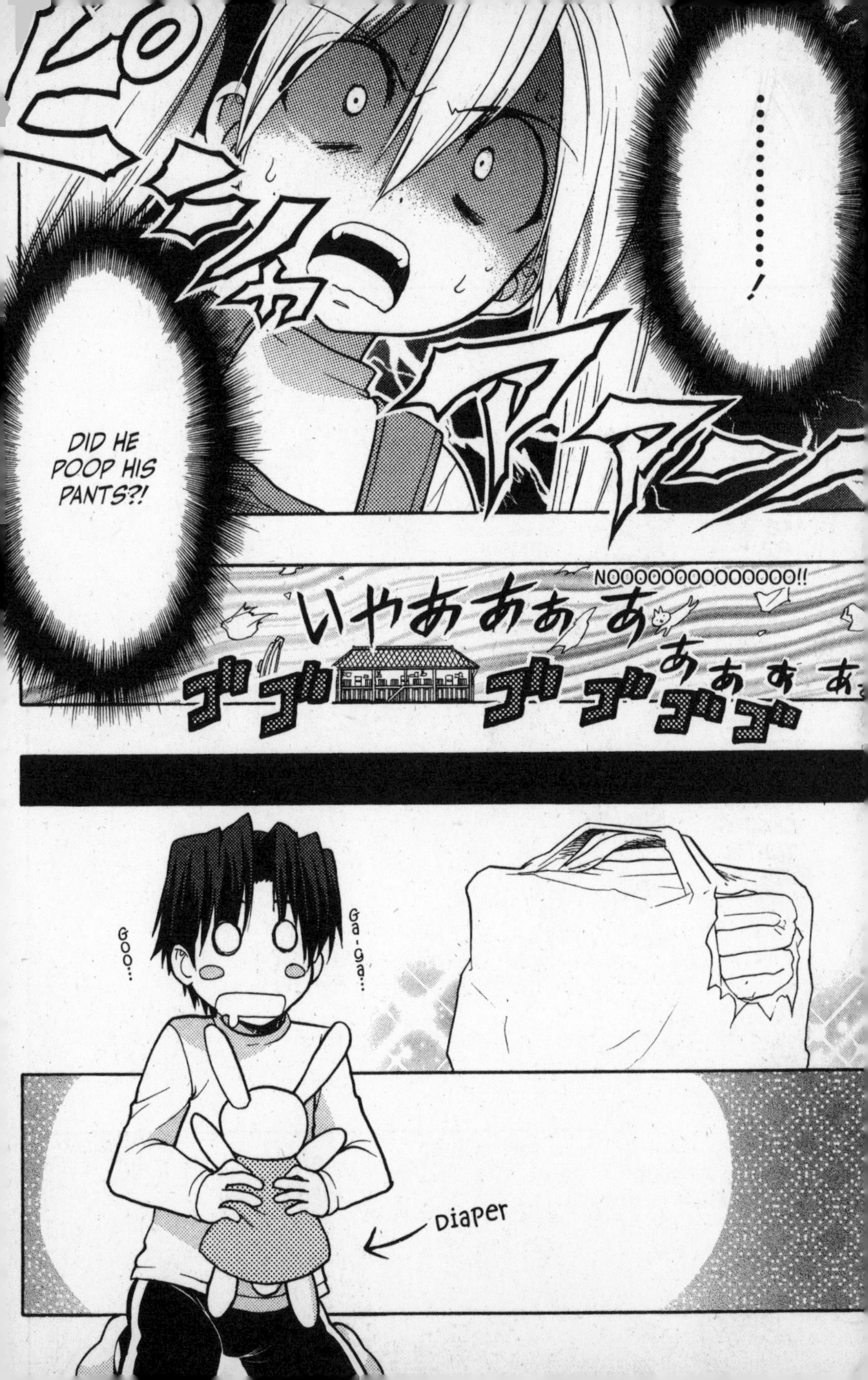
......!
DID HE POOP HIS PANTS?!
NOOOOOOOOOOOOOO!!
いやあああああああああ
ゴゴゴゴゴゴ
Ga-ga...
Goo...
Diaper

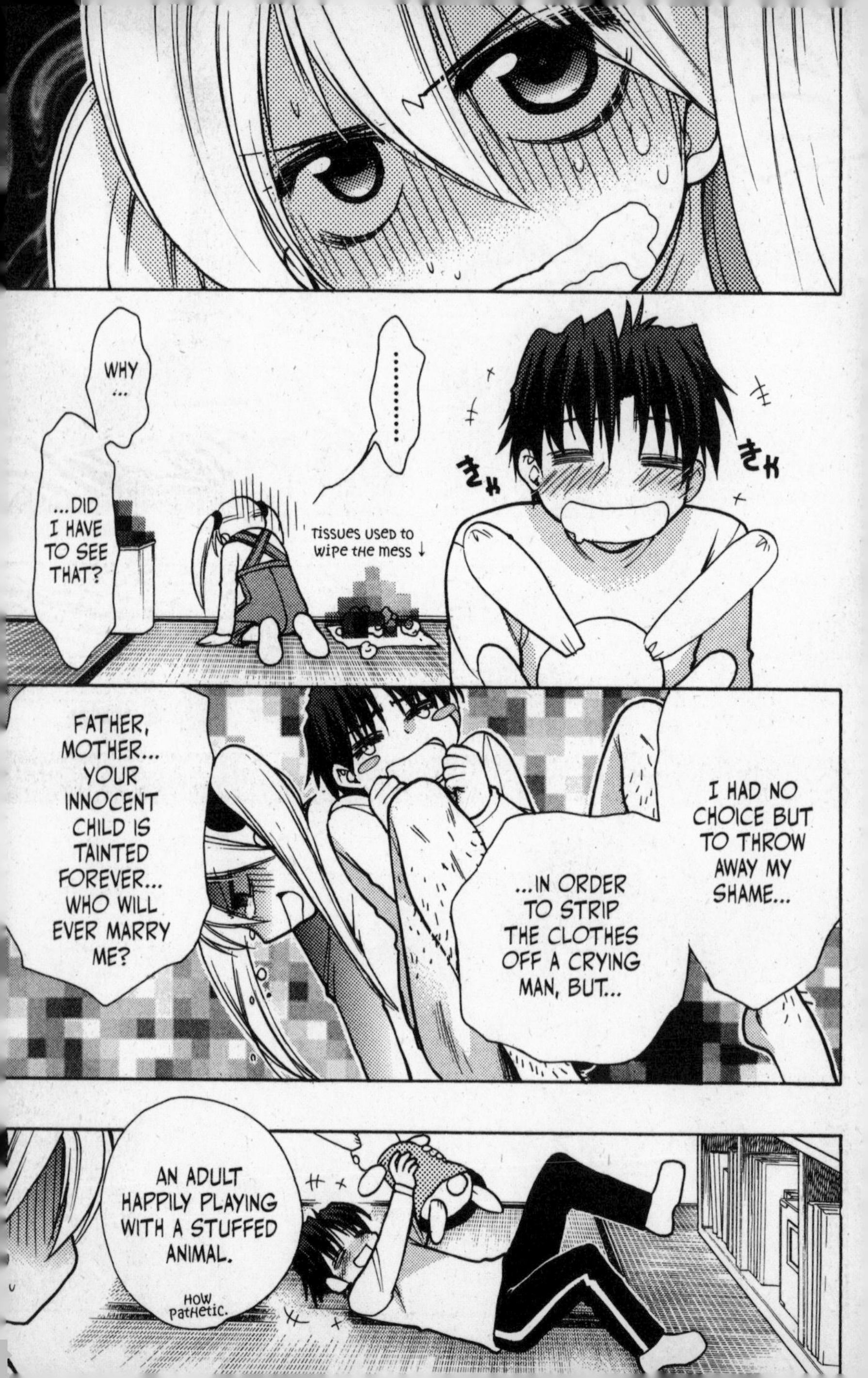
......
TISSUES USED TO WIPE THE MESS ↓
WHY...
...DID I HAVE TO SEE THAT?
I HAD NO CHOICE BUT TO THROW AWAY MY SHAME...
...IN ORDER TO STRIP THE CLOTHES OFF A CRYING MAN, BUT...
FATHER, MOTHER... YOUR INNOCENT CHILD IS TAINTED FOREVER... WHO WILL EVER MARRY ME?
AN ADULT HAPPILY PLAYING WITH A STUFFED ANIMAL.
HOW PATHETIC.

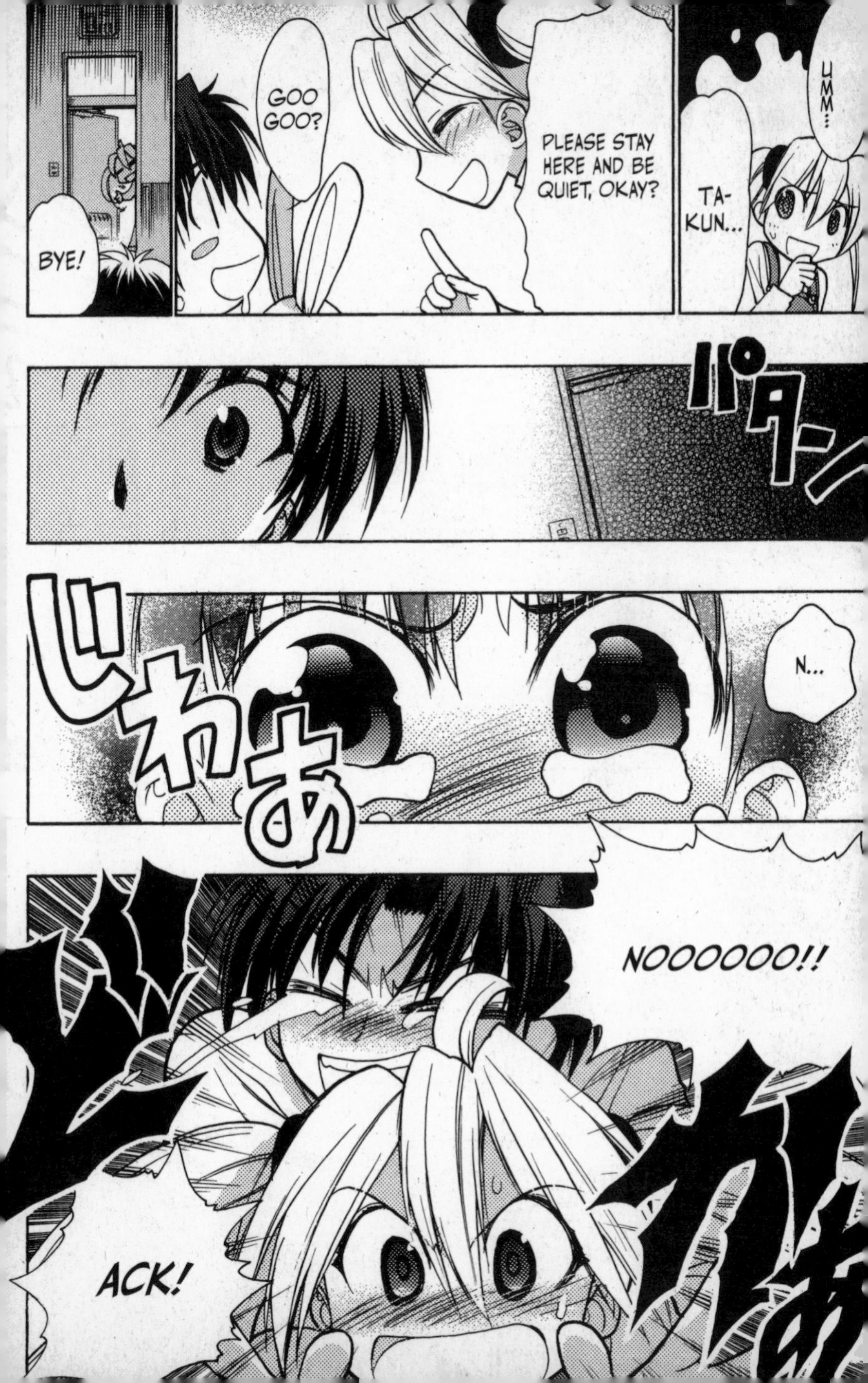
UMM...
TA-KUN...
PLEASE STAY HERE AND BE QUIET, OKAY?
GOO GOO?
BYE!
パターン
N...
じわあ
NOOOOOO!!
ACK!

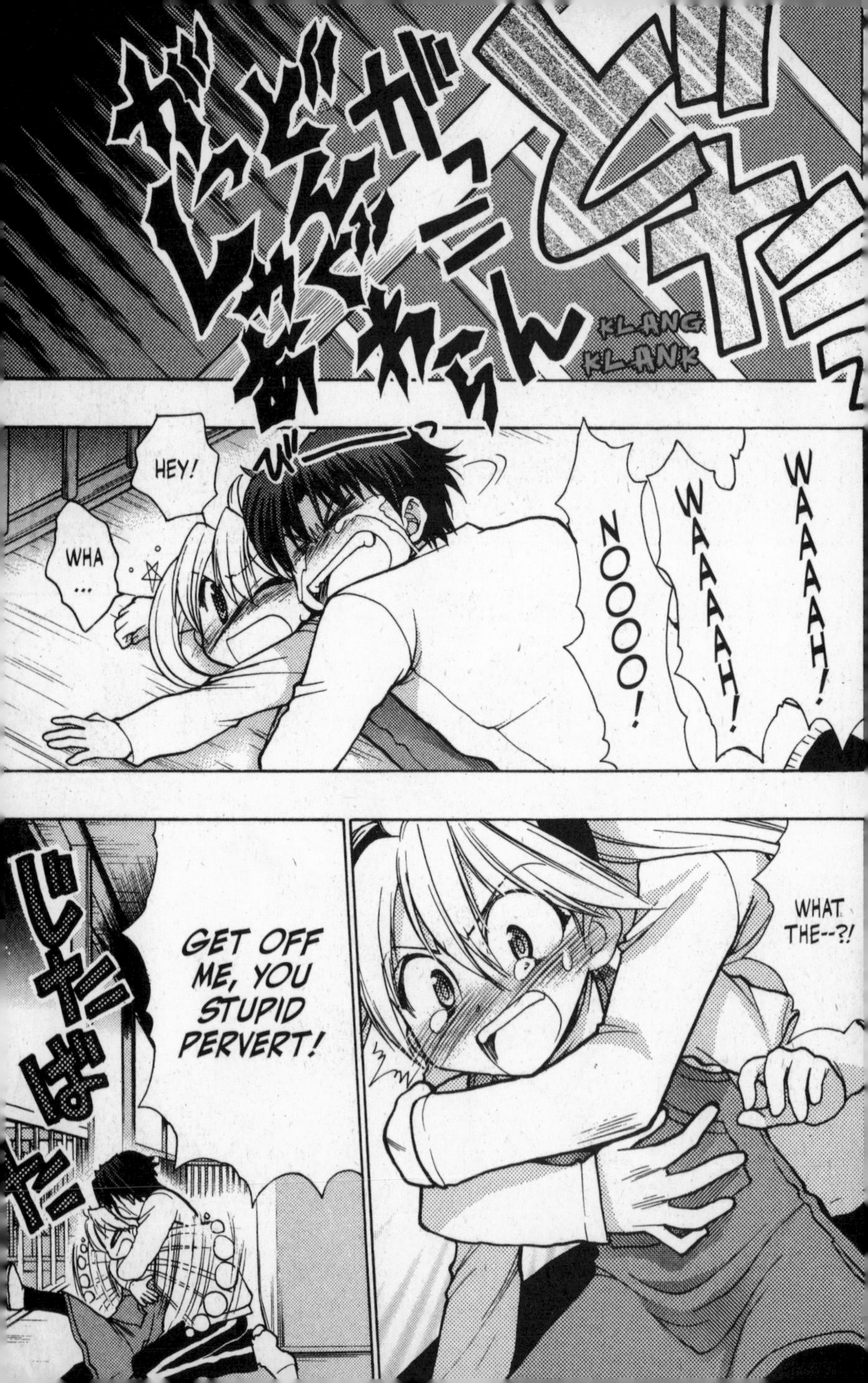
KLANG
KLANK
WAAAAAH!
WAAAAAH!
NOOOOO!
HEY!
WHA...
WHAT THE--?!
GET OFF ME, YOU STUPID PERVERT!

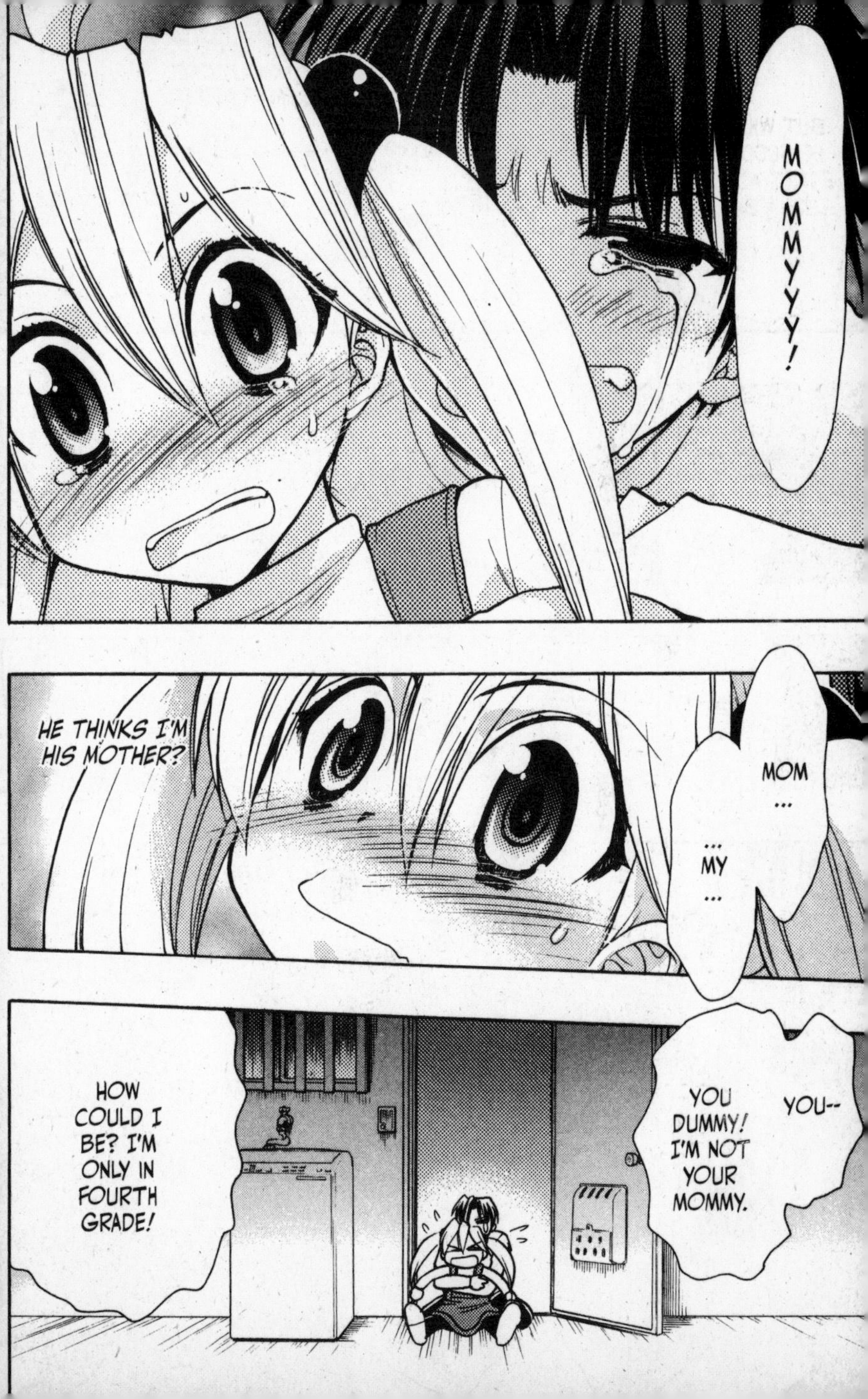
MOMMYYY!
MOM ...
... MY ...
HE THINKS I'M HIS MOTHER?
YOU--
YOU DUMMY! I'M NOT YOUR MOMMY.
HOW COULD I BE? I'M ONLY IN FOURTH GRADE!

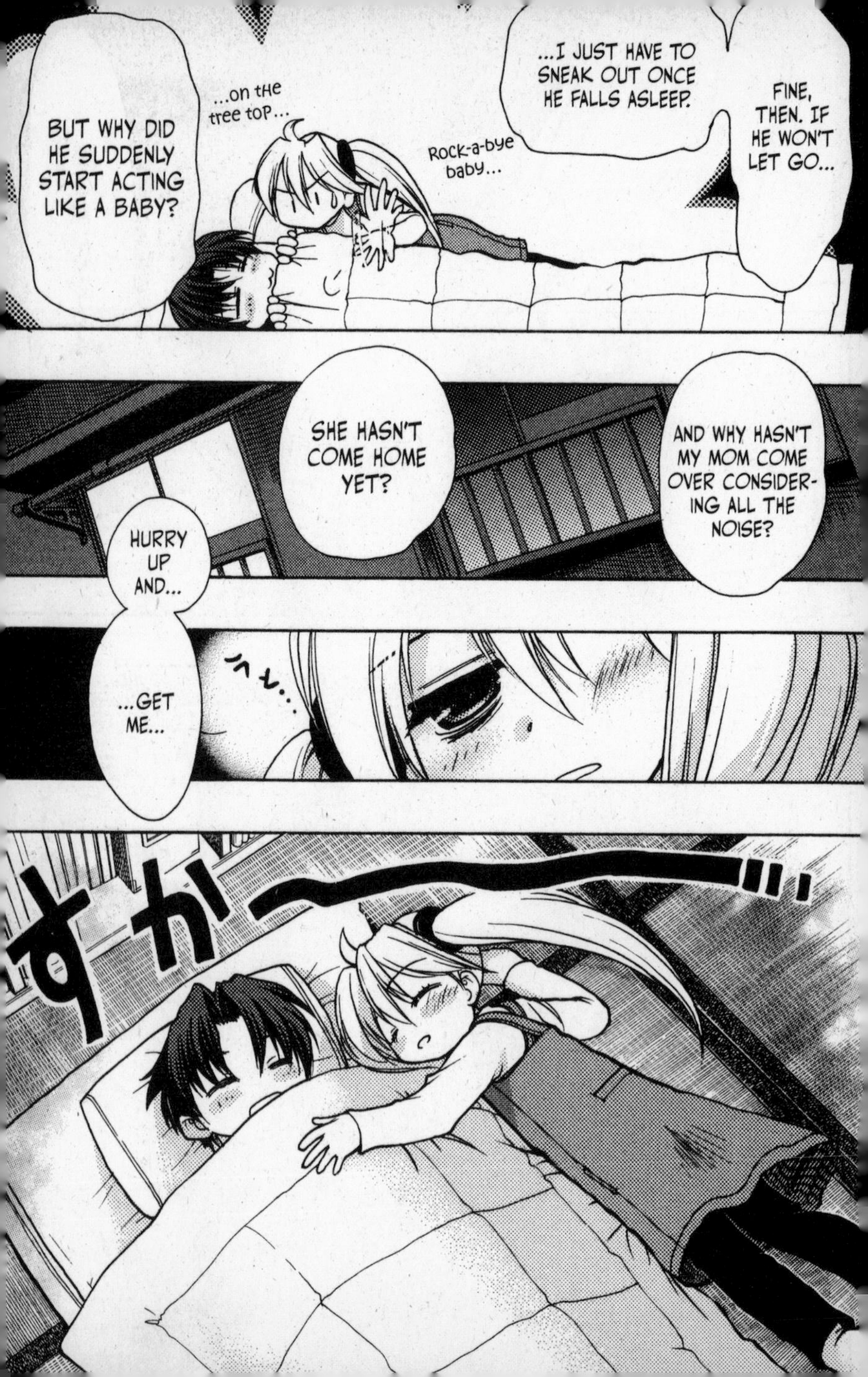
FINE, THEN. IF HE WON'T LET GO...
...I JUST HAVE TO SNEAK OUT ONCE HE FALLS ASLEEP.
Rock-a-bye baby...
...on the tree top...
BUT WHY DID HE SUDDENLY START ACTING LIKE A BABY?
AND WHY HASN'T MY MOM COME OVER CONSIDERING ALL THE NOISE?
SHE HASN'T COME HOME YET?
HURRY UP AND...
...GET ME...
すかー

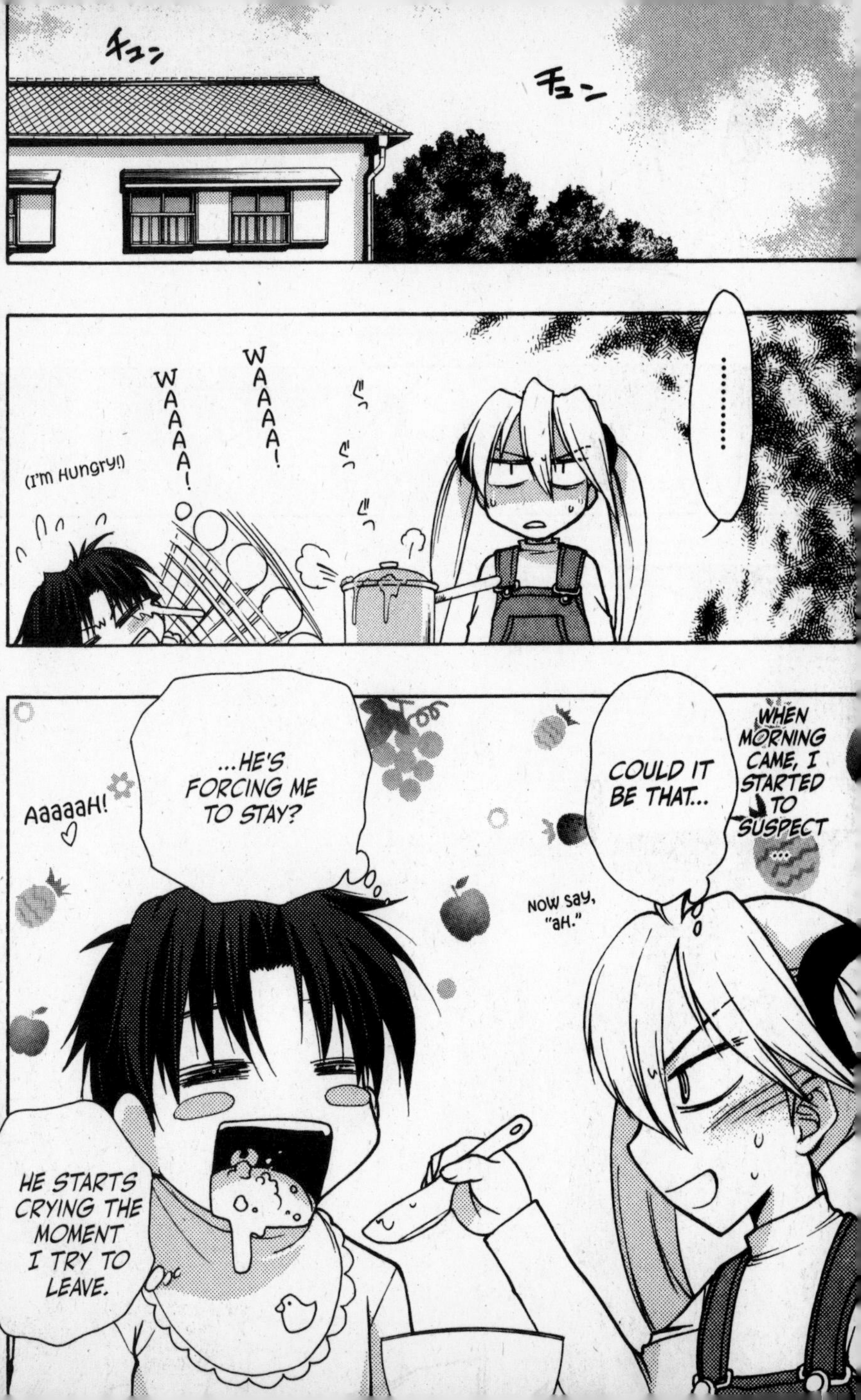
チュン
チュン
......
WAAAA!
WAAAA!
ぐっ
ぐっ
ぐっ
(I'm Hungry!)
WHEN MORNING CAME, I STARTED TO SUSPECT
COULD IT BE THAT...
...HE'S FORCING ME TO STAY?
NOW SAY, "AH."
AaaaaH!
HE STARTS CRYING THE MOMENT I TRY TO LEAVE.

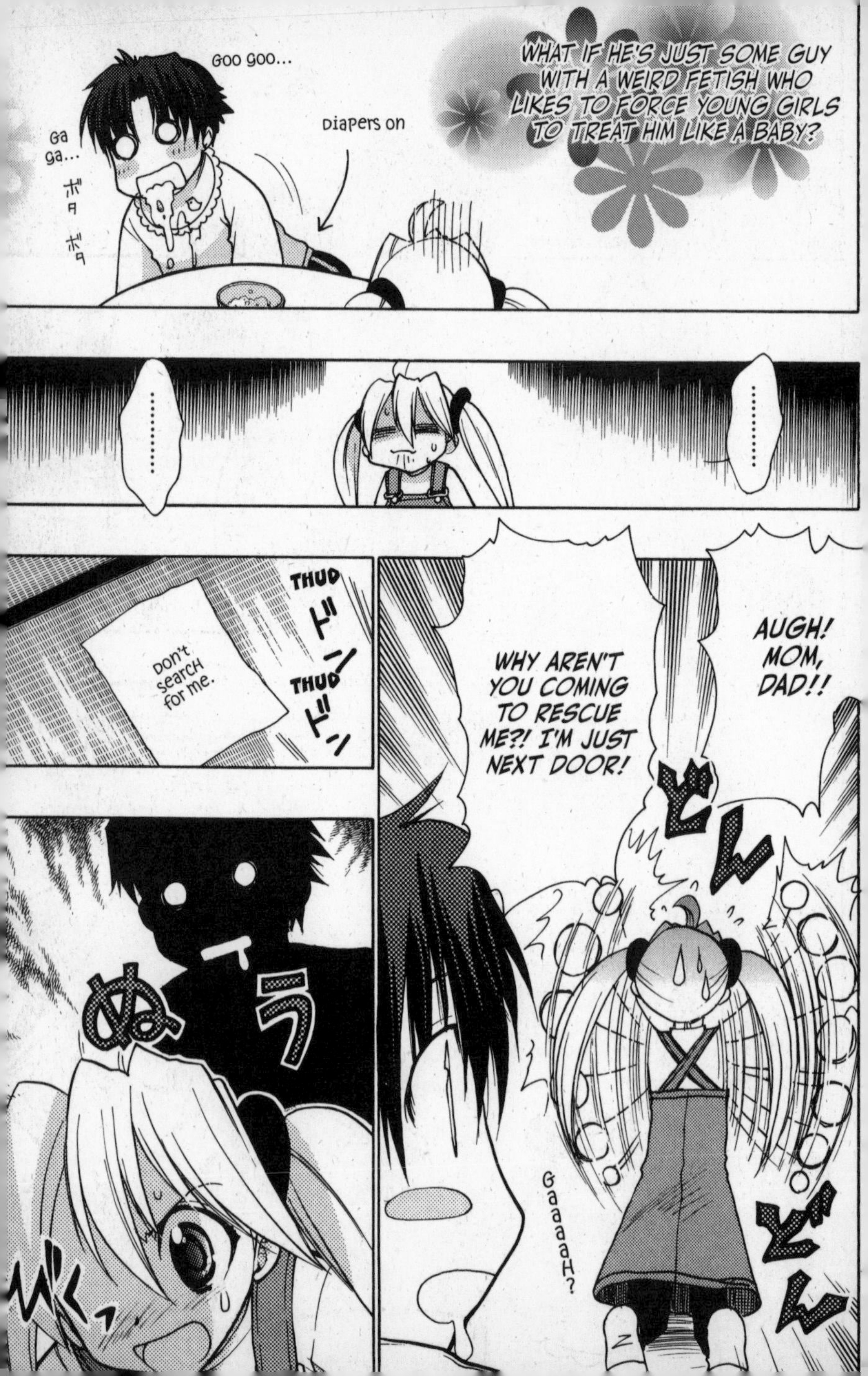
WHAT IF HE'S JUST SOME GUY WITH A WEIRD FETISH WHO LIKES TO FORCE YOUNG GIRLS TO TREAT HIM LIKE A BABY?
Goo goo...
Diapers on
Ga ga...
ボタ ボタ
......
......
AUGH! MOM, DAD!!
WHY AREN'T YOU COMING TO RESCUE ME?! I'M JUST NEXT DOOR!
どん
Gaaaaah?
どん
THUD ドン
THUD ドン
Don't search for me.
ぬう

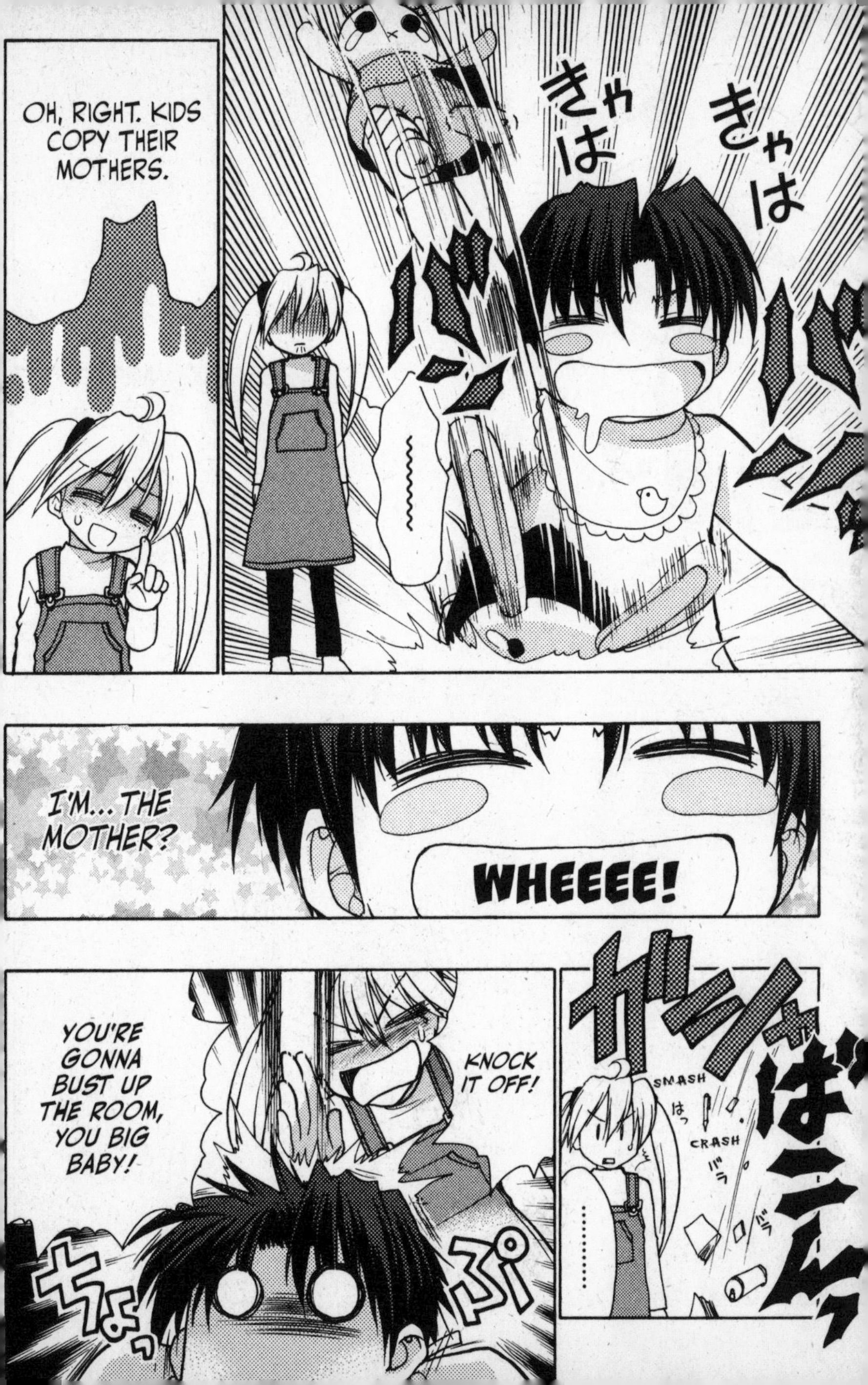
きゃは
きゃは
OH, RIGHT. KIDS COPY THEIR MOTHERS.
WHEEEE!
I'M... THE MOTHER?
ガシャ
SMASH
はっ
CRASH
バラ
バラ
......
KNOCK IT OFF!
YOU'RE GONNA BUST UP THE ROOM, YOU BIG BABY!
ちょっ
ぷ

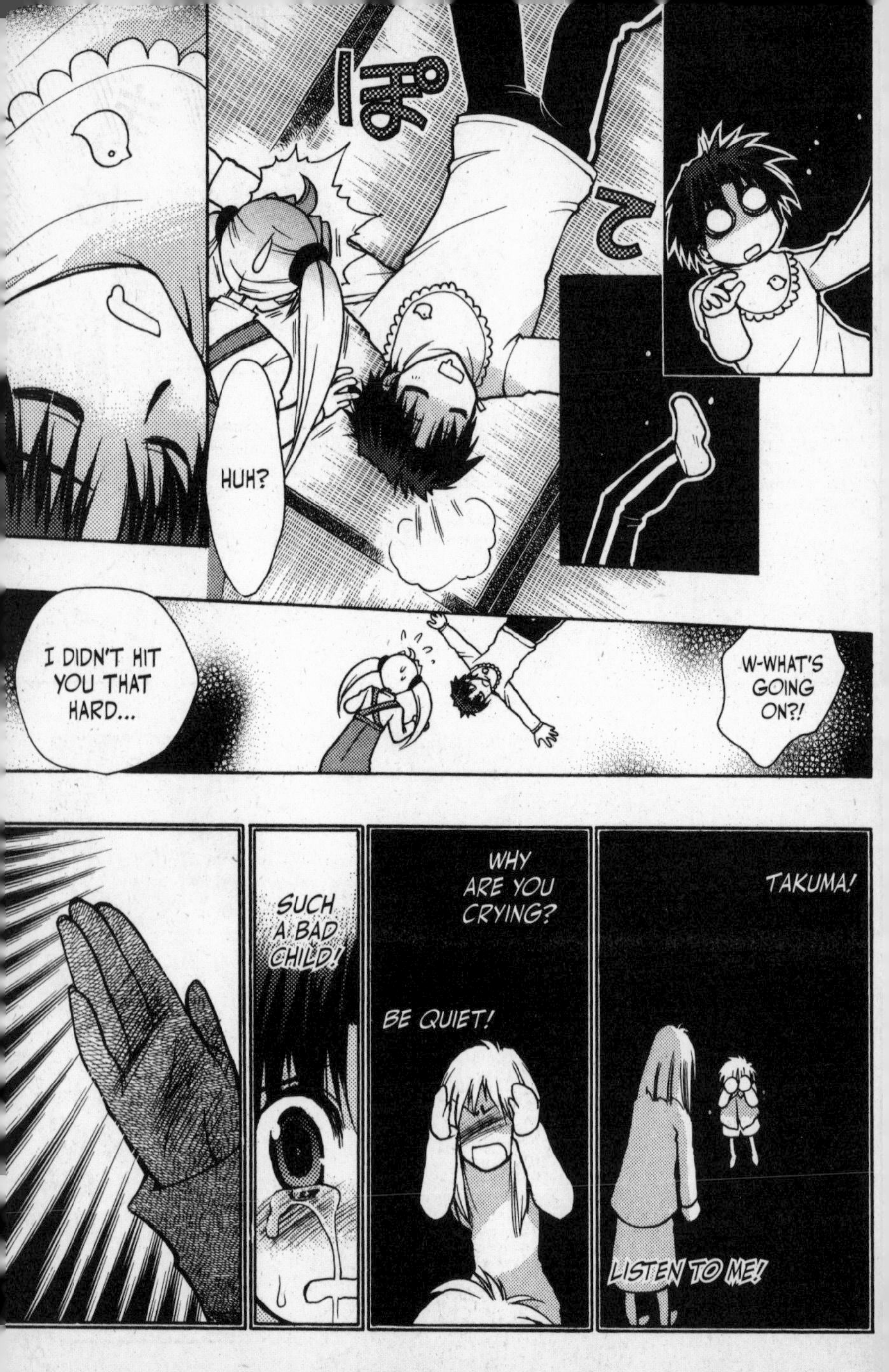
ぽて
HUH?
W-WHAT'S GOING ON?!
I DIDN'T HIT YOU THAT HARD...
TAKUMA!
LISTEN TO ME!
WHY ARE YOU CRYING?
BE QUIET!
SUCH A BAD CHILD!

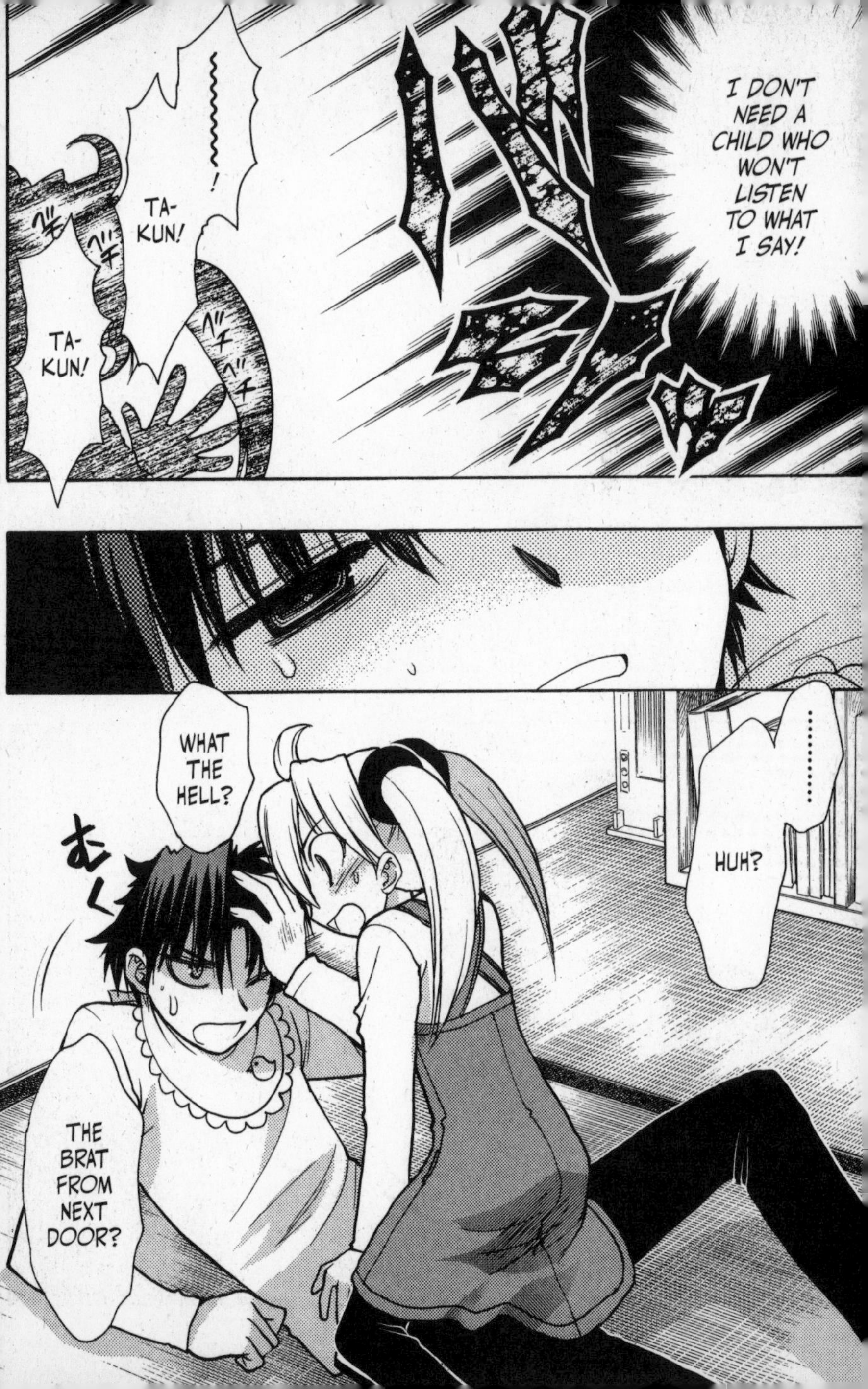

I DON'T NEED A CHILD WHO WON'T LISTEN TO WHAT I SAY!
~~~~~~!
TA-KUN!
TA-KUN!
ベチ
ベチ
ベチ
ベチ
......
HUH?
WHAT THE HELL?
むく
THE BRAT FROM NEXT DOOR?
~~~~~~

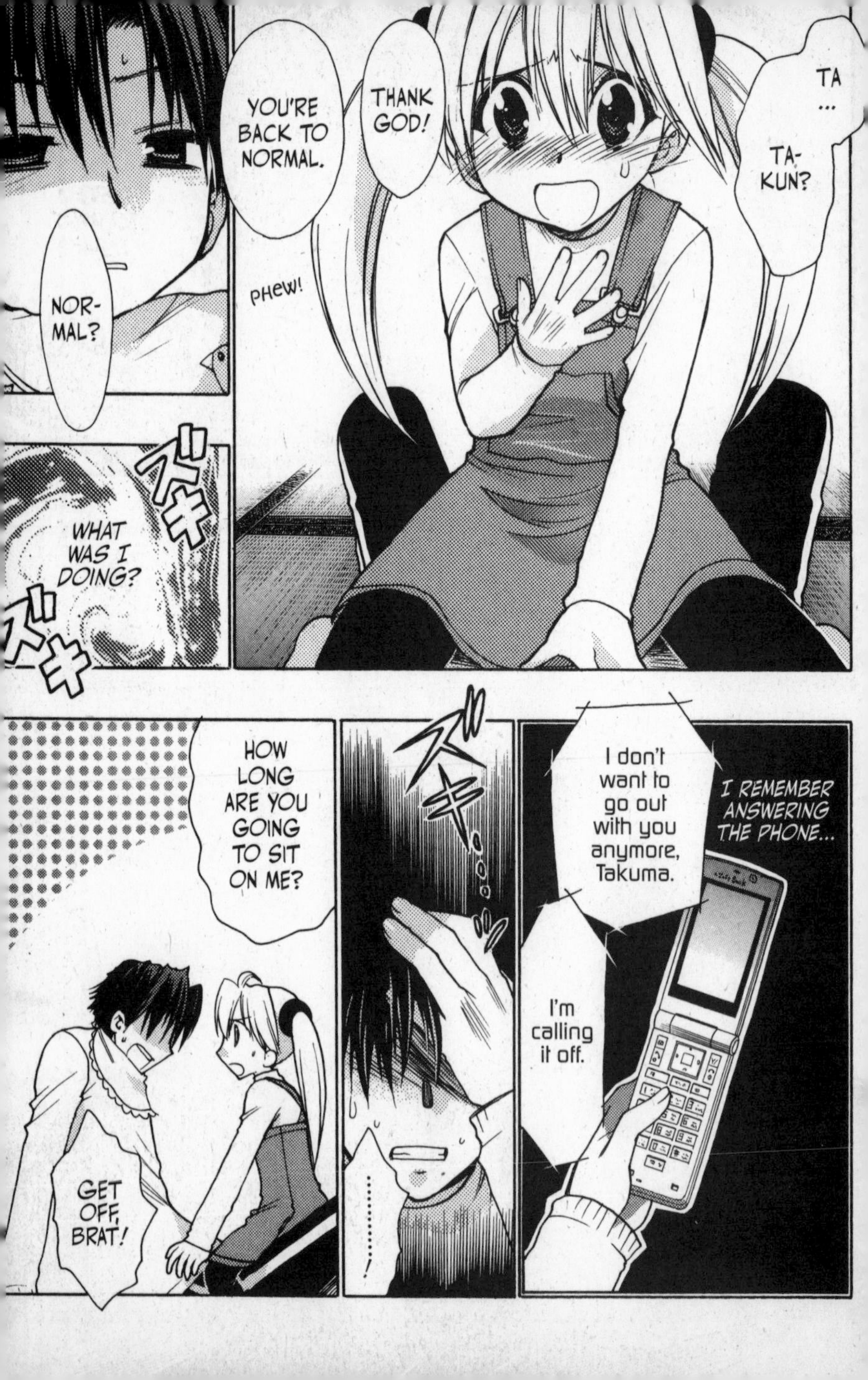
TA ... TA-KUN?
THANK GOD!
YOU'RE BACK TO NORMAL.
PHEW!
NOR-MAL?
ズキ
WHAT WAS I DOING?
ズキ
I REMEMBER ANSWERING THE PHONE...
I don't want to go out with you anymore, Takuma.
I'm calling it off.
ズキ
......!
HOW LONG ARE YOU GOING TO SIT ON ME?
GET OFF, BRAT!

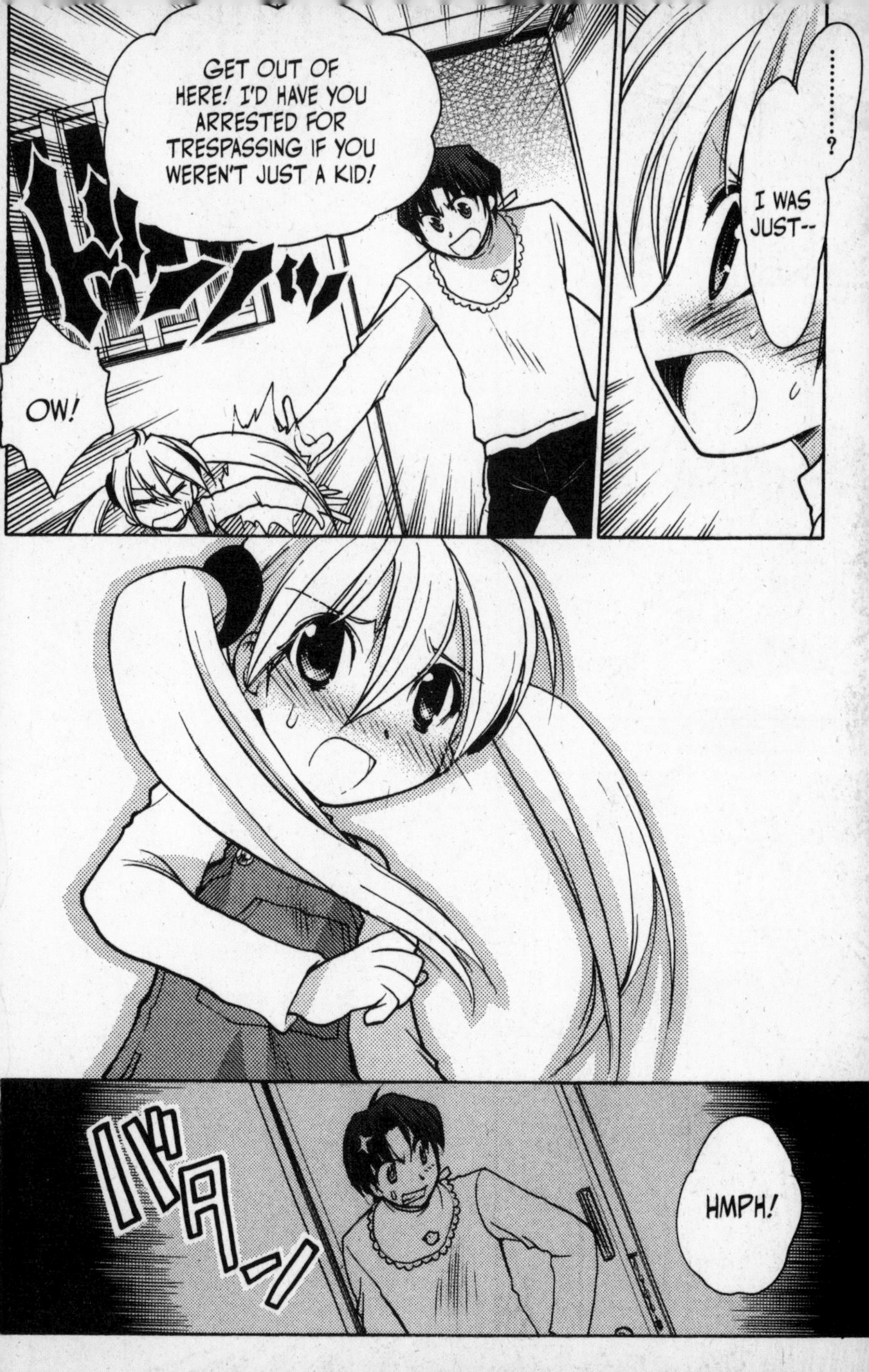
......?
I WAS JUST--
GET OUT OF HERE! I'D HAVE YOU ARRESTED FOR TRESPASSING IF YOU WEREN'T JUST A KID!
OW!
HMPH!

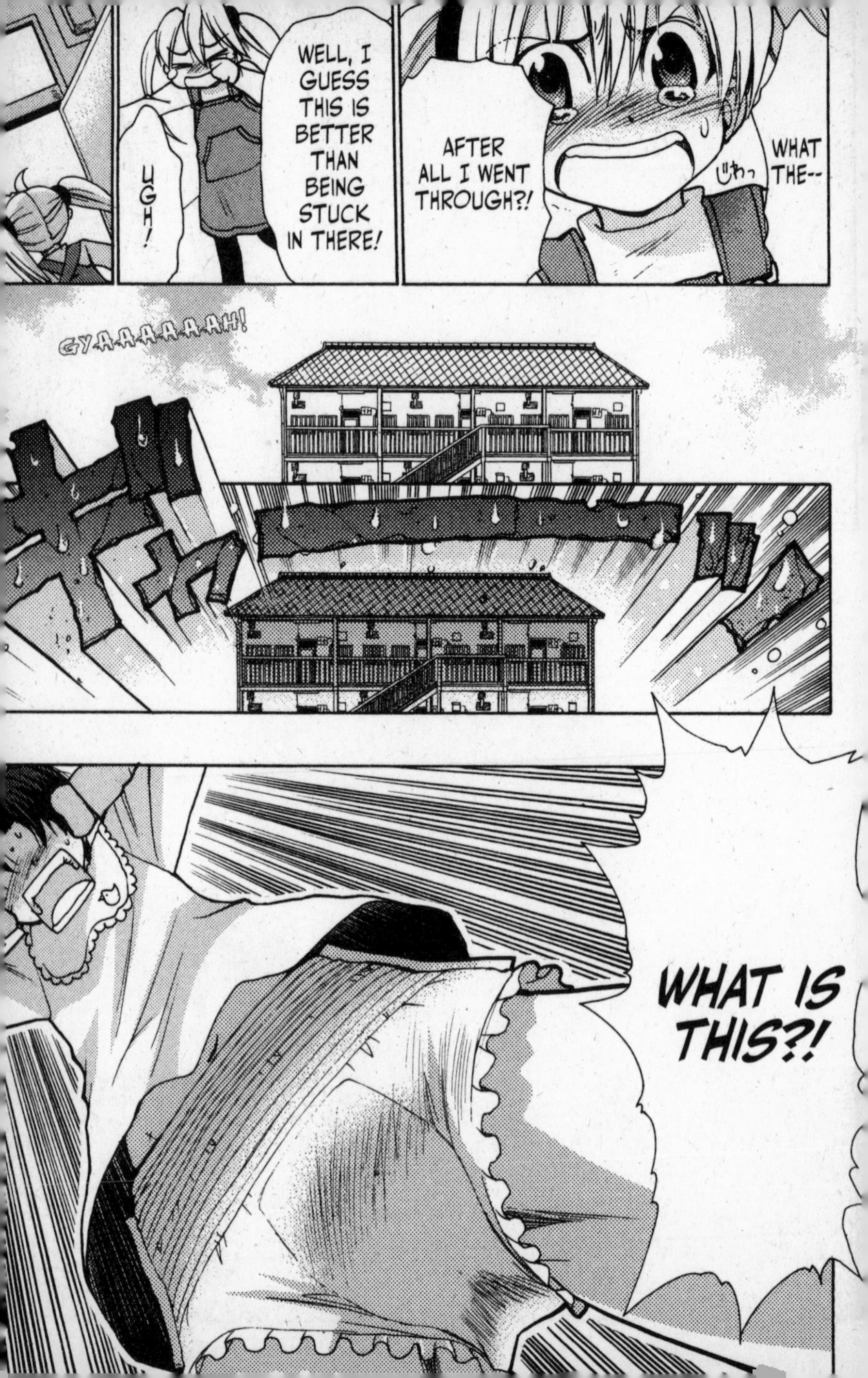
WHAT THE--
じわっ
AFTER ALL I WENT THROUGH?!
WELL, I GUESS THIS IS BETTER THAN BEING STUCK IN THERE!
UGH!
GYAAAAAAAH!
WHAT IS THIS?!

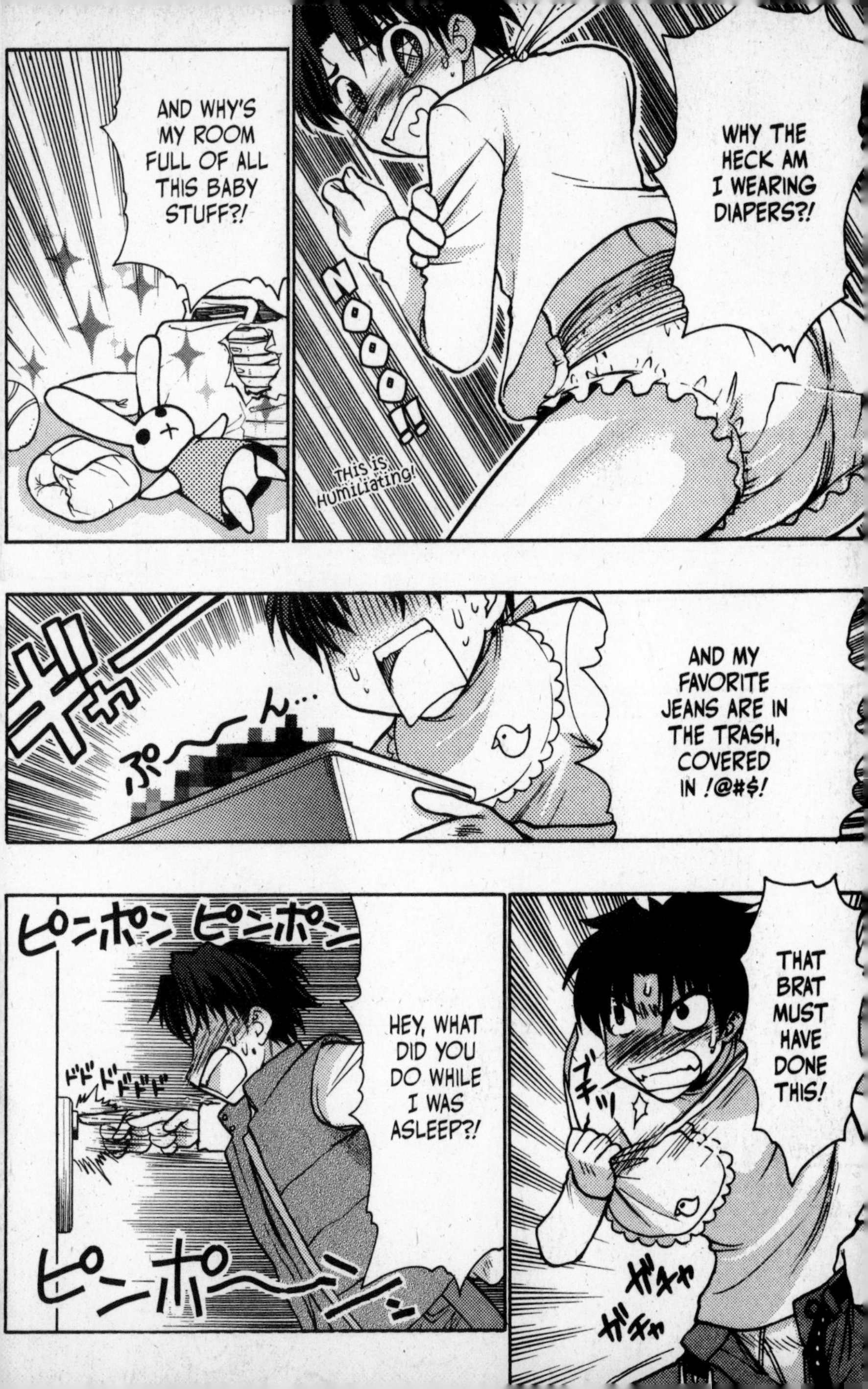
WHY THE HECK AM I WEARING DIAPERS?!
NOOOO!!
THIS IS HUMILIATING!
AND WHY'S MY ROOM FULL OF ALL THIS BABY STUFF?!
AND MY FAVORITE JEANS ARE IN THE TRASH, COVERED IN !@#$!
ぷ〜〜ん…
THAT BRAT MUST HAVE DONE THIS!
ガチャ
ガチャ
ピンポン ピンポン
HEY, WHAT DID YOU DO WHILE I WAS ASLEEP?!
ドドドドド
ピンポ〜〜ン

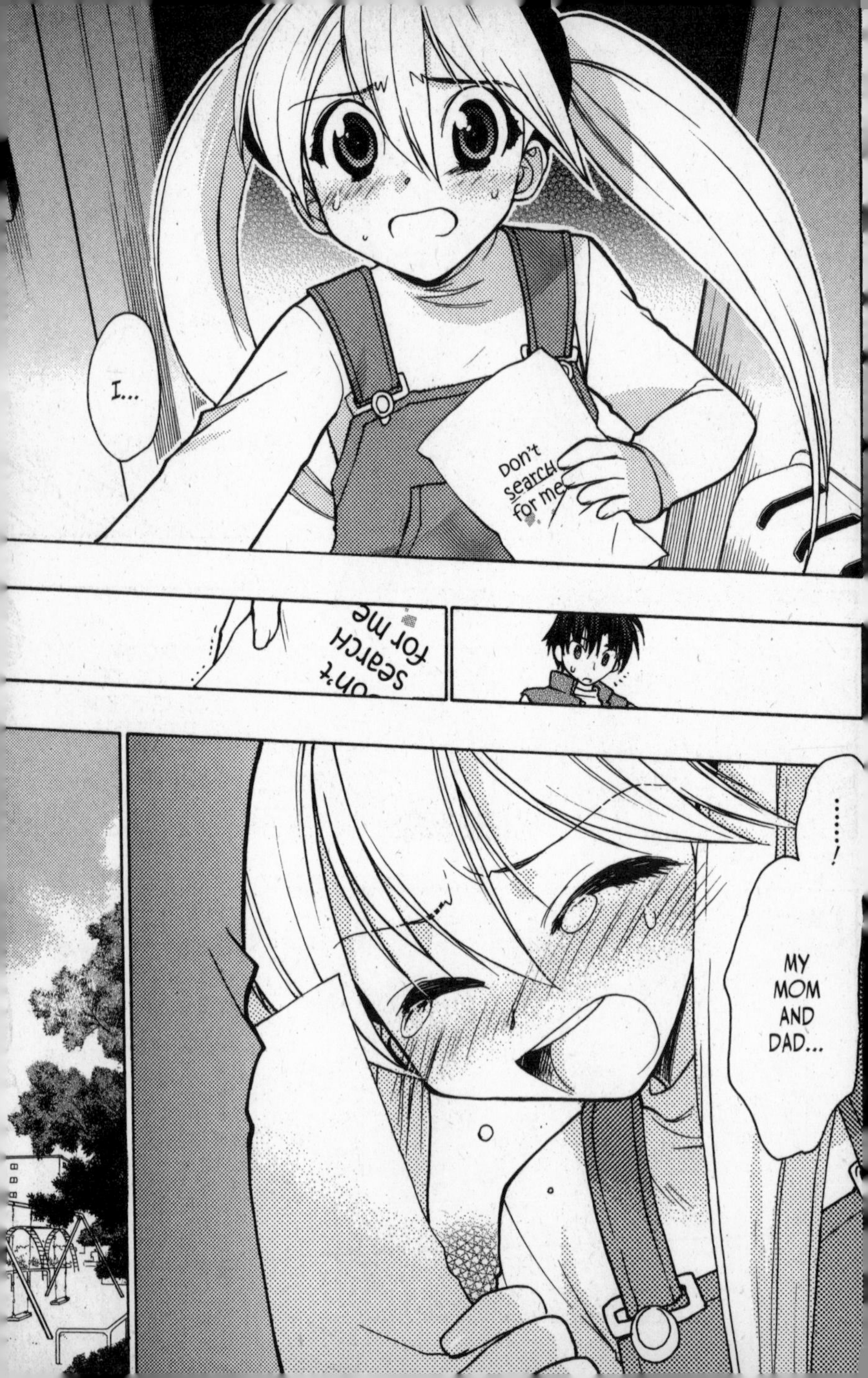
I...
Don't search for me
......!
MY MOM AND DAD...

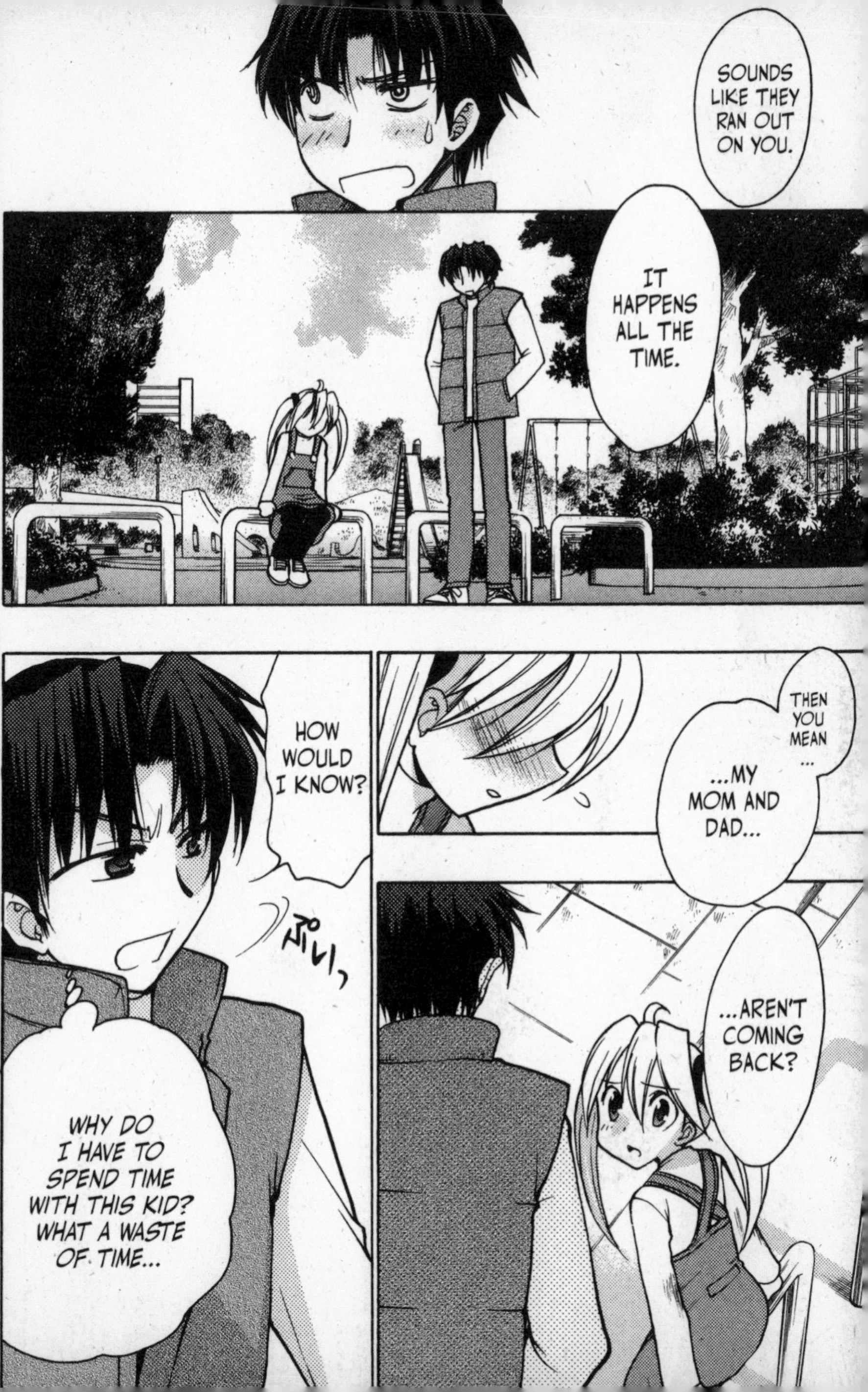
SOUNDS LIKE THEY RAN OUT ON YOU.
IT HAPPENS ALL THE TIME.
THEN YOU MEAN ...
...MY MOM AND DAD...
...AREN'T COMING BACK?
HOW WOULD I KNOW?
WHY DO I HAVE TO SPEND TIME WITH THIS KID? WHAT A WASTE OF TIME...

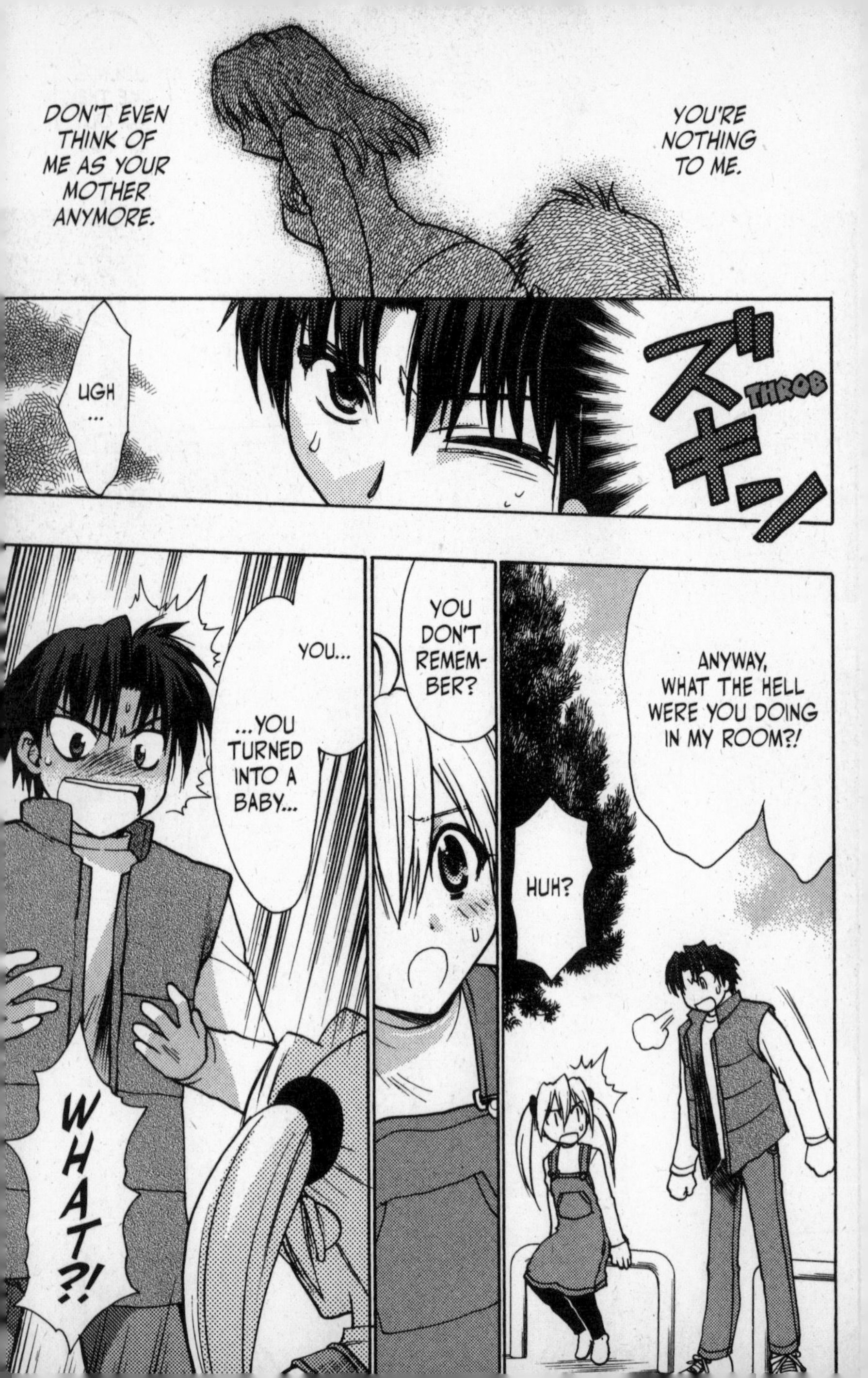
YOU'RE NOTHING TO ME.
DON'T EVEN THINK OF ME AS YOUR MOTHER ANYMORE.
ズキッ
THROB
UGH...
ANYWAY, WHAT THE HELL WERE YOU DOING IN MY ROOM?!
HUH?
YOU DON'T REMEMBER?
YOU...
...YOU TURNED INTO A BABY...
WHAT?!

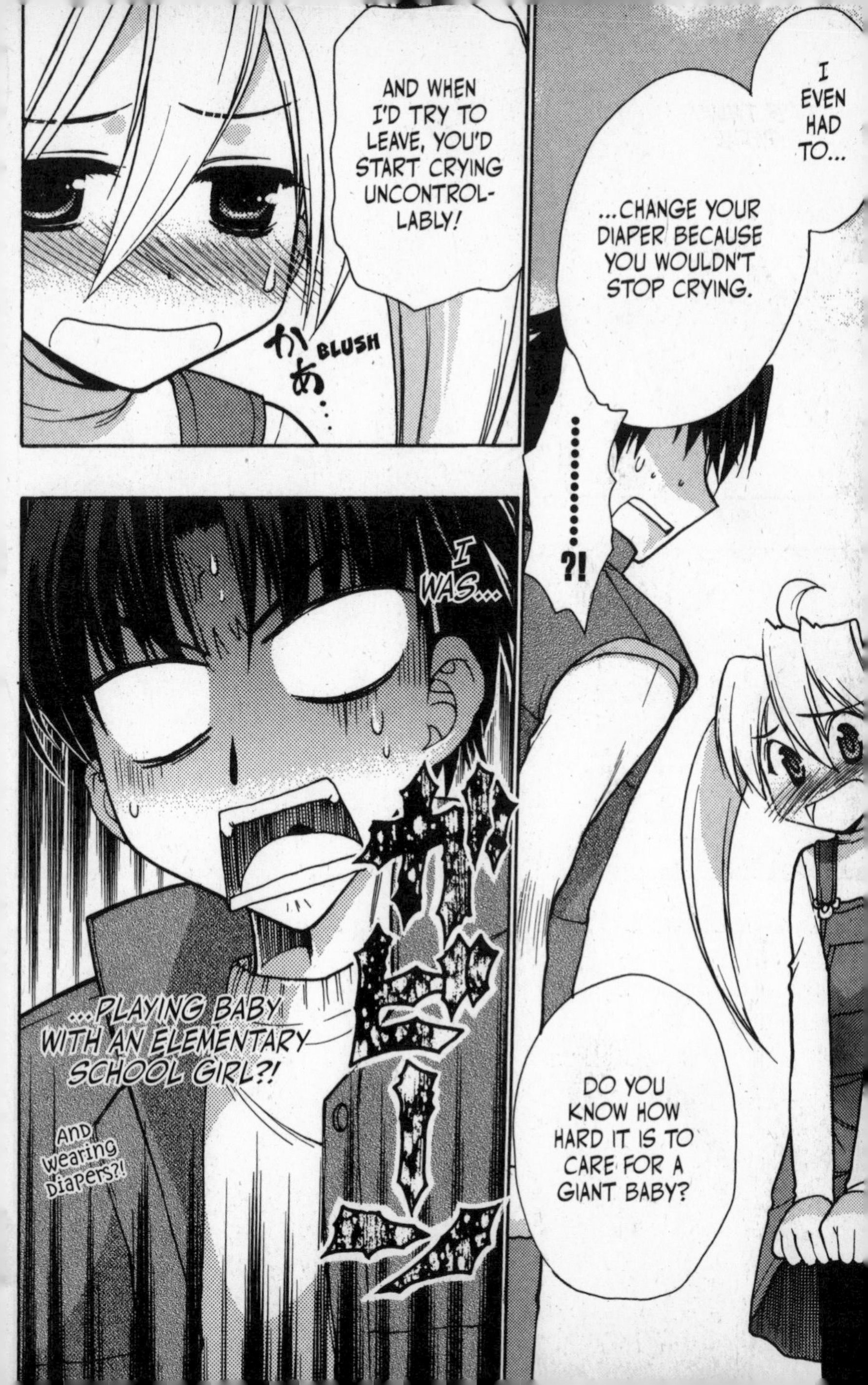
I EVEN HAD TO...
...CHANGE YOUR DIAPER BECAUSE YOU WOULDN'T STOP CRYING.
......?!
DO YOU KNOW HOW HARD IT IS TO CARE FOR A GIANT BABY?
AND WHEN I'D TRY TO LEAVE, YOU'D START CRYING UNCONTROL-LABLY!
かあ... BLUSH
I WAS...
...PLAYING BABY WITH AN ELEMENTARY SCHOOL GIRL?!
AND WEARING DIAPERS?!

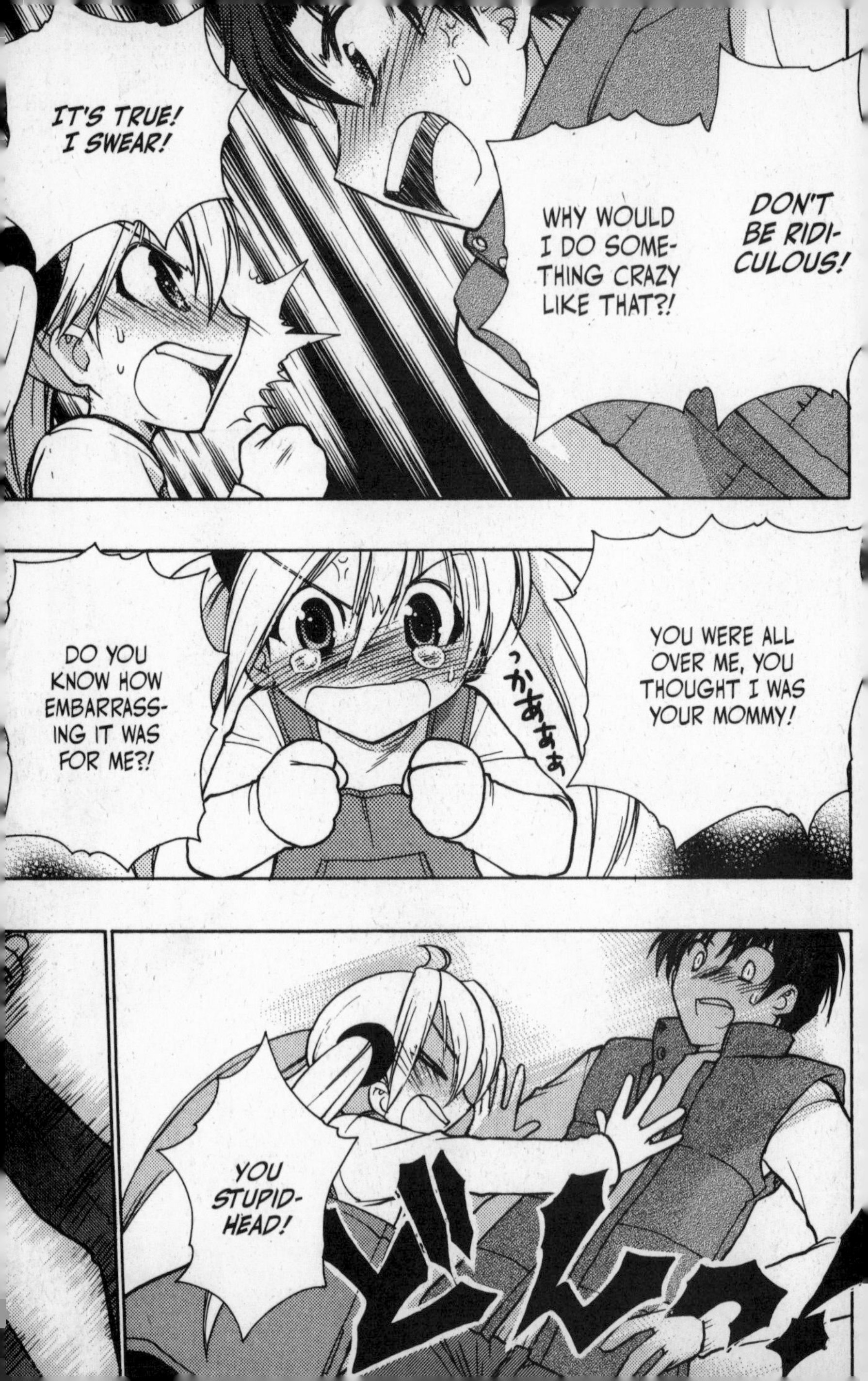
DON'T BE RIDI-CULOUS!
WHY WOULD I DO SOME-THING CRAZY LIKE THAT?!
IT'S TRUE! I SWEAR!
YOU WERE ALL OVER ME, YOU THOUGHT I WAS YOUR MOMMY!
っかあああ
DO YOU KNOW HOW EMBARRASS-ING IT WAS FOR ME?!
YOU STUPID-HEAD!

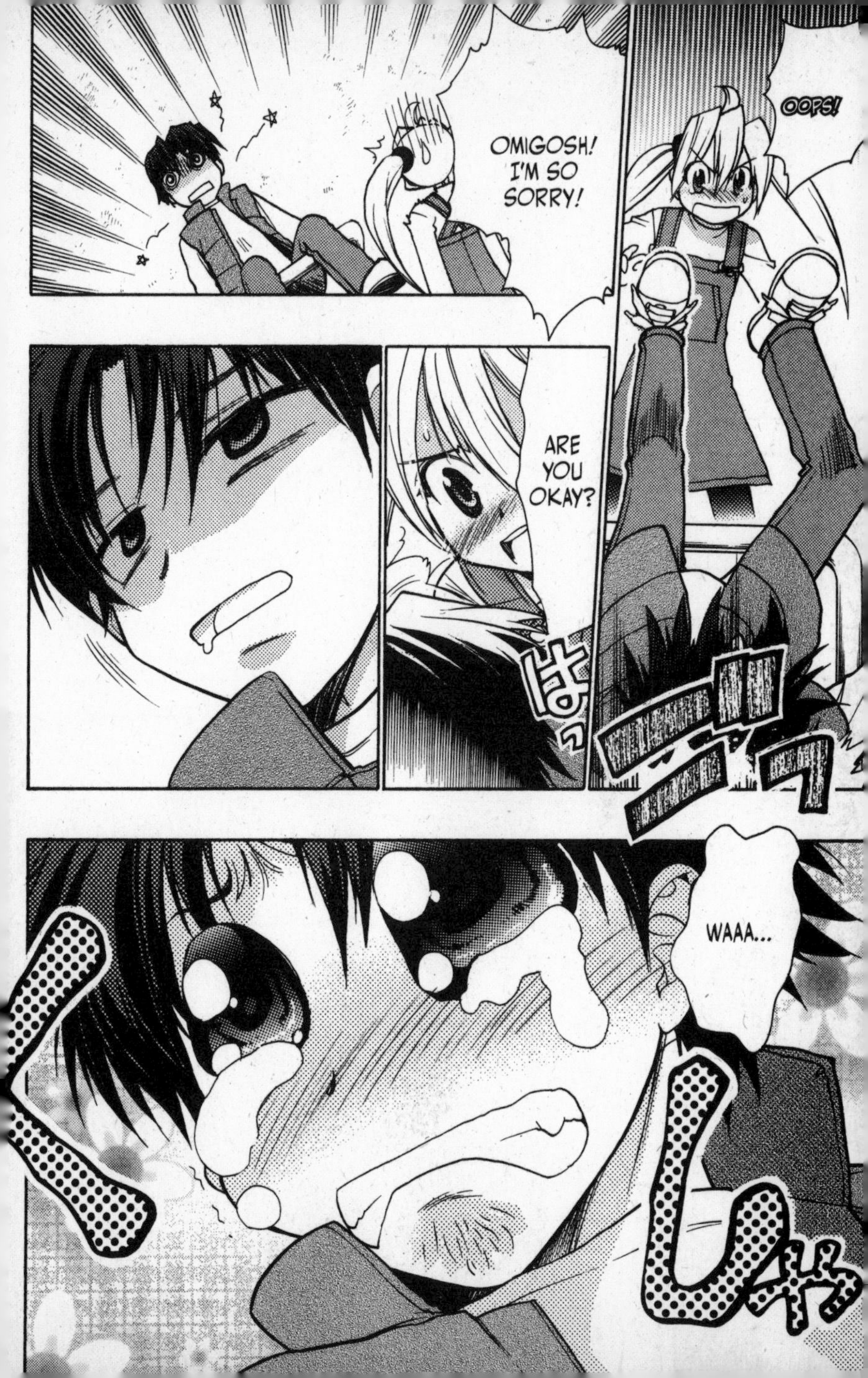
OOPS!
OMIGOSH! I'M SO SORRY!
ARE YOU OKAY?
WAAA...

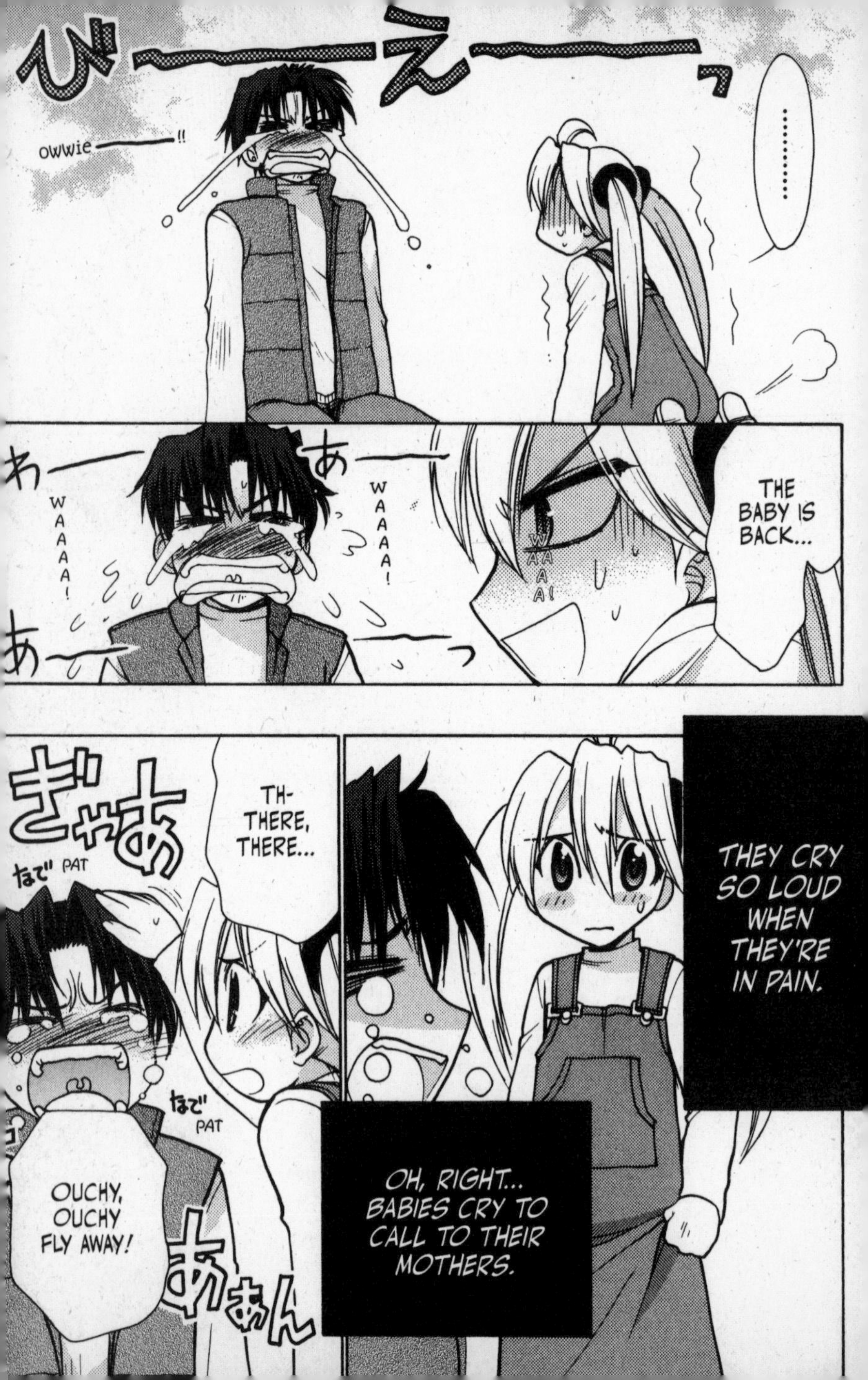
……
び～～え～～っ
OWWIE——!!
THE BABY IS BACK...
WAAAA!
あーーーっ
WAAAA!
わーーー
WAAAA!
あーー
THEY CRY SO LOUD WHEN THEY'RE IN PAIN.
OH, RIGHT... BABIES CRY TO CALL TO THEIR MOTHERS.
TH- THERE, THERE...
ぎゃあ
なで PAT
なで PAT
OUCHY, OUCHY FLY AWAY!
あぁん

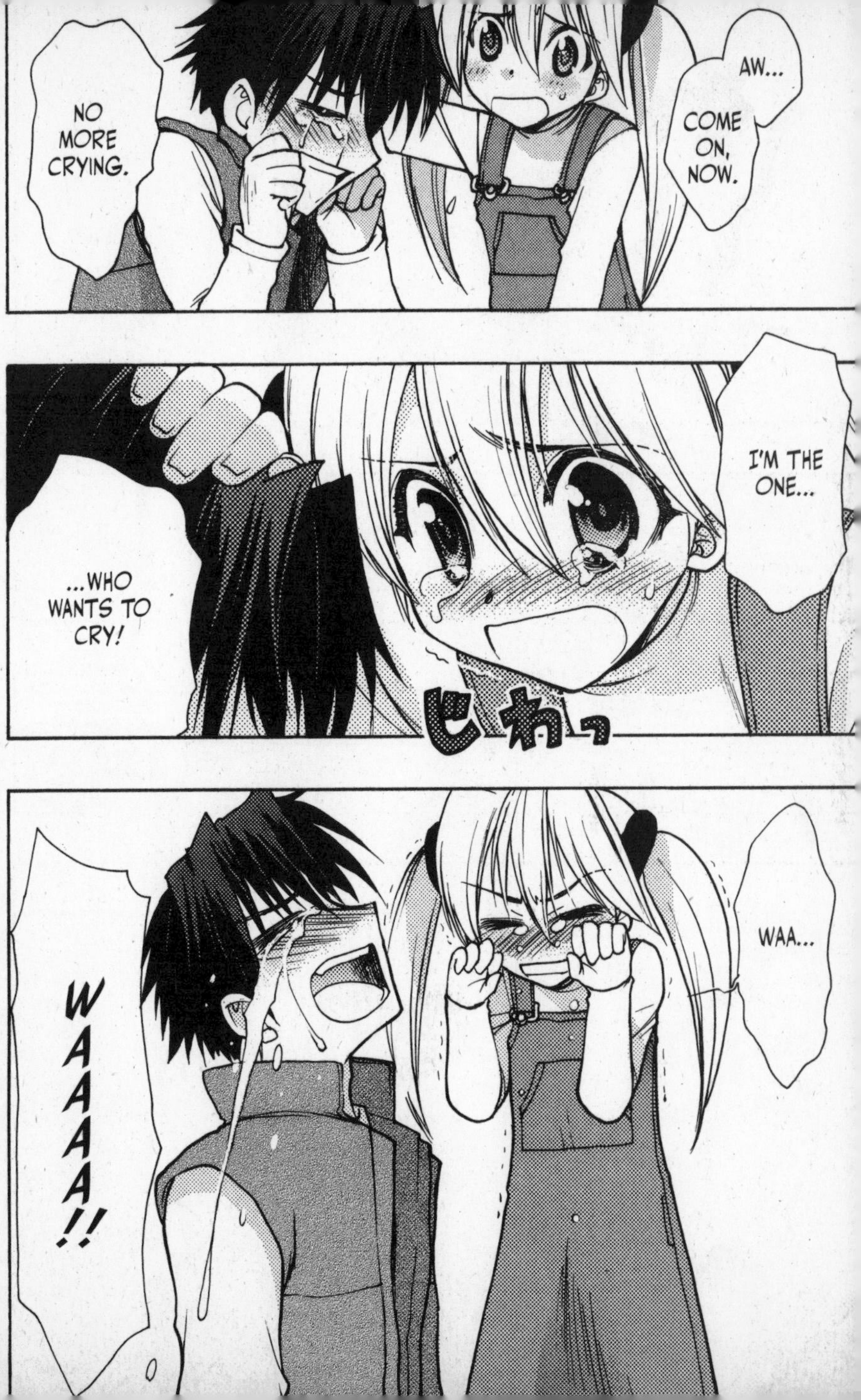
AW... COME ON, NOW.
NO MORE CRYING.
I'M THE ONE...
...WHO WANTS TO CRY!
じわっ
WAA...
WAAAAA!!

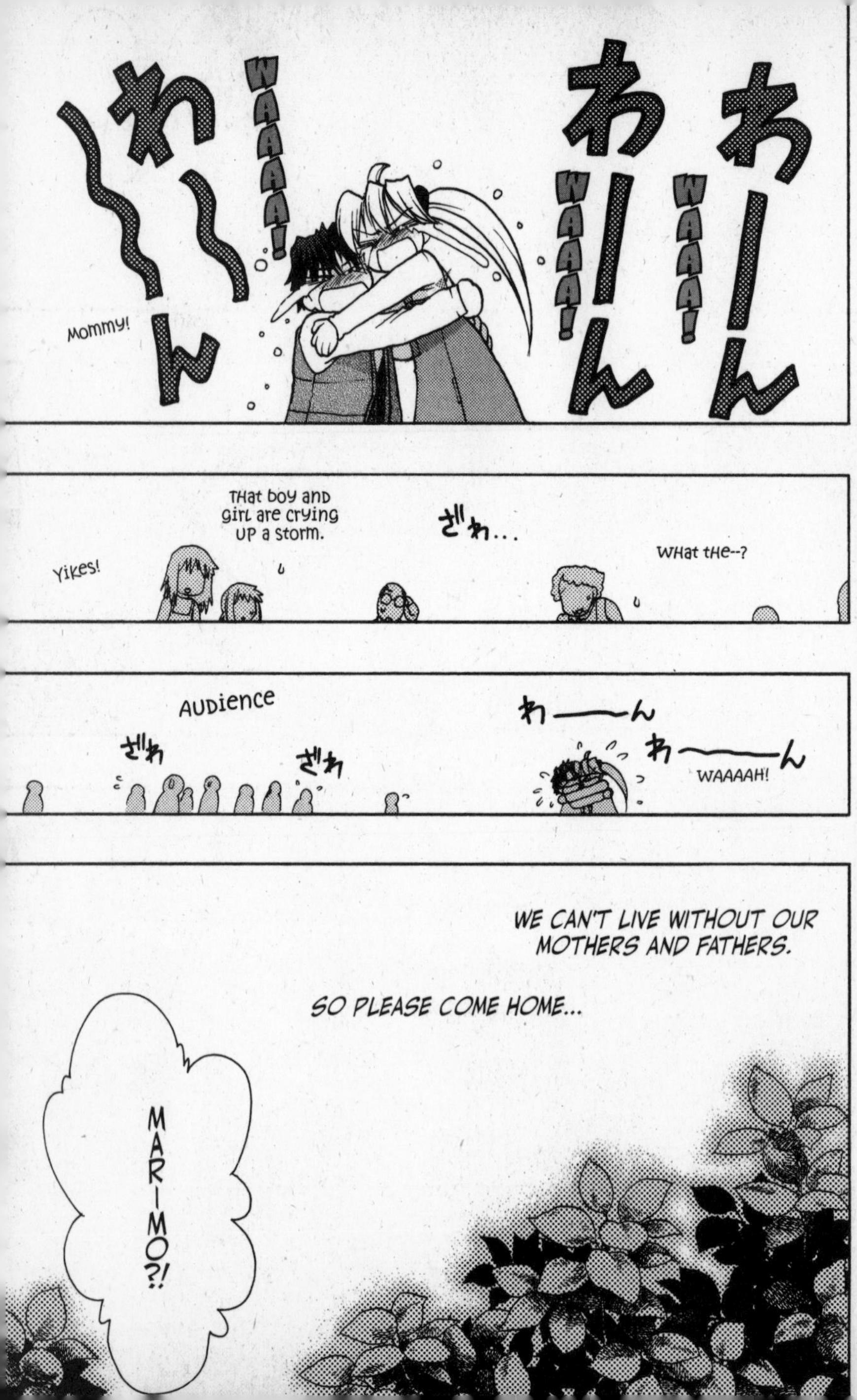
わーん
WAAAA!
わーん
WAAAA!
わ〜〜ん
WAAAA!
Mommy!
What the--?
ざわ...
That boy and girl are crying up a storm.
Yikes!
わ──ん
わ───ん
WAAAAH!
ざわ
ざわ
AUDIENCE
WE CAN'T LIVE WITHOUT OUR MOTHERS AND FATHERS.
SO PLEASE COME HOME...
MARIMO?!

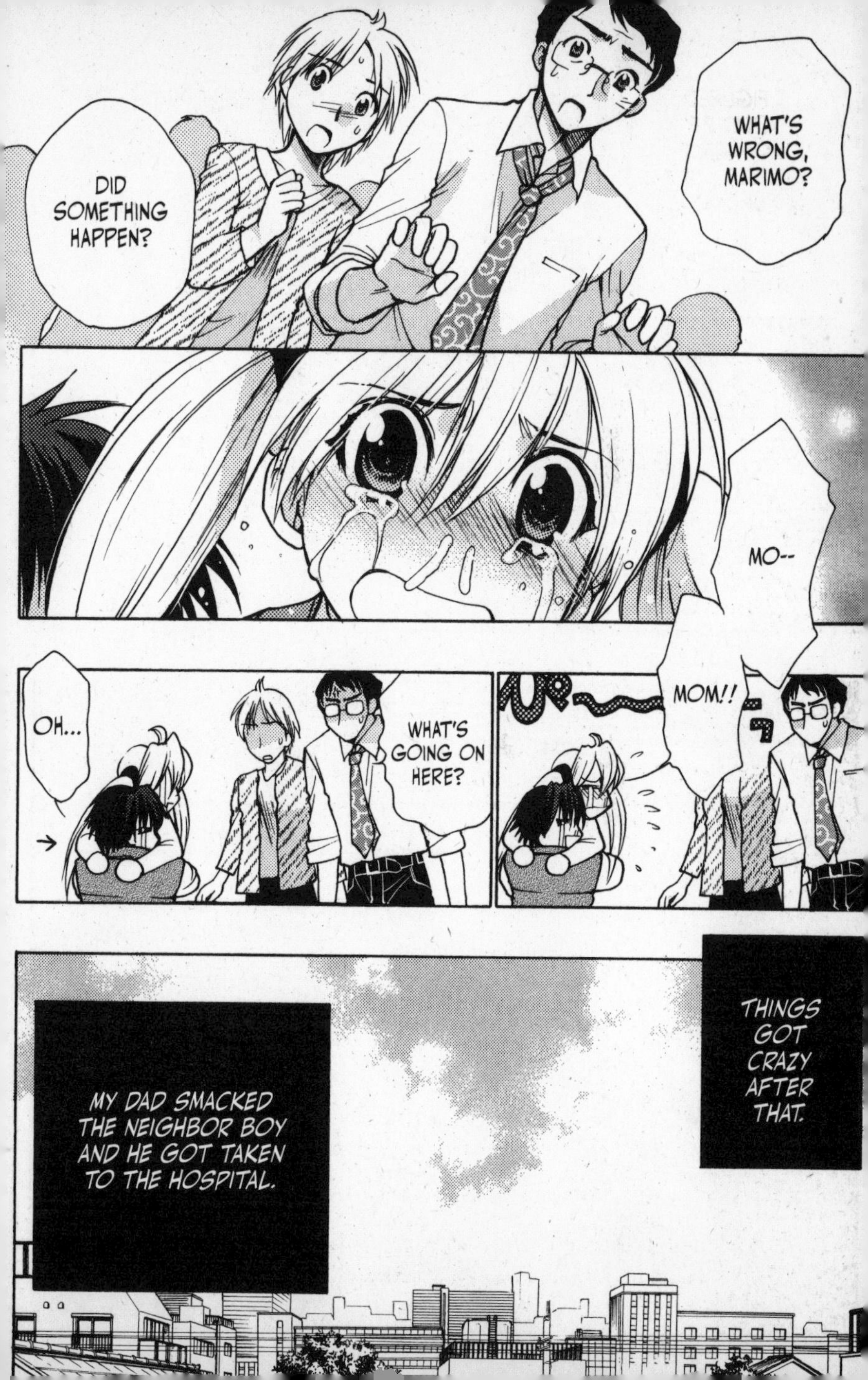
WHAT'S WRONG, MARIMO?
DID SOMETHING HAPPEN?
MO--
MOM!!
WHAT'S GOING ON HERE?
OH...
THINGS GOT CRAZY AFTER THAT.
MY DAD SMACKED THE NEIGHBOR BOY AND HE GOT TAKEN TO THE HOSPITAL.

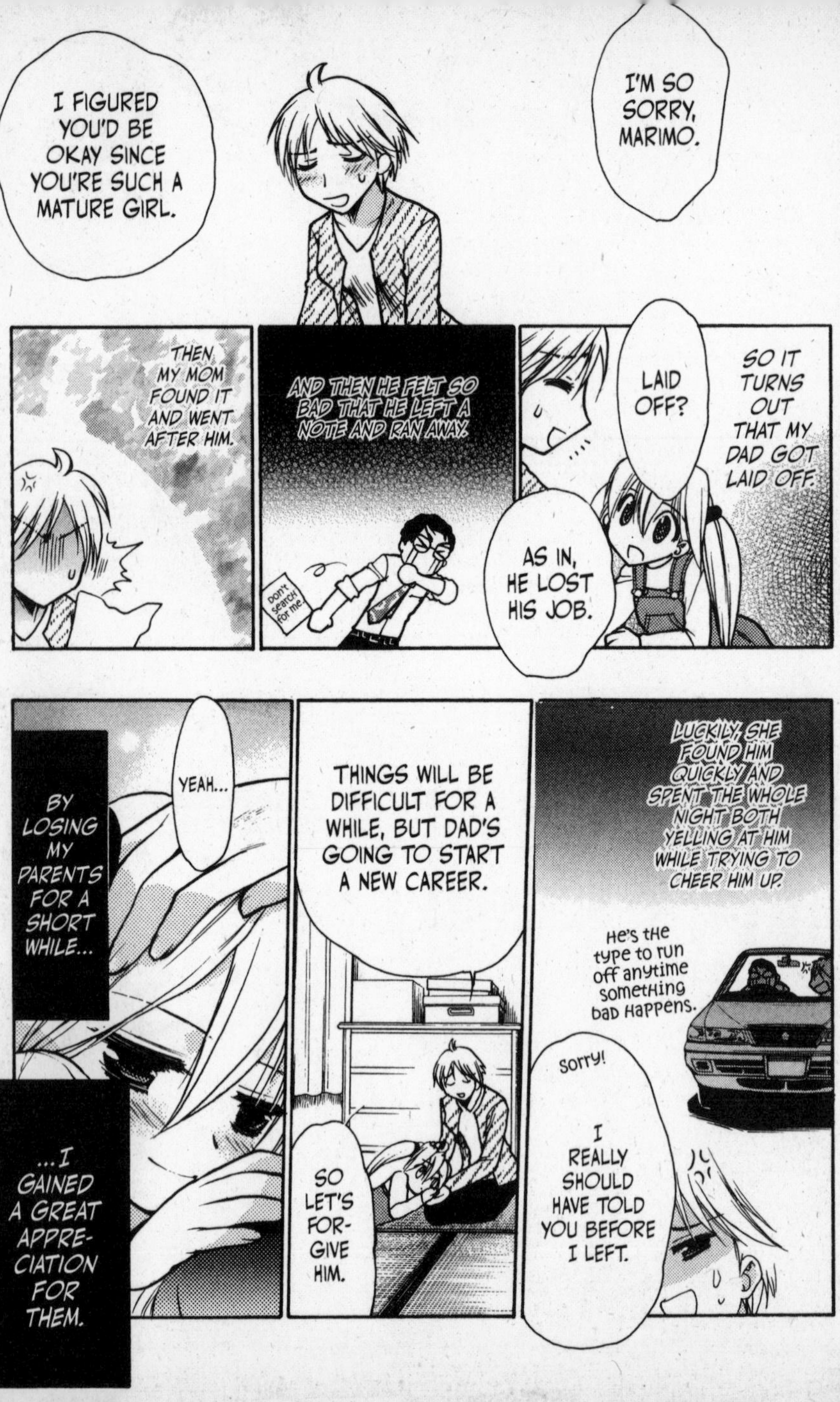
I'M SO SORRY, MARIMO.
I FIGURED YOU'D BE OKAY SINCE YOU'RE SUCH A MATURE GIRL.
SO IT TURNS OUT THAT MY DAD GOT LAID OFF.
LAID OFF?
AS IN, HE LOST HIS JOB.
AND THEN HE FELT SO BAD THAT HE LEFT A NOTE AND RAN AWAY.
Don't search for me.
THEN MY MOM FOUND IT AND WENT AFTER HIM.
LUCKILY, SHE FOUND HIM QUICKLY AND SPENT THE WHOLE NIGHT BOTH YELLING AT HIM WHILE TRYING TO CHEER HIM UP.
He's the type to run off anytime something bad happens.
Sorry!
I REALLY SHOULD HAVE TOLD YOU BEFORE I LEFT.
THINGS WILL BE DIFFICULT FOR A WHILE, BUT DAD'S GOING TO START A NEW CAREER.
SO LET'S FOR-GIVE HIM.
YEAH...
BY LOSING MY PARENTS FOR A SHORT WHILE...
...I GAINED A GREAT APPRE-CIATION FOR THEM.

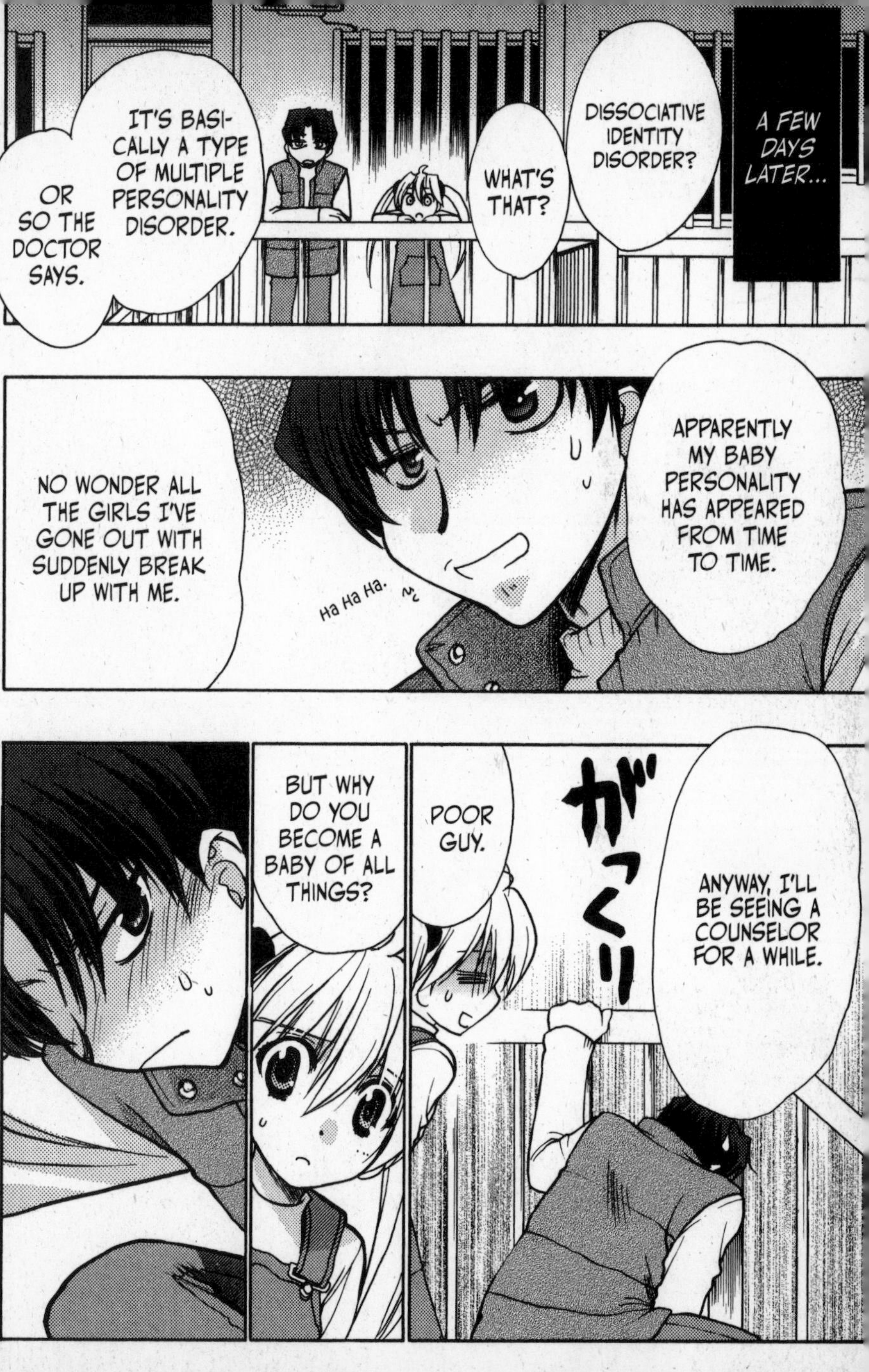
A FEW DAYS LATER...
DISSOCIATIVE IDENTITY DISORDER?
WHAT'S THAT?
IT'S BASI-CALLY A TYPE OF MULTIPLE PERSONALITY DISORDER.
OR SO THE DOCTOR SAYS.
APPARENTLY MY BABY PERSONALITY HAS APPEARED FROM TIME TO TIME.
Ha Ha Ha.
NO WONDER ALL THE GIRLS I'VE GONE OUT WITH SUDDENLY BREAK UP WITH ME.
ANYWAY, I'LL BE SEEING A COUNSELOR FOR A WHILE.
がっくり
POOR GUY.
BUT WHY DO YOU BECOME A BABY OF ALL THINGS?

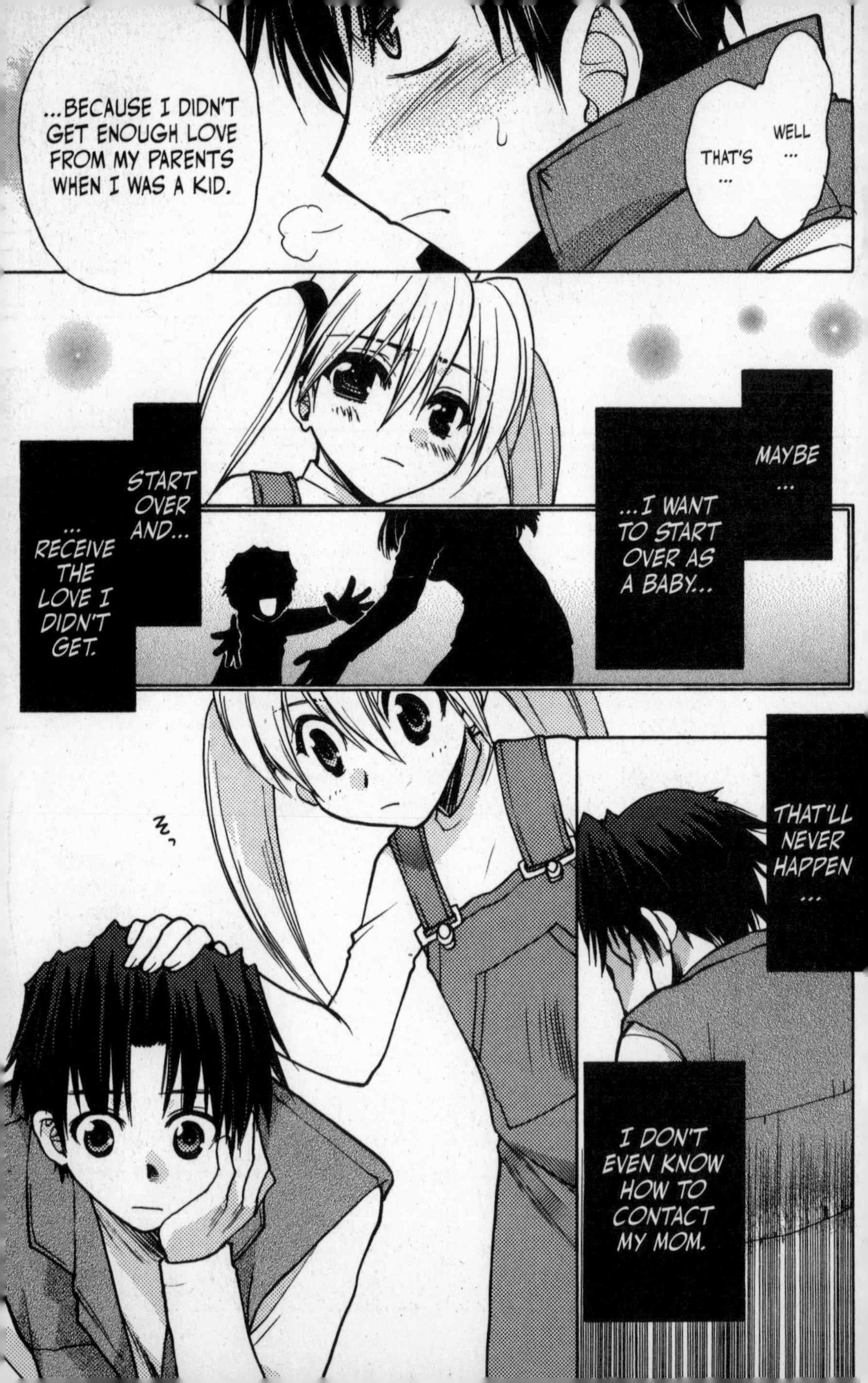
...BECAUSE I DIDN'T GET ENOUGH LOVE FROM MY PARENTS WHEN I WAS A KID.
WELL...
THAT'S...
MAYBE...
...I WANT TO START OVER AS A BABY...
START OVER AND...
...RECEIVE THE LOVE I DIDN'T GET.
THAT'LL NEVER HAPPEN...
I DON'T EVEN KNOW HOW TO CONTACT MY MOM.

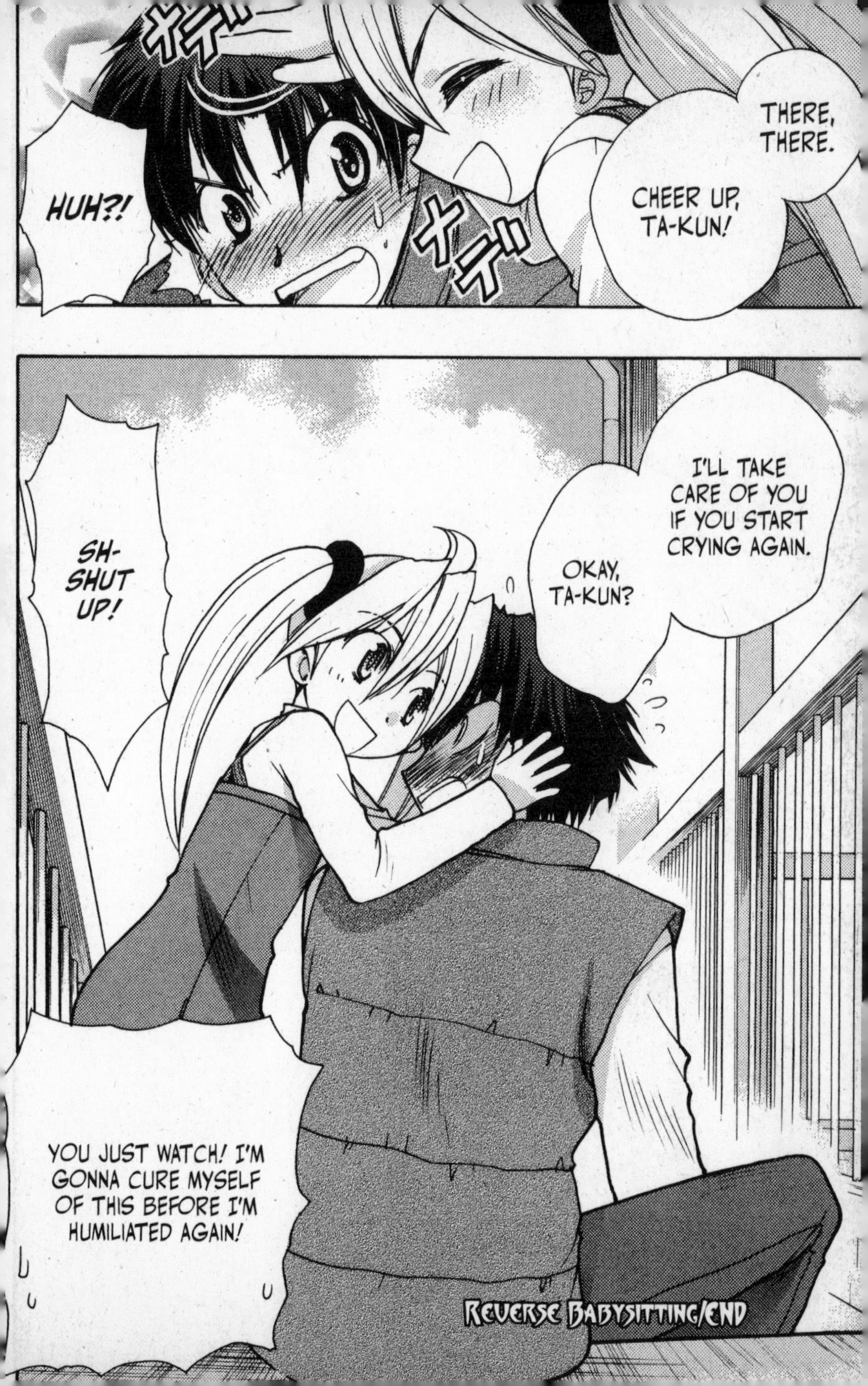
THERE, THERE.
CHEER UP, TA-KUN!
HUH?!
I'LL TAKE CARE OF YOU IF YOU START CRYING AGAIN.
OKAY, TA-KUN?
SH- SHUT UP!
YOU JUST WATCH! I'M GONNA CURE MYSELF OF THIS BEFORE I'M HUMILIATED AGAIN!
REVERSE BABYSITTING/END

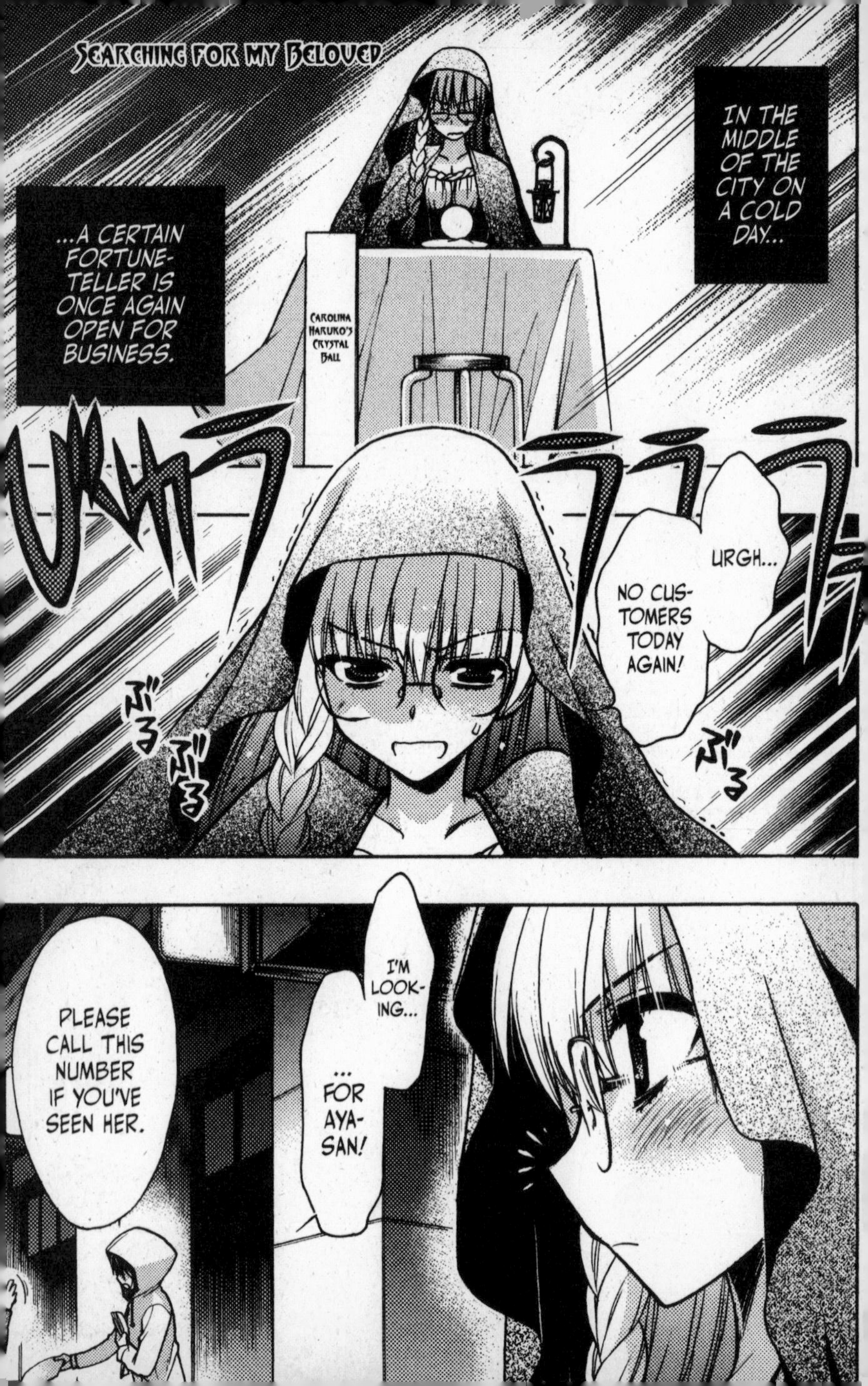
Searching for my Beloved
IN THE MIDDLE OF THE CITY ON A COLD DAY...
...A CERTAIN FORTUNE-TELLER IS ONCE AGAIN OPEN FOR BUSINESS.
Carolina Haruko's Crystal Ball
URGH...
NO CUS-TOMERS TODAY AGAIN!
ぶる
ぶる ぶる
I'M LOOK-ING...
...FOR AYA-SAN!
PLEASE CALL THIS NUMBER IF YOU'VE SEEN HER.

Searching for my Beloved

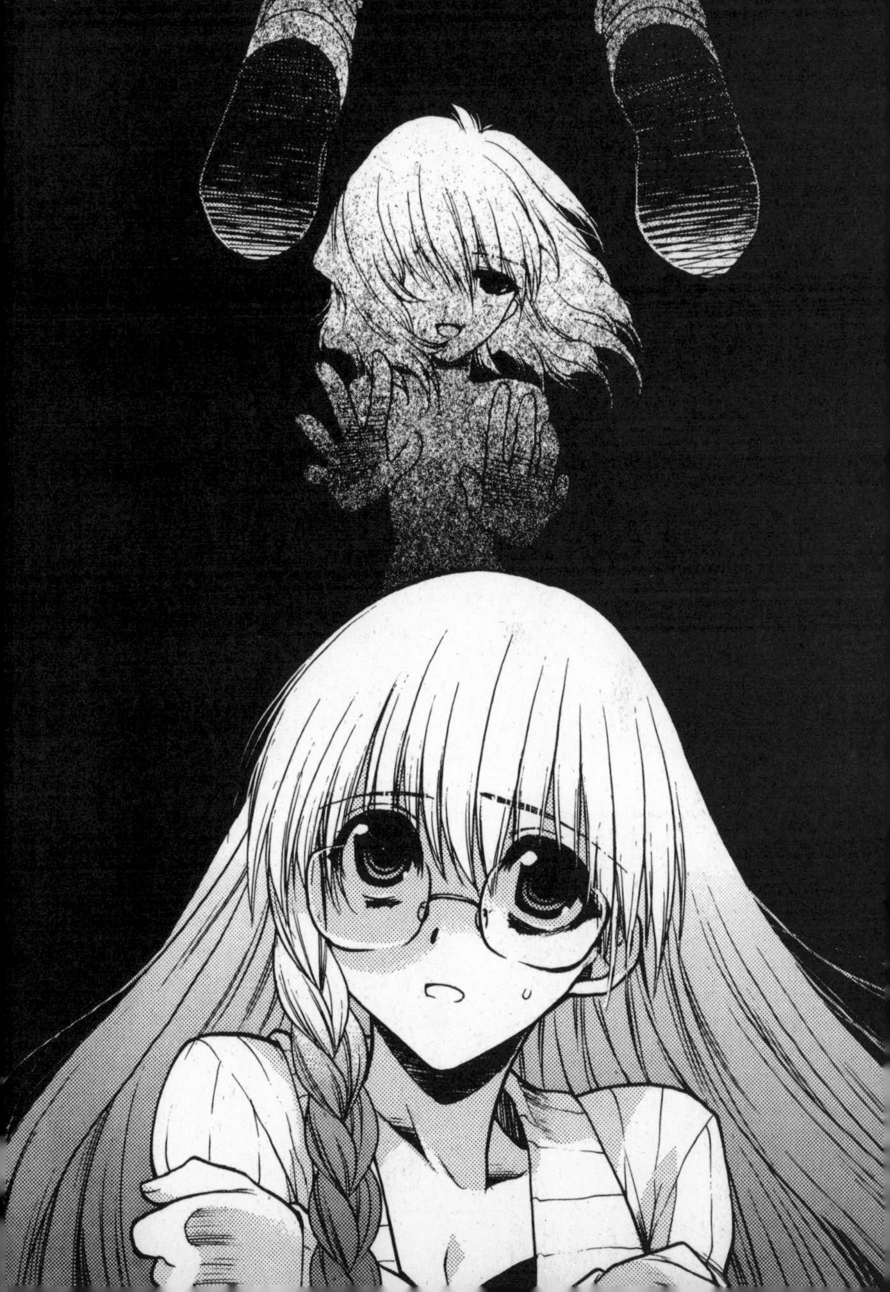

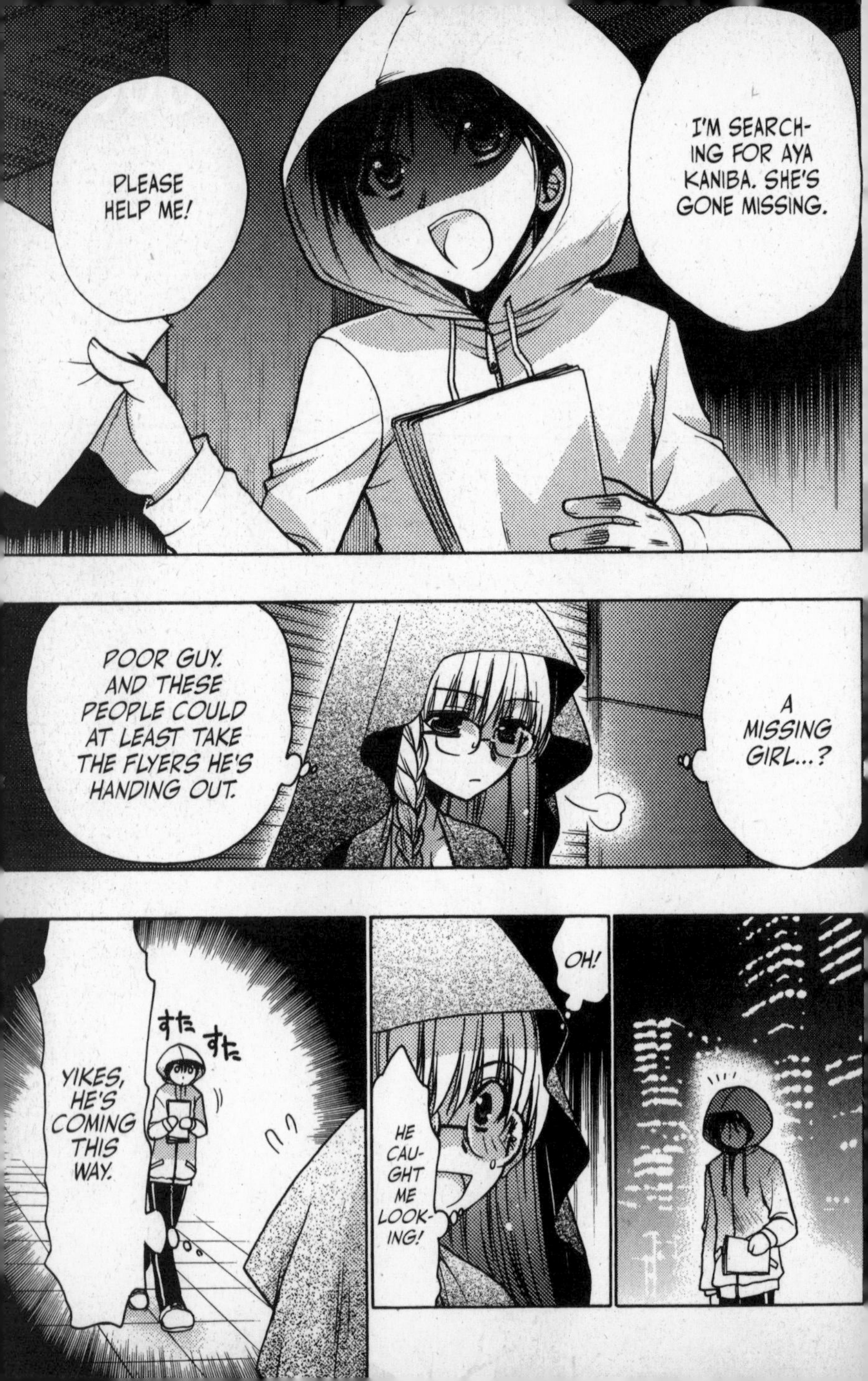
I'M SEARCH-ING FOR AYA KANIBA. SHE'S GONE MISSING.
PLEASE HELP ME!
A MISSING GIRL...?
POOR GUY. AND THESE PEOPLE COULD AT LEAST TAKE THE FLYERS HE'S HANDING OUT.
OH!
HE CAU-GHT ME LOOK-ING!
すた すた
YIKES, HE'S COMING THIS WAY.

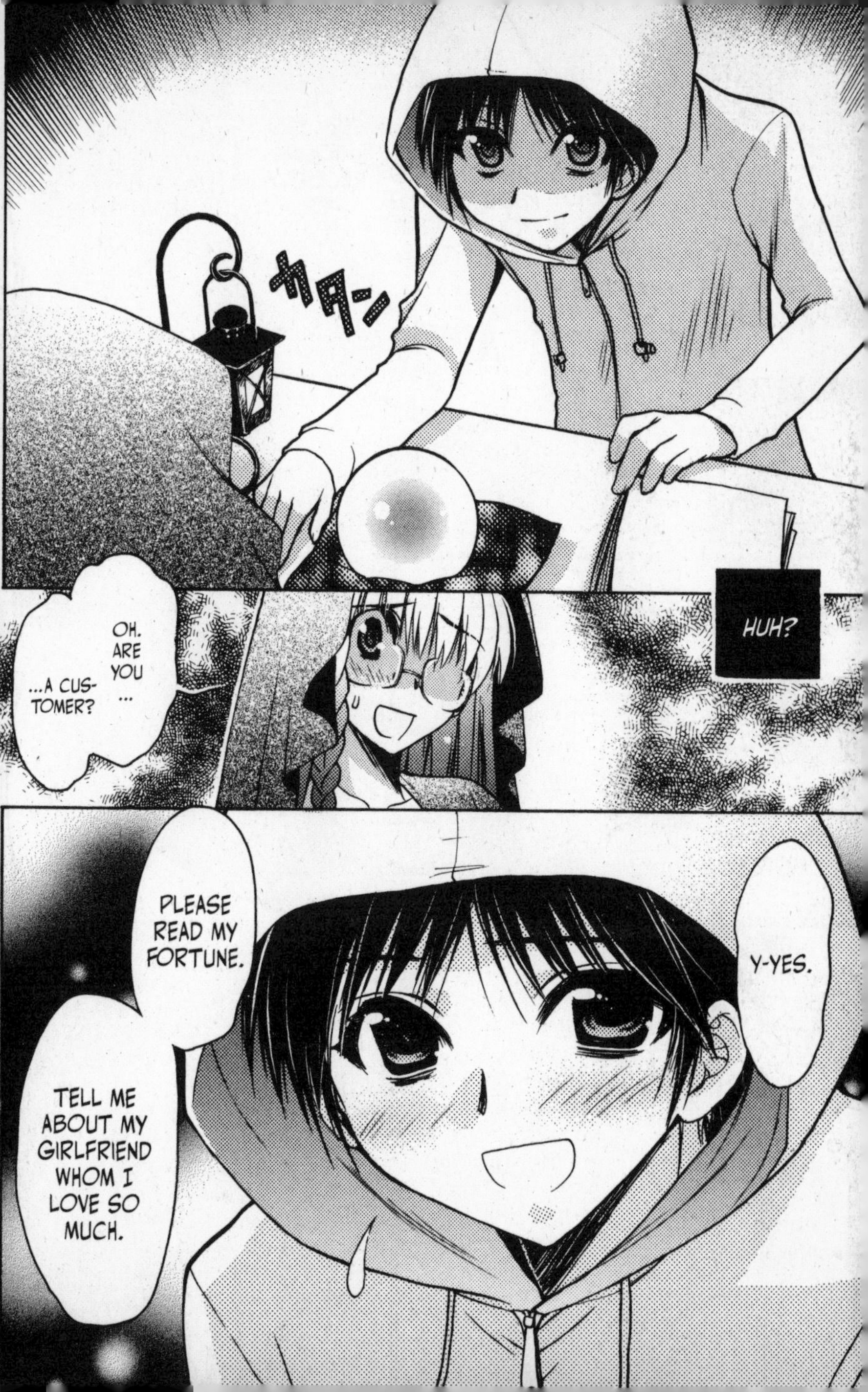
カタン
HUH?
OH. ARE YOU ...
...A CUS-TOMER?
Y-YES.
PLEASE READ MY FORTUNE.
TELL ME ABOUT MY GIRLFRIEND WHOM I LOVE SO MUCH.

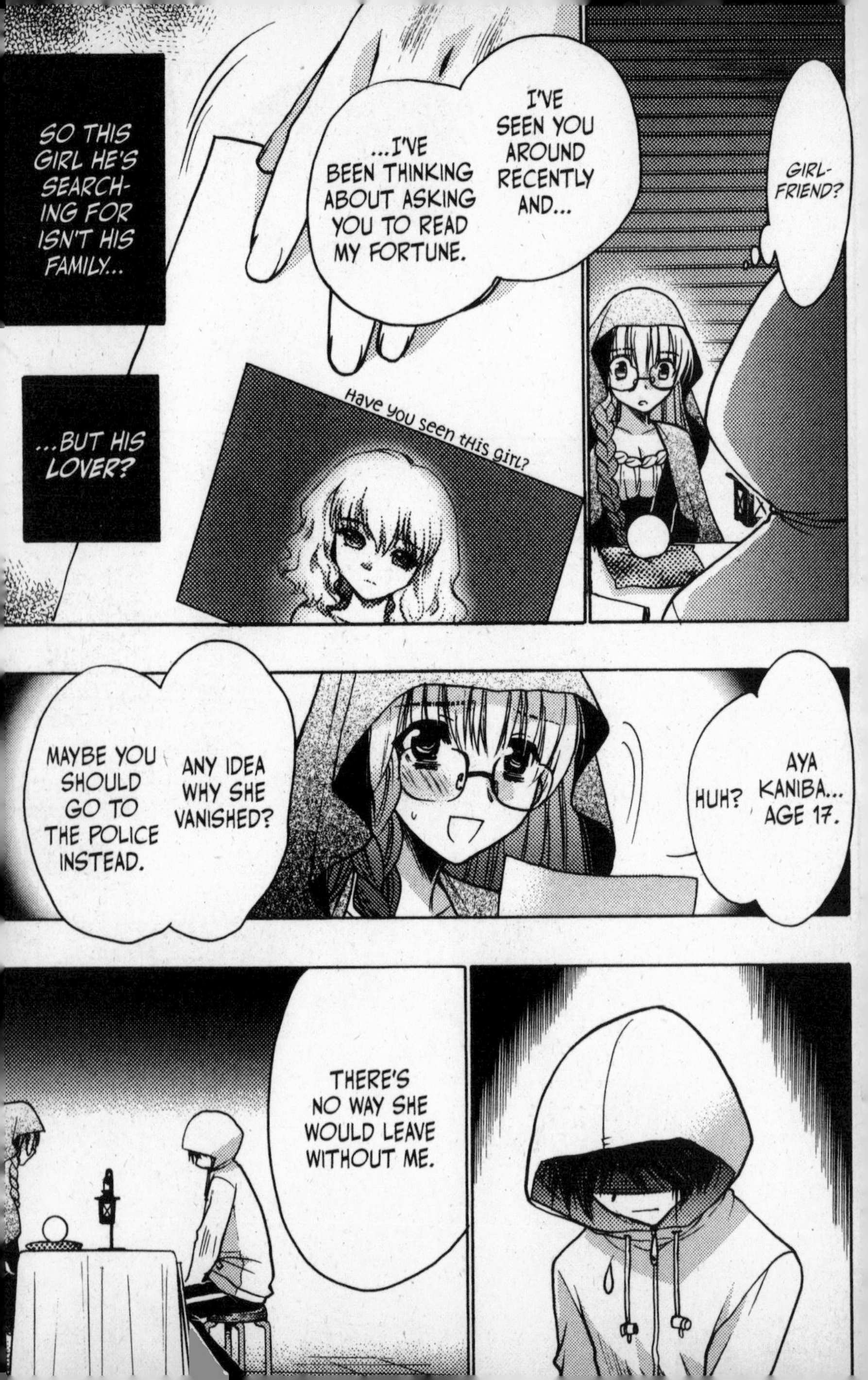
GIRL-FRIEND?
I'VE SEEN YOU AROUND RECENTLY AND...
...I'VE BEEN THINKING ABOUT ASKING YOU TO READ MY FORTUNE.
Have you seen this girl?
SO THIS GIRL HE'S SEARCHING FOR ISN'T HIS FAMILY...
...BUT HIS LOVER?
AYA KANIBA... AGE 17.
HUH?
ANY IDEA WHY SHE VANISHED?
MAYBE YOU SHOULD GO TO THE POLICE INSTEAD.
THERE'S NO WAY SHE WOULD LEAVE WITHOUT ME.

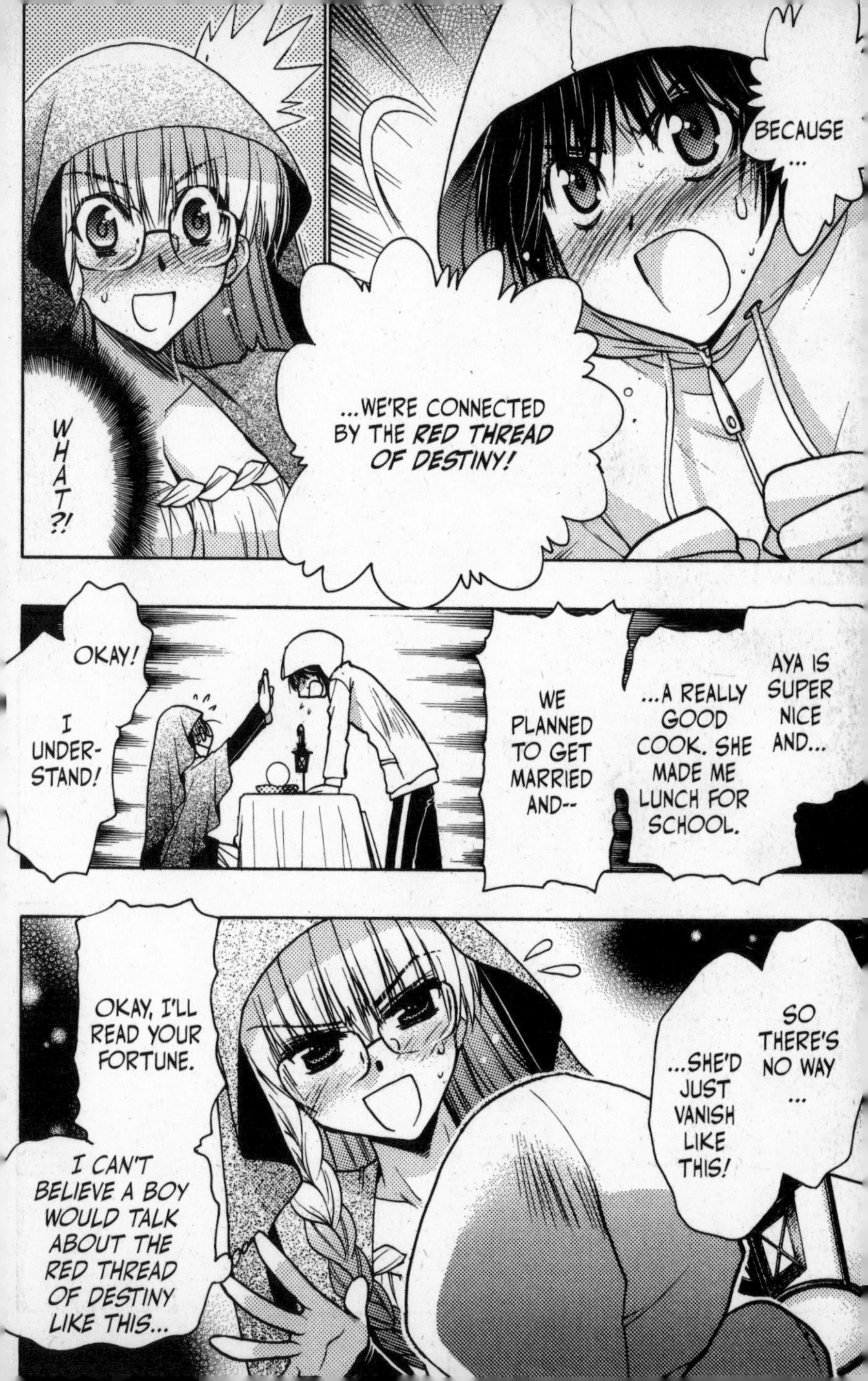
BECAUSE ...
...WE'RE CONNECTED BY THE RED THREAD OF DESTINY!
WHAT?!
AYA IS SUPER NICE AND...
...A REALLY GOOD COOK. SHE MADE ME LUNCH FOR SCHOOL.
WE PLANNED TO GET MARRIED AND--
OKAY!
I UNDER-STAND!
SO THERE'S NO WAY ...
...SHE'D JUST VANISH LIKE THIS!
OKAY, I'LL READ YOUR FORTUNE.
I CAN'T BELIEVE A BOY WOULD TALK ABOUT THE RED THREAD OF DESTINY LIKE THIS...

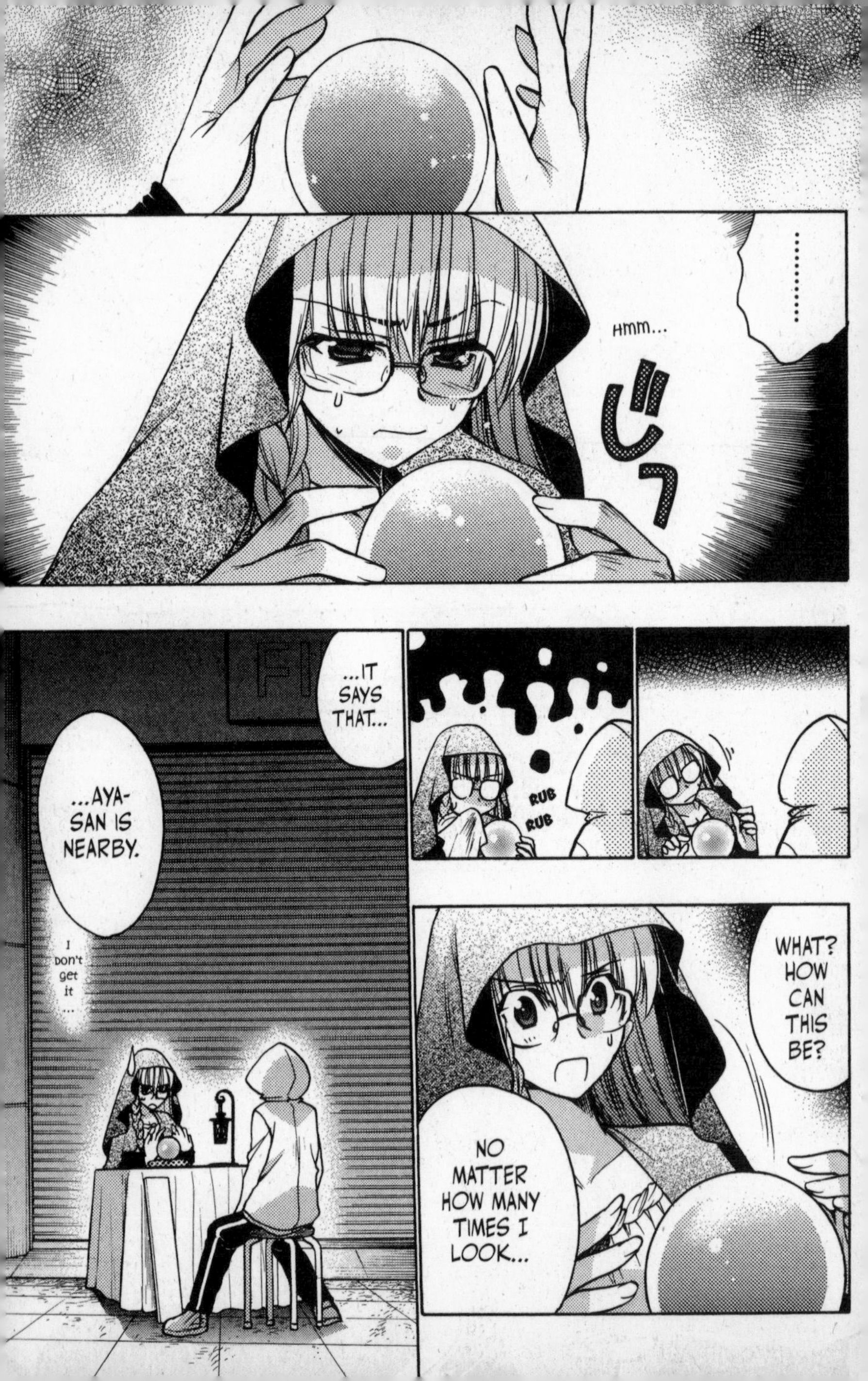
......
HMM...
じっ
RUB RUB
WHAT? HOW CAN THIS BE?
NO MATTER HOW MANY TIMES I LOOK...
...IT SAYS THAT...
...AYA-SAN IS NEARBY.
I don't get it ...

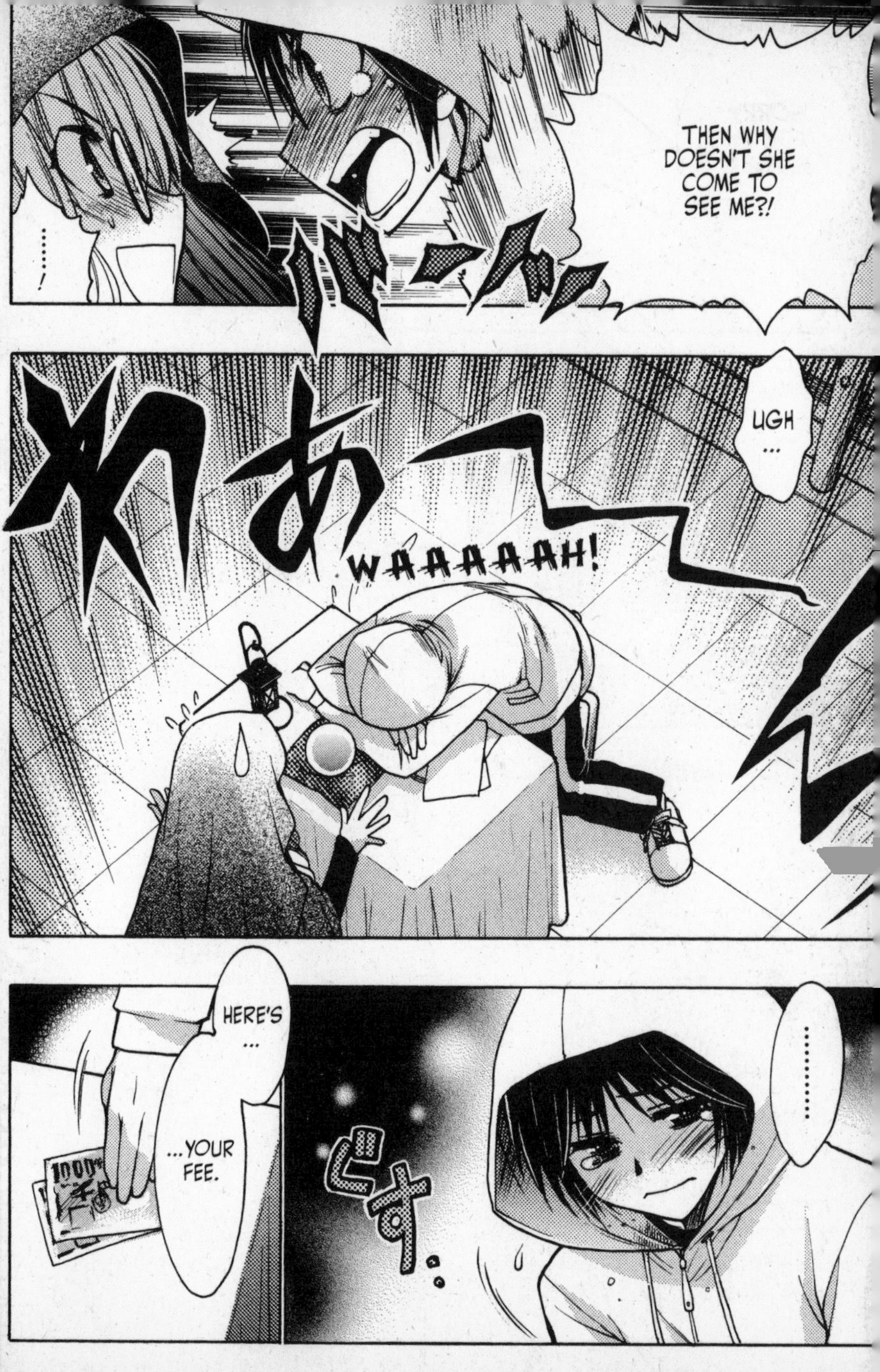
THEN WHY DOESN'T SHE COME TO SEE ME?!
……!
UGH …
わあ～
WAAAAAAH!
……
どす
HERE'S …
…YOUR FEE.

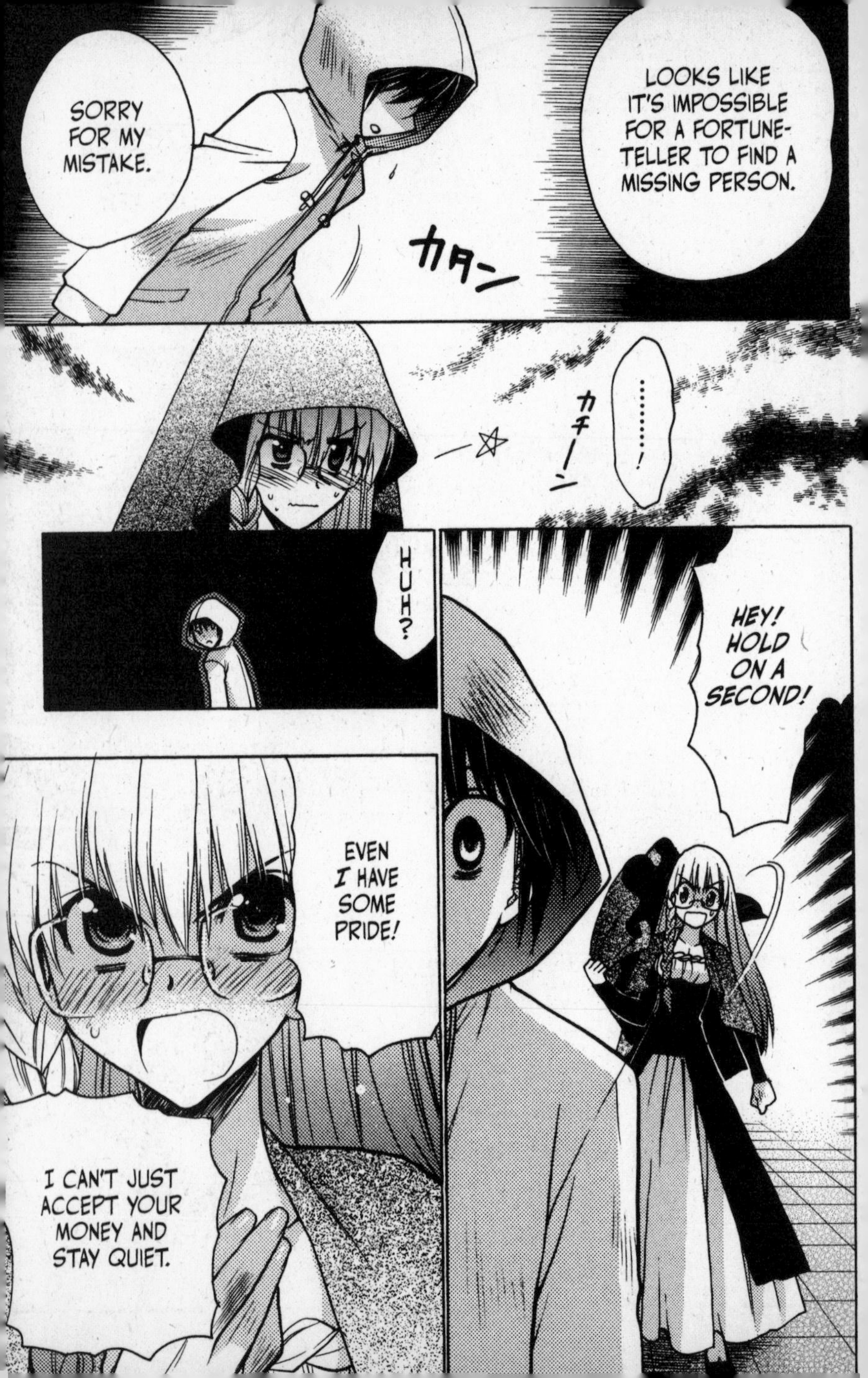
LOOKS LIKE IT'S IMPOSSIBLE FOR A FORTUNE-TELLER TO FIND A MISSING PERSON.
カタン
SORRY FOR MY MISTAKE.
......!
カチーン
HEY! HOLD ON A SECOND!
HUH?
EVEN I HAVE SOME PRIDE!
I CAN'T JUST ACCEPT YOUR MONEY AND STAY QUIET.

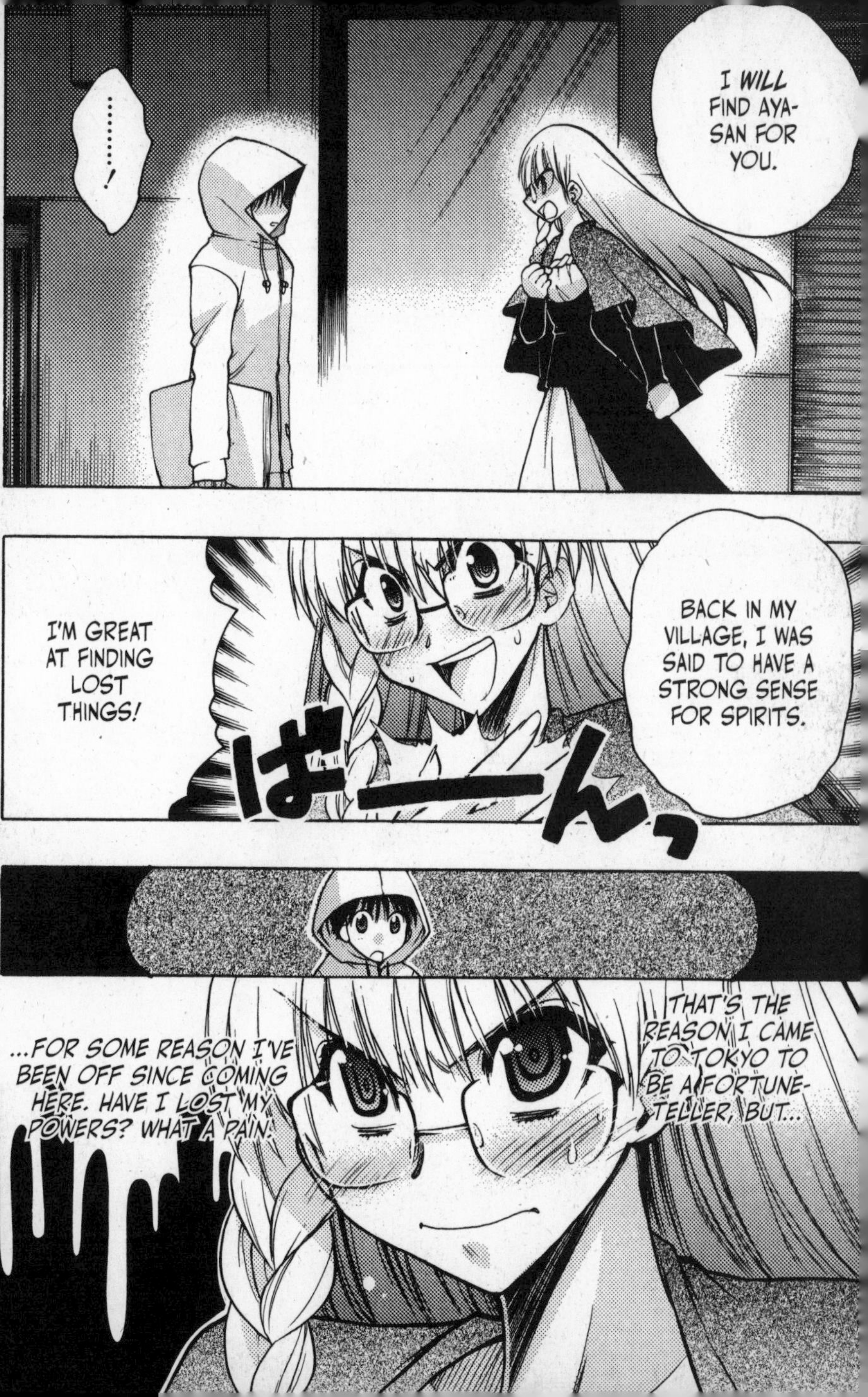
I WILL FIND AYA-SAN FOR YOU.
......!
BACK IN MY VILLAGE, I WAS SAID TO HAVE A STRONG SENSE FOR SPIRITS.
I'M GREAT AT FINDING LOST THINGS!
ばーーん
THAT'S THE REASON I CAME TO TOKYO TO BE A FORTUNE-TELLER, BUT...
...FOR SOME REASON I'VE BEEN OFF SINCE COMING HERE. HAVE I LOST MY POWERS? WHAT A PAIN.

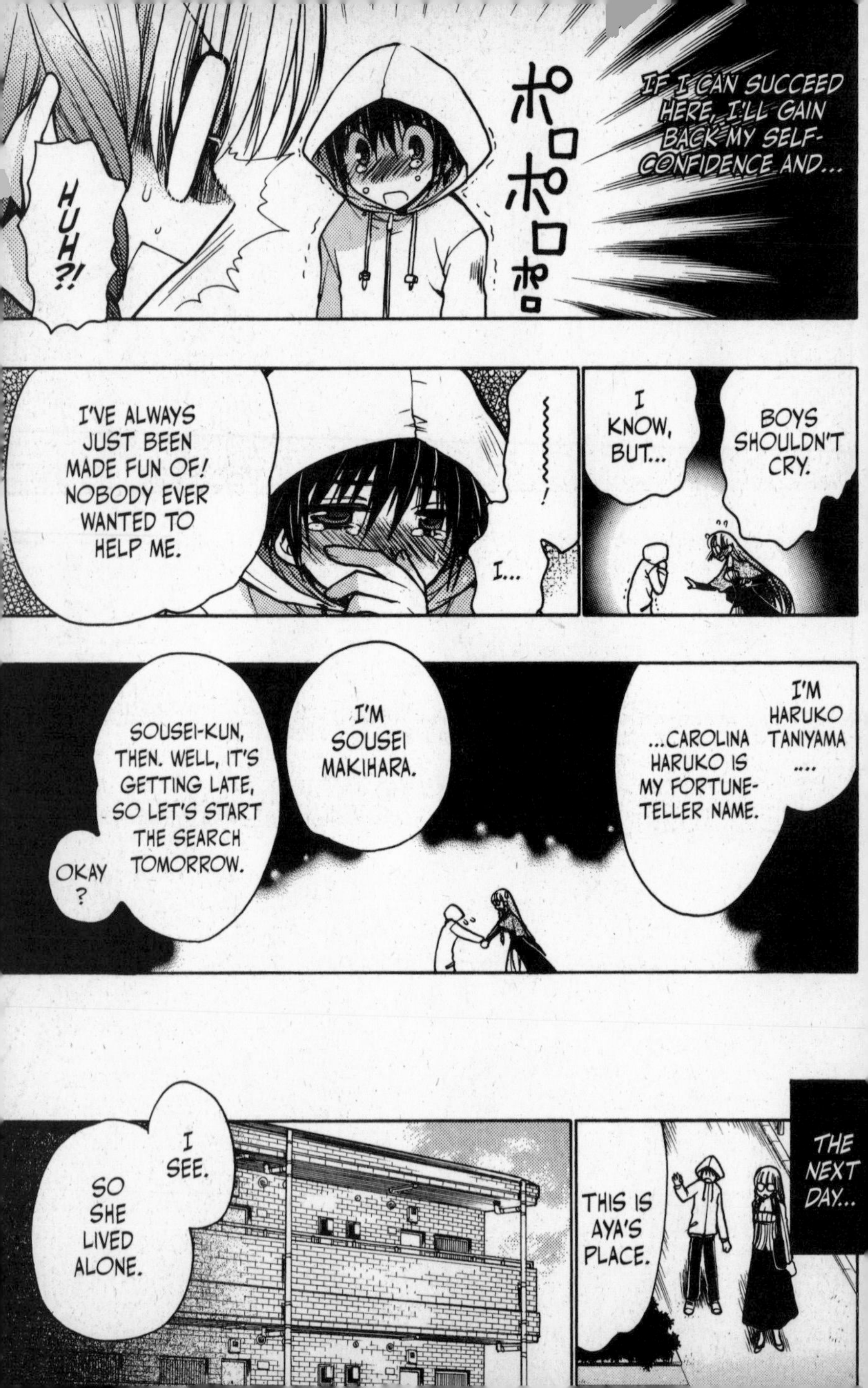
IF I CAN SUCCEED HERE, I'LL GAIN BACK MY SELF-CONFIDENCE AND...
ポロポロポロ
HUH?!
BOYS SHOULDN'T CRY.
I KNOW, BUT...
I...
I'VE ALWAYS JUST BEEN MADE FUN OF! NOBODY EVER WANTED TO HELP ME.
I'M HARUKO TANIYAMA ....
...CAROLINA HARUKO IS MY FORTUNE-TELLER NAME.
I'M SOUSEI MAKIHARA.
SOUSEI-KUN, THEN. WELL, IT'S GETTING LATE, SO LET'S START THE SEARCH TOMORROW.
OKAY ?
THE NEXT DAY...
THIS IS AYA'S PLACE.
I SEE.
SO SHE LIVED ALONE.

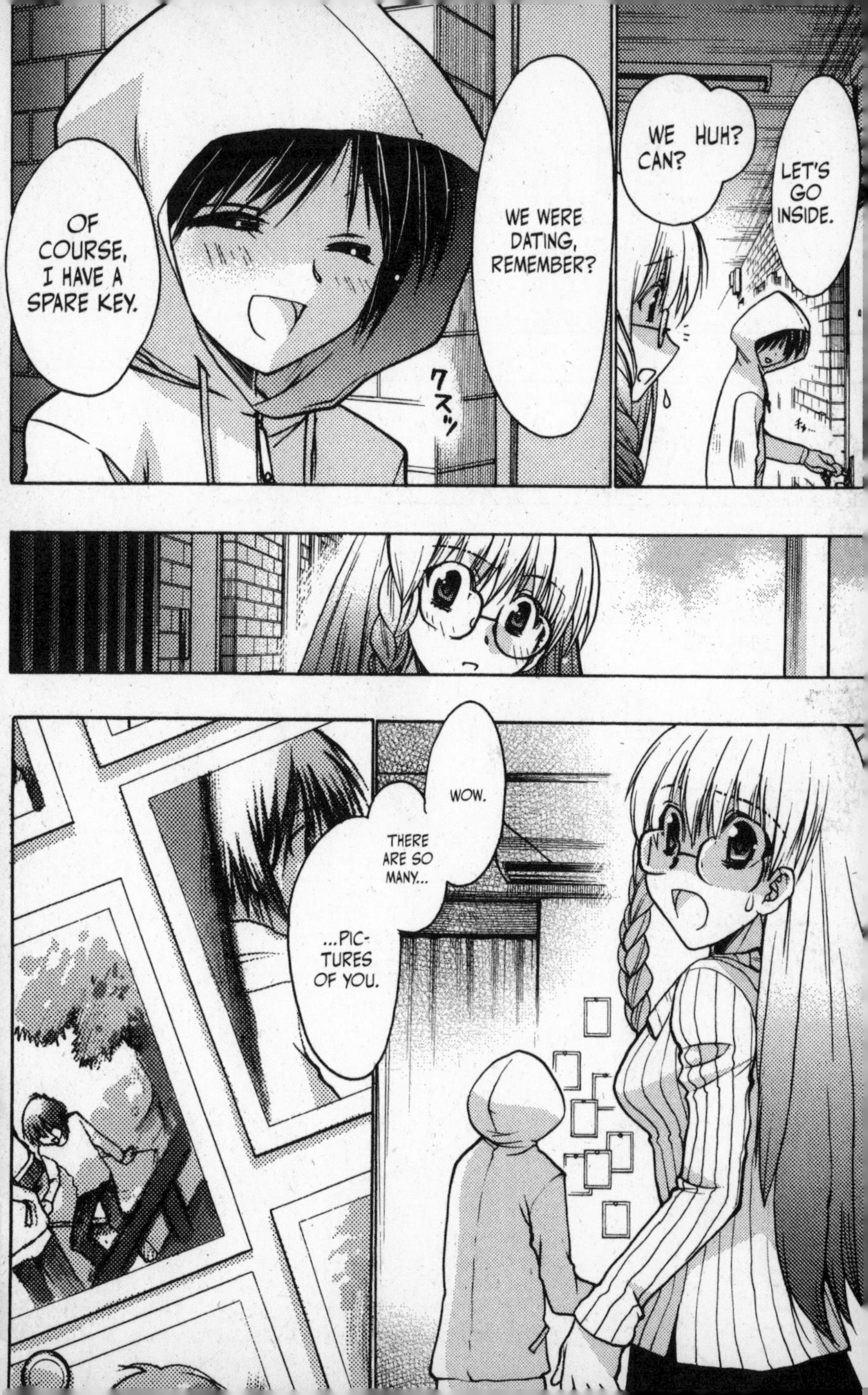
LET'S GO INSIDE.
HUH?
WE CAN?
WE WERE DATING, REMEMBER?
クスッ
OF COURSE, I HAVE A SPARE KEY.
WOW.
THERE ARE SO MANY...
...PIC-TURES OF YOU.

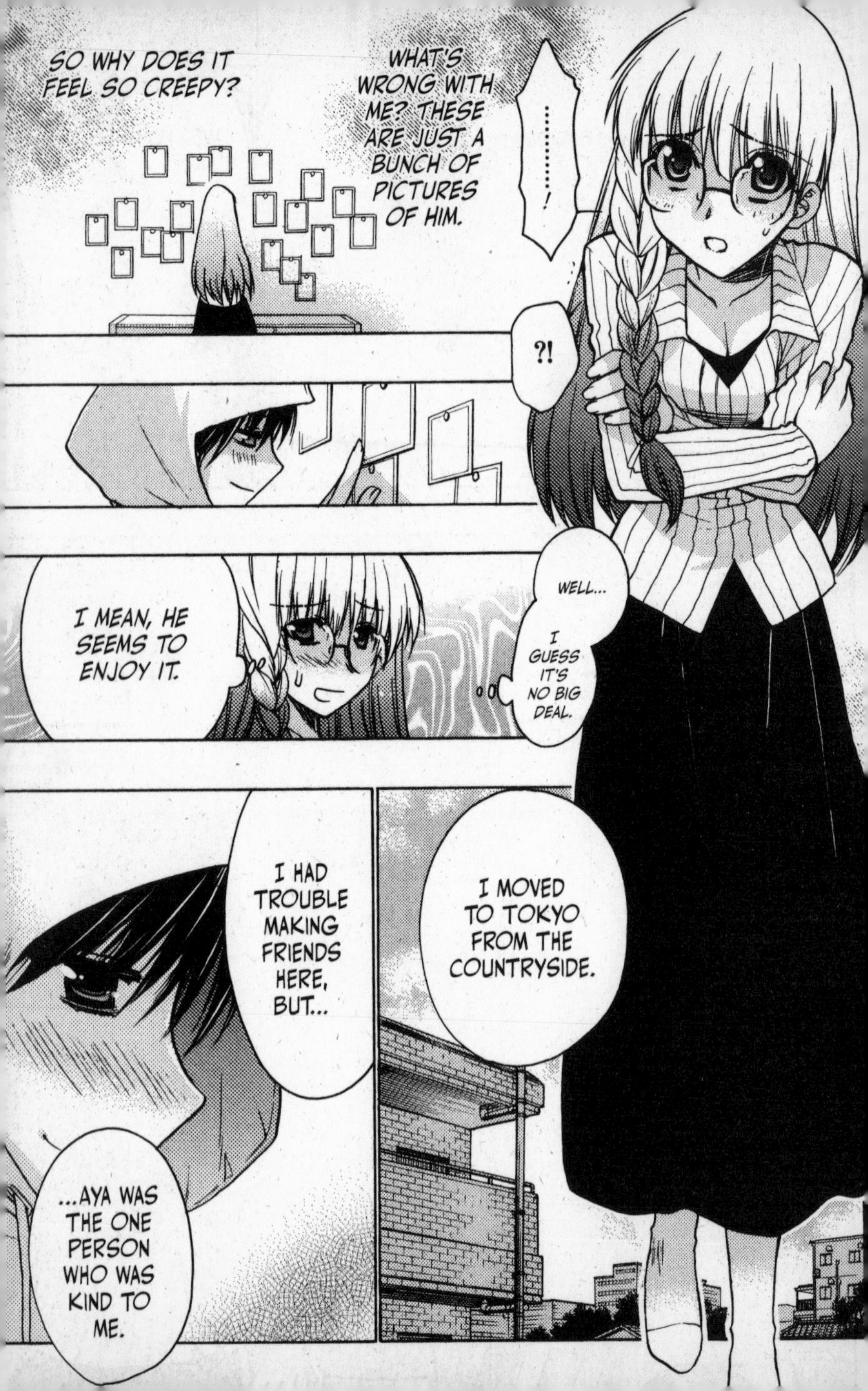
WHAT'S WRONG WITH ME? THESE ARE JUST A BUNCH OF PICTURES OF HIM.
SO WHY DOES IT FEEL SO CREEPY?
......!
?!
I MEAN, HE SEEMS TO ENJOY IT.
WELL... I GUESS IT'S NO BIG DEAL.
I MOVED TO TOKYO FROM THE COUNTRYSIDE.
I HAD TROUBLE MAKING FRIENDS HERE, BUT...
...AYA WAS THE ONE PERSON WHO WAS KIND TO ME.

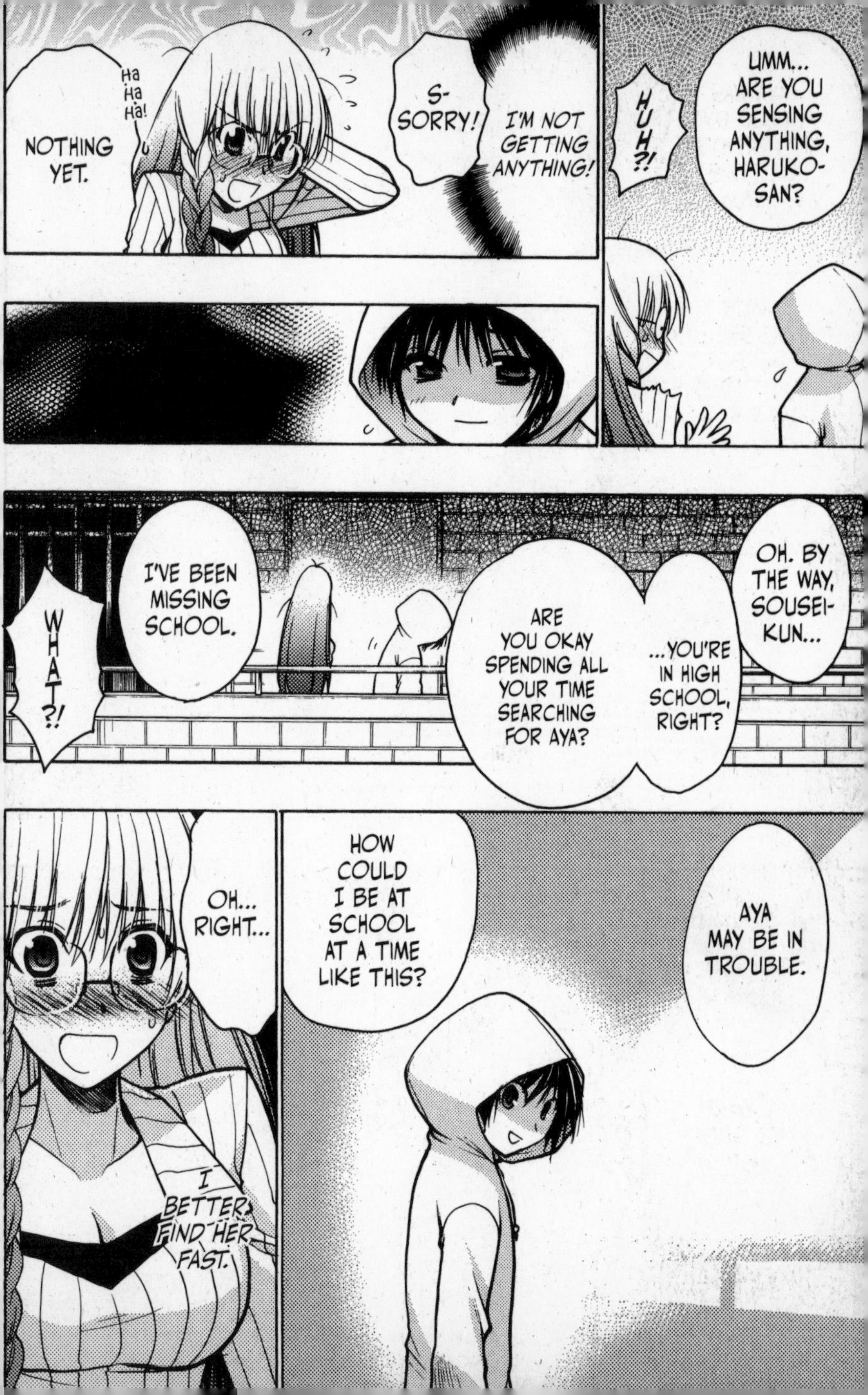
UMM... ARE YOU SENSING ANYTHING, HARUKO-SAN?
HUH?!
S-SORRY!
I'M NOT GETTING ANYTHING!
Ha Ha Ha!
NOTHING YET.
OH. BY THE WAY, SOUSEI-KUN...
...YOU'RE IN HIGH SCHOOL, RIGHT?
ARE YOU OKAY SPENDING ALL YOUR TIME SEARCHING FOR AYA?
I'VE BEEN MISSING SCHOOL.
WHAT?!
AYA MAY BE IN TROUBLE.
HOW COULD I BE AT SCHOOL AT A TIME LIKE THIS?
OH... RIGHT...
I BETTER FIND HER FAST.

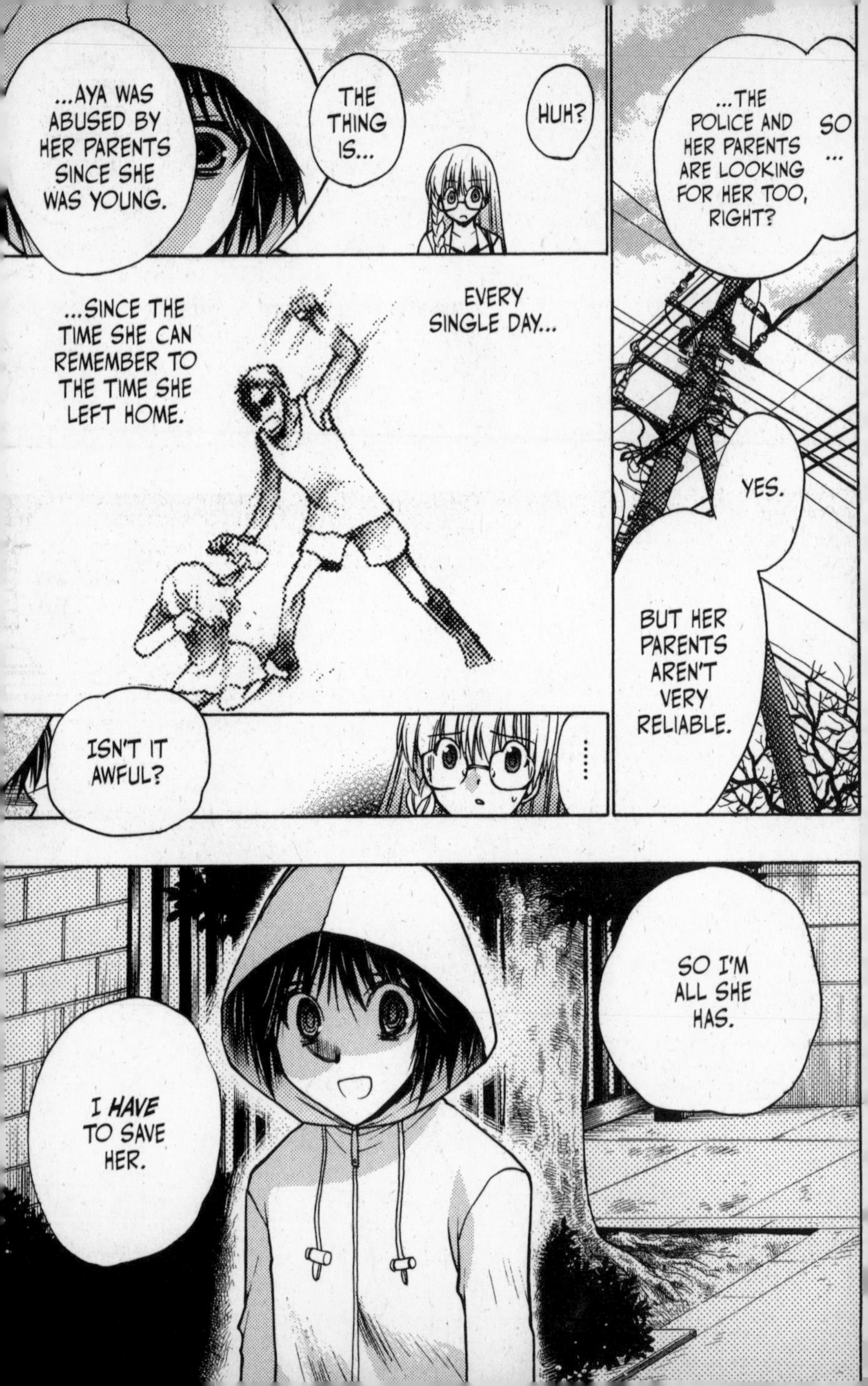
SO ...
...THE POLICE AND HER PARENTS ARE LOOKING FOR HER TOO, RIGHT?
YES.
BUT HER PARENTS AREN'T VERY RELIABLE.
HUH?
THE THING IS...
...AYA WAS ABUSED BY HER PARENTS SINCE SHE WAS YOUNG.
EVERY SINGLE DAY...
...SINCE THE TIME SHE CAN REMEMBER TO THE TIME SHE LEFT HOME.
......
ISN'T IT AWFUL?
SO I'M ALL SHE HAS.
I *HAVE* TO SAVE HER.

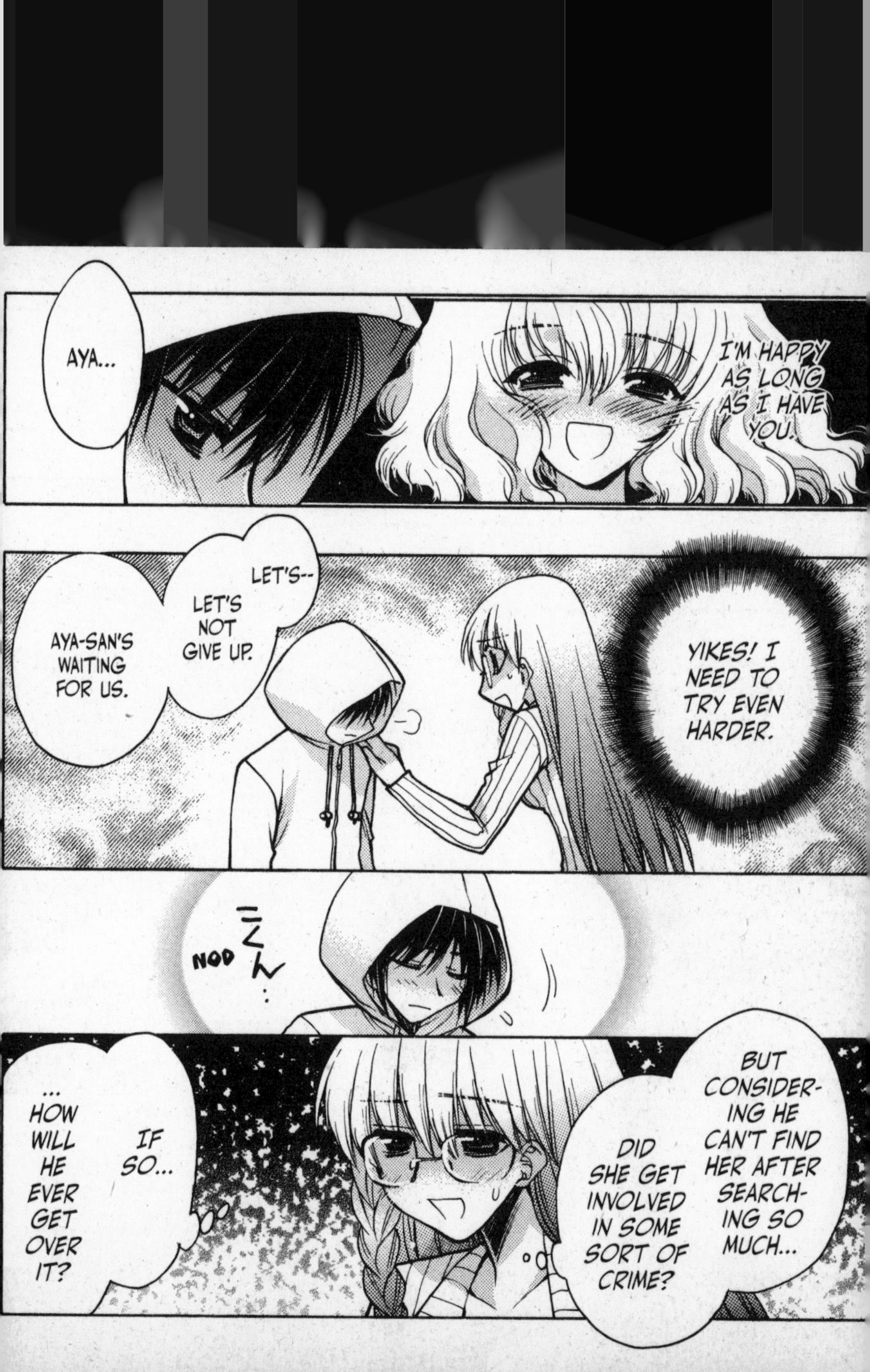
I'M HAPPY AS LONG AS I HAVE YOU.
AYA...
YIKES! I NEED TO TRY EVEN HARDER.
LET'S--
LET'S NOT GIVE UP.
AYA-SAN'S WAITING FOR US.
NOD
BUT CONSIDER-ING HE CAN'T FIND HER AFTER SEARCH-ING SO MUCH...
DID SHE GET INVOLVED IN SOME SORT OF CRIME?
IF SO...
... HOW WILL HE EVER GET OVER IT?

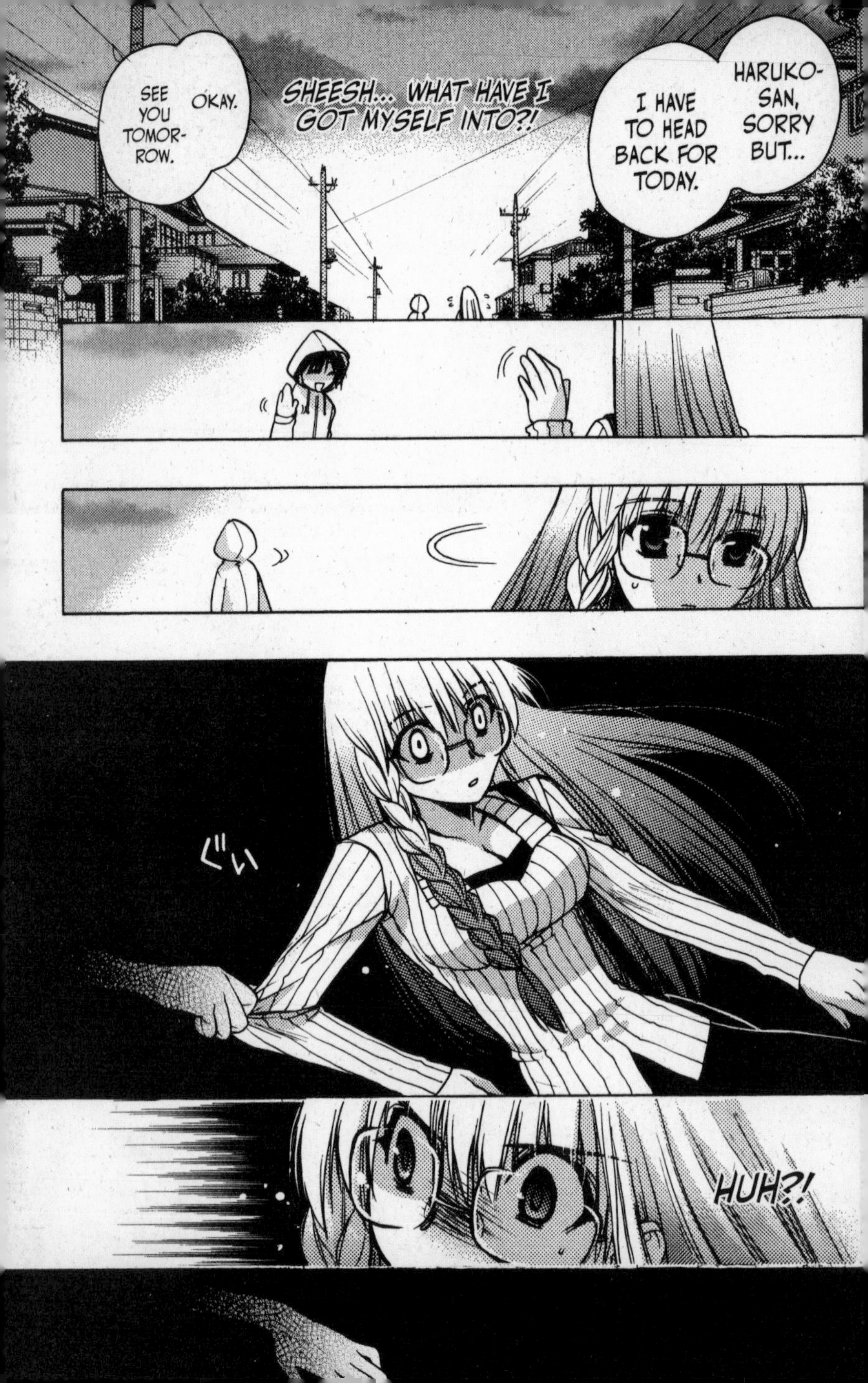
HARUKO-SAN, SORRY BUT... I HAVE TO HEAD BACK FOR TODAY.
SHEESH... WHAT HAVE I GOT MYSELF INTO?!
OKAY. SEE YOU TOMOR-ROW.
ぐい
HUH?!

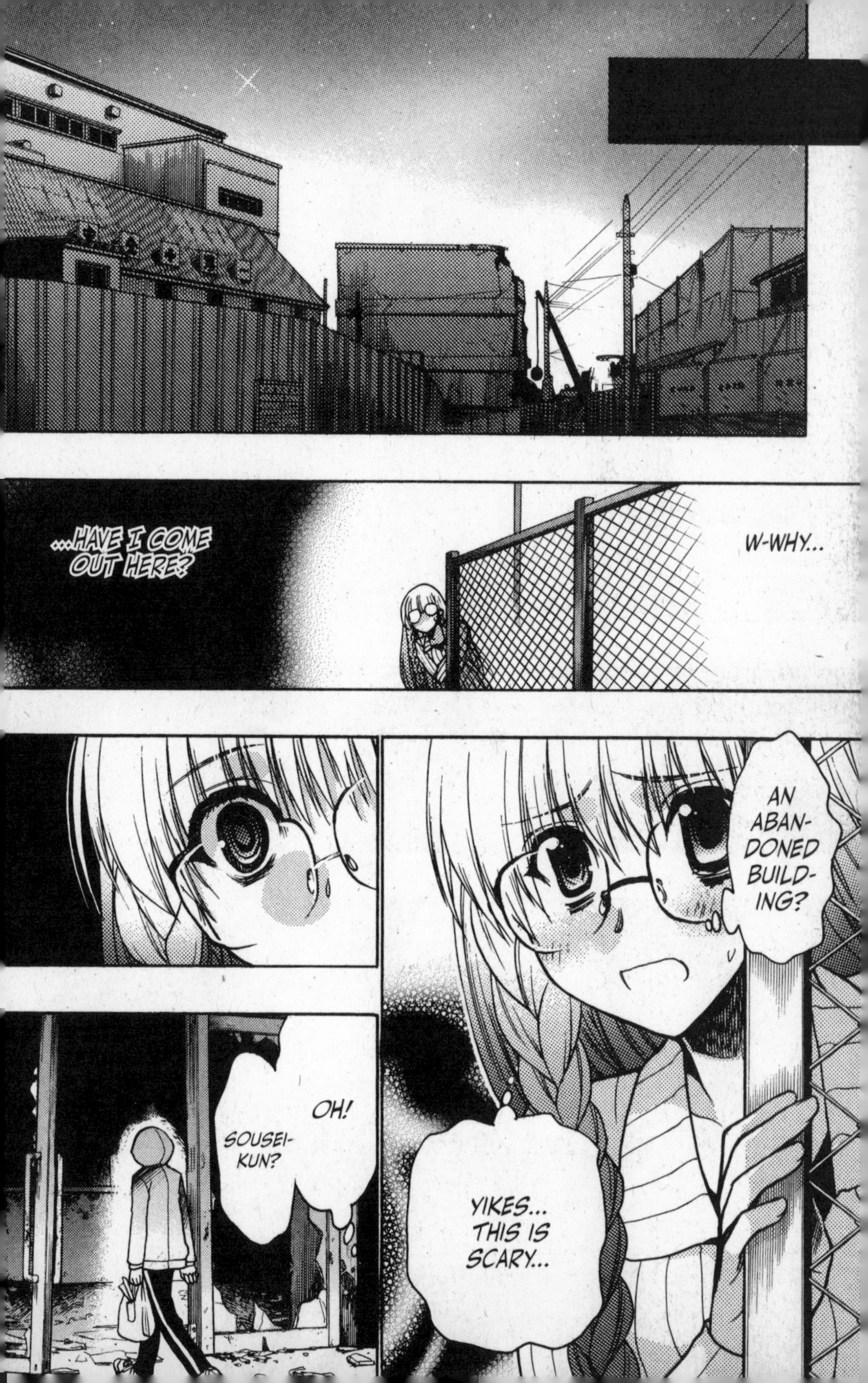
W-WHY...
...HAVE I COME OUT HERE?
AN ABAN-DONED BUILD-ING?
YIKES... THIS IS SCARY...
OH!
SOUSEI-KUN?

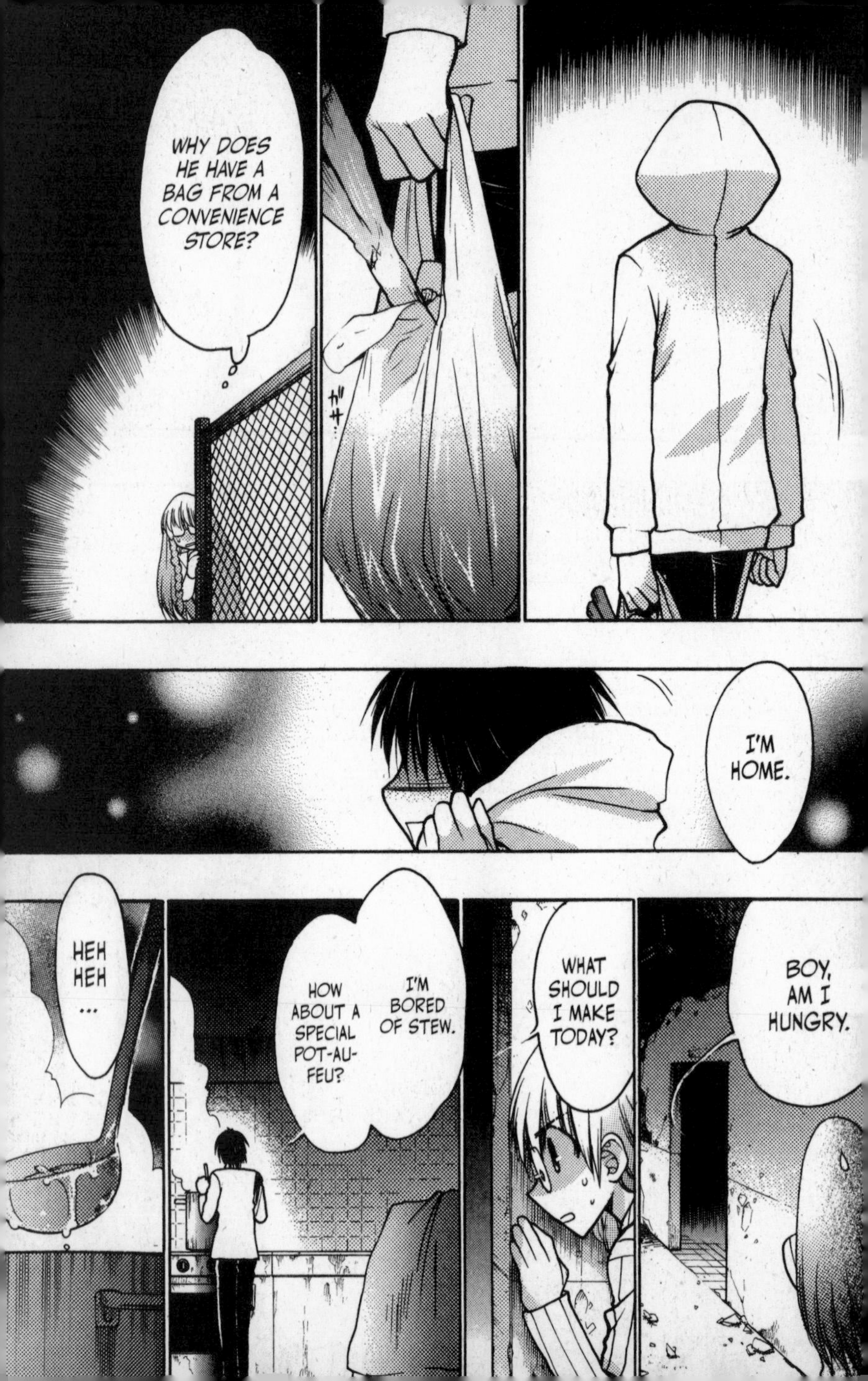
ガサ
WHY DOES HE HAVE A BAG FROM A CONVENIENCE STORE?
I'M HOME.
BOY, AM I HUNGRY.
WHAT SHOULD I MAKE TODAY?
I'M BORED OF STEW.
HOW ABOUT A SPECIAL POT-AU-FEU?
HEH HEH ...

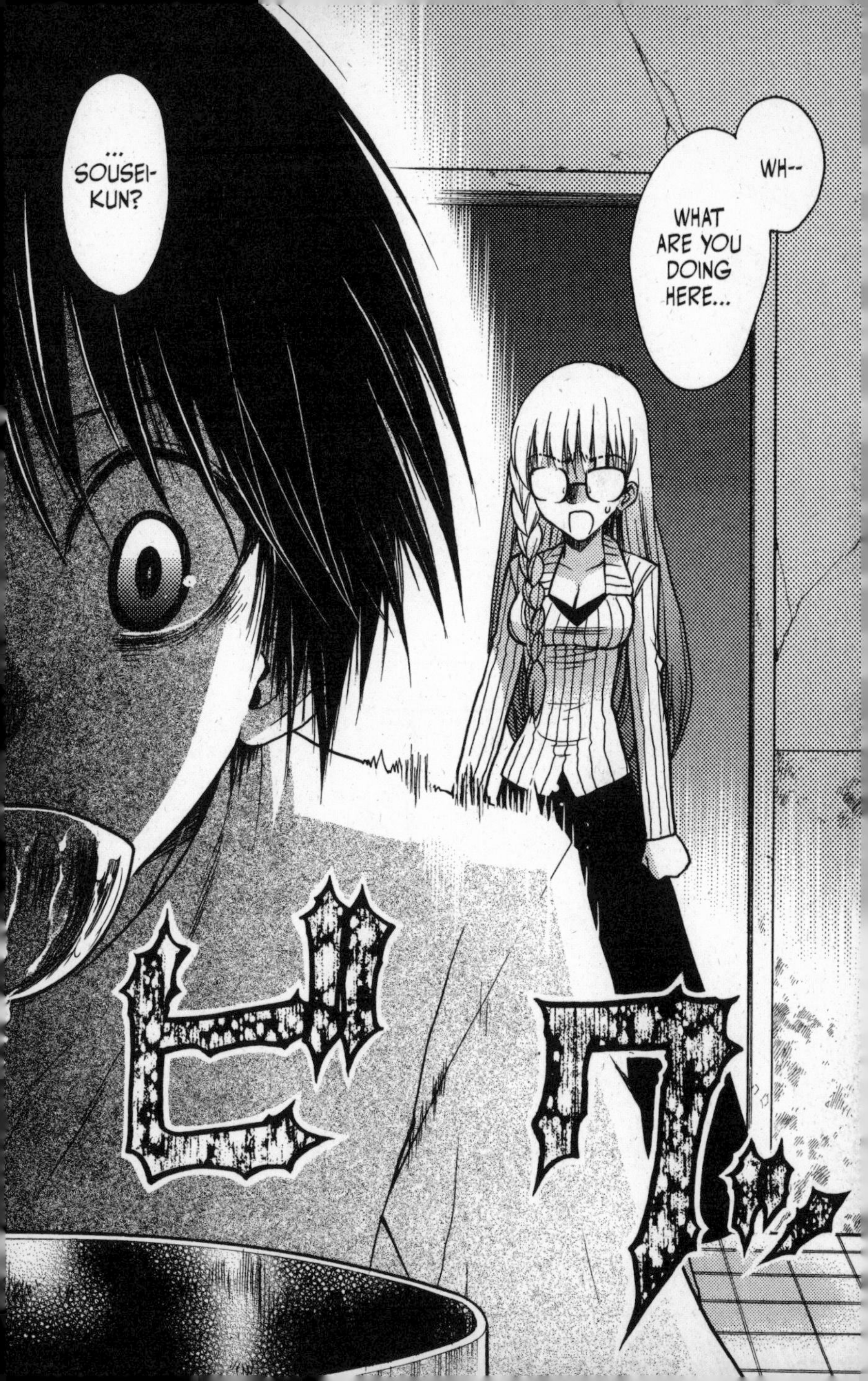
WH-- WHAT ARE YOU DOING HERE...
... SOUSEI-KUN?
ヒクッ

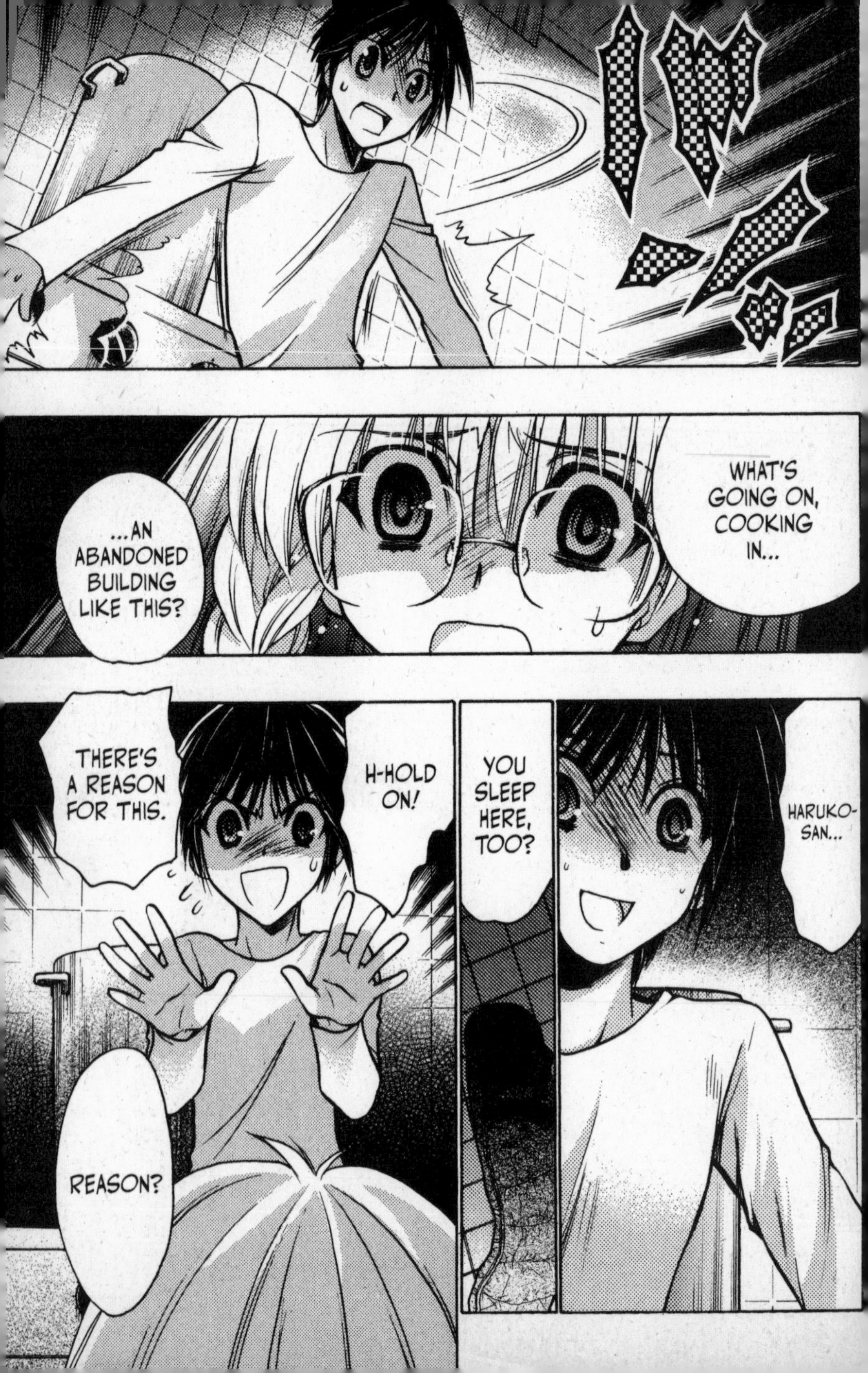
WHAT'S GOING ON, COOKING IN...
...AN ABANDONED BUILDING LIKE THIS?
HARUKO-SAN...
YOU SLEEP HERE, TOO?
H-HOLD ON!
THERE'S A REASON FOR THIS.
REASON?

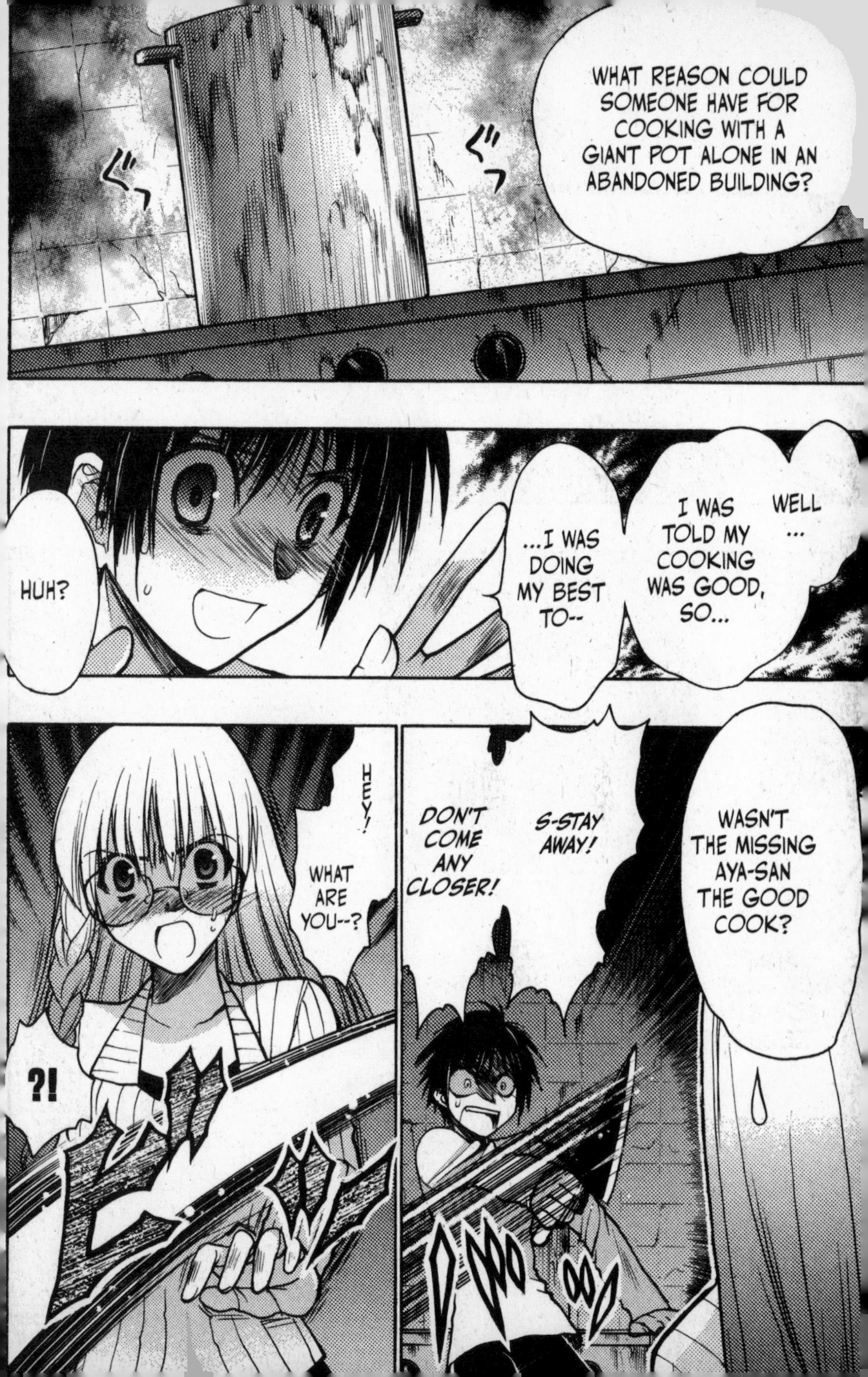

WHAT REASON COULD SOMEONE HAVE FOR COOKING WITH A GIANT POT ALONE IN AN ABANDONED BUILDING?
WELL ...
I WAS TOLD MY COOKING WAS GOOD, SO...
...I WAS DOING MY BEST TO--
HUH?
WASN'T THE MISSING AYA-SAN THE GOOD COOK?
S-STAY AWAY!
DON'T COME ANY CLOSER!
HEY!
WHAT ARE YOU--?
?!

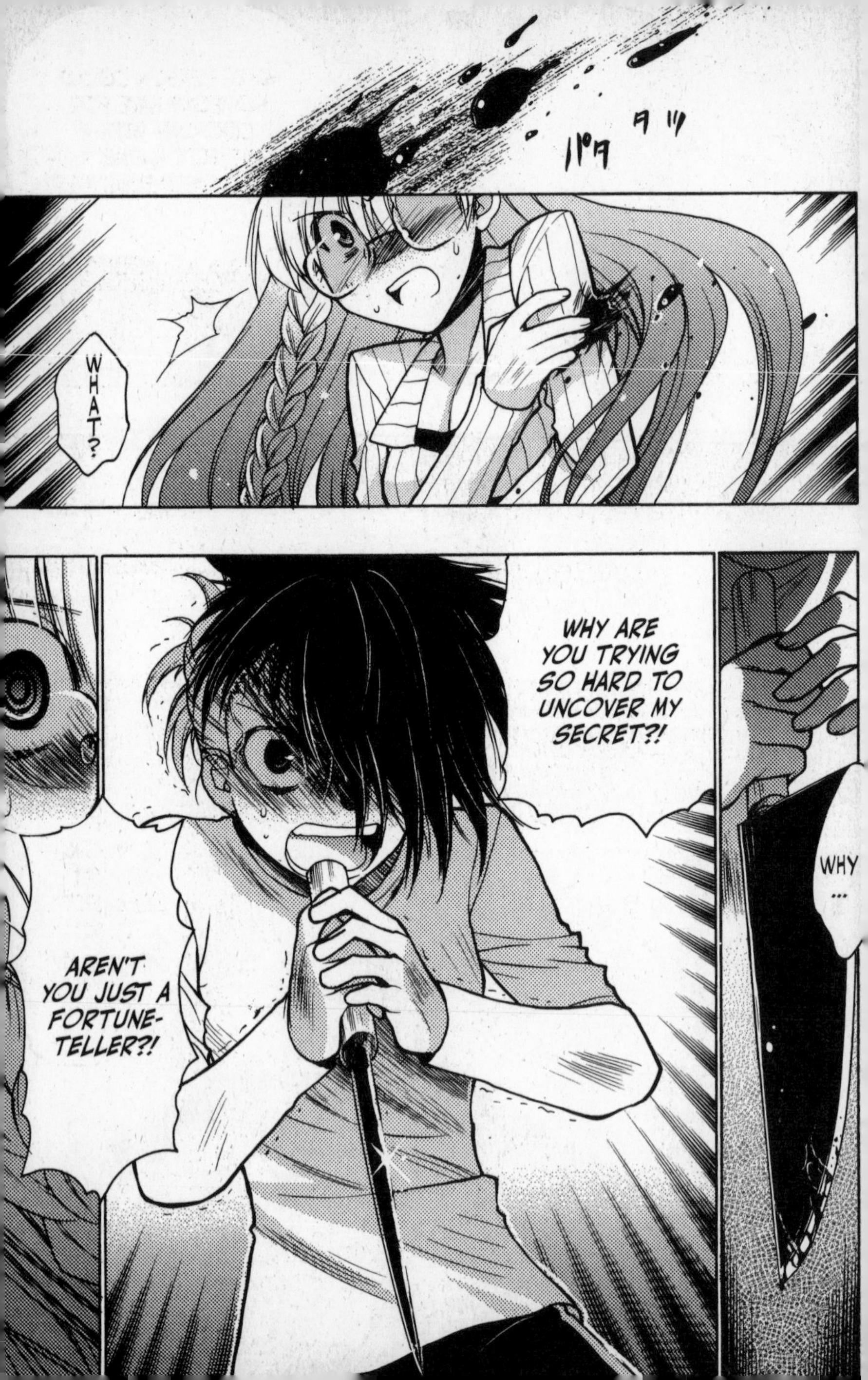
タッ
パタ
WHAT?!
WHY ...
WHY ARE YOU TRYING SO HARD TO UNCOVER MY SECRET?!
AREN'T YOU JUST A FORTUNE-TELLER?!

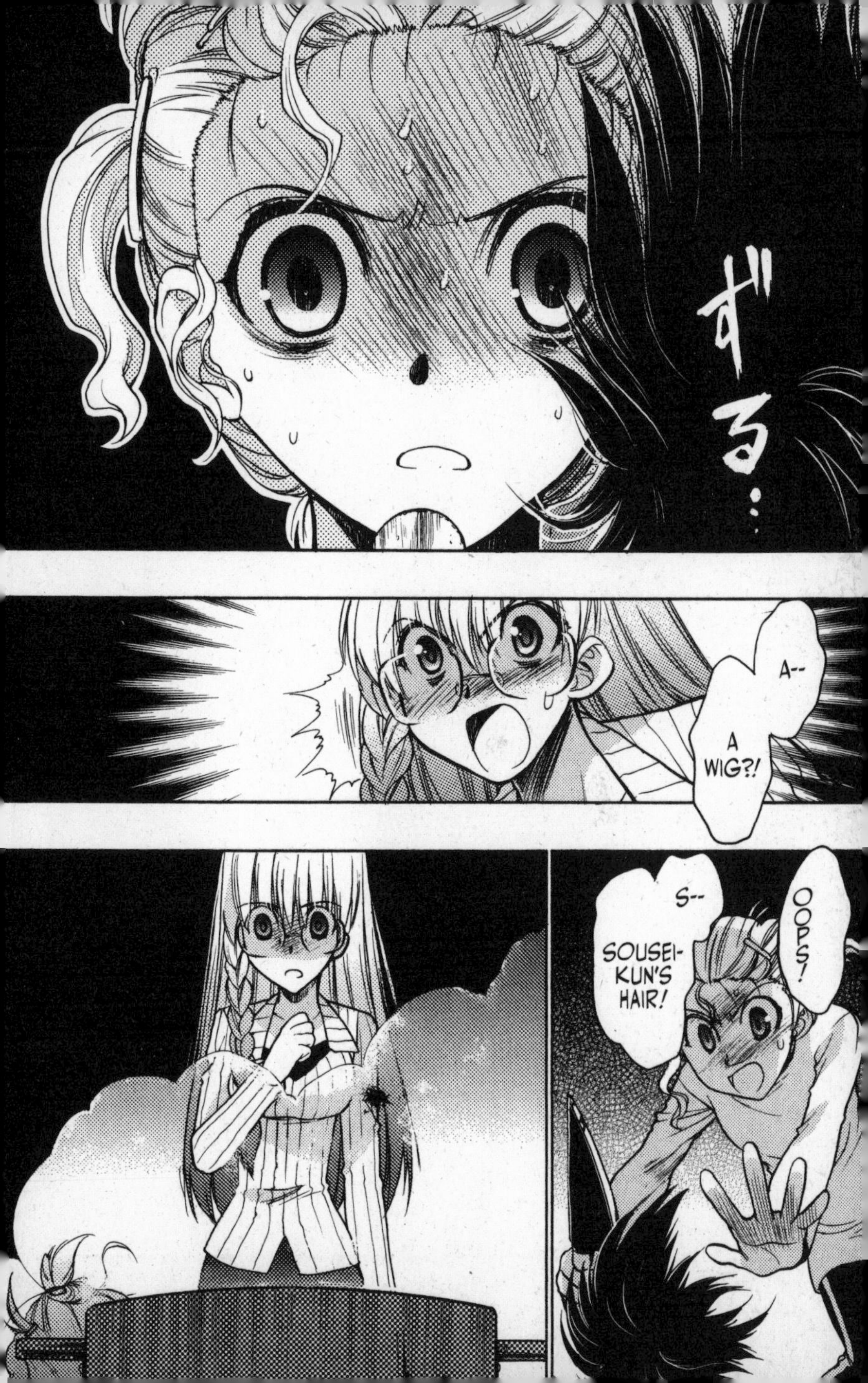
ずる…
A--
A WIG?!
OOPS?!
S--
SOUSEI-KUN'S HAIR!

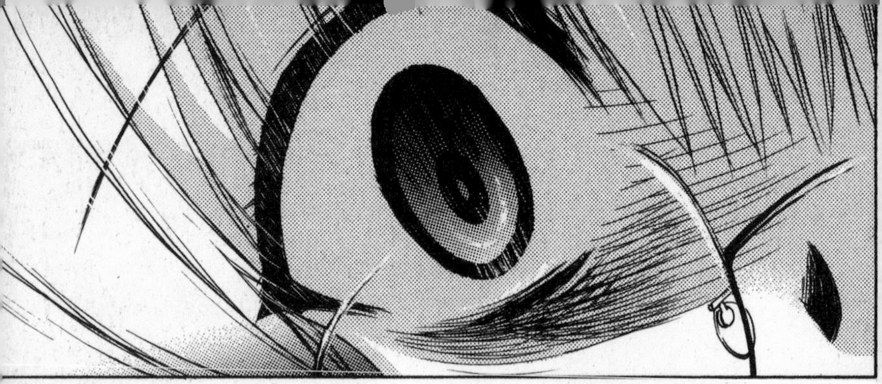

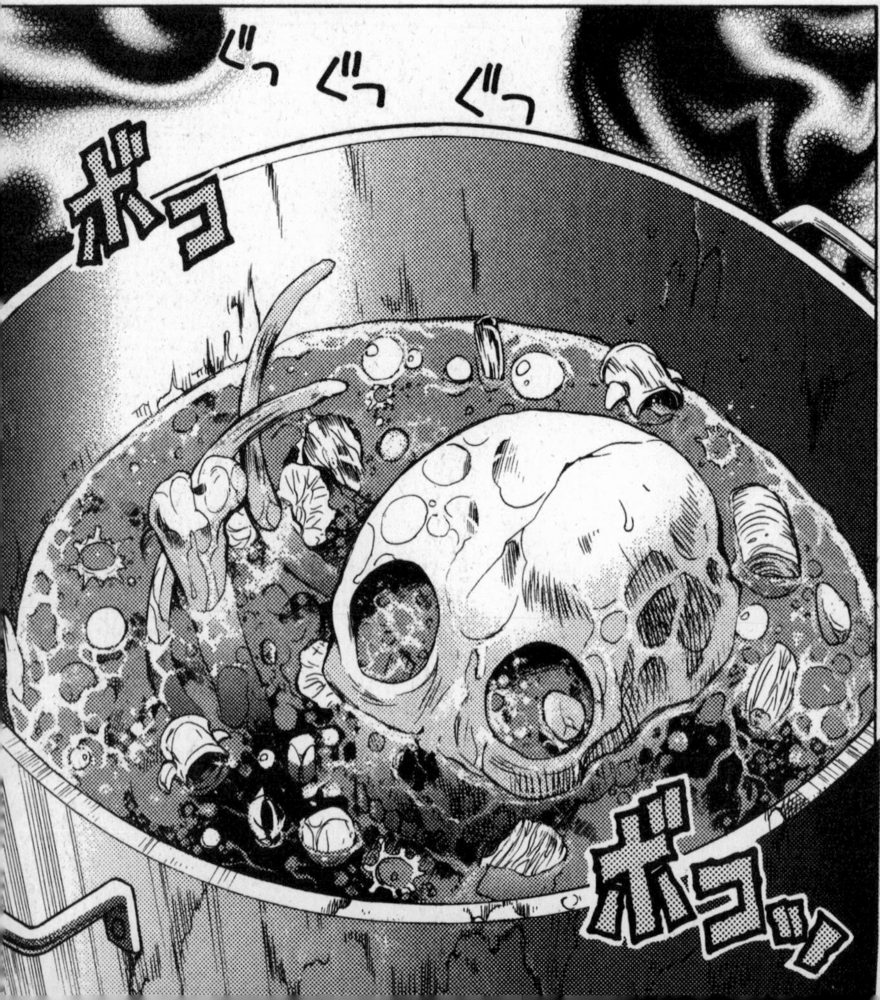
ぐつ ぐつ ぐつ
ボコ
ボコッ

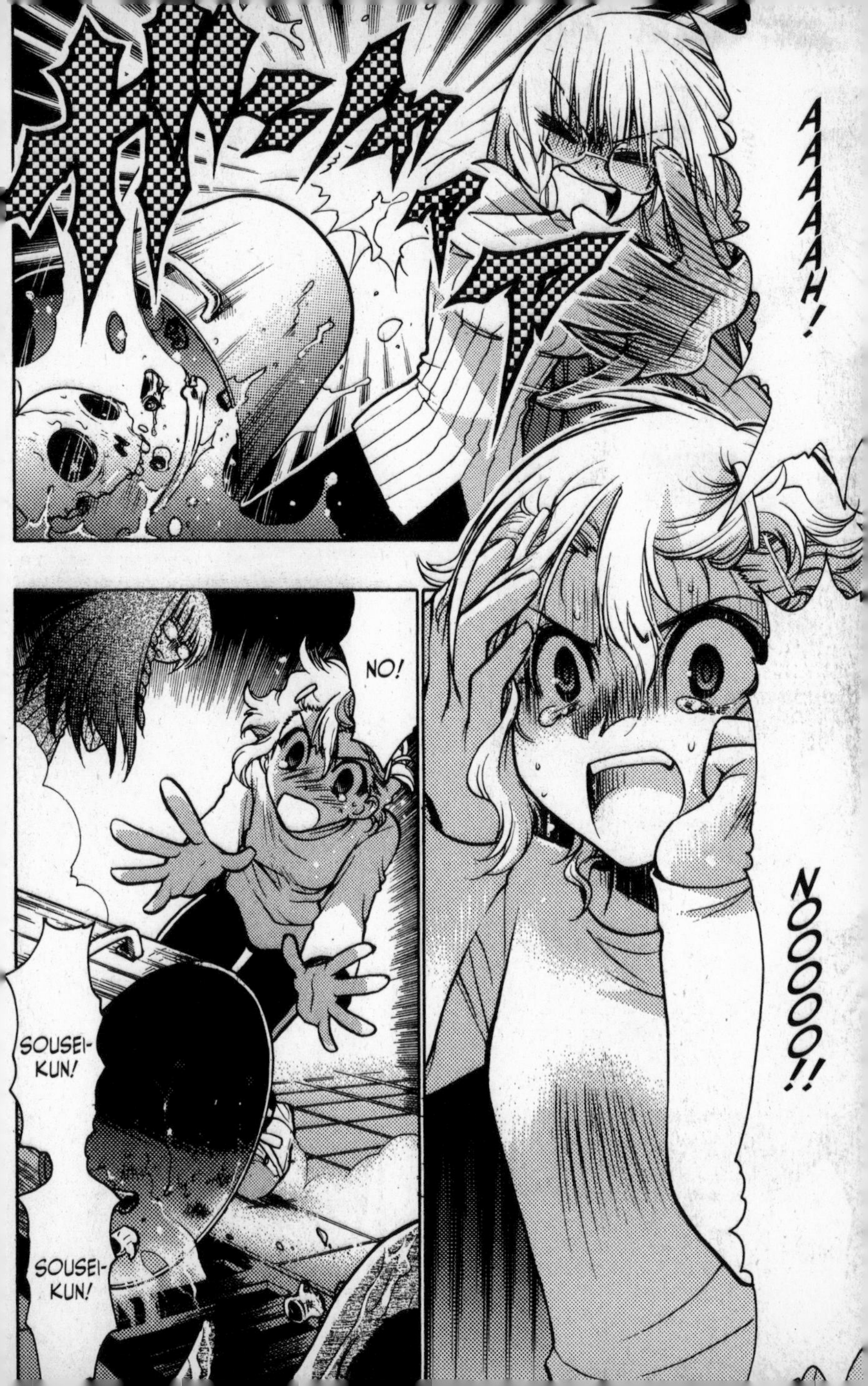
AAAAAH!
NOOOOOO!!
NO!
SOUSEI-KUN!
SOUSEI-KUN!

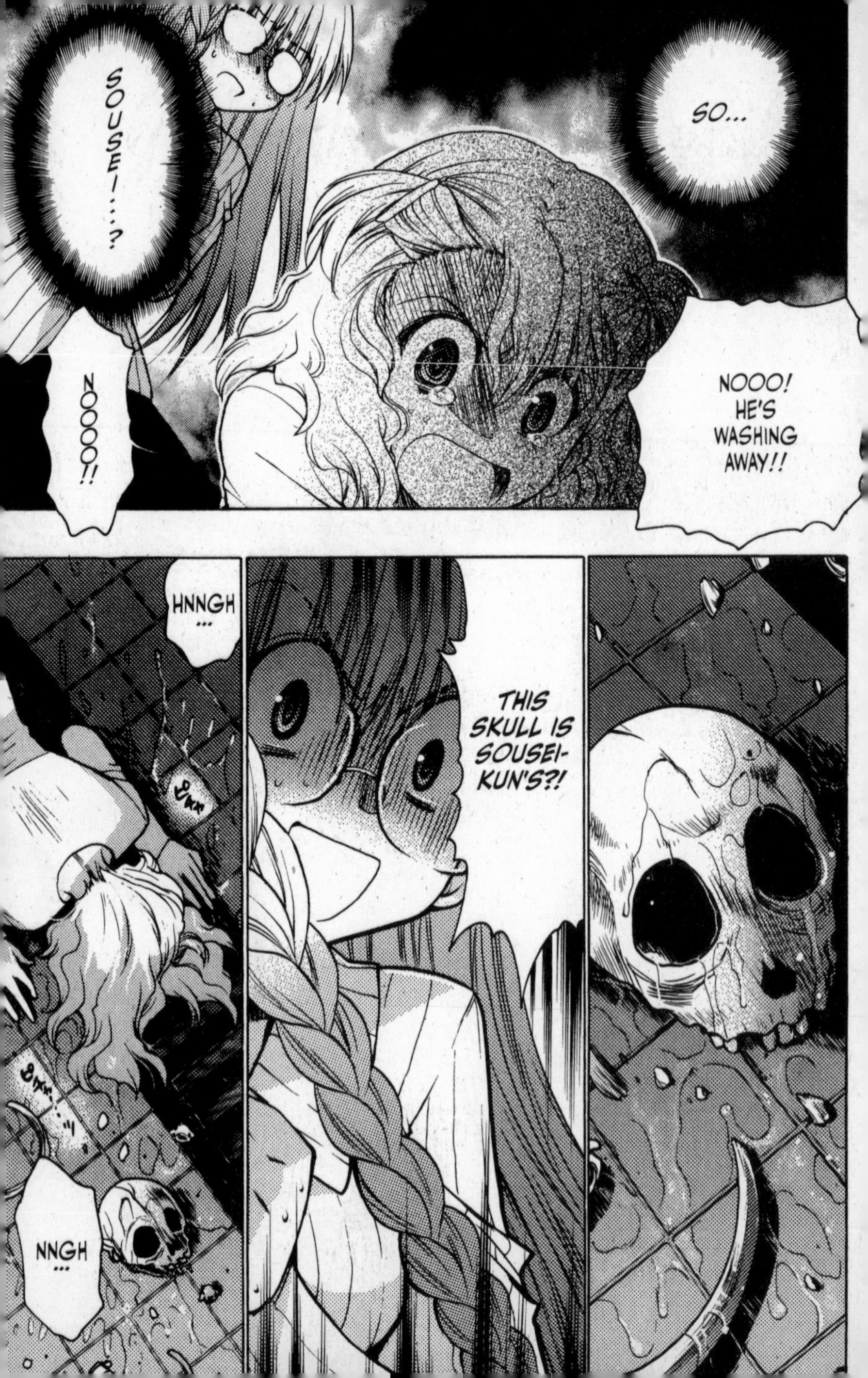
SO...
SOUSEI...?
NOOO! HE'S WASHING AWAY!!
NOOOO!!
THIS SKULL IS SOUSEI-KUN'S?!
HNNGH...
NNGH...

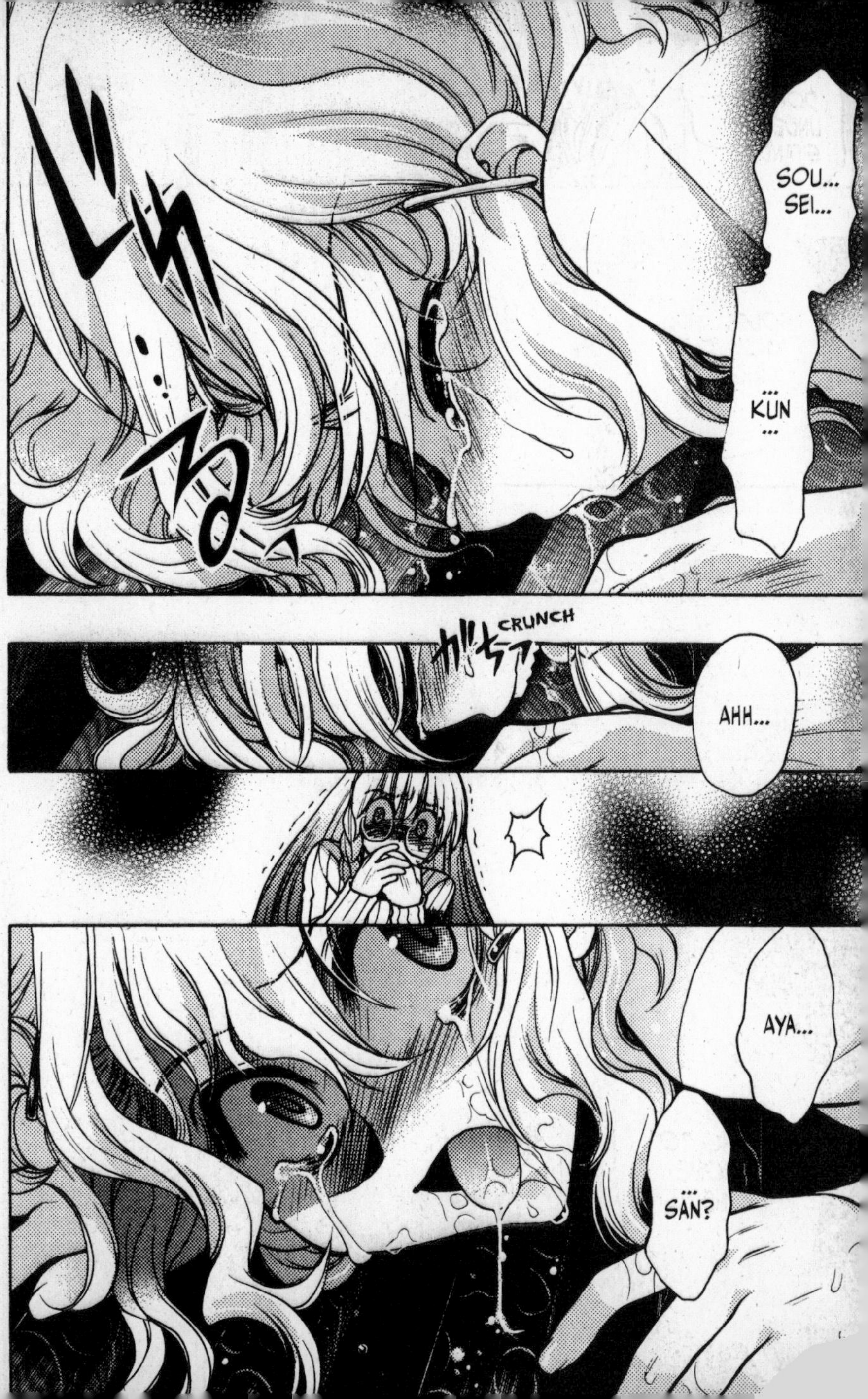
SOU... SEI...
...KUN...
AHH...
CRUNCH
AYA...
...SAN?

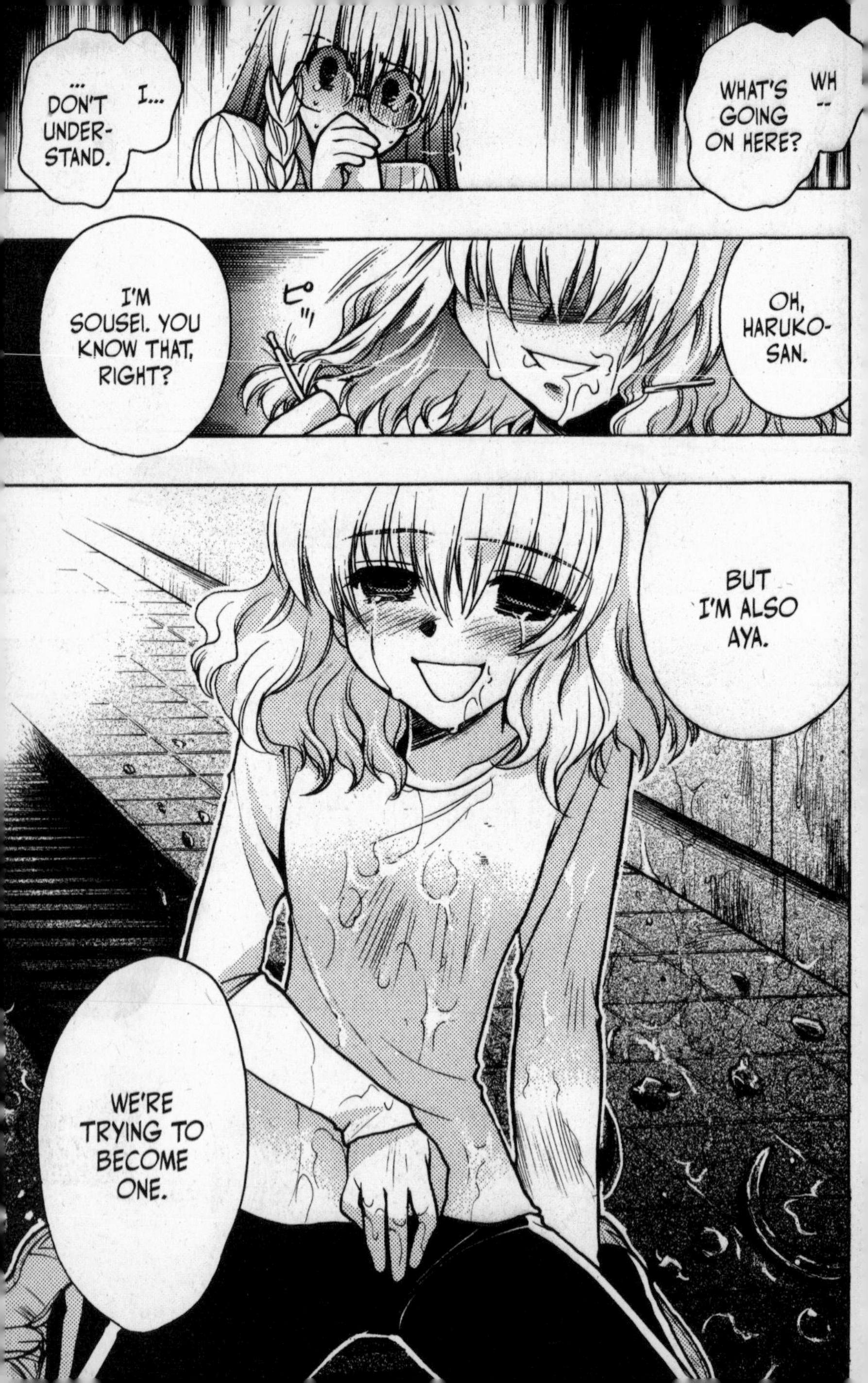
WH --
WHAT'S GOING ON HERE?
I...
... DON'T UNDER-STAND.
OH, HARUKO-SAN.
ピッ
I'M SOUSEI. YOU KNOW THAT, RIGHT?
BUT I'M ALSO AYA.
WE'RE TRYING TO BECOME ONE.

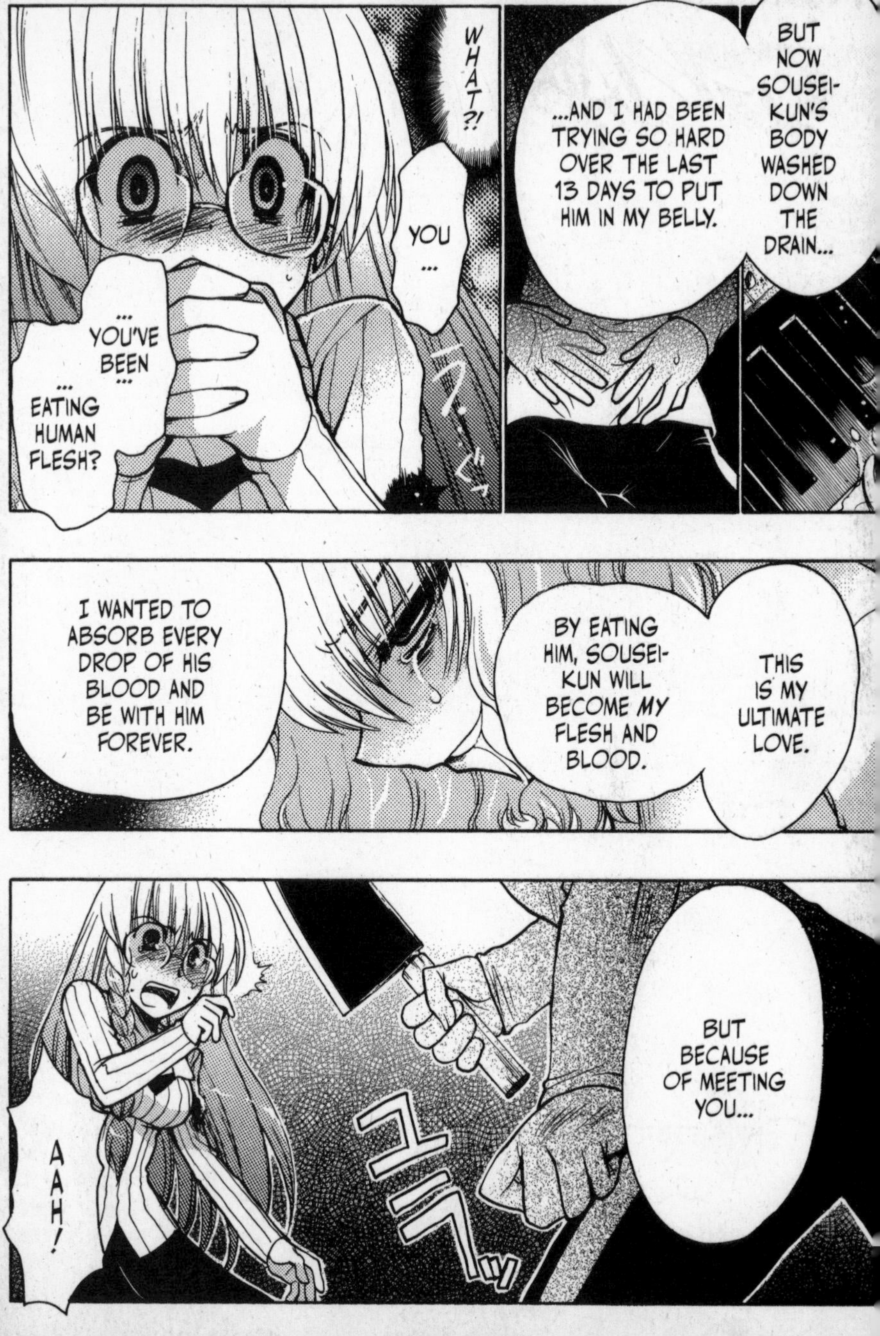
BUT NOW SOUSEI-KUN'S BODY WASHED DOWN THE DRAIN...
...AND I HAD BEEN TRYING SO HARD OVER THE LAST 13 DAYS TO PUT HIM IN MY BELLY.
WHAT?!
YOU...
...YOU'VE BEEN... EATING HUMAN FLESH?
THIS IS MY ULTIMATE LOVE.
BY EATING HIM, SOUSEI-KUN WILL BECOME *MY* FLESH AND BLOOD.
I WANTED TO ABSORB EVERY DROP OF HIS BLOOD AND BE WITH HIM FOREVER.
BUT BECAUSE OF MEETING YOU...
AAH!

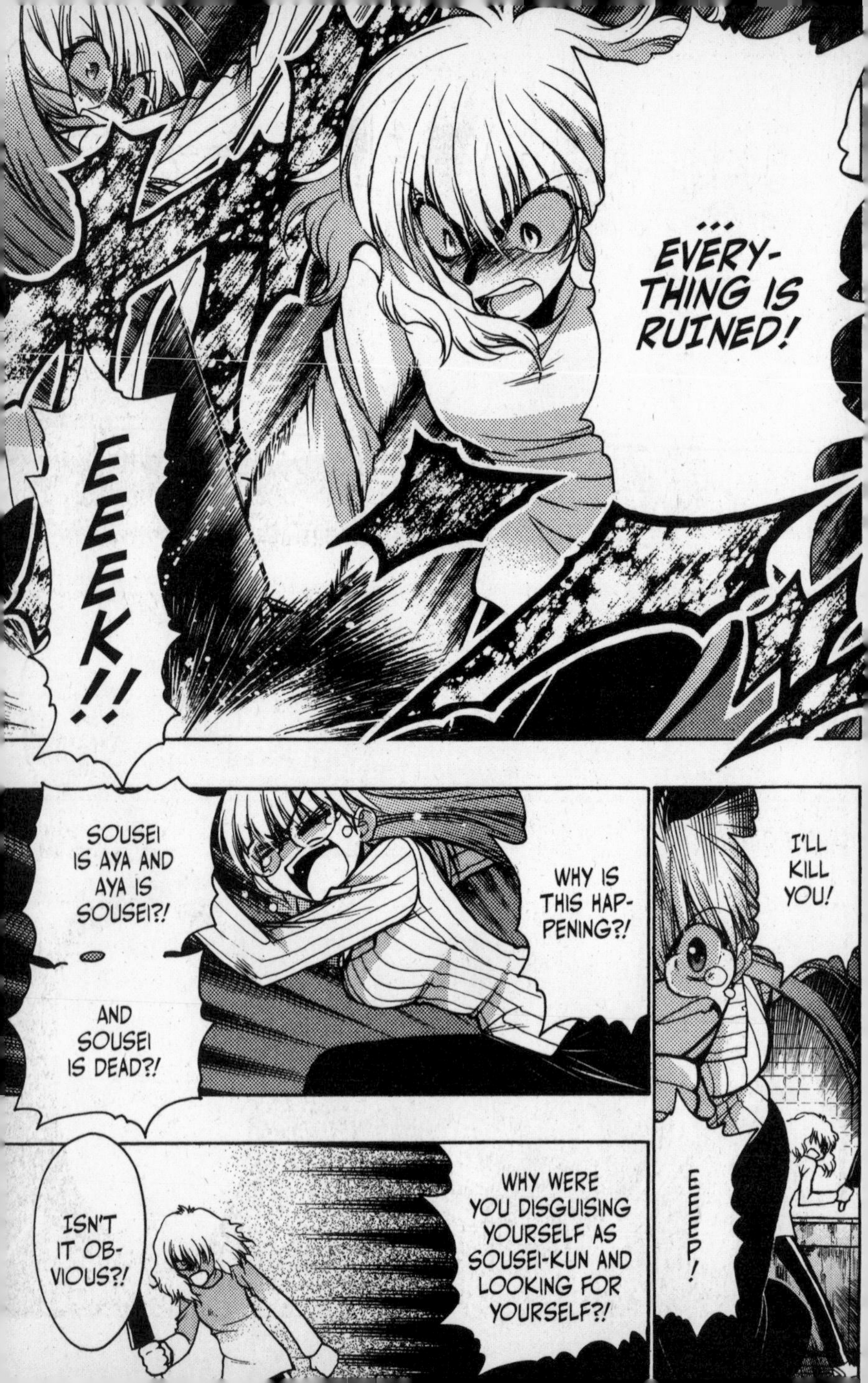
...EVERYTHING IS RUINED!
EEEEK!!
I'LL KILL YOU!
EEEP!
WHY IS THIS HAPPENING?!
SOUSEI IS AYA AND AYA IS SOUSEI?!
...
AND SOUSEI IS DEAD?!
WHY WERE YOU DISGUISING YOURSELF AS SOUSEI-KUN AND LOOKING FOR YOURSELF?!
ISN'T IT OBVIOUS?!

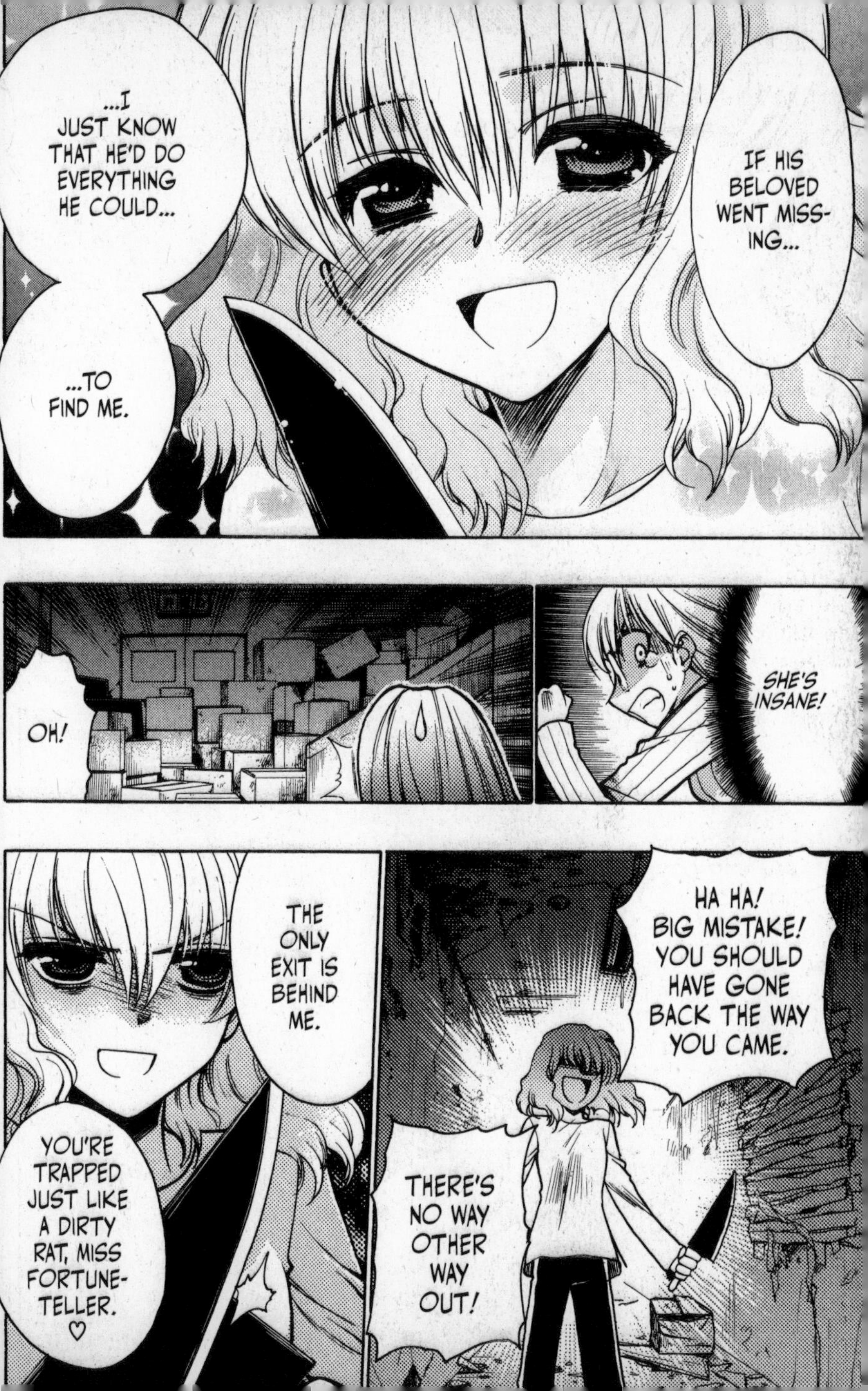
IF HIS BELOVED WENT MISSING...
...I JUST KNOW THAT HE'D DO EVERYTHING HE COULD...
...TO FIND ME.
SHE'S INSANE!
OH!
HA HA! BIG MISTAKE! YOU SHOULD HAVE GONE BACK THE WAY YOU CAME.
THERE'S NO WAY OTHER WAY OUT!
THE ONLY EXIT IS BEHIND ME.
YOU'RE TRAPPED JUST LIKE A DIRTY RAT, MISS FORTUNE-TELLER. ♡

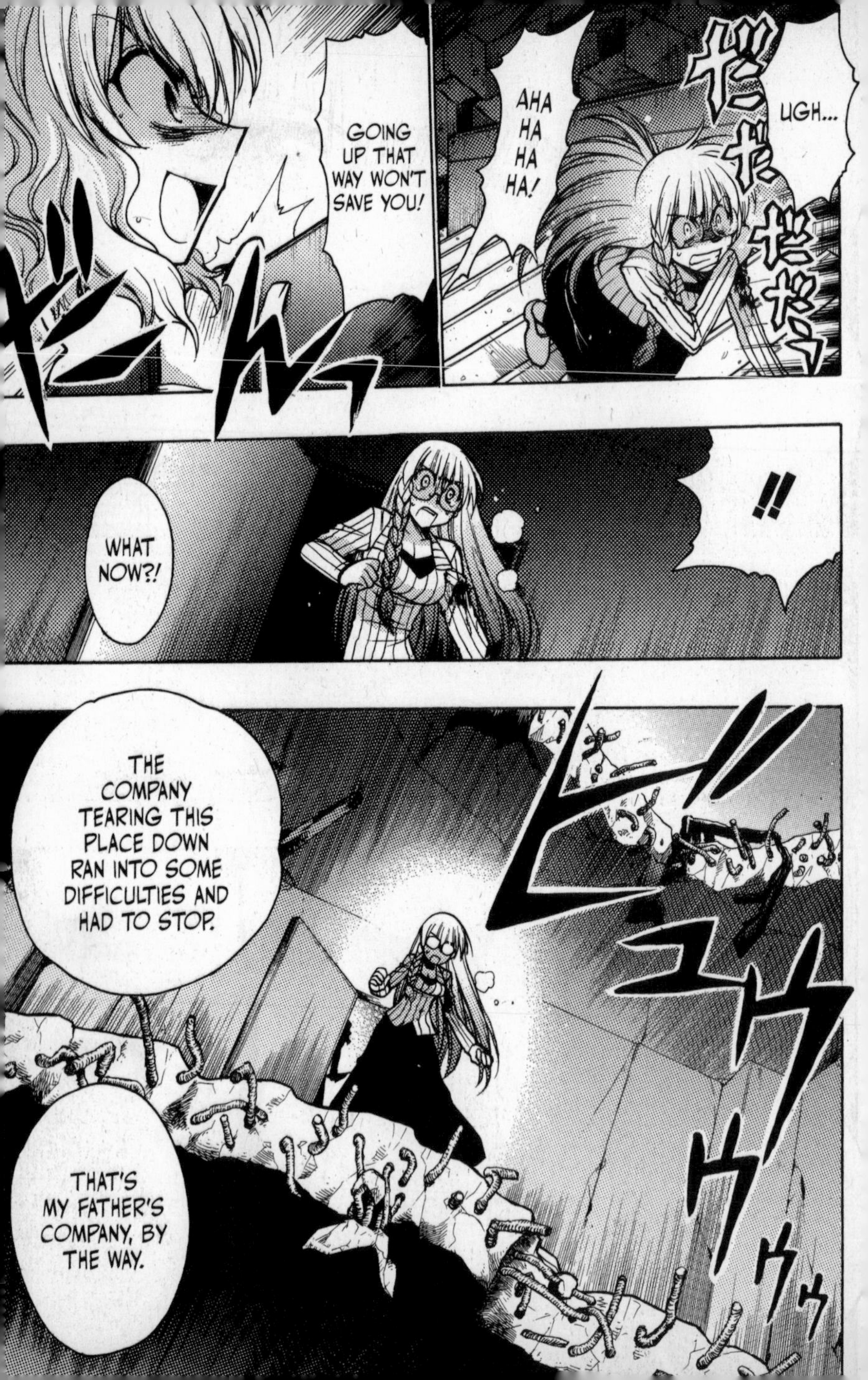
UGH...
AHA HA HA HA!
GOING UP THAT WAY WON'T SAVE YOU!
!!
WHAT NOW?!
THE COMPANY TEARING THIS PLACE DOWN RAN INTO SOME DIFFICULTIES AND HAD TO STOP.
THAT'S MY FATHER'S COMPANY, BY THE WAY.

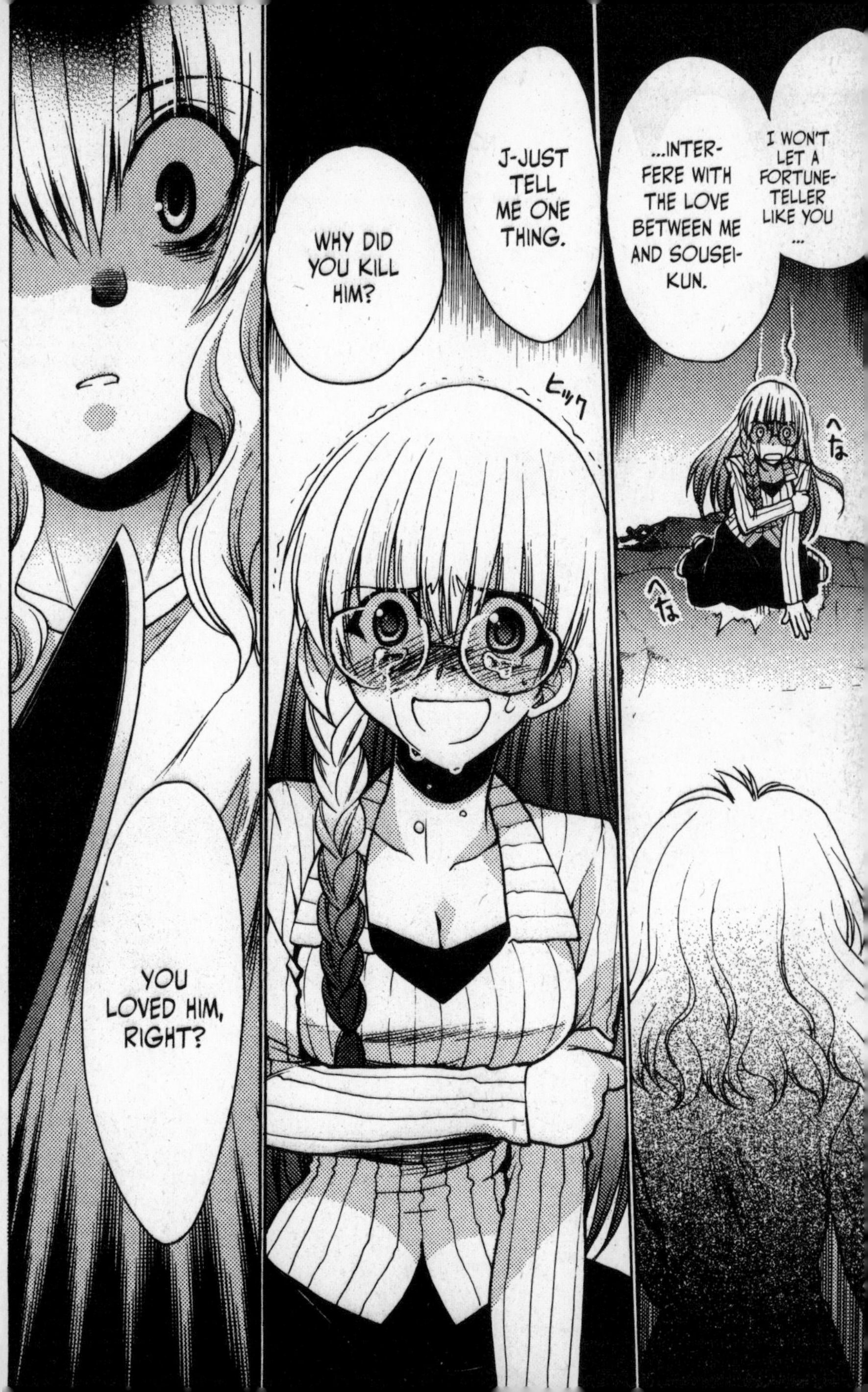
I WON'T LET A FORTUNE-TELLER LIKE YOU ...
...INTER-FERE WITH THE LOVE BETWEEN ME AND SOUSEI-KUN.
へな
へな
J-JUST TELL ME ONE THING.
WHY DID YOU KILL HIM?
YOU LOVED HIM, RIGHT?

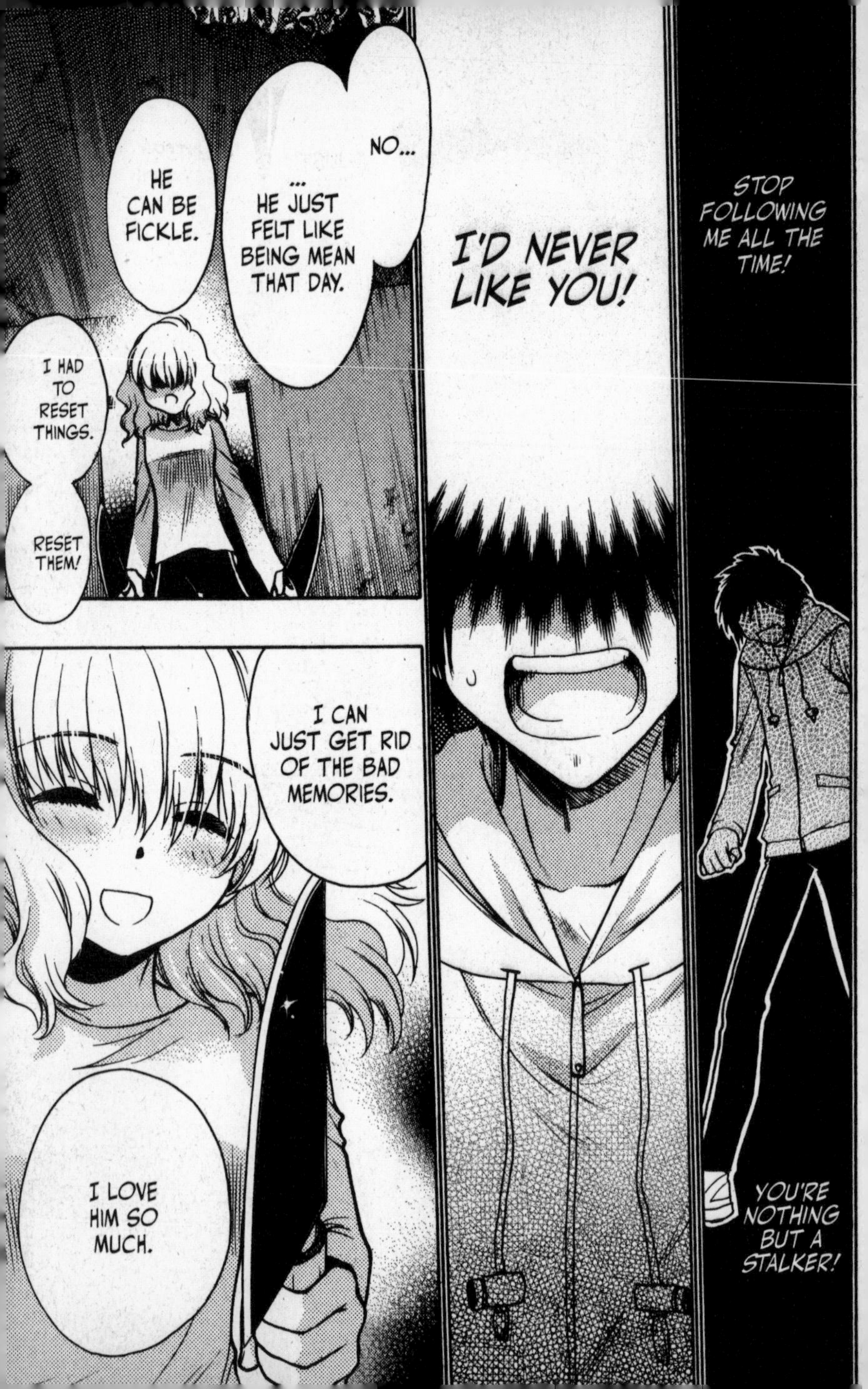
STOP FOLLOWING ME ALL THE TIME!
YOU'RE NOTHING BUT A STALKER!
I'D NEVER LIKE YOU!
NO...
... HE JUST FELT LIKE BEING MEAN THAT DAY.
HE CAN BE FICKLE.
I HAD TO RESET THINGS.
RESET THEM!
I CAN JUST GET RID OF THE BAD MEMORIES.
I LOVE HIM SO MUCH.

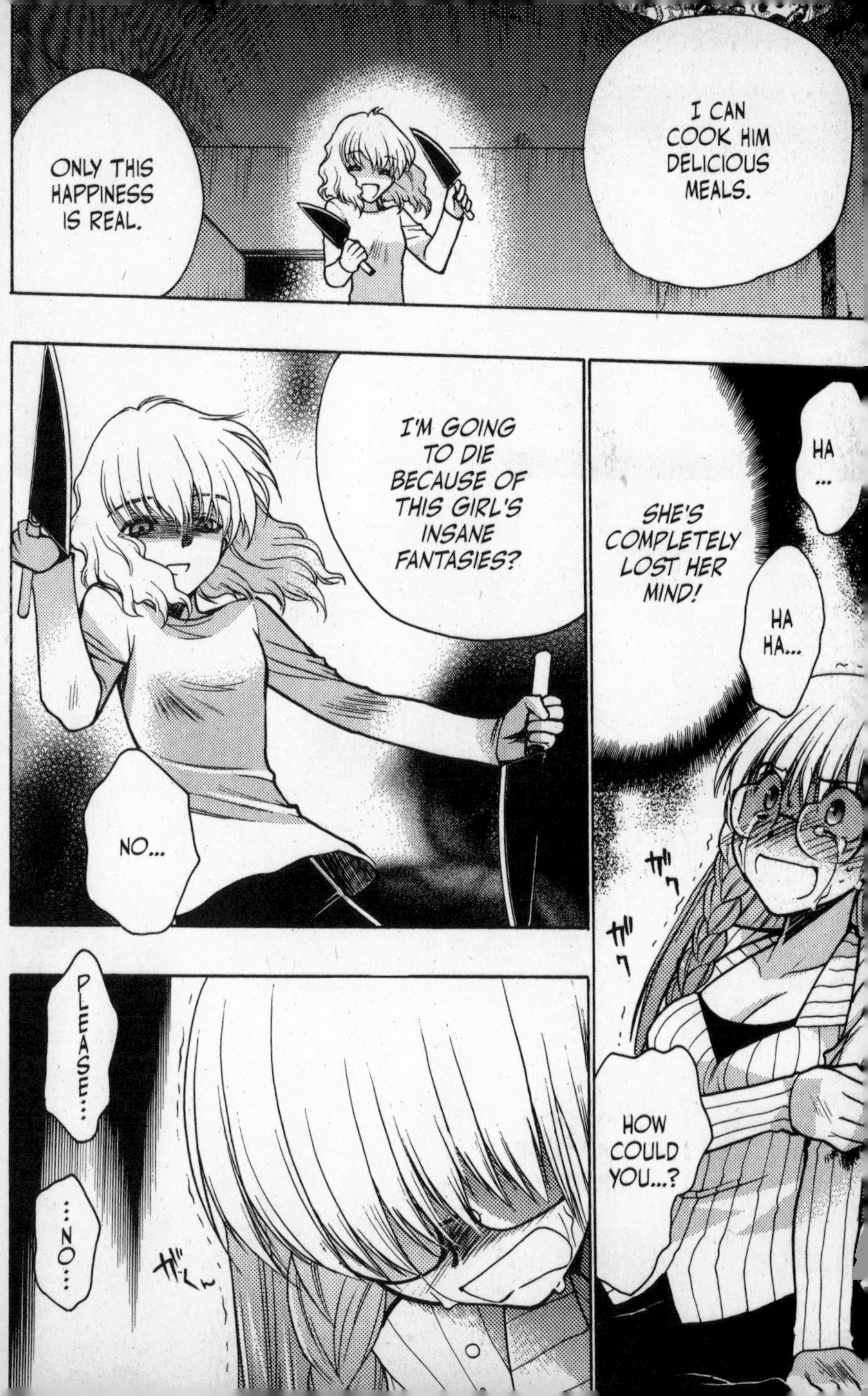
I CAN COOK HIM DELICIOUS MEALS.
ONLY THIS HAPPINESS IS REAL.
HA ...
SHE'S COMPLETELY LOST HER MIND!
HA HA...
HOW COULD YOU...?
I'M GOING TO DIE BECAUSE OF THIS GIRL'S INSANE FANTASIES?
NO...
PLEASE...
...NO...

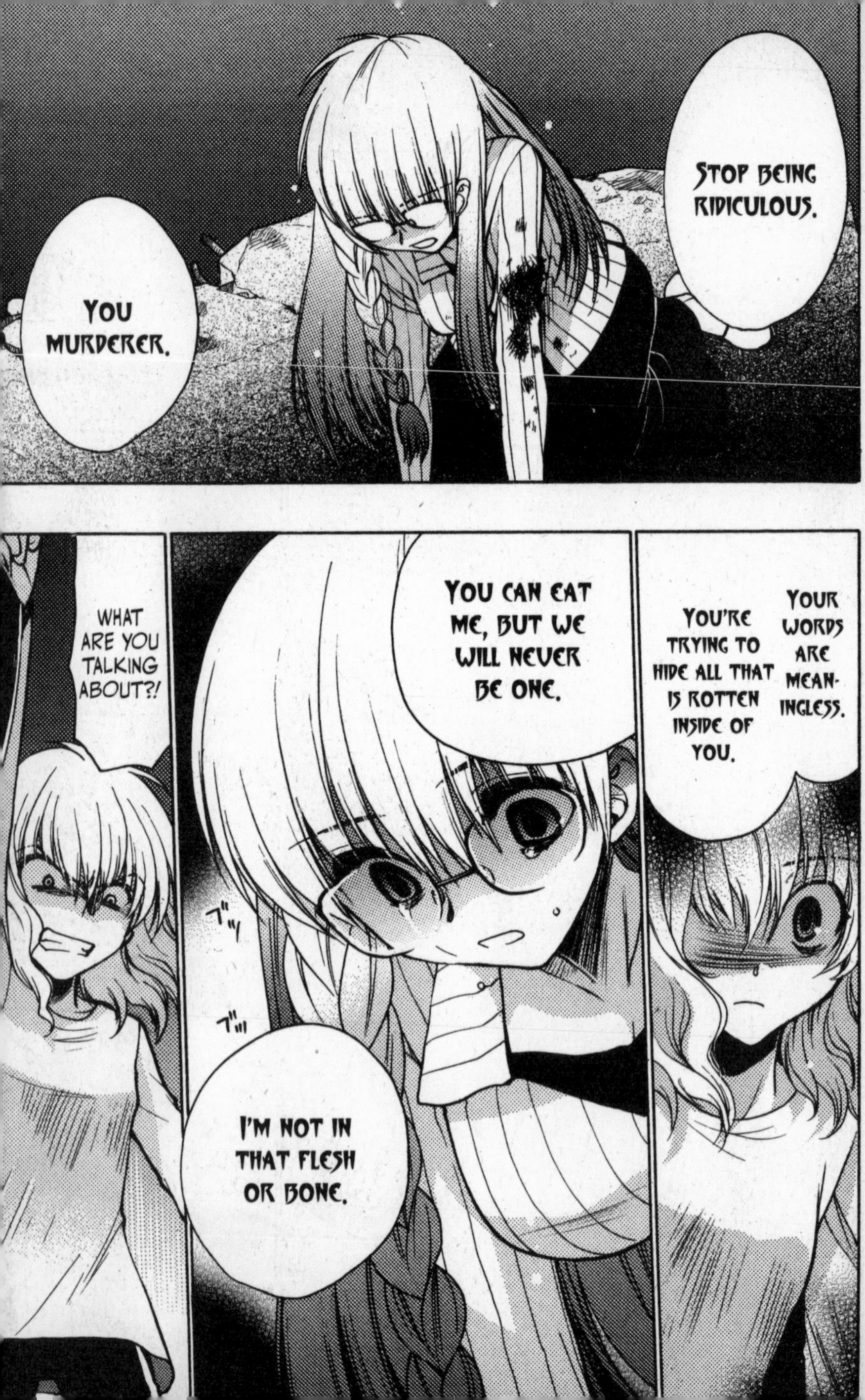
STOP BEING RIDICULOUS.
YOU MURDERER.
YOUR WORDS ARE MEAN-INGLESS.
YOU'RE TRYING TO HIDE ALL THAT IS ROTTEN INSIDE OF YOU.
YOU CAN EAT ME, BUT WE WILL NEVER BE ONE.
I'M NOT IN THAT FLESH OR BONE.
WHAT ARE YOU TALKING ABOUT?!

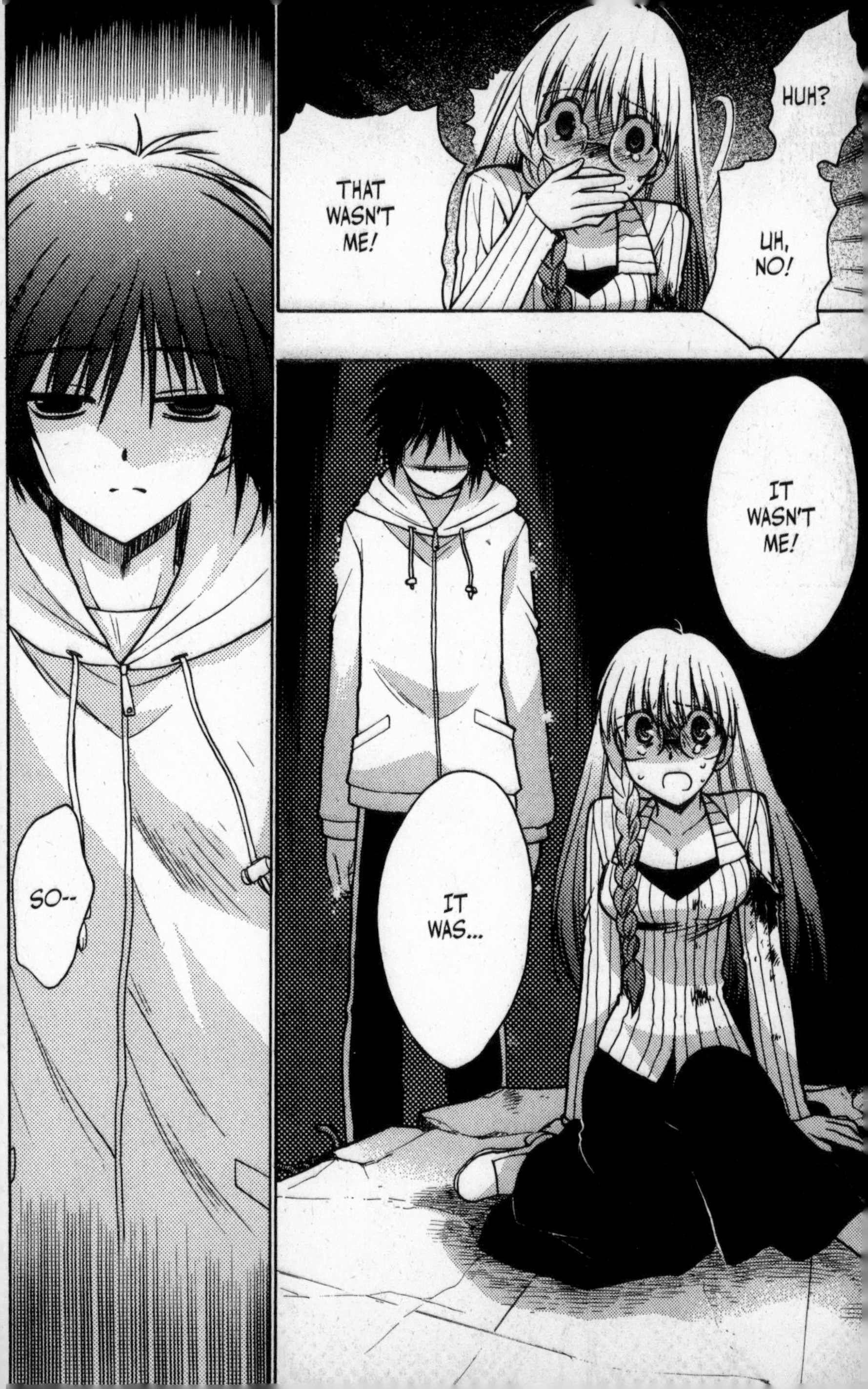
HUH?
UH, NO!
THAT WASN'T ME!
IT WASN'T ME!
IT WAS...
SO--

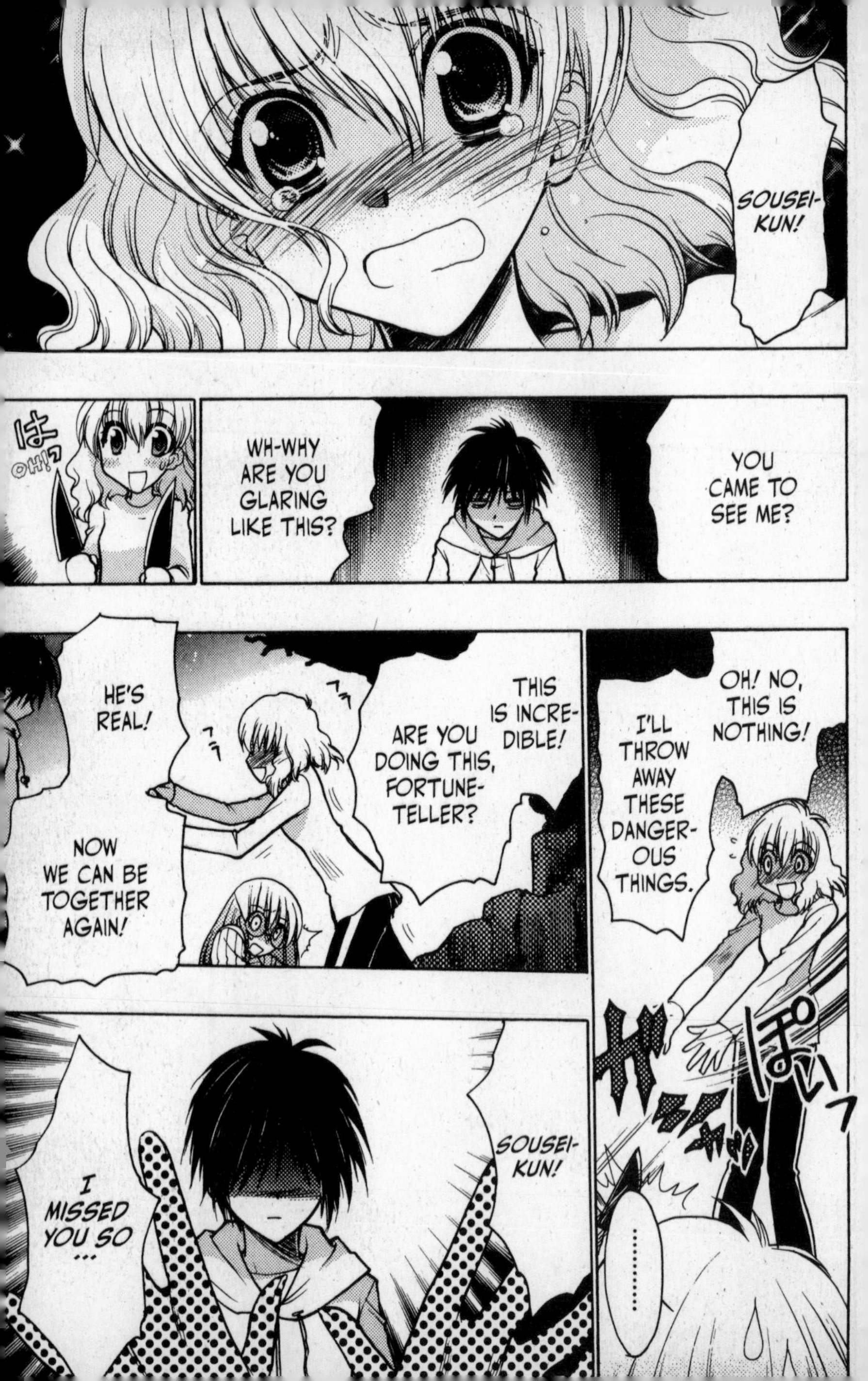
SOUSEI-KUN!
YOU CAME TO SEE ME?
WH-WHY ARE YOU GLARING LIKE THIS?
は
OH!?
OH! NO, THIS IS NOTHING!
I'LL THROW AWAY THESE DANGEROUS THINGS.
ぽいっ
THIS IS INCREDIBLE!
ARE YOU DOING THIS, FORTUNE-TELLER?
HE'S REAL!
NOW WE CAN BE TOGETHER AGAIN!
......
SOUSEI-KUN!
I MISSED YOU SO ...

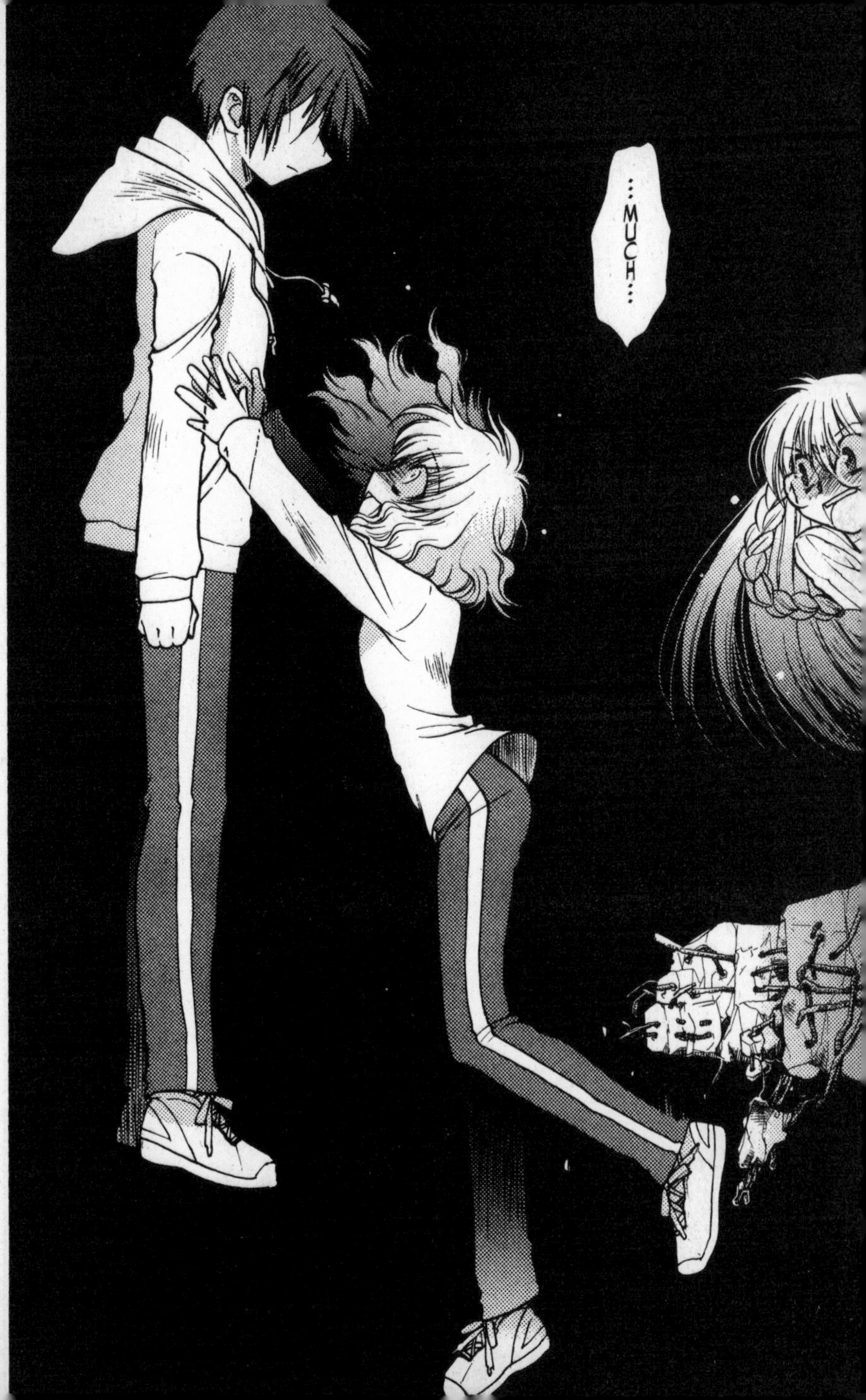
...MUCH...

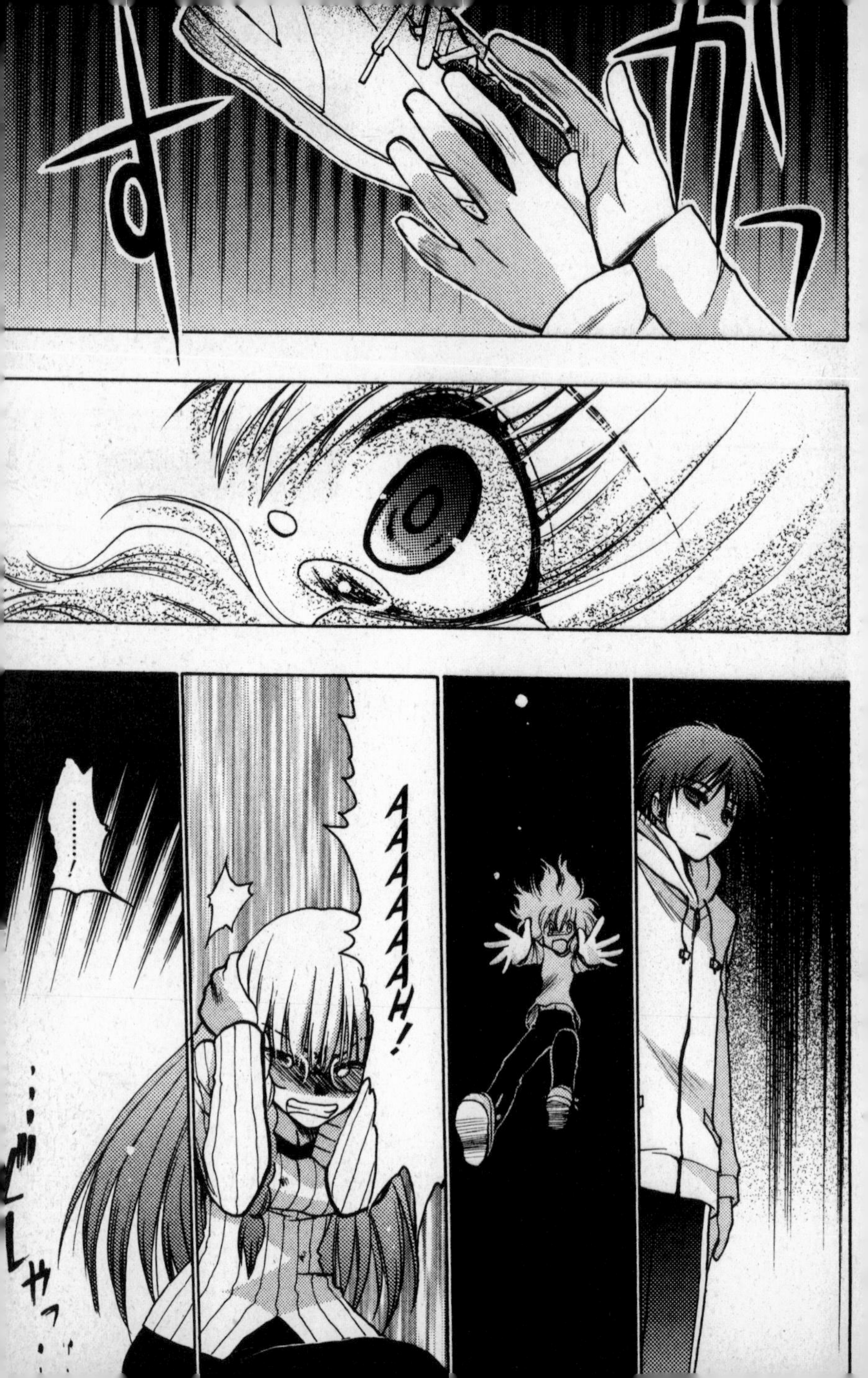
カッ
すっ
AAAAAAH!
……!
…ぐしゃっ…

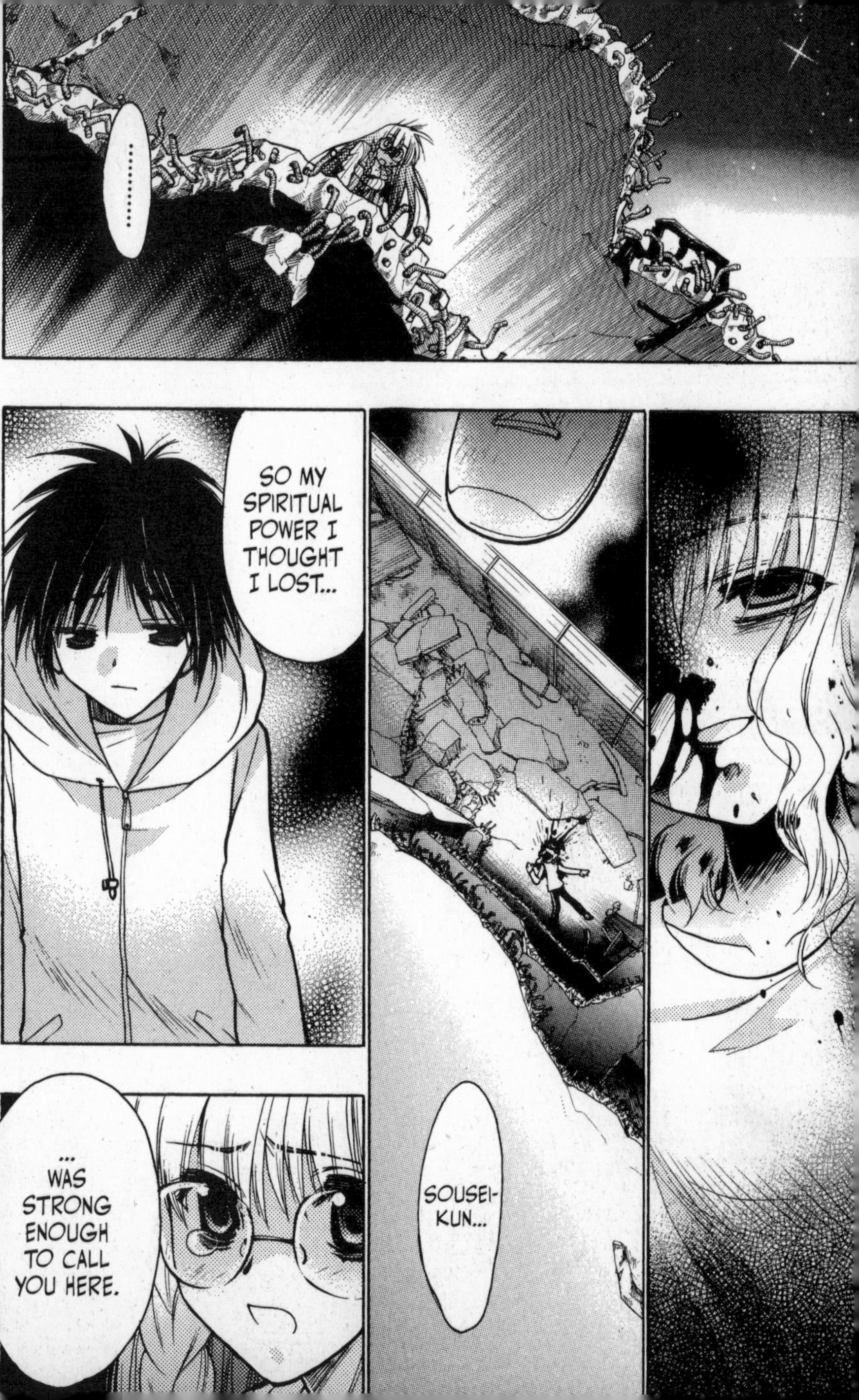
......
SOUSEI-KUN...
SO MY SPIRITUAL POWER I THOUGHT I LOST...
... WAS STRONG ENOUGH TO CALL YOU HERE.

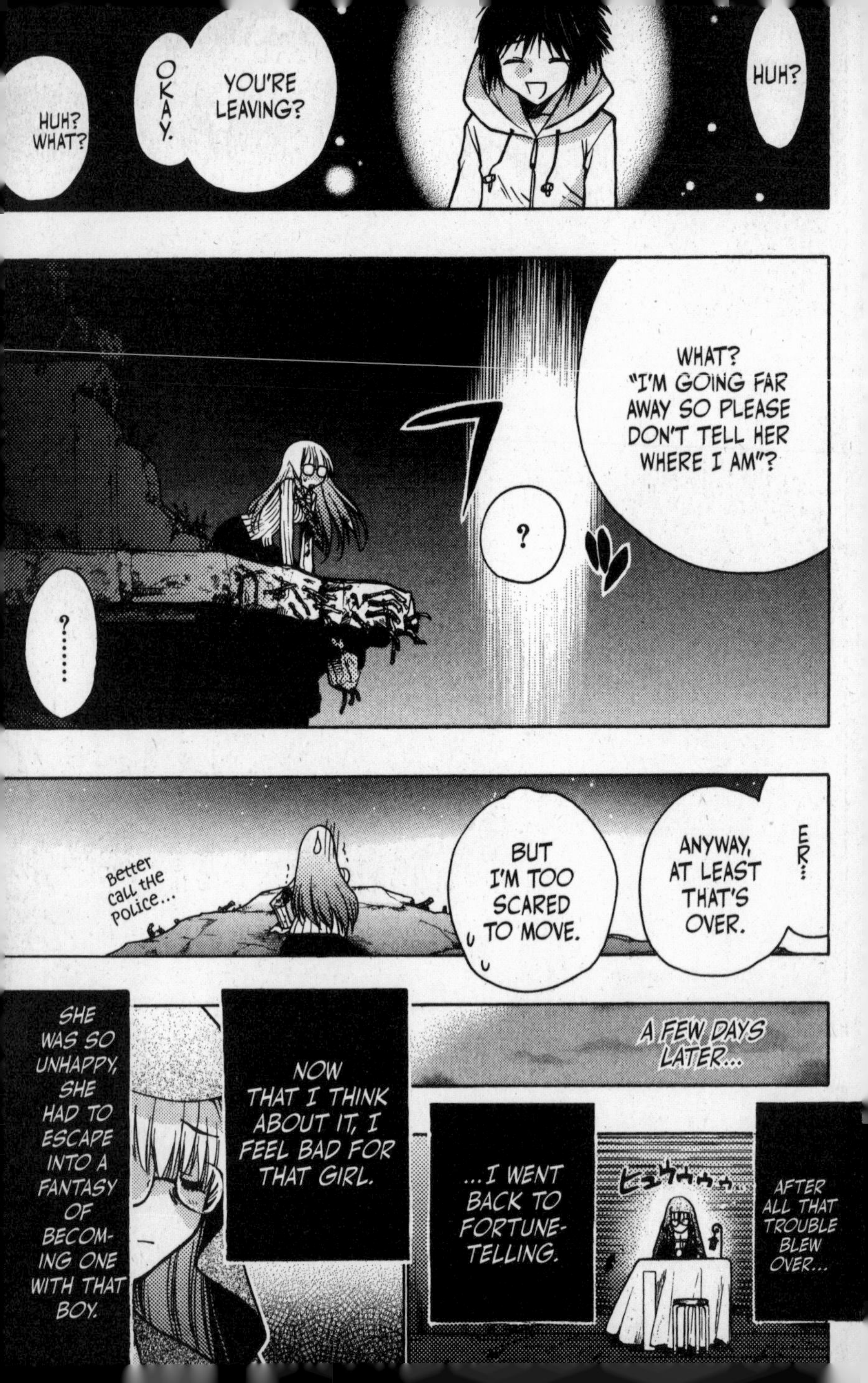
HUH?
YOU'RE LEAVING?
OKAY.
HUH? WHAT?
WHAT? "I'M GOING FAR AWAY SO PLEASE DON'T TELL HER WHERE I AM"?
?
?......
ER...
ANYWAY, AT LEAST THAT'S OVER.
BUT I'M TOO SCARED TO MOVE.
Better call the police...
A FEW DAYS LATER...
AFTER ALL THAT TROUBLE BLEW OVER...
ヒュウウウゥ...
...I WENT BACK TO FORTUNE-TELLING.
NOW THAT I THINK ABOUT IT, I FEEL BAD FOR THAT GIRL.
SHE WAS SO UNHAPPY, SHE HAD TO ESCAPE INTO A FANTASY OF BECOMING ONE WITH THAT BOY.

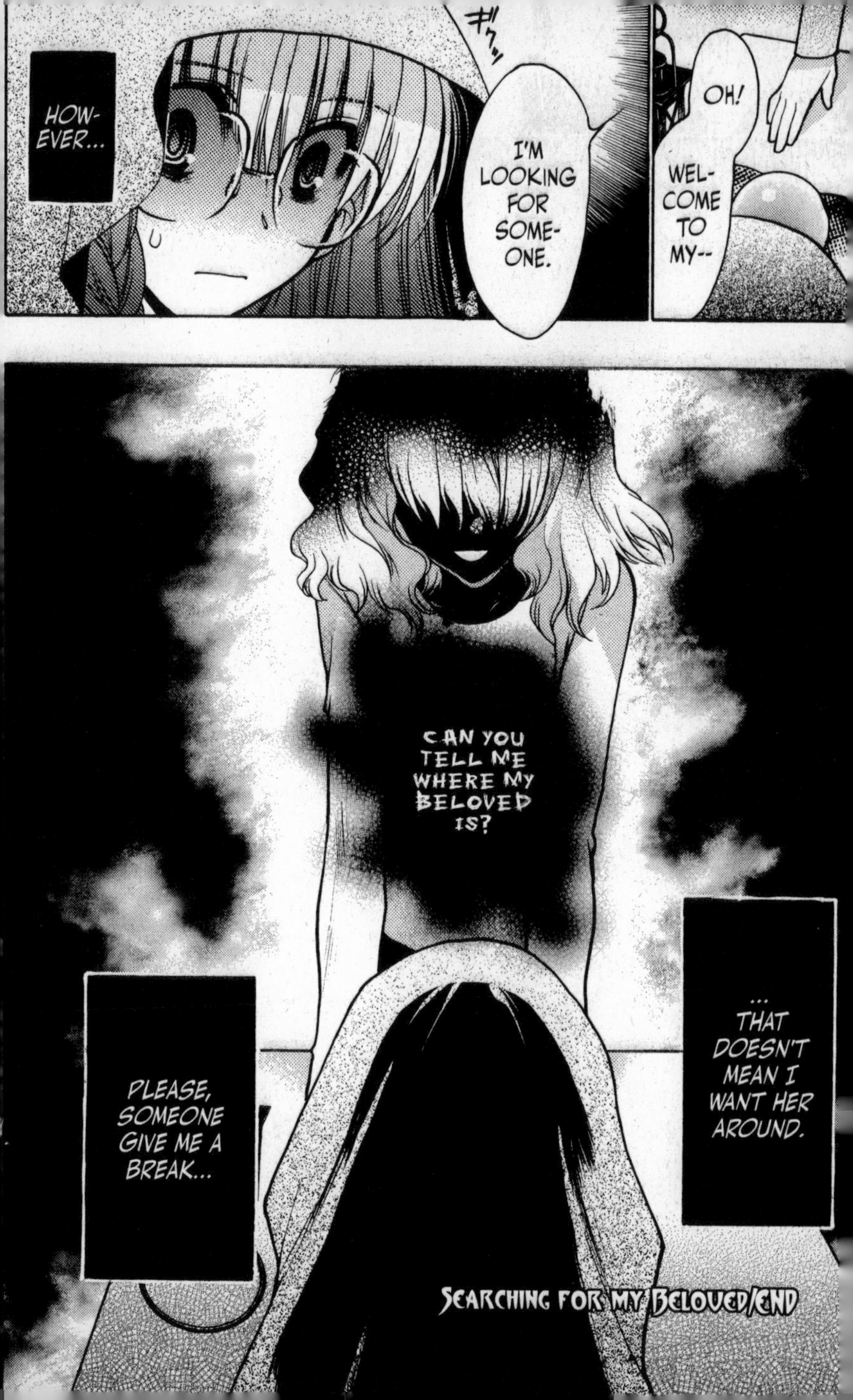
OH!
WEL-COME TO MY--
I'M LOOKING FOR SOME-ONE.
HOW-EVER...
CAN YOU TELL ME WHERE MY BELOVED IS?
... THAT DOESN'T MEAN I WANT HER AROUND.
PLEASE, SOMEONE GIVE ME A BREAK...
SEARCHING FOR MY BELOVED/END

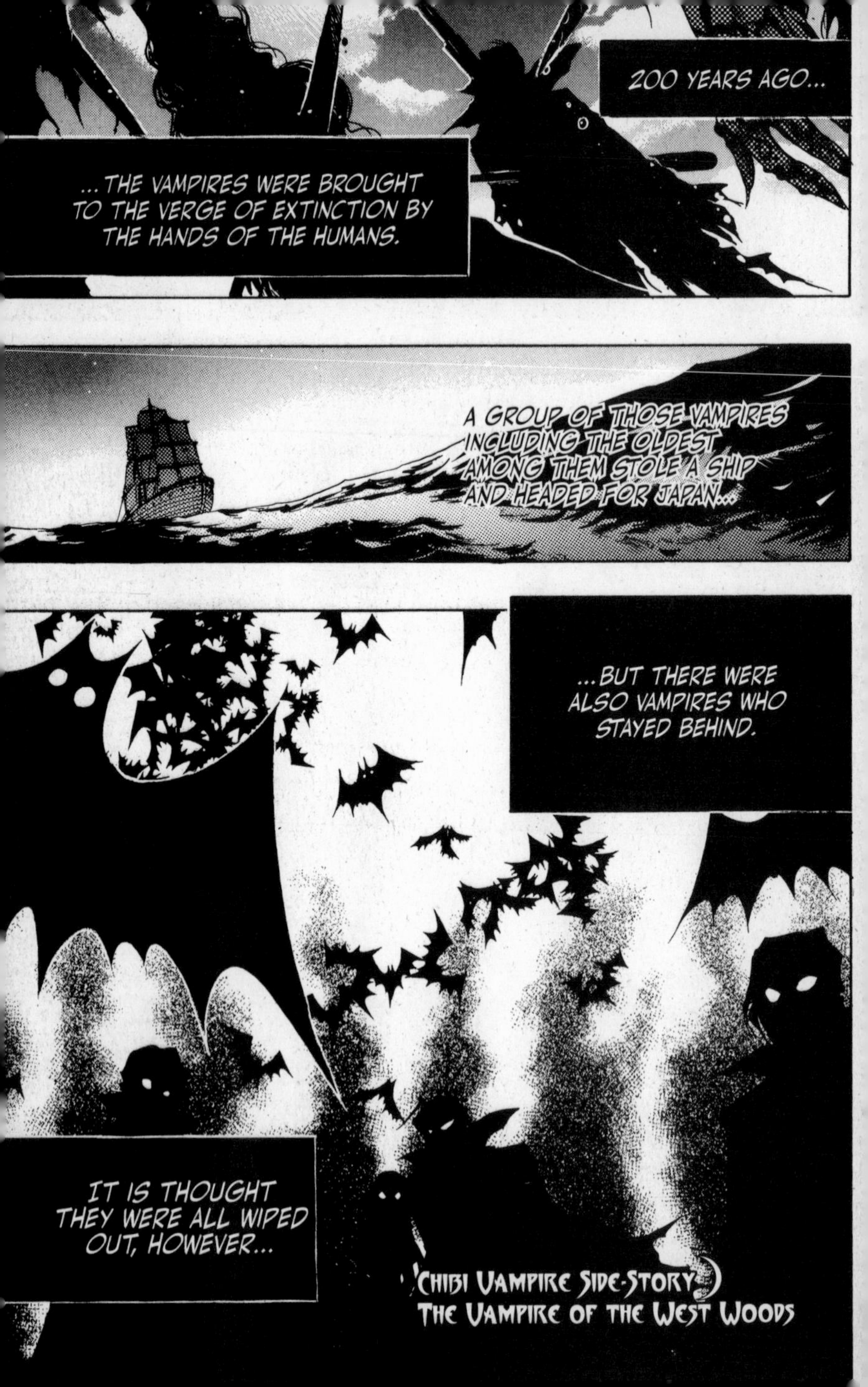
200 YEARS AGO...
...THE VAMPIRES WERE BROUGHT TO THE VERGE OF EXTINCTION BY THE HANDS OF THE HUMANS.
A GROUP OF THOSE VAMPIRES INCLUDING THE OLDEST AMONG THEM STOLE A SHIP AND HEADED FOR JAPAN...
...BUT THERE WERE ALSO VAMPIRES WHO STAYED BEHIND.
IT IS THOUGHT THEY WERE ALL WIPED OUT, HOWEVER...
CHIBI VAMPIRE SIDE-STORY
THE VAMPIRE OF THE WEST WOODS

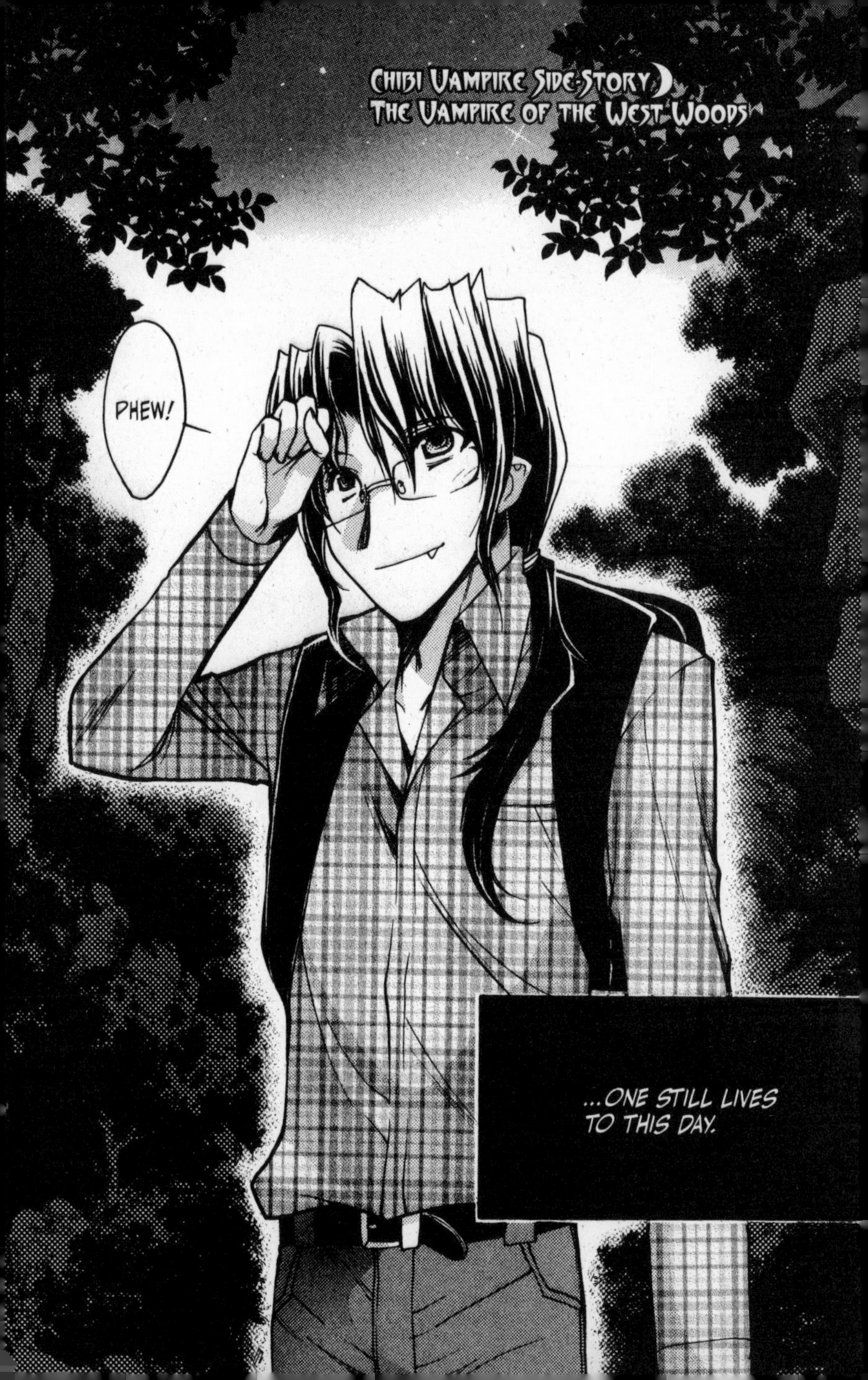
CHIBI VAMPIRE SIDE STORY
THE VAMPIRE OF THE WEST WOODS
PHEW!
...ONE STILL LIVES TO THIS DAY.

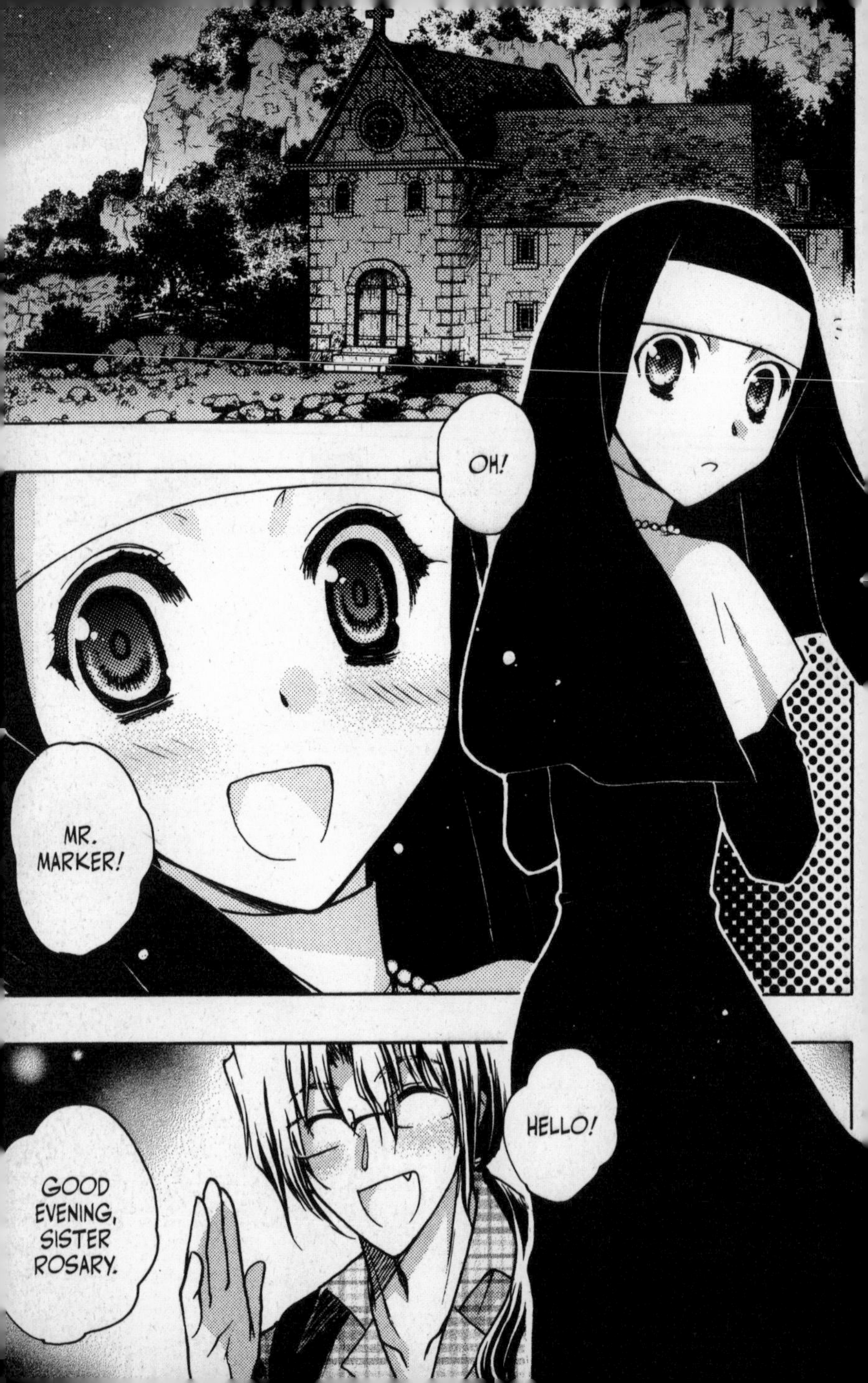
OH!
MR. MARKER!
HELLO!
GOOD EVENING, SISTER ROSARY.

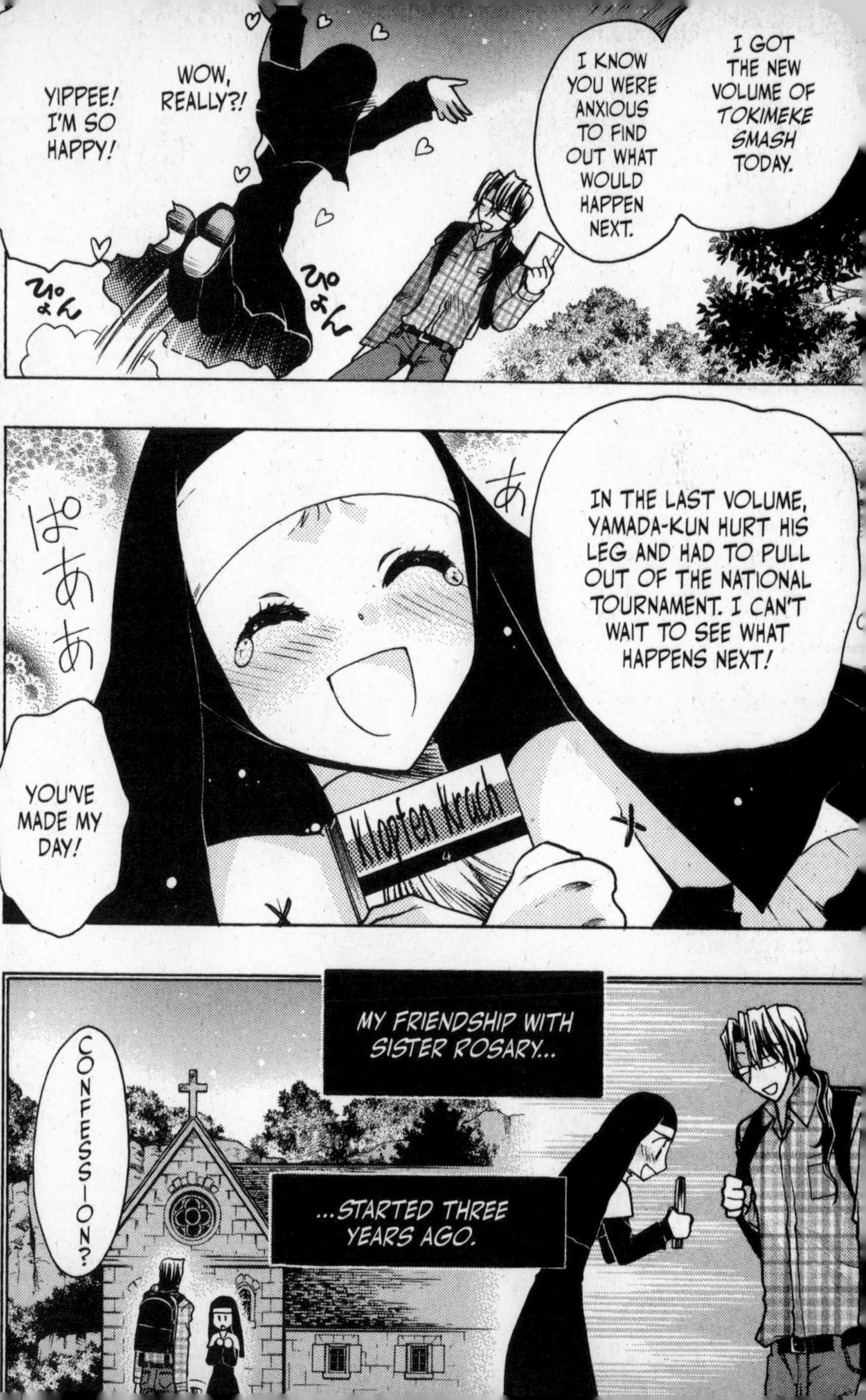
I GOT THE NEW VOLUME OF *TOKIMEKE SMASH* TODAY.
I KNOW YOU WERE ANXIOUS TO FIND OUT WHAT WOULD HAPPEN NEXT.
WOW, REALLY?!
YIPPEE! I'M SO HAPPY!
ぴょん
ぴょん
IN THE LAST VOLUME, YAMADA-KUN HURT HIS LEG AND HAD TO PULL OUT OF THE NATIONAL TOURNAMENT. I CAN'T WAIT TO SEE WHAT HAPPENS NEXT!
あ
ぱああ
Klopfen Krach
YOU'VE MADE MY DAY!
MY FRIENDSHIP WITH SISTER ROSARY...
...STARTED THREE YEARS AGO.
CONFESSION?

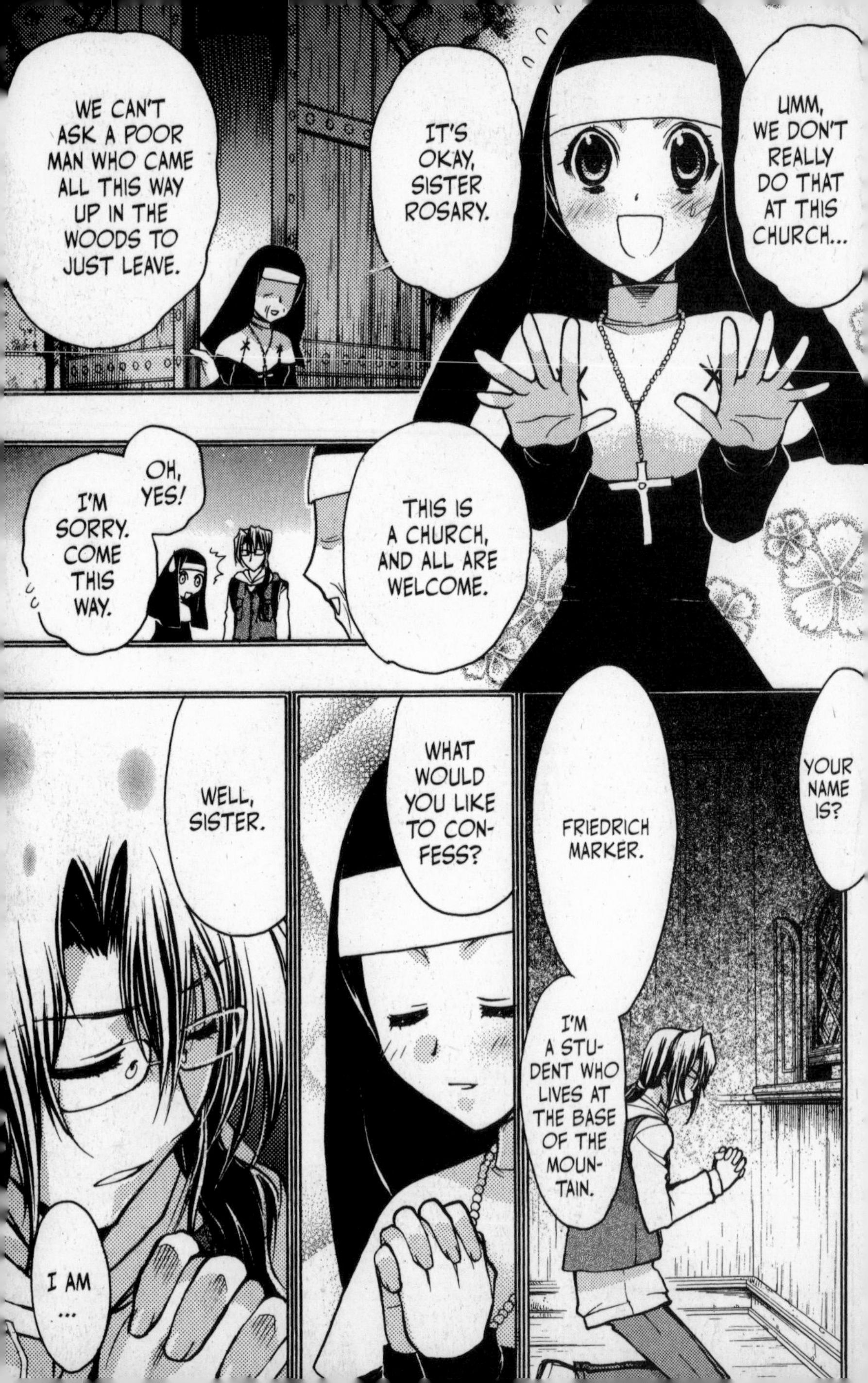
UMM, WE DON'T REALLY DO THAT AT THIS CHURCH...
IT'S OKAY, SISTER ROSARY.
WE CAN'T ASK A POOR MAN WHO CAME ALL THIS WAY UP IN THE WOODS TO JUST LEAVE.
THIS IS A CHURCH, AND ALL ARE WELCOME.
OH, YES!
I'M SORRY. COME THIS WAY.
YOUR NAME IS?
FRIEDRICH MARKER.
I'M A STUDENT WHO LIVES AT THE BASE OF THE MOUNTAIN.
WHAT WOULD YOU LIKE TO CONFESS?
WELL, SISTER.
I AM ...

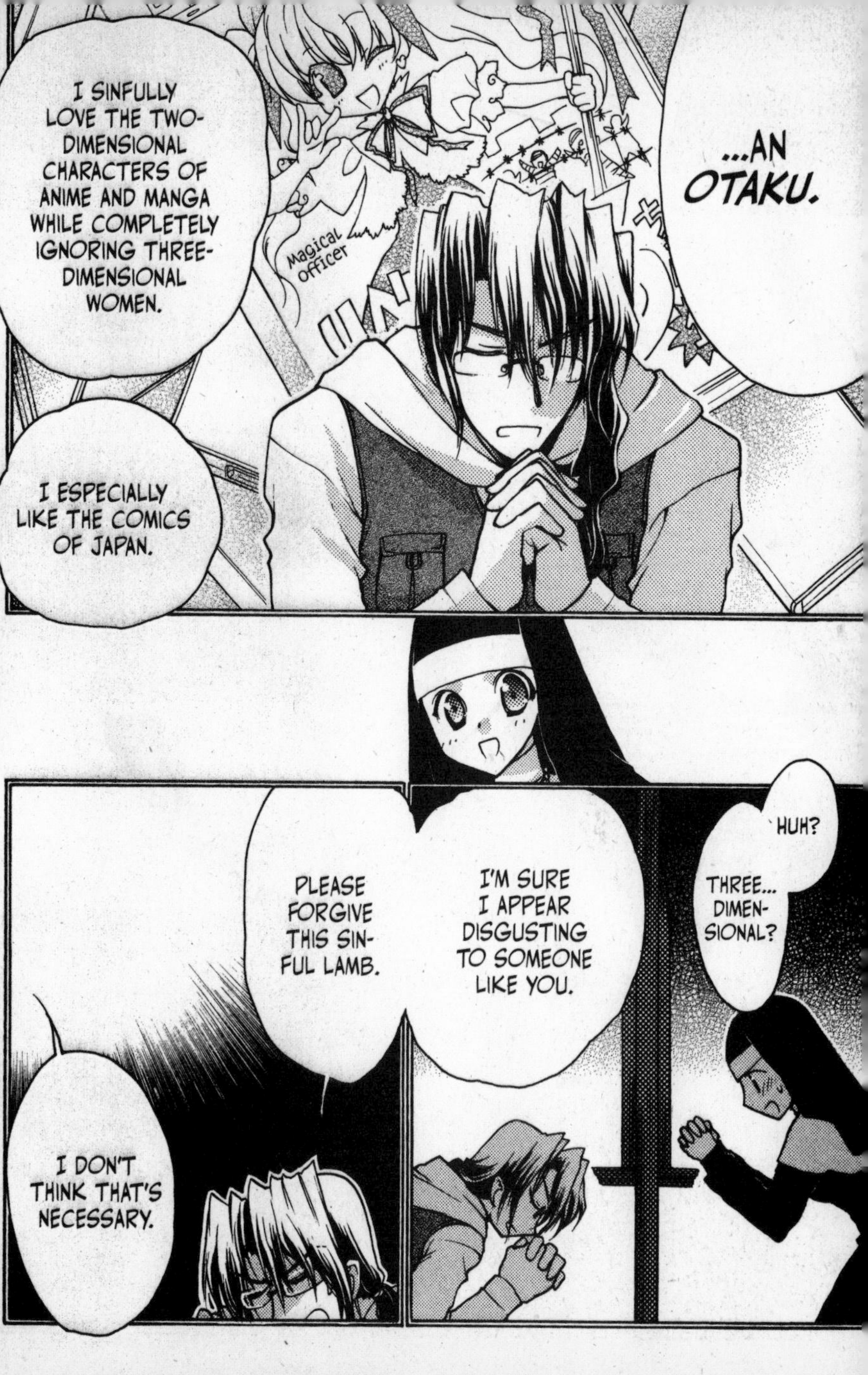
...AN OTAKU.
I SINFULLY LOVE THE TWO-DIMENSIONAL CHARACTERS OF ANIME AND MANGA WHILE COMPLETELY IGNORING THREE-DIMENSIONAL WOMEN.
Magical officer
I ESPECIALLY LIKE THE COMICS OF JAPAN.
HUH?
THREE... DIMEN-SIONAL?
I'M SURE I APPEAR DISGUSTING TO SOMEONE LIKE YOU.
PLEASE FORGIVE THIS SIN-FUL LAMB.
I DON'T THINK THAT'S NECESSARY.

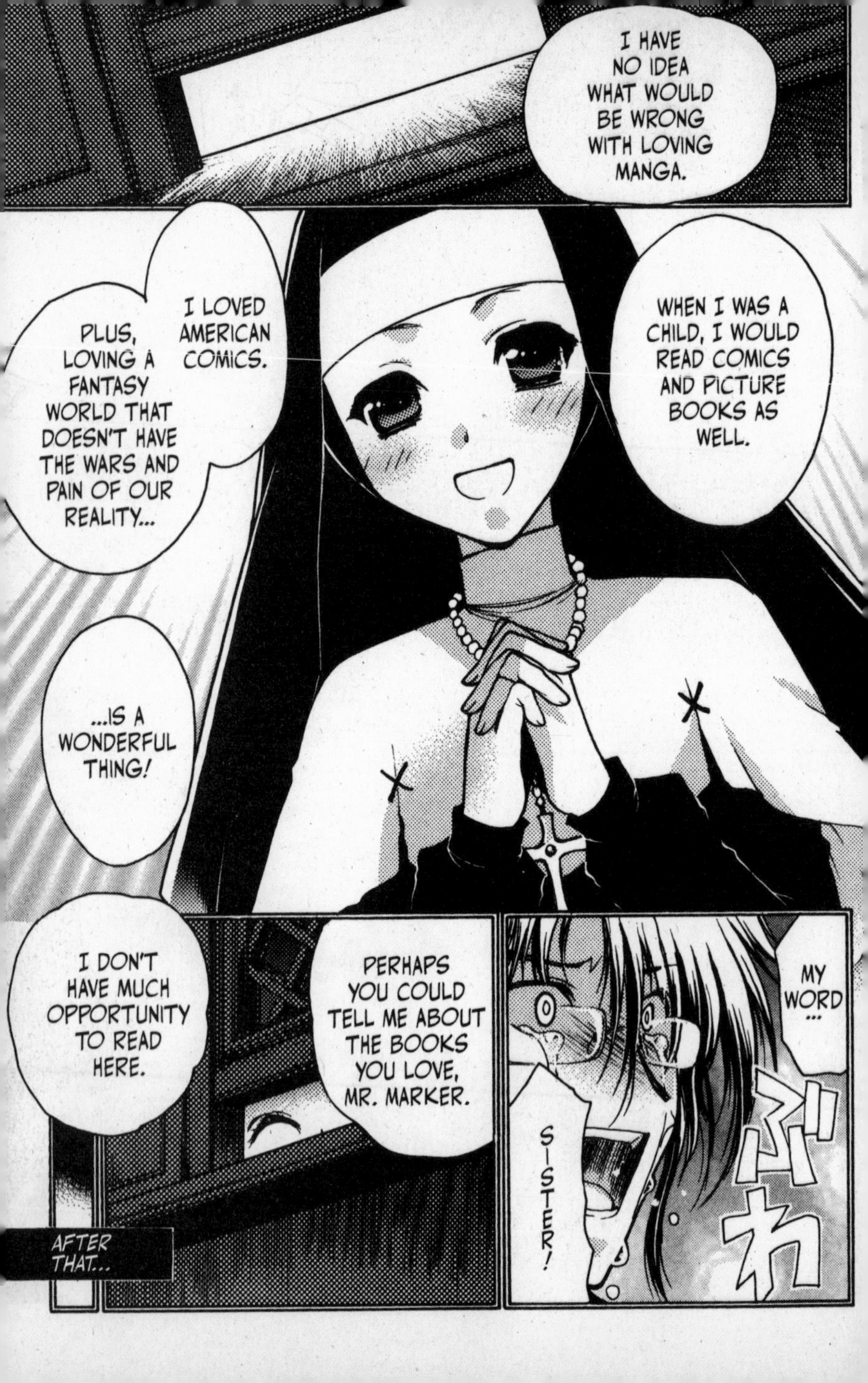
I HAVE NO IDEA WHAT WOULD BE WRONG WITH LOVING MANGA.
WHEN I WAS A CHILD, I WOULD READ COMICS AND PICTURE BOOKS AS WELL.
I LOVED AMERICAN COMICS.
PLUS, LOVING A FANTASY WORLD THAT DOESN'T HAVE THE WARS AND PAIN OF OUR REALITY...
...IS A WONDERFUL THING!
MY WORD...
SISTER!
PERHAPS YOU COULD TELL ME ABOUT THE BOOKS YOU LOVE, MR. MARKER.
I DON'T HAVE MUCH OPPORTUNITY TO READ HERE.
AFTER THAT...

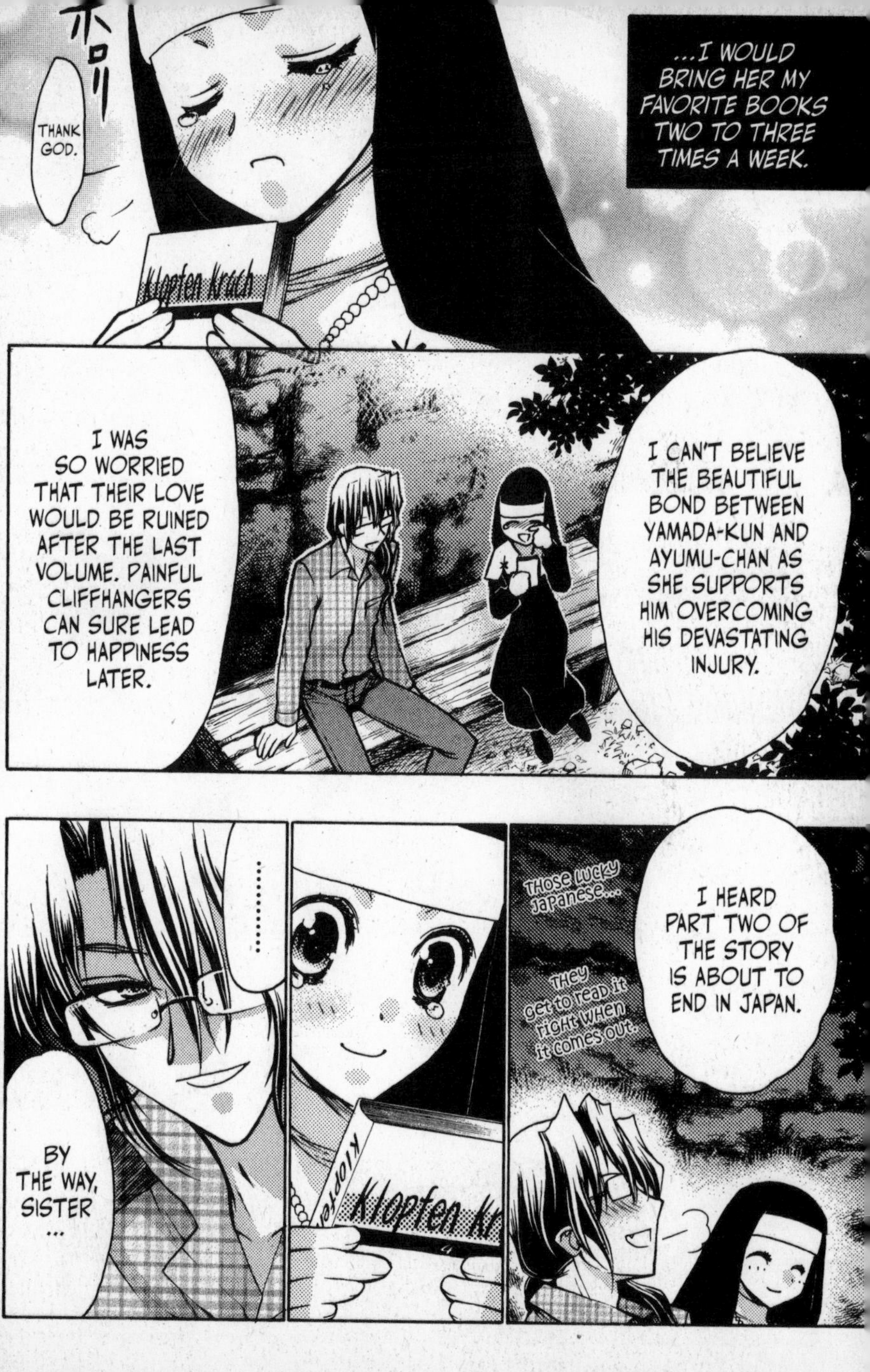
...I WOULD BRING HER MY FAVORITE BOOKS TWO TO THREE TIMES A WEEK.
ホロリ
THANK GOD.
Klopfen Krach
I CAN'T BELIEVE THE BEAUTIFUL BOND BETWEEN YAMADA-KUN AND AYUMU-CHAN AS SHE SUPPORTS HIM OVERCOMING HIS DEVASTATING INJURY.
I WAS SO WORRIED THAT THEIR LOVE WOULD BE RUINED AFTER THE LAST VOLUME. PAINFUL CLIFFHANGERS CAN SURE LEAD TO HAPPINESS LATER.
I HEARD PART TWO OF THE STORY IS ABOUT TO END IN JAPAN.
THOSE LUCKY JAPANESE...
THEY GET TO READ IT RIGHT WHEN IT COMES OUT.
......
Klopfen Kr
BY THE WAY, SISTER...

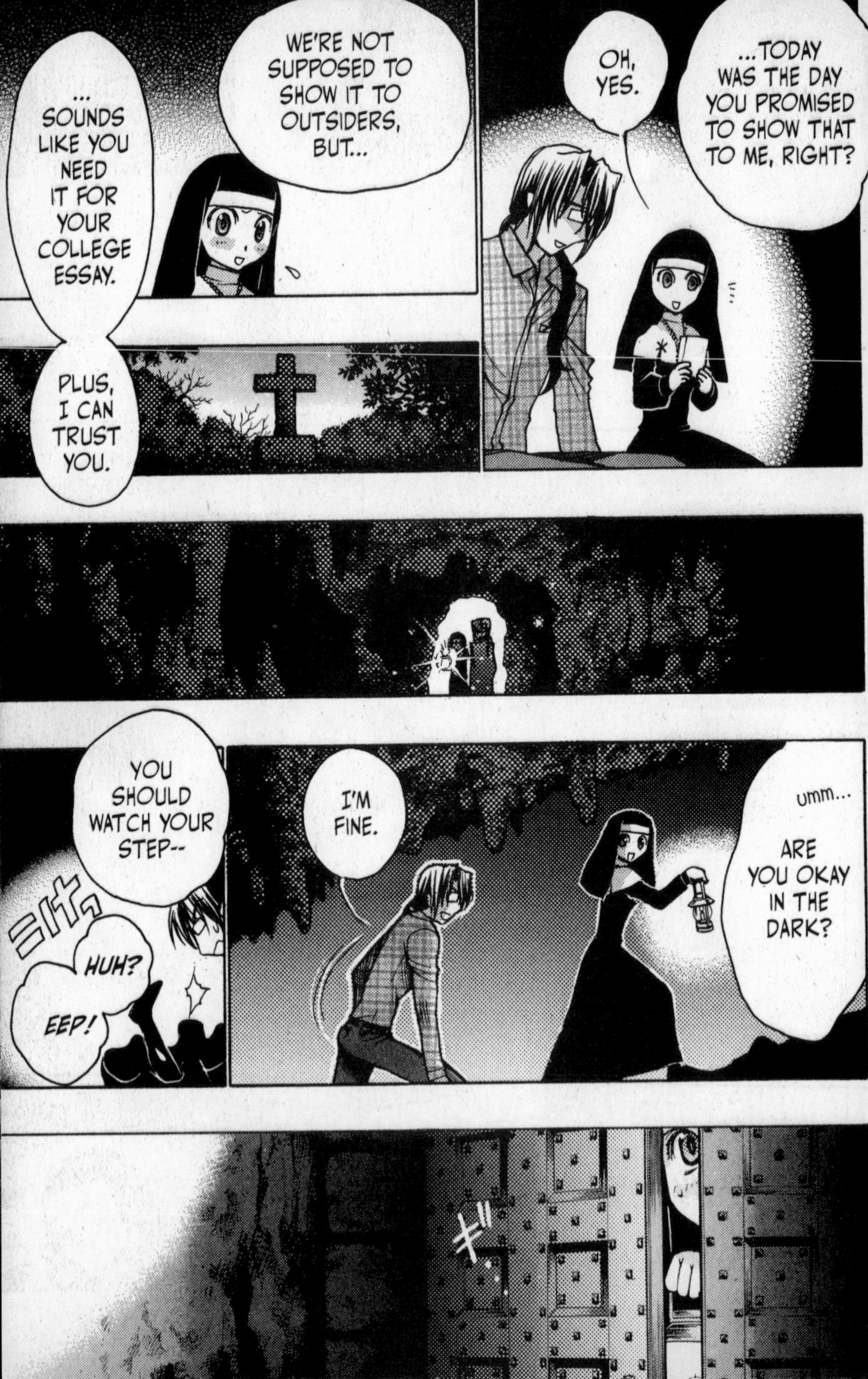
...TODAY WAS THE DAY YOU PROMISED TO SHOW THAT TO ME, RIGHT?
OH, YES.
WE'RE NOT SUPPOSED TO SHOW IT TO OUTSIDERS, BUT...
... SOUNDS LIKE YOU NEED IT FOR YOUR COLLEGE ESSAY.
PLUS, I CAN TRUST YOU.
umm...
ARE YOU OKAY IN THE DARK?
I'M FINE.
YOU SHOULD WATCH YOUR STEP--
HUH?
EEP!

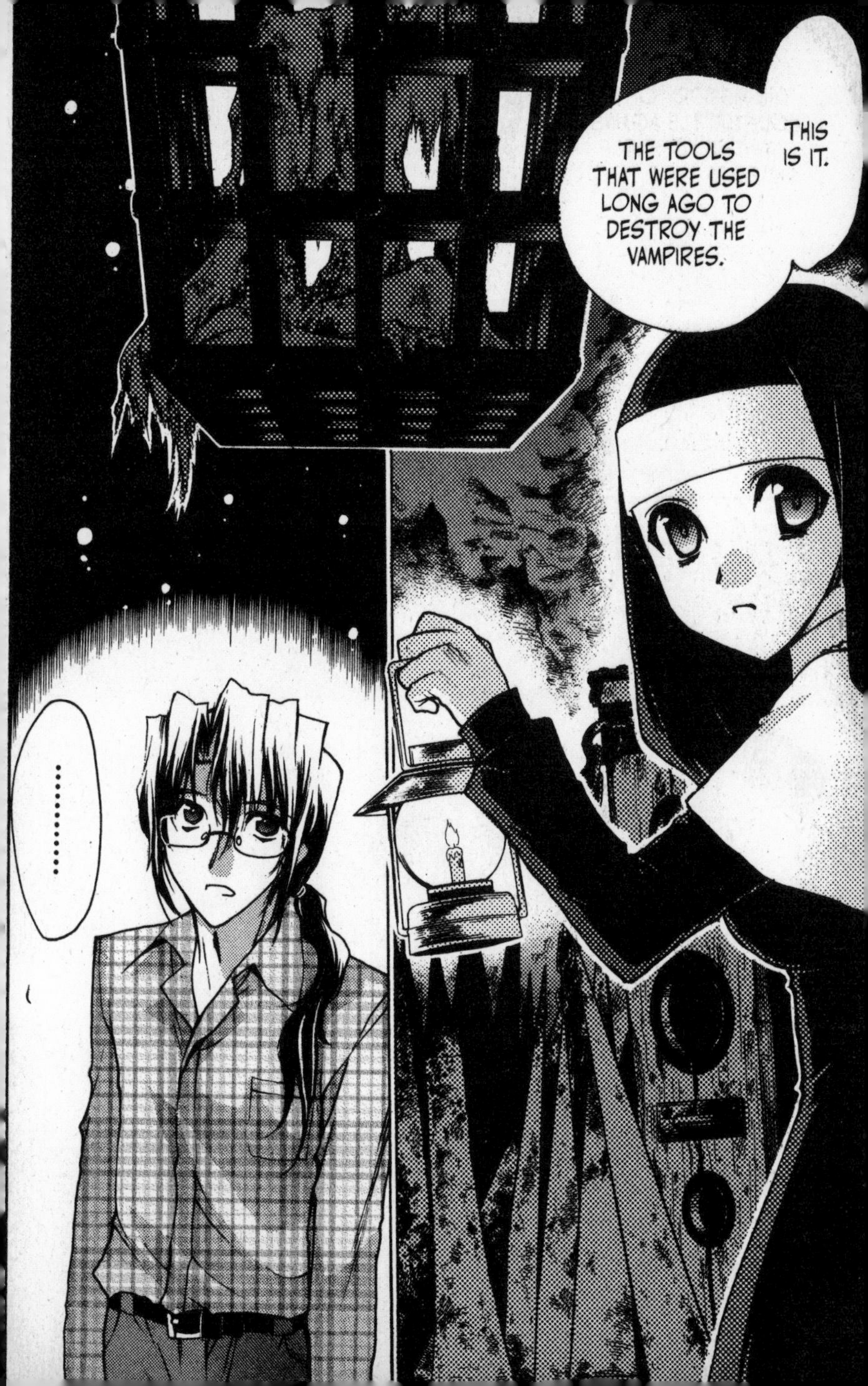
THIS IS IT.
THE TOOLS THAT WERE USED LONG AGO TO DESTROY THE VAMPIRES.
....

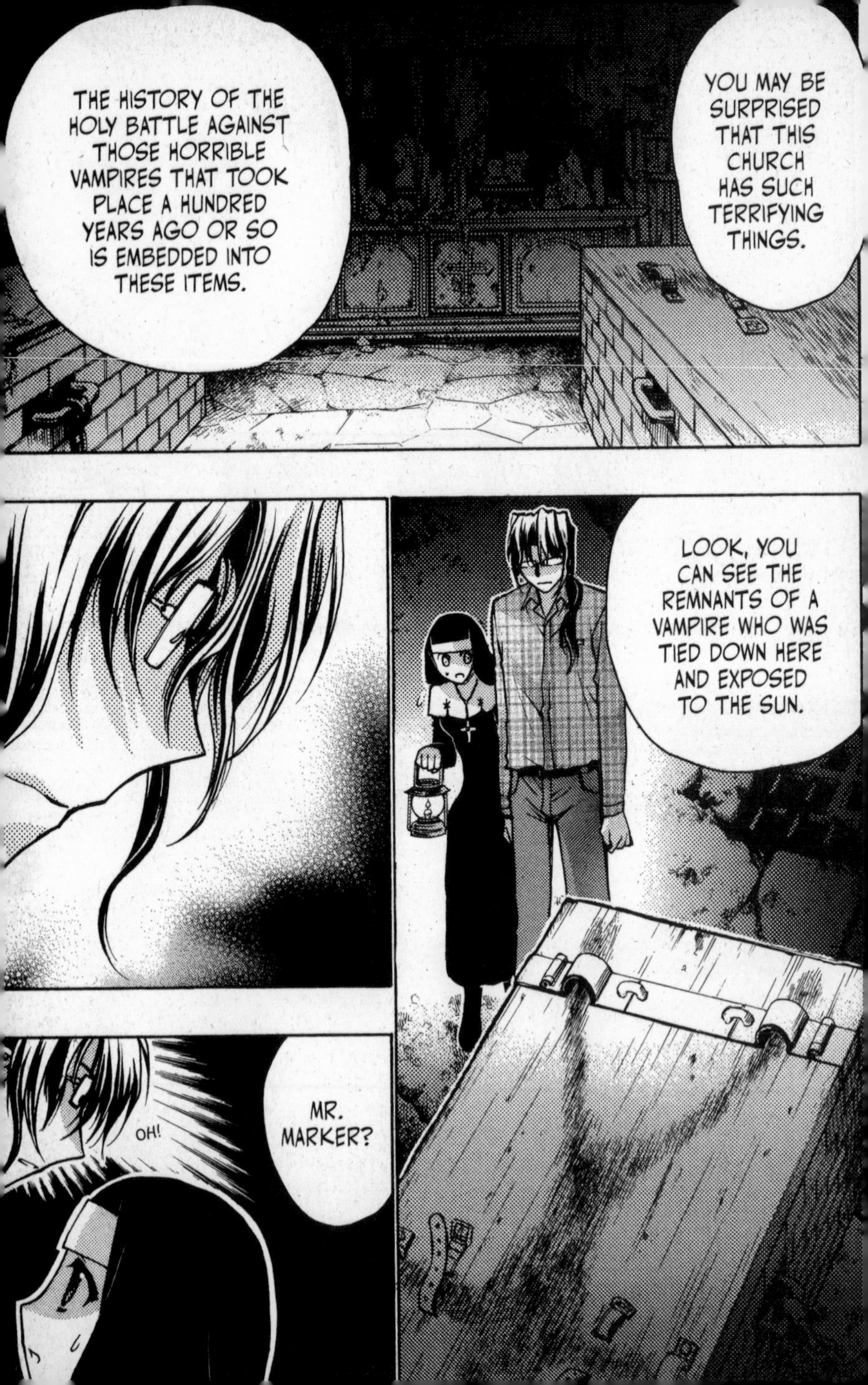
YOU MAY BE SURPRISED THAT THIS CHURCH HAS SUCH TERRIFYING THINGS.
THE HISTORY OF THE HOLY BATTLE AGAINST THOSE HORRIBLE VAMPIRES THAT TOOK PLACE A HUNDRED YEARS AGO OR SO IS EMBEDDED INTO THESE ITEMS.
LOOK, YOU CAN SEE THE REMNANTS OF A VAMPIRE WHO WAS TIED DOWN HERE AND EXPOSED TO THE SUN.
MR. MARKER?
OH!

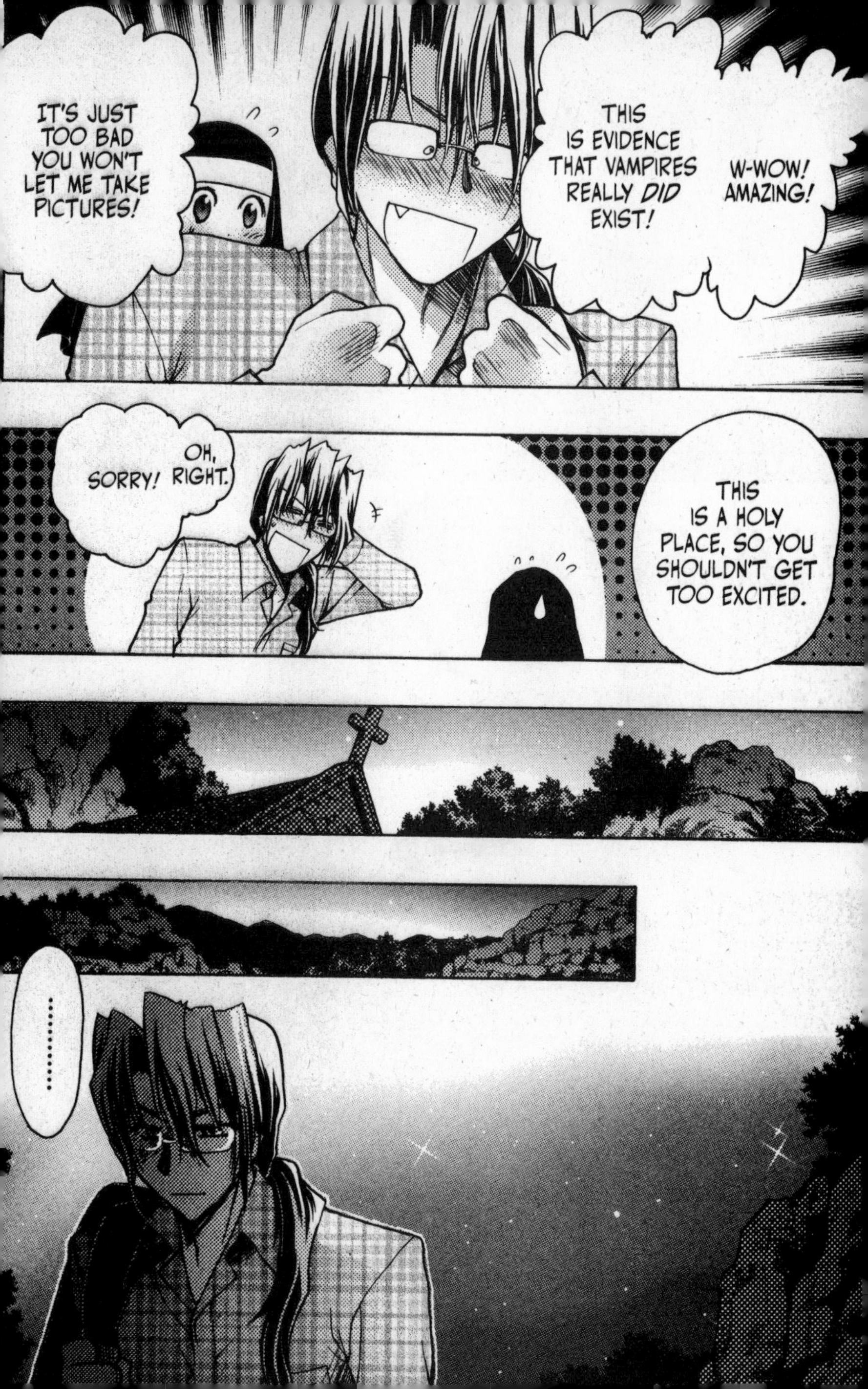
W-WOW! AMAZING!
THIS IS EVIDENCE THAT VAMPIRES REALLY *DID* EXIST!
IT'S JUST TOO BAD YOU WON'T LET ME TAKE PICTURES!
THIS IS A HOLY PLACE, SO YOU SHOULDN'T GET TOO EXCITED.
OH, RIGHT.
SORRY!
……

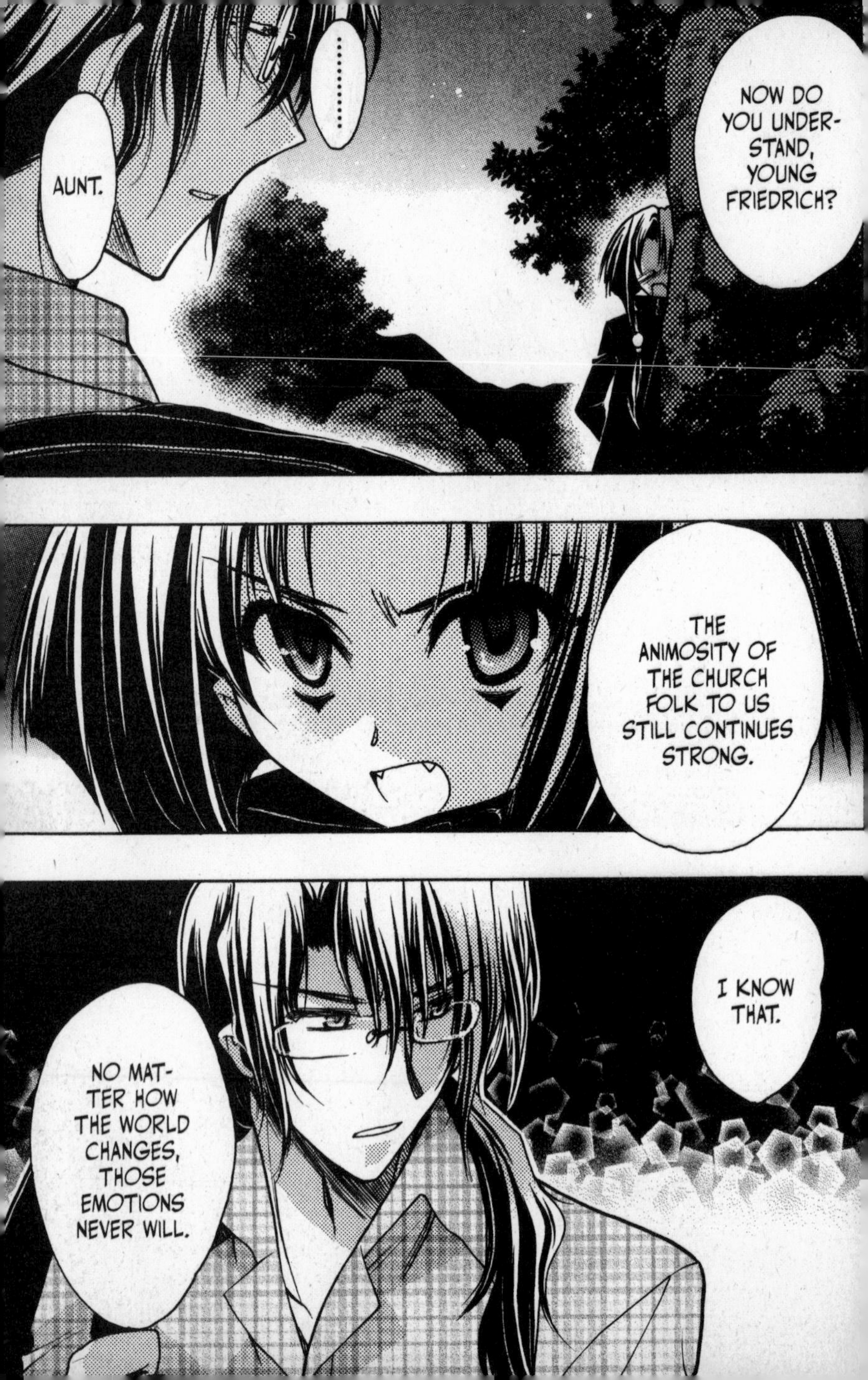
NOW DO YOU UNDER-STAND, YOUNG FRIEDRICH?
....
AUNT.
THE ANIMOSITY OF THE CHURCH FOLK TO US STILL CONTINUES STRONG.
I KNOW THAT.
NO MAT-TER HOW THE WORLD CHANGES, THOSE EMOTIONS NEVER WILL.

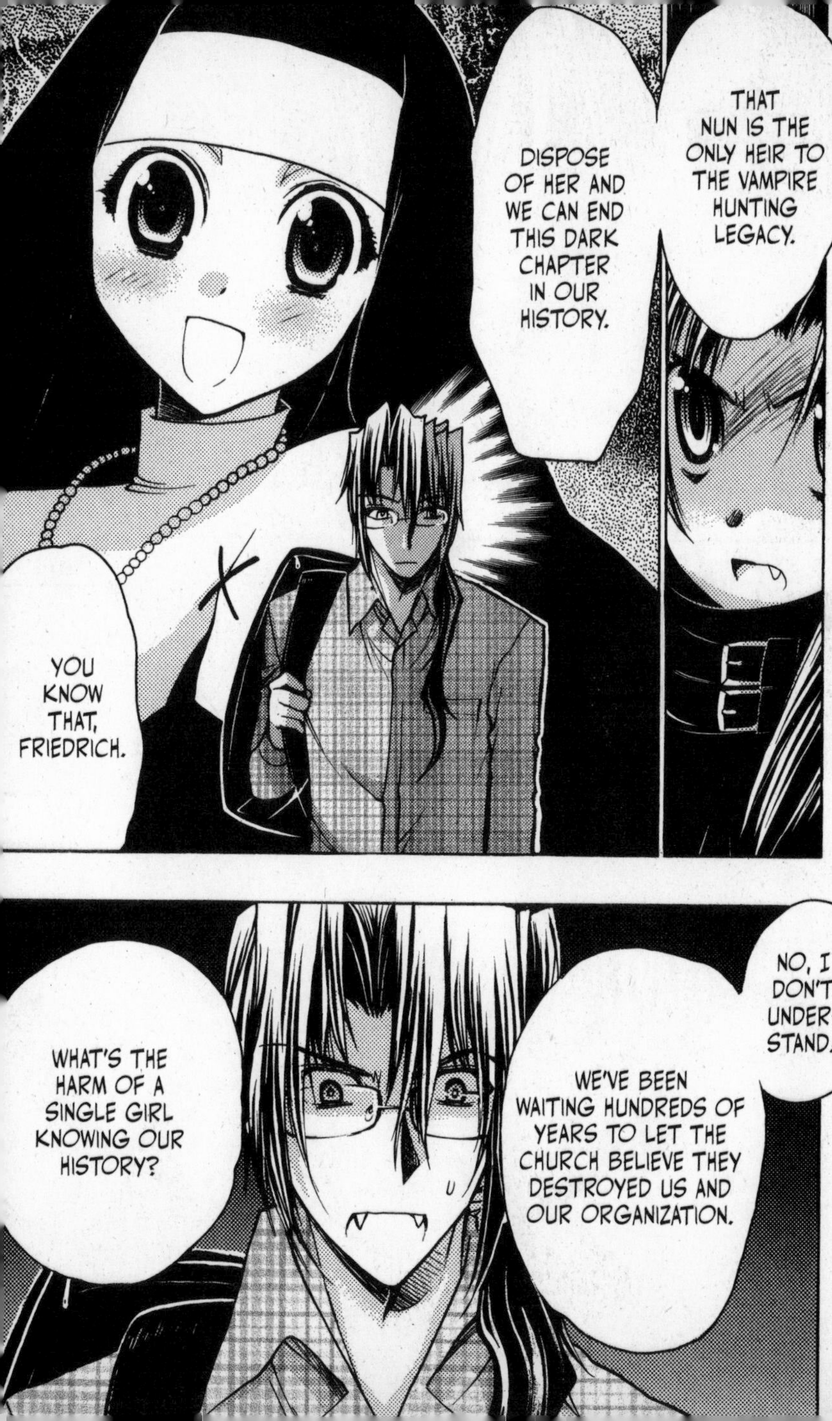
THAT NUN IS THE ONLY HEIR TO THE VAMPIRE HUNTING LEGACY.
DISPOSE OF HER AND WE CAN END THIS DARK CHAPTER IN OUR HISTORY.
YOU KNOW THAT, FRIEDRICH.
NO, I DON'T UNDER-STAND!
WE'VE BEEN WAITING HUNDREDS OF YEARS TO LET THE CHURCH BELIEVE THEY DESTROYED US AND OUR ORGANIZATION.
WHAT'S THE HARM OF A SINGLE GIRL KNOWING OUR HISTORY?

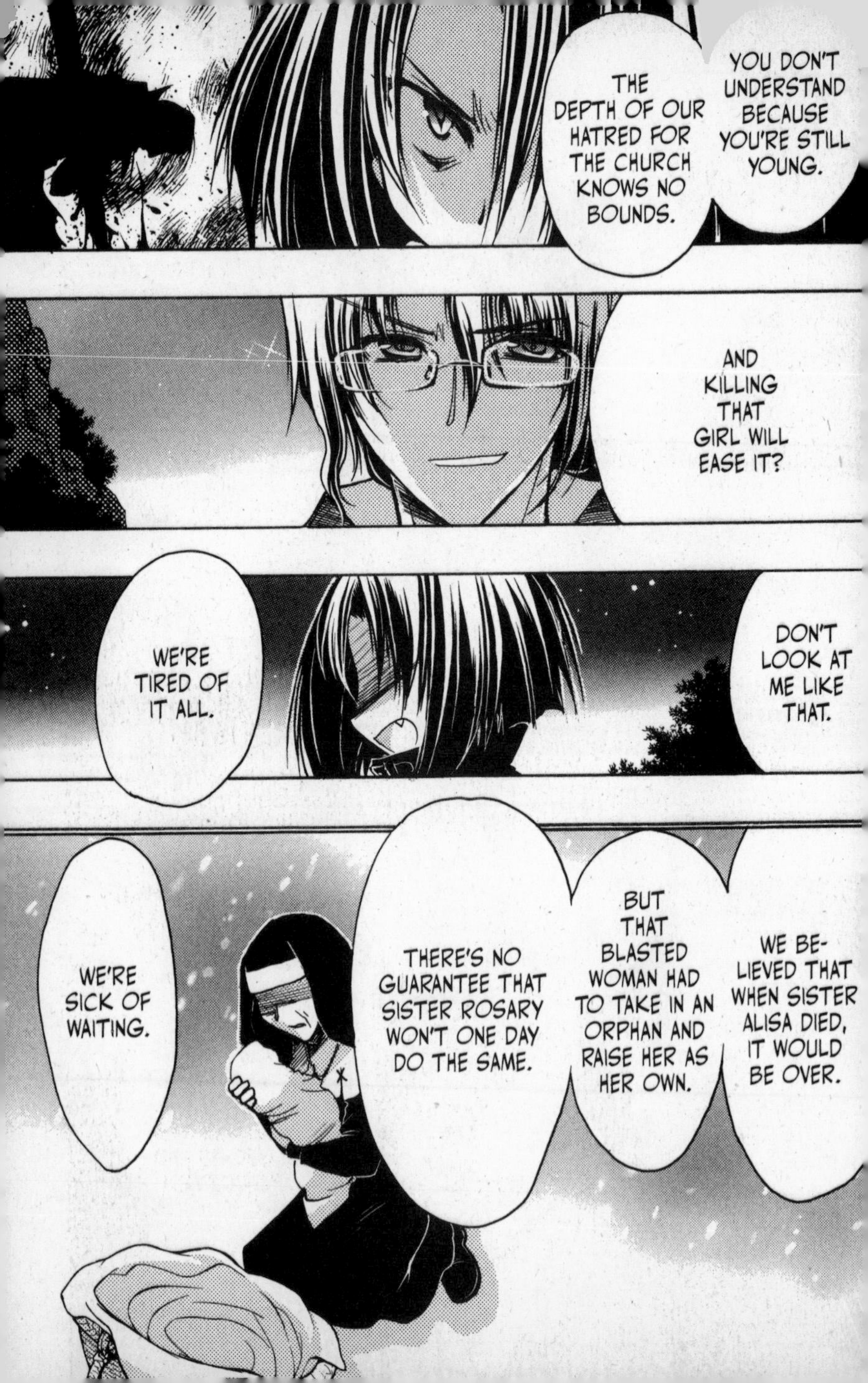
YOU DON'T UNDERSTAND BECAUSE YOU'RE STILL YOUNG.
THE DEPTH OF OUR HATRED FOR THE CHURCH KNOWS NO BOUNDS.
AND KILLING THAT GIRL WILL EASE IT?
DON'T LOOK AT ME LIKE THAT.
WE'RE TIRED OF IT ALL.
WE BE-LIEVED THAT WHEN SISTER ALISA DIED, IT WOULD BE OVER.
BUT THAT BLASTED WOMAN HAD TO TAKE IN AN ORPHAN AND RAISE HER AS HER OWN.
THERE'S NO GUARANTEE THAT SISTER ROSARY WON'T ONE DAY DO THE SAME.
WE'RE SICK OF WAITING.

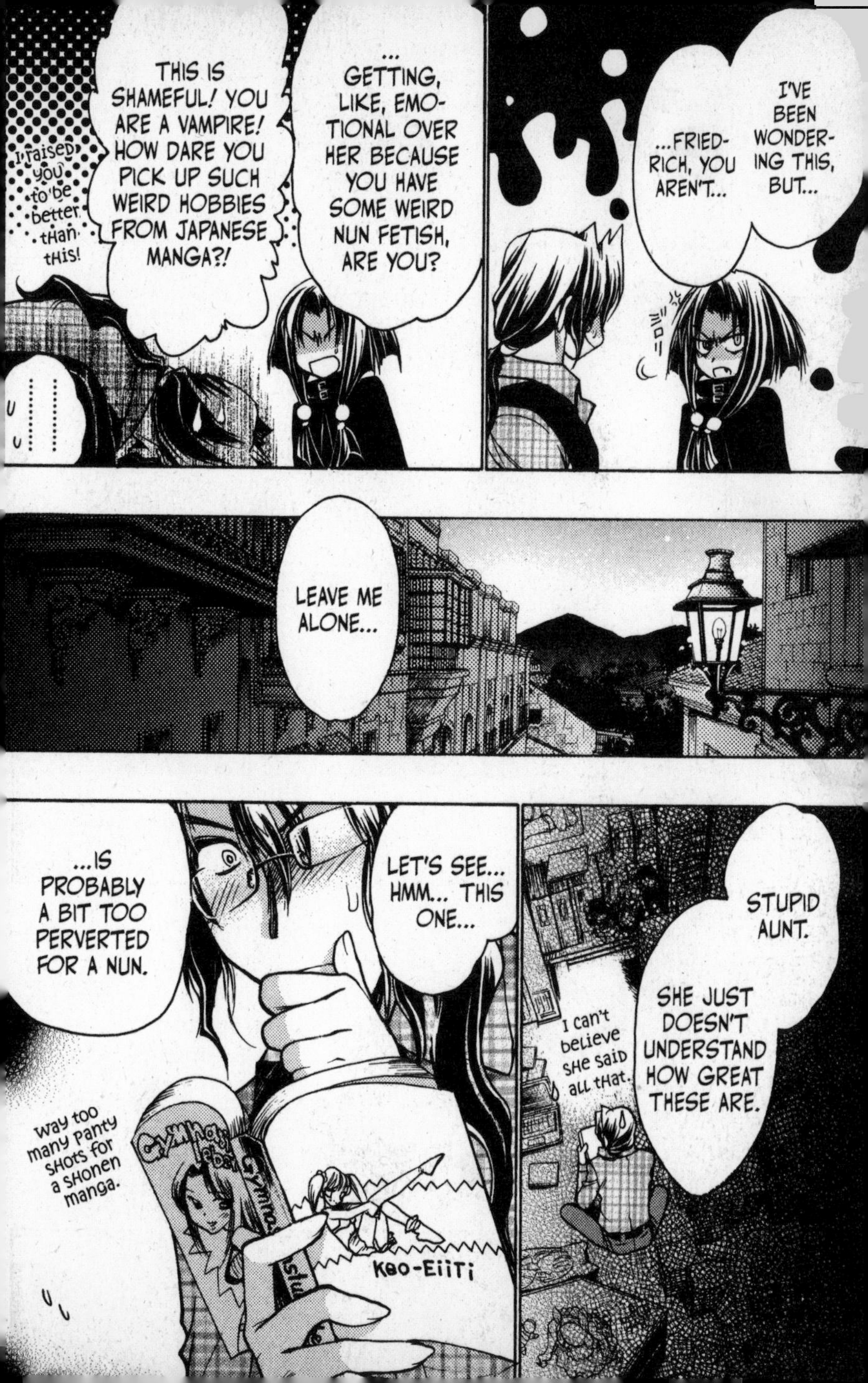
I'VE BEEN WONDERING THIS, BUT...
...FRIEDRICH, YOU AREN'T...
...GETTING, LIKE, EMOTIONAL OVER HER BECAUSE YOU HAVE SOME WEIRD NUN FETISH, ARE YOU?
THIS IS SHAMEFUL! YOU ARE A VAMPIRE! HOW DARE YOU PICK UP SUCH WEIRD HOBBIES FROM JAPANESE MANGA?!
I raised you to be better than this!
......
LEAVE ME ALONE...
STUPID AUNT.
SHE JUST DOESN'T UNDERSTAND HOW GREAT THESE ARE.
I can't believe she said all that.
LET'S SEE... HMM... THIS ONE...
...IS PROBABLY A BIT TOO PERVERTED FOR A NUN.
Way too many panty shots for a shonen manga.
Keo-EiiTi

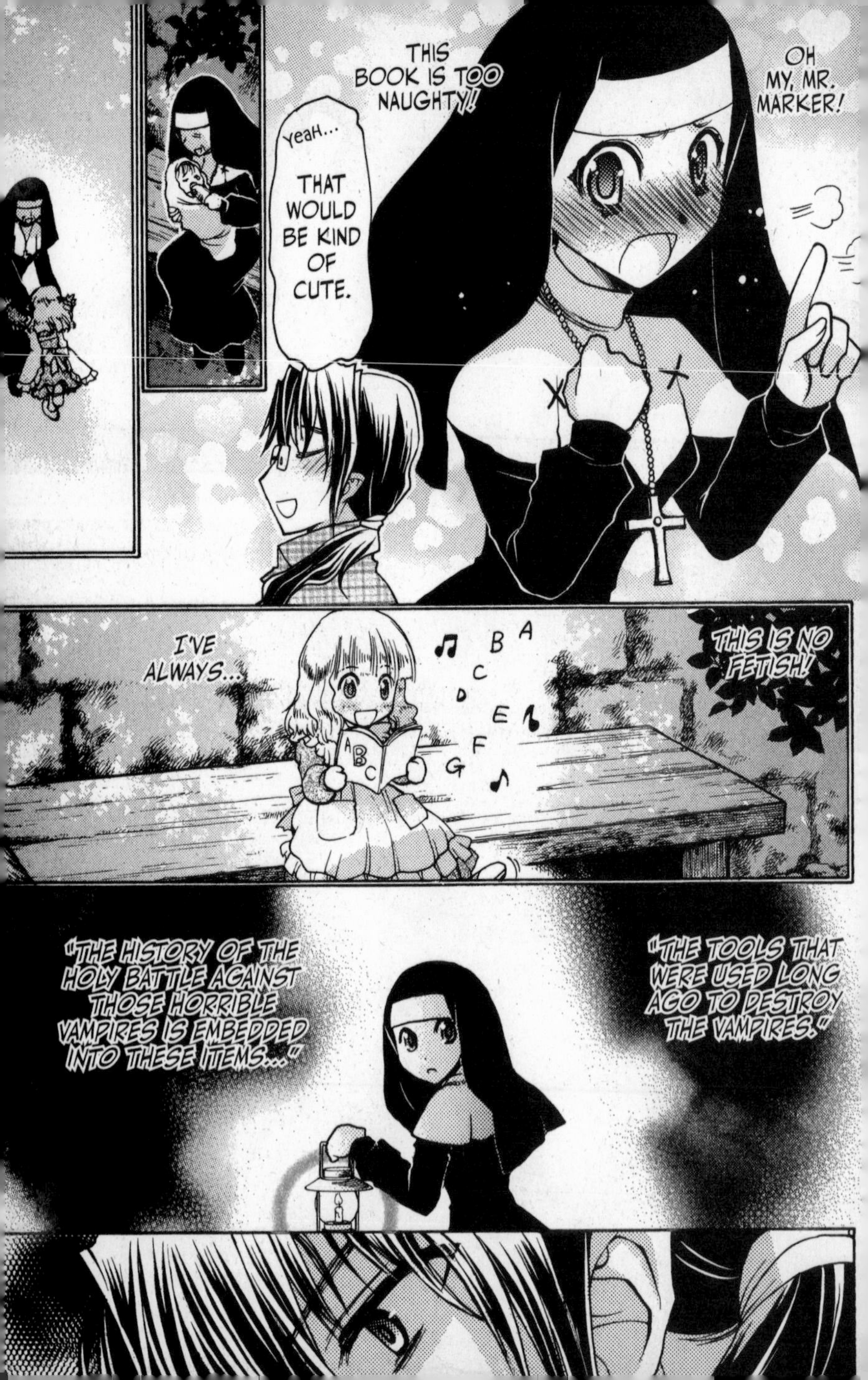
OH MY, MR. MARKER!
THIS BOOK IS TOO NAUGHTY!
Yeah... THAT WOULD BE KIND OF CUTE.
THIS IS NO FETISH!
I'VE ALWAYS...
ABC
A B C D E F G
"THE TOOLS THAT WERE USED LONG AGO TO DESTROY THE VAMPIRES."
"THE HISTORY OF THE HOLY BATTLE AGAINST THOSE HORRIBLE VAMPIRES IS EMBEDDED INTO THESE ITEMS..."

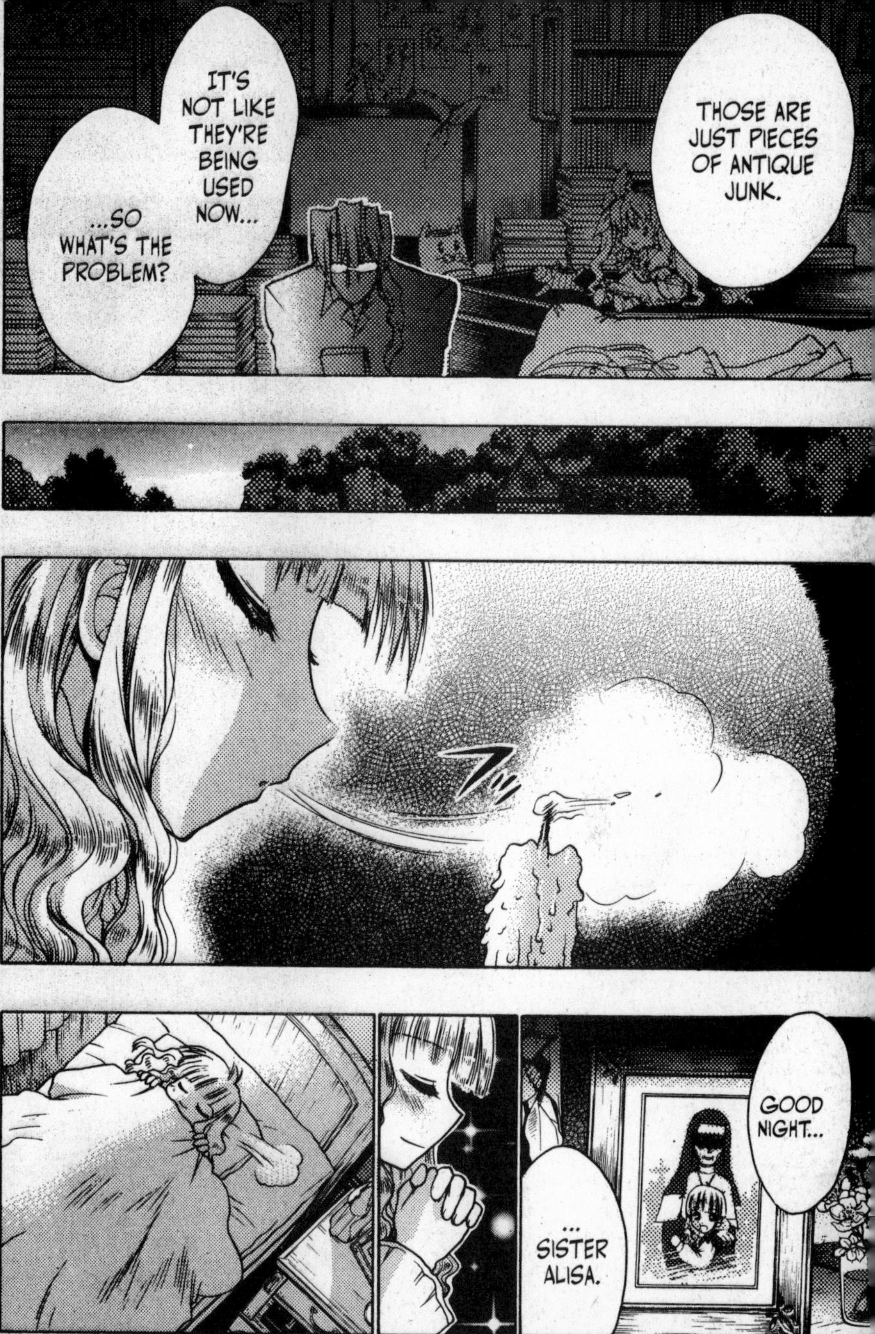
THOSE ARE JUST PIECES OF ANTIQUE JUNK.
IT'S NOT LIKE THEY'RE BEING USED NOW...
...SO WHAT'S THE PROBLEM?
GOOD NIGHT...
... SISTER ALISA.

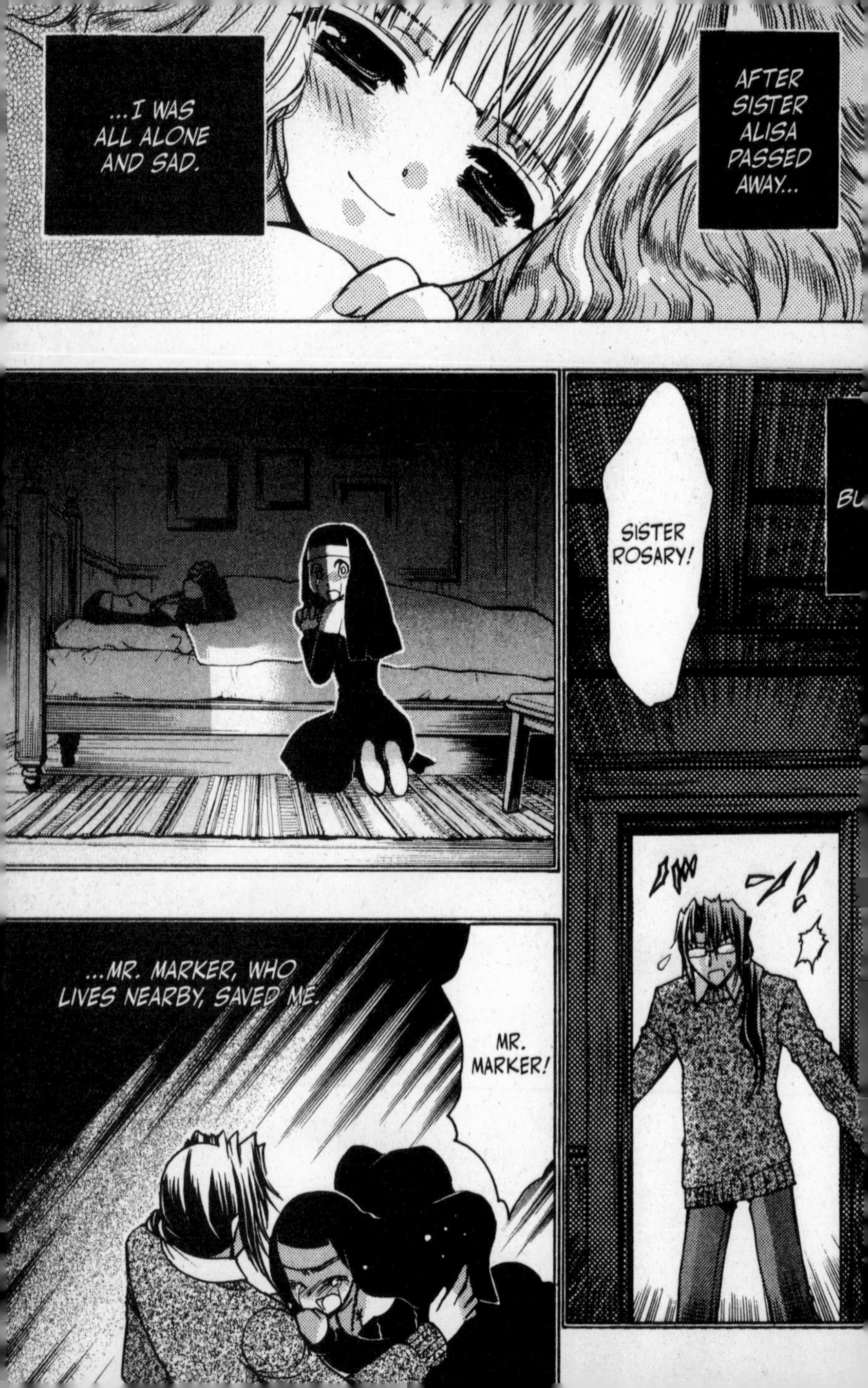
AFTER SISTER ALISA PASSED AWAY...
...I WAS ALL ALONE AND SAD.
BU
SISTER ROSARY!
...MR. MARKER, WHO LIVES NEARBY, SAVED ME.
MR. MARKER!

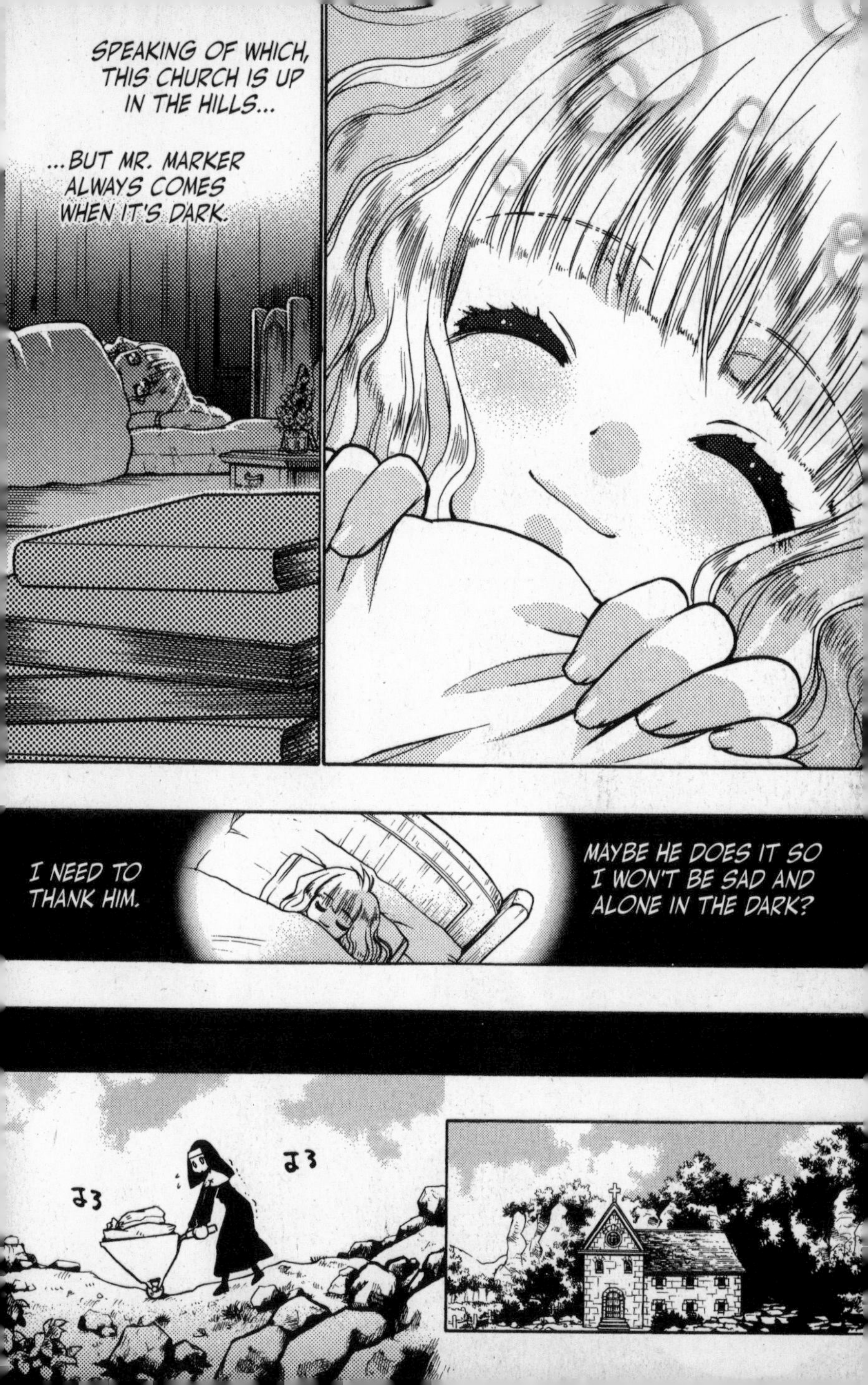
SPEAKING OF WHICH, THIS CHURCH IS UP IN THE HILLS...
...BUT MR. MARKER ALWAYS COMES WHEN IT'S DARK.
MAYBE HE DOES IT SO I WON'T BE SAD AND ALONE IN THE DARK?
I NEED TO THANK HIM.
よろ
よろ

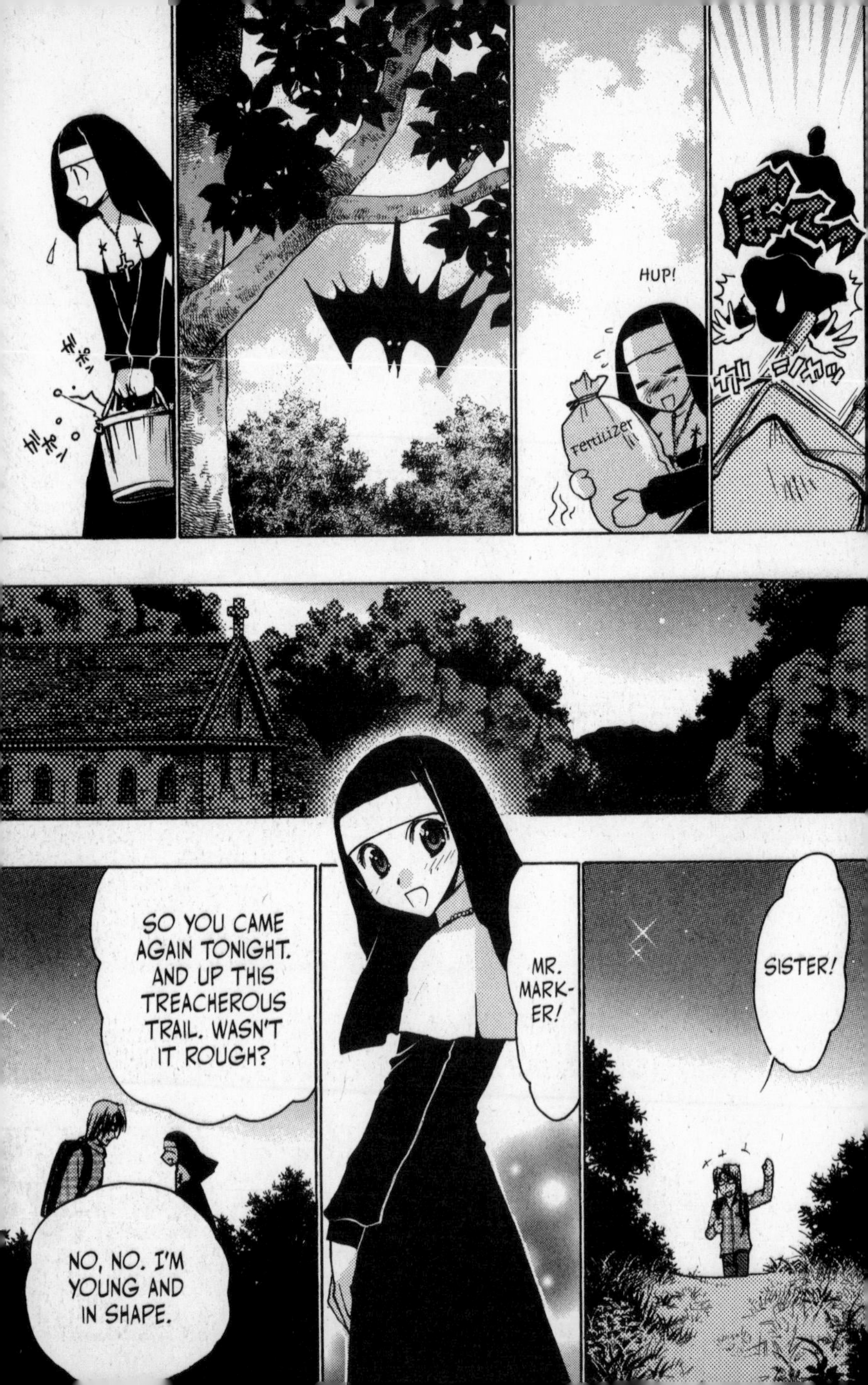
HUP!
Fertilizer
SISTER!
MR. MARKER!
SO YOU CAME AGAIN TONIGHT. AND UP THIS TREACHEROUS TRAIL. WASN'T IT ROUGH?
NO, NO. I'M YOUNG AND IN SHAPE.

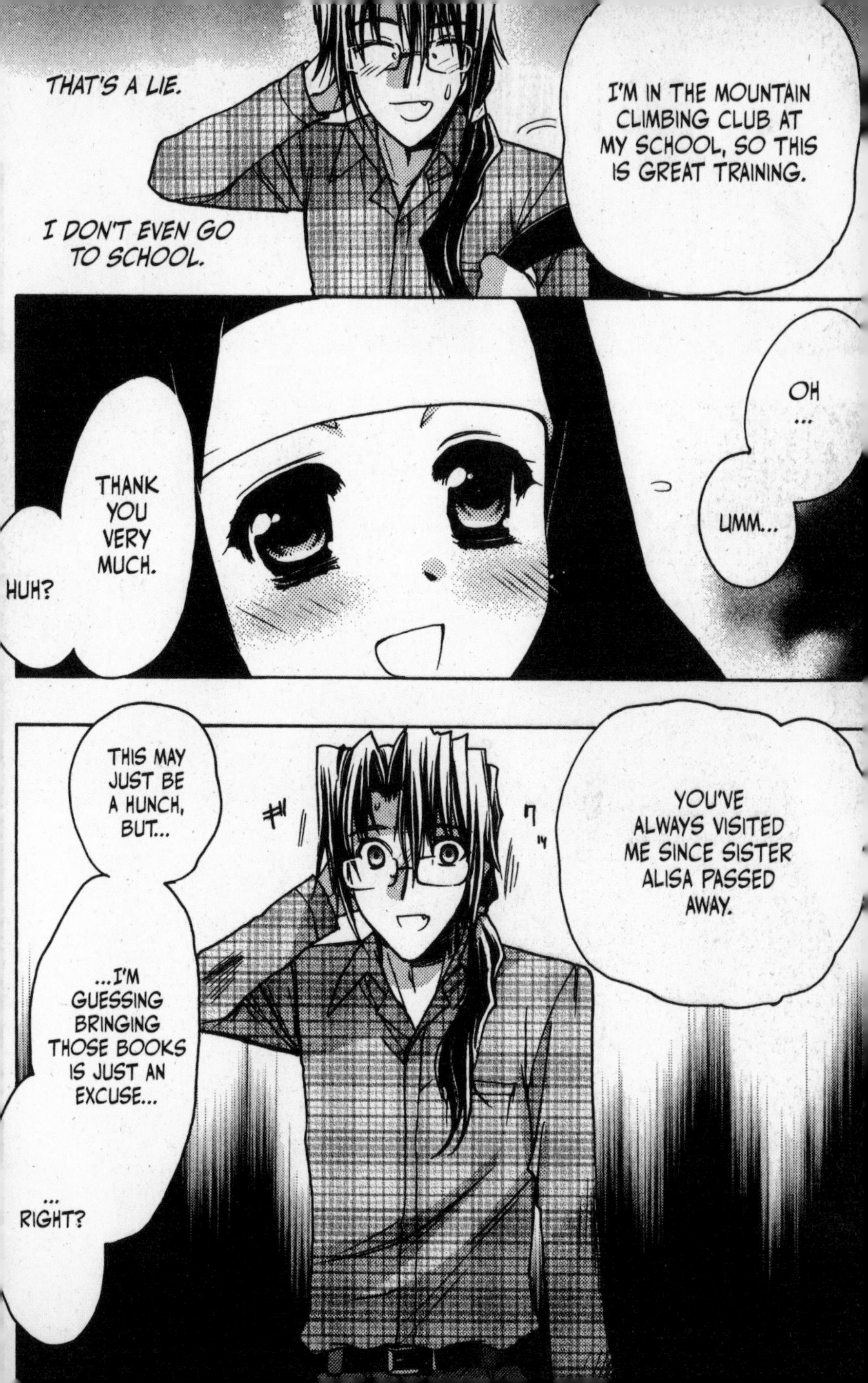
I'M IN THE MOUNTAIN CLIMBING CLUB AT MY SCHOOL, SO THIS IS GREAT TRAINING.
THAT'S A LIE.
I DON'T EVEN GO TO SCHOOL.
OH ... UMM...
THANK YOU VERY MUCH.
HUH?
YOU'VE ALWAYS VISITED ME SINCE SISTER ALISA PASSED AWAY.
THIS MAY JUST BE A HUNCH, BUT...
...I'M GUESSING BRINGING THOSE BOOKS IS JUST AN EXCUSE...
... RIGHT?

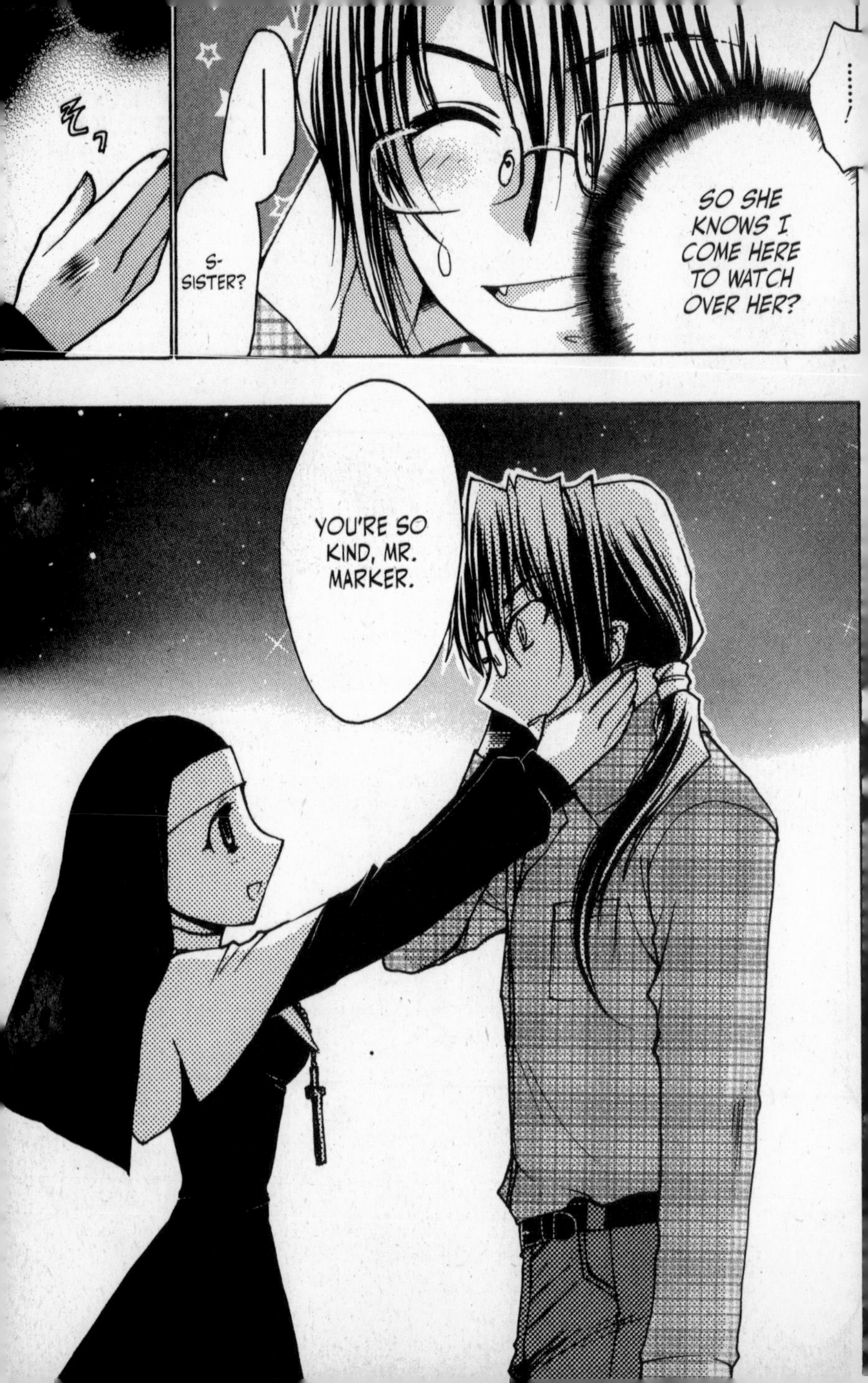
......!
SO SHE KNOWS I COME HERE TO WATCH OVER HER?
S-SISTER?
YOU'RE SO KIND, MR. MARKER.

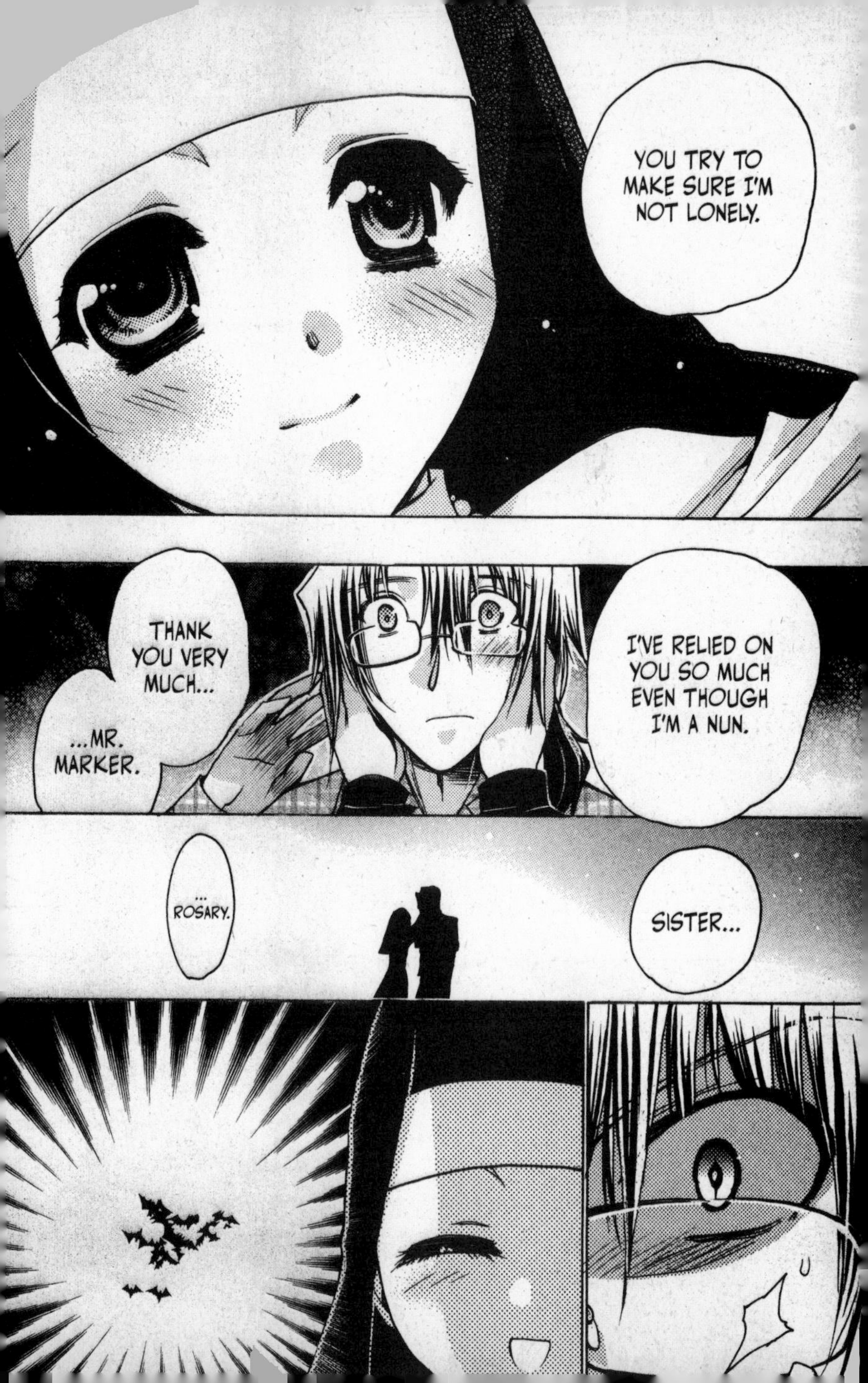
YOU TRY TO MAKE SURE I'M NOT LONELY.
I'VE RELIED ON YOU SO MUCH EVEN THOUGH I'M A NUN.
THANK YOU VERY MUCH...
...MR. MARKER.
SISTER...
... ROSARY.

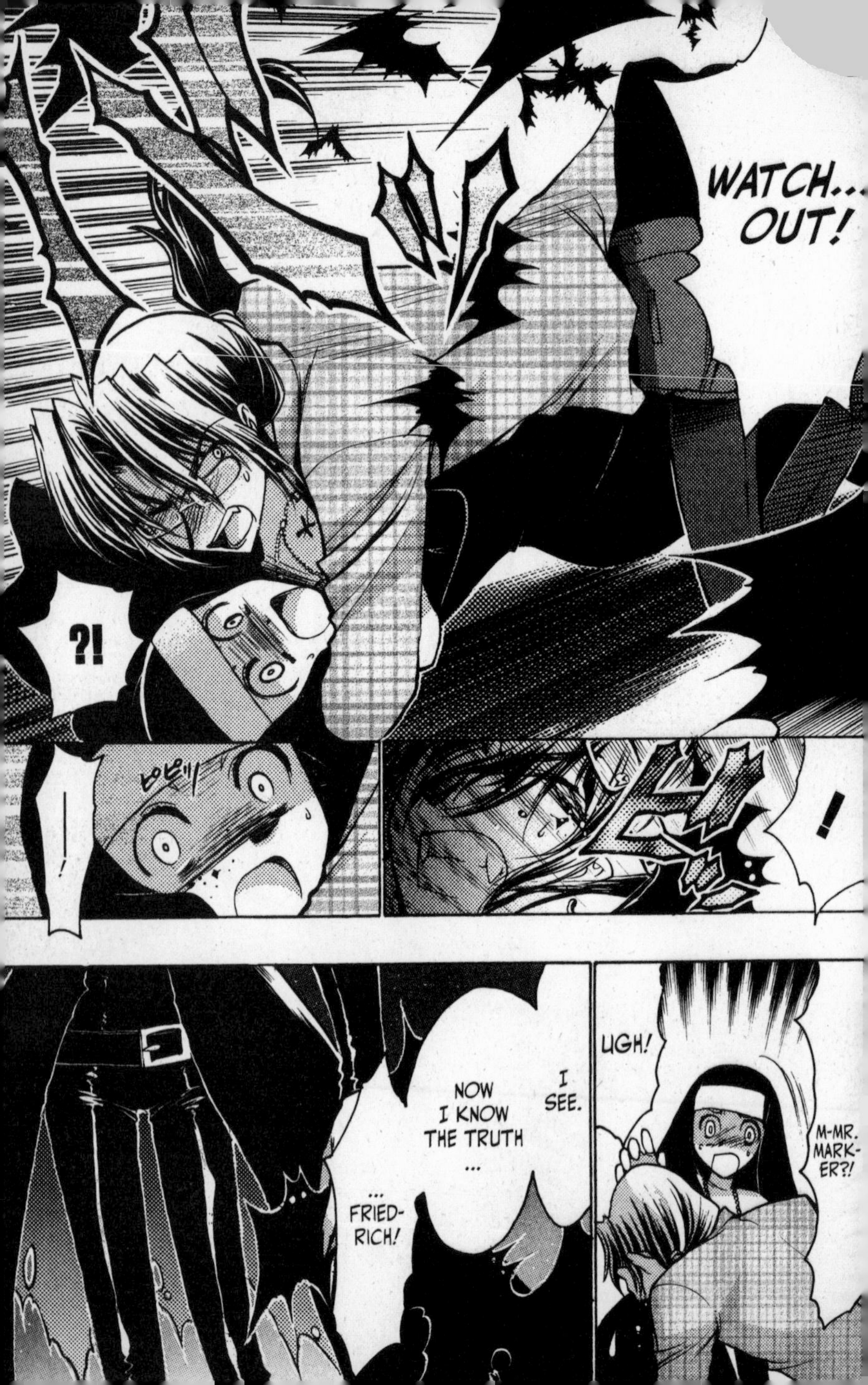
WATCH... OUT!
?!
!
UGH!
M-MR. MARKER?!
I SEE.
NOW I KNOW THE TRUTH ...
... FRIED-RICH!

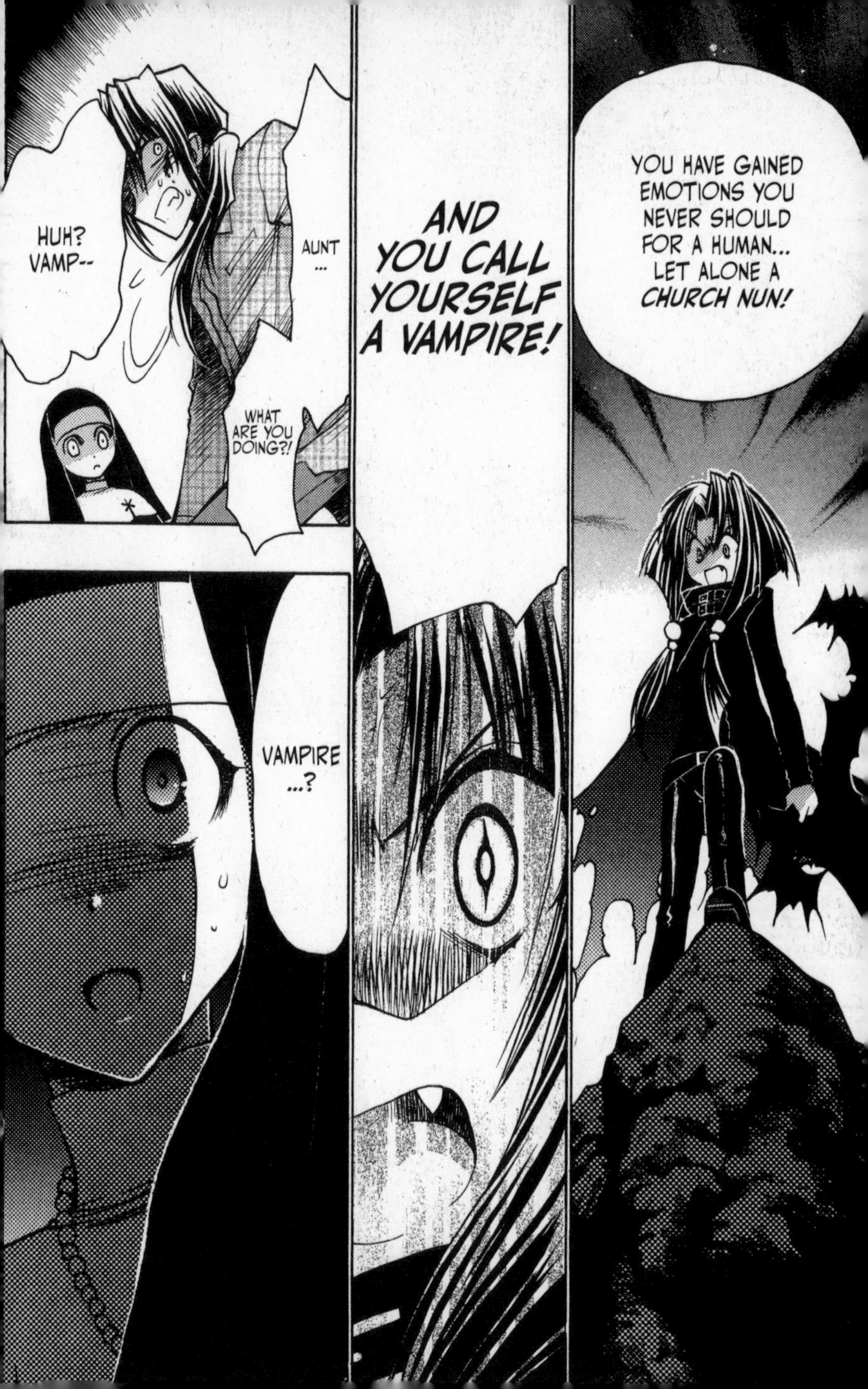

YOU HAVE GAINED EMOTIONS YOU NEVER SHOULD FOR A HUMAN... LET ALONE A CHURCH NUN!
AND YOU CALL YOURSELF A VAMPIRE!
AUNT ...
WHAT ARE YOU DOING?!
HUH? VAMP--
VAMPIRE ...?

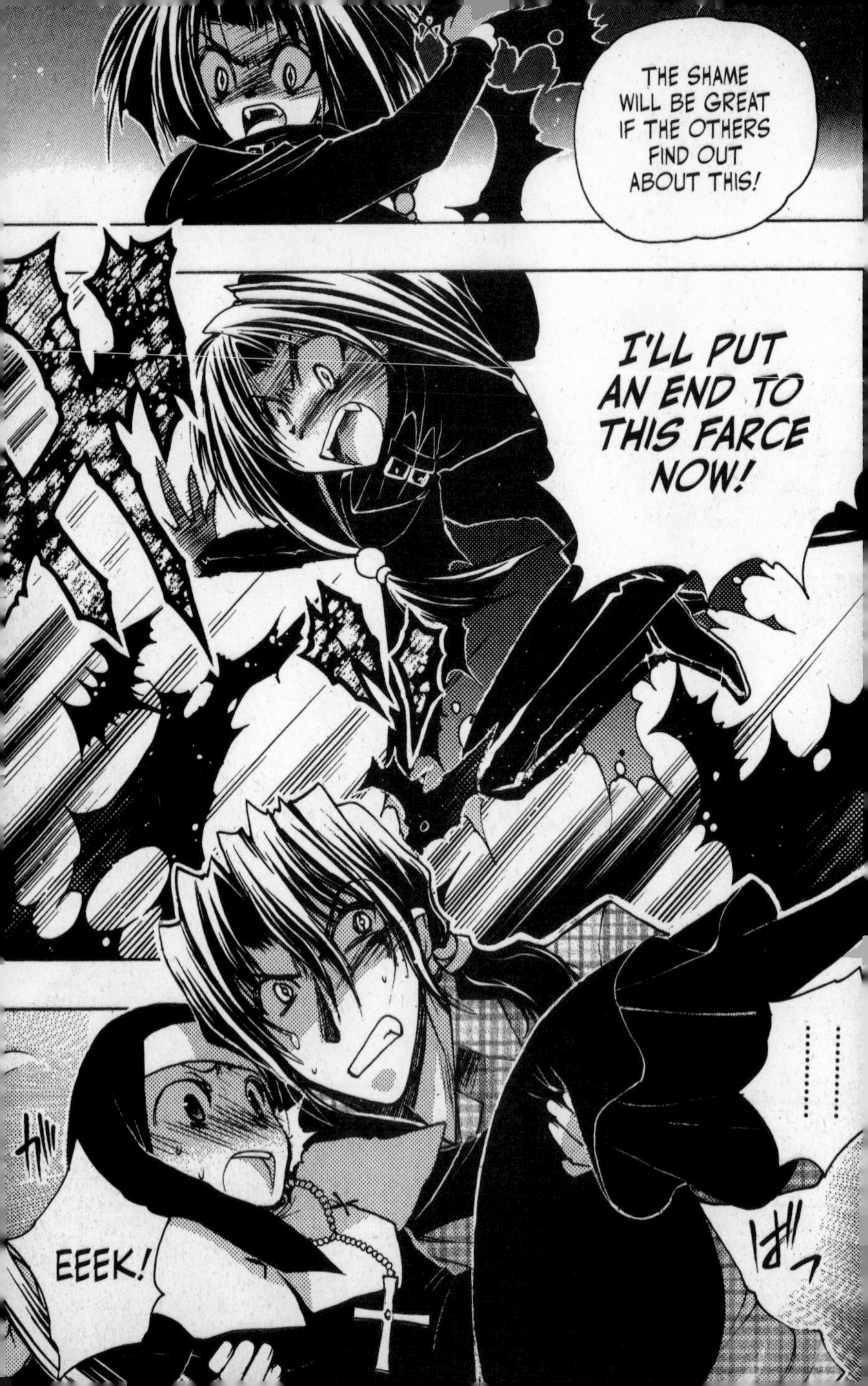
THE SHAME WILL BE GREAT IF THE OTHERS FIND OUT ABOUT THIS!
I'LL PUT AN END TO THIS FARCE NOW!
EEEK!

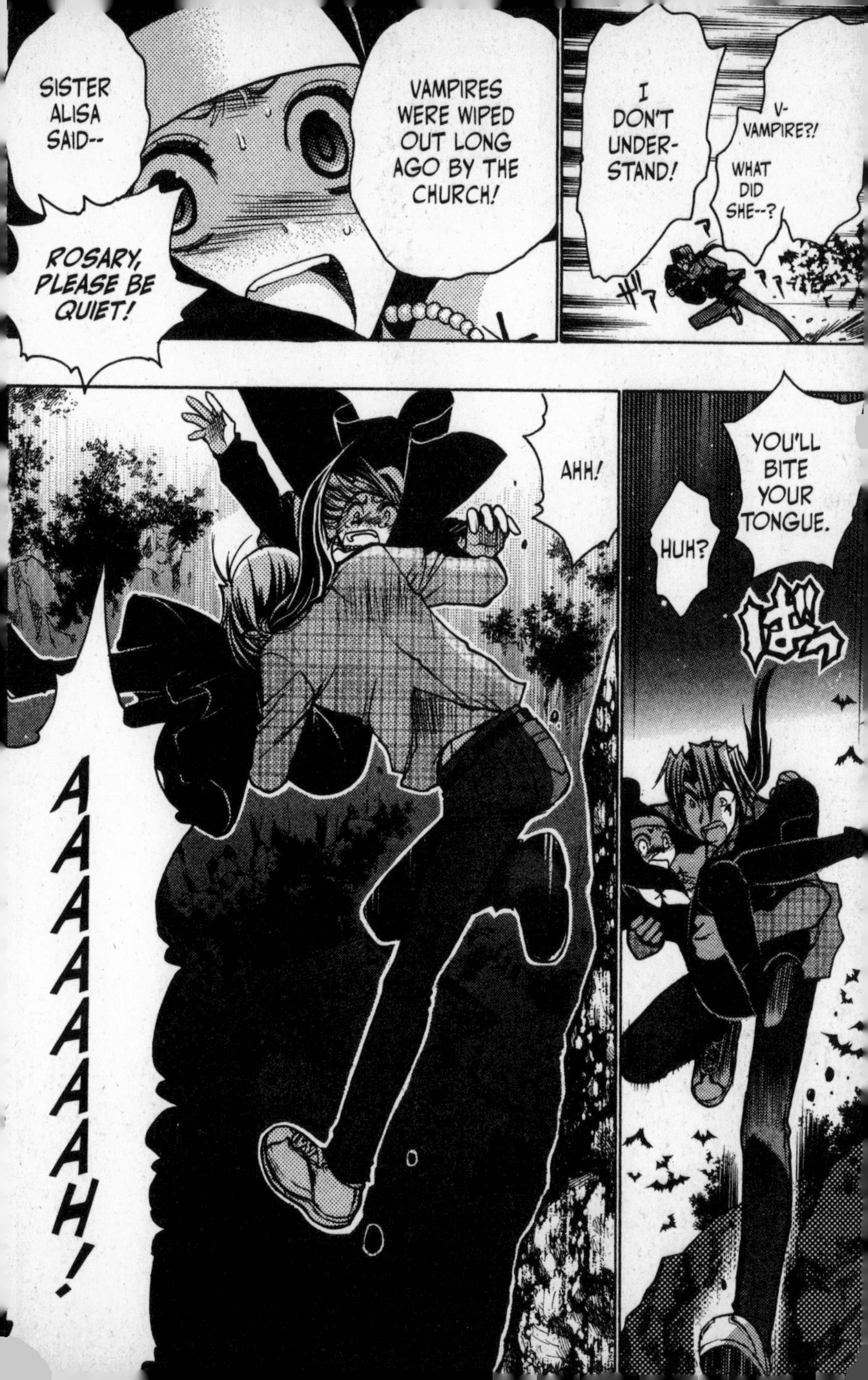
V-VAMPIRE?!
WHAT DID SHE--?
I DON'T UNDERSTAND!
SISTER ALISA SAID--
VAMPIRES WERE WIPED OUT LONG AGO BY THE CHURCH!
ROSARY, PLEASE BE QUIET!
YOU'LL BITE YOUR TONGUE.
HUH?
AHH!
AAAAAAAH!

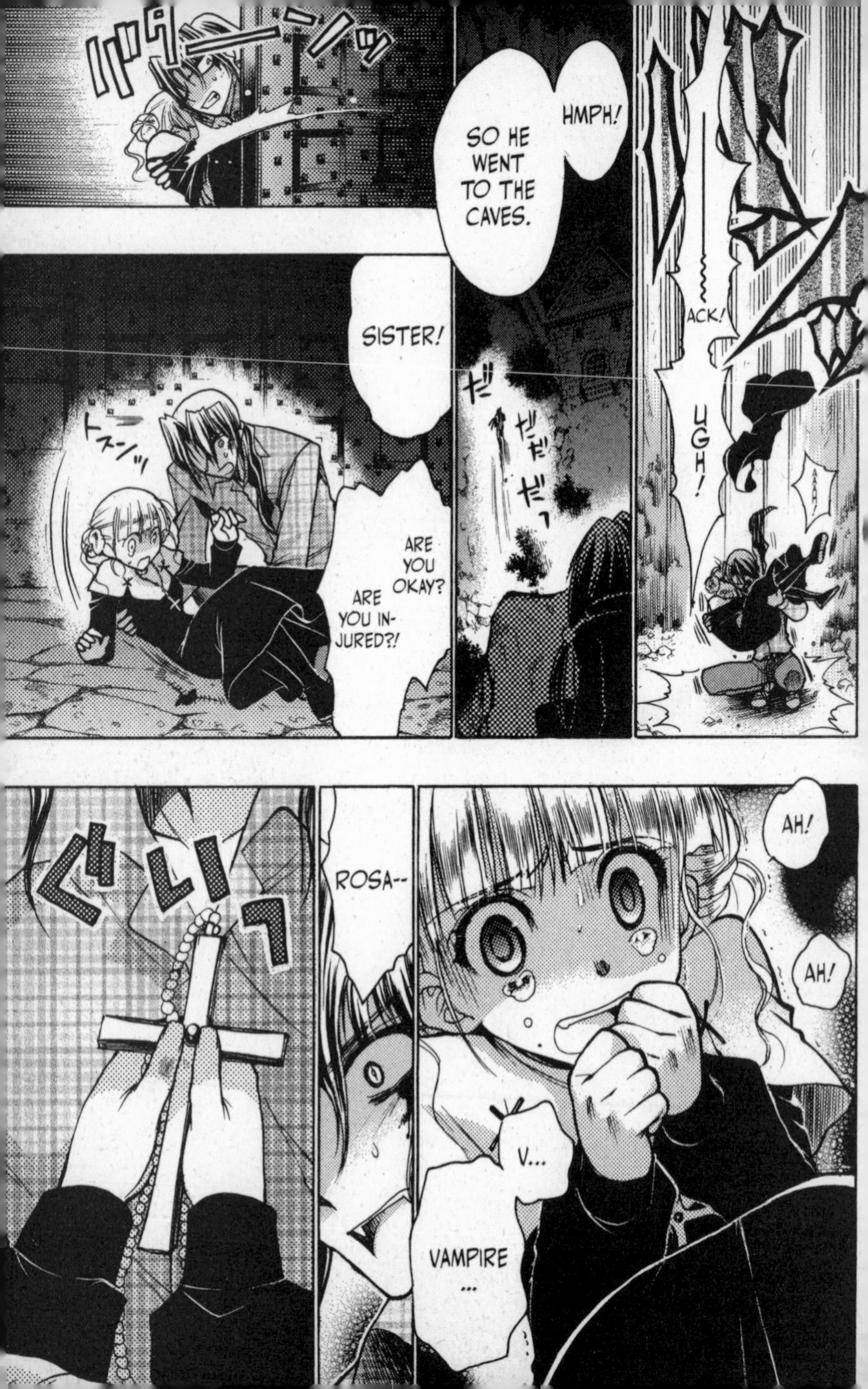
ACK!
UGH!
AAAH!
HMPH!
SO HE WENT TO THE CAVES.
SISTER!
ARE YOU OKAY?
ARE YOU INJURED?!
AH!
AH!
V...
VAMPIRE ...
ROSA--

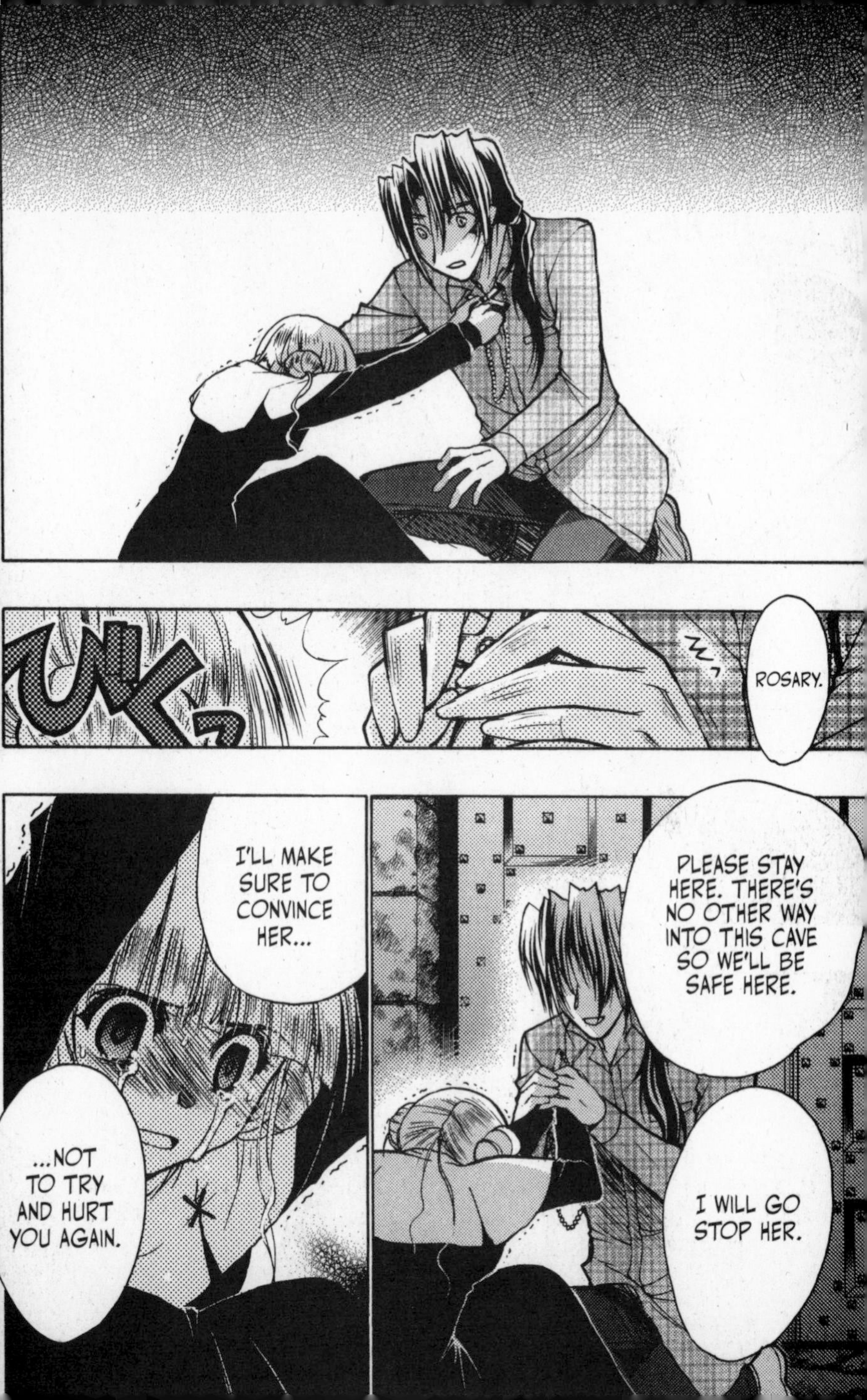
ROSARY.
PLEASE STAY HERE. THERE'S NO OTHER WAY INTO THIS CAVE SO WE'LL BE SAFE HERE.
I WILL GO STOP HER.
I'LL MAKE SURE TO CONVINCE HER...
...NOT TO TRY AND HURT YOU AGAIN.

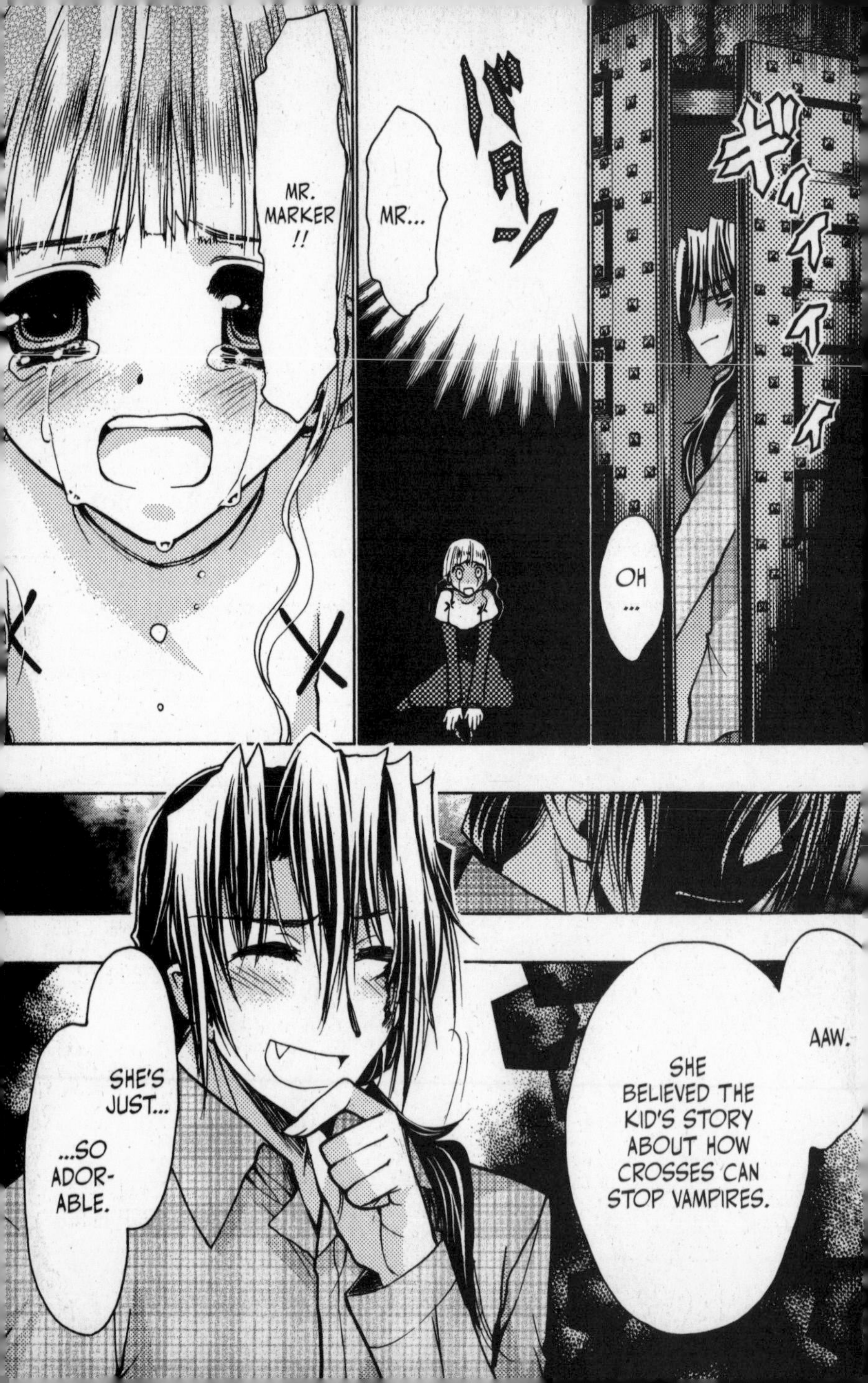
ギィィィィ
OH ...
バタン
MR...
MR. MARKER !!
AAW.
SHE BELIEVED THE KID'S STORY ABOUT HOW CROSSES CAN STOP VAMPIRES.
SHE'S JUST...
...SO ADORABLE.

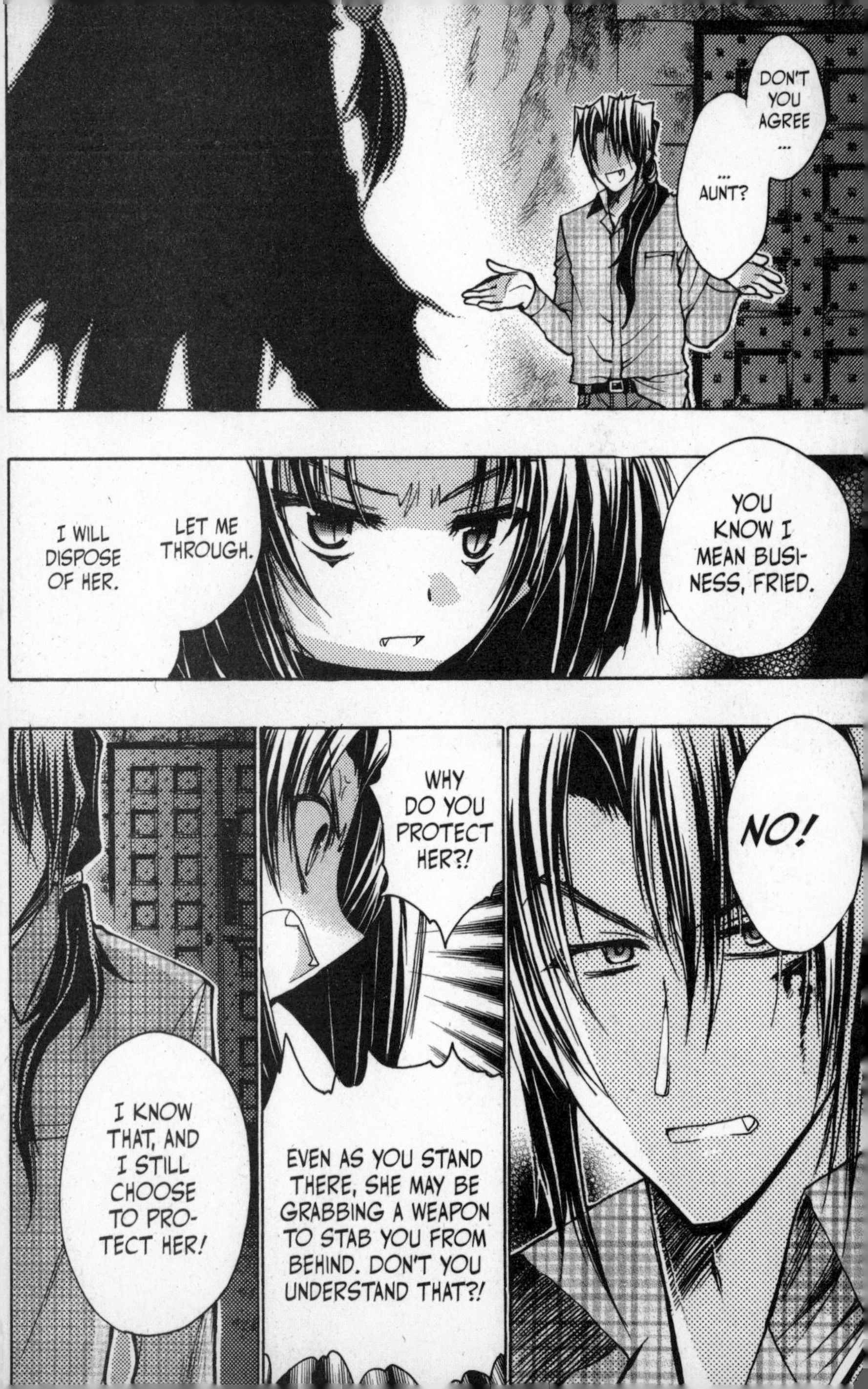
DON'T YOU AGREE ...
... AUNT?
YOU KNOW I MEAN BUSINESS, FRIED.
LET ME THROUGH.
I WILL DISPOSE OF HER.
NO!
WHY DO YOU PROTECT HER?!
EVEN AS YOU STAND THERE, SHE MAY BE GRABBING A WEAPON TO STAB YOU FROM BEHIND. DON'T YOU UNDERSTAND THAT?!
I KNOW THAT, AND I STILL CHOOSE TO PROTECT HER!

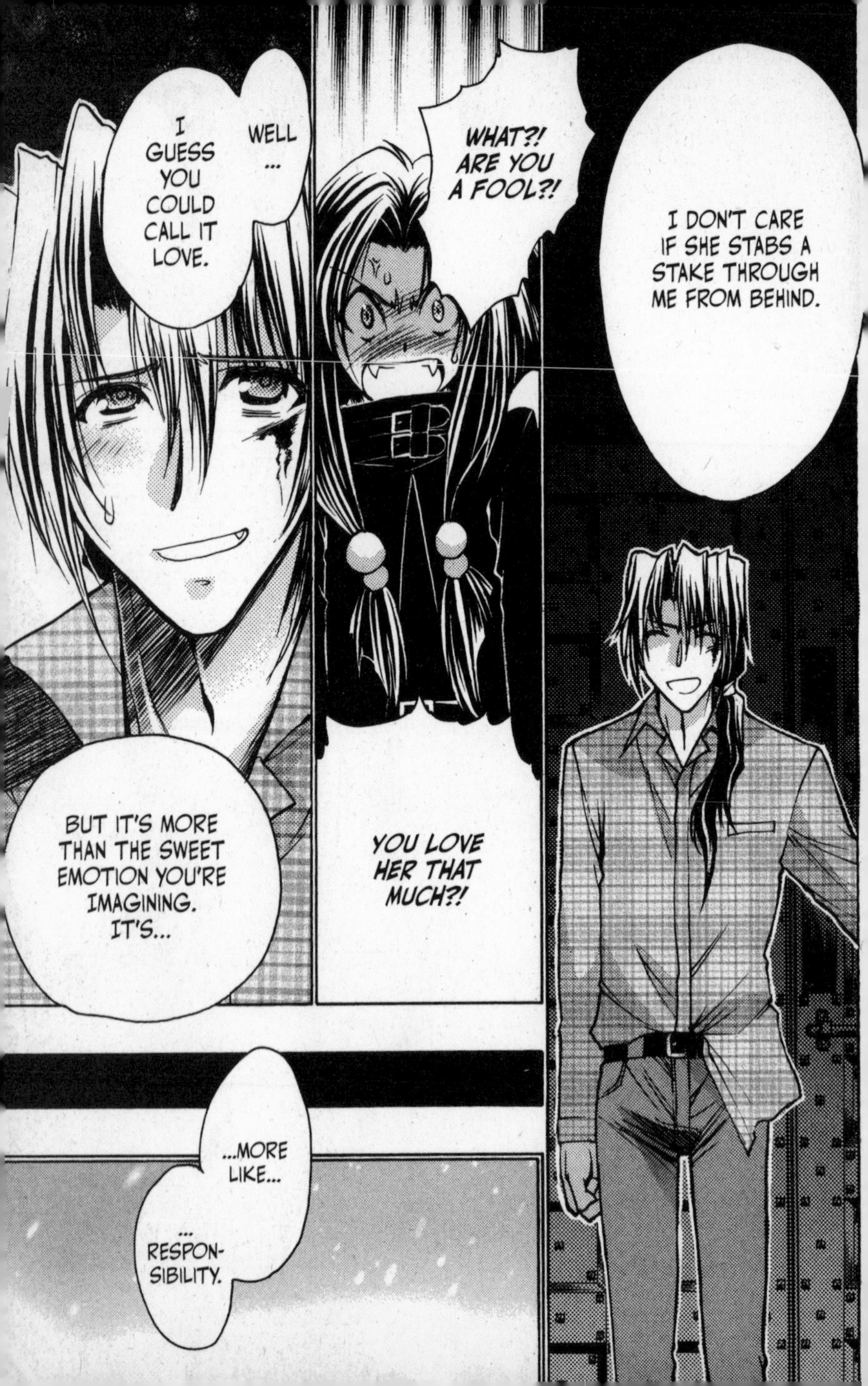
I DON'T CARE IF SHE STABS A STAKE THROUGH ME FROM BEHIND.
WHAT?! ARE YOU A FOOL?!
YOU LOVE HER THAT MUCH?!
WELL...
I GUESS YOU COULD CALL IT LOVE.
BUT IT'S MORE THAN THE SWEET EMOTION YOU'RE IMAGINING. IT'S...
...MORE LIKE...
...RESPON-SIBILITY.

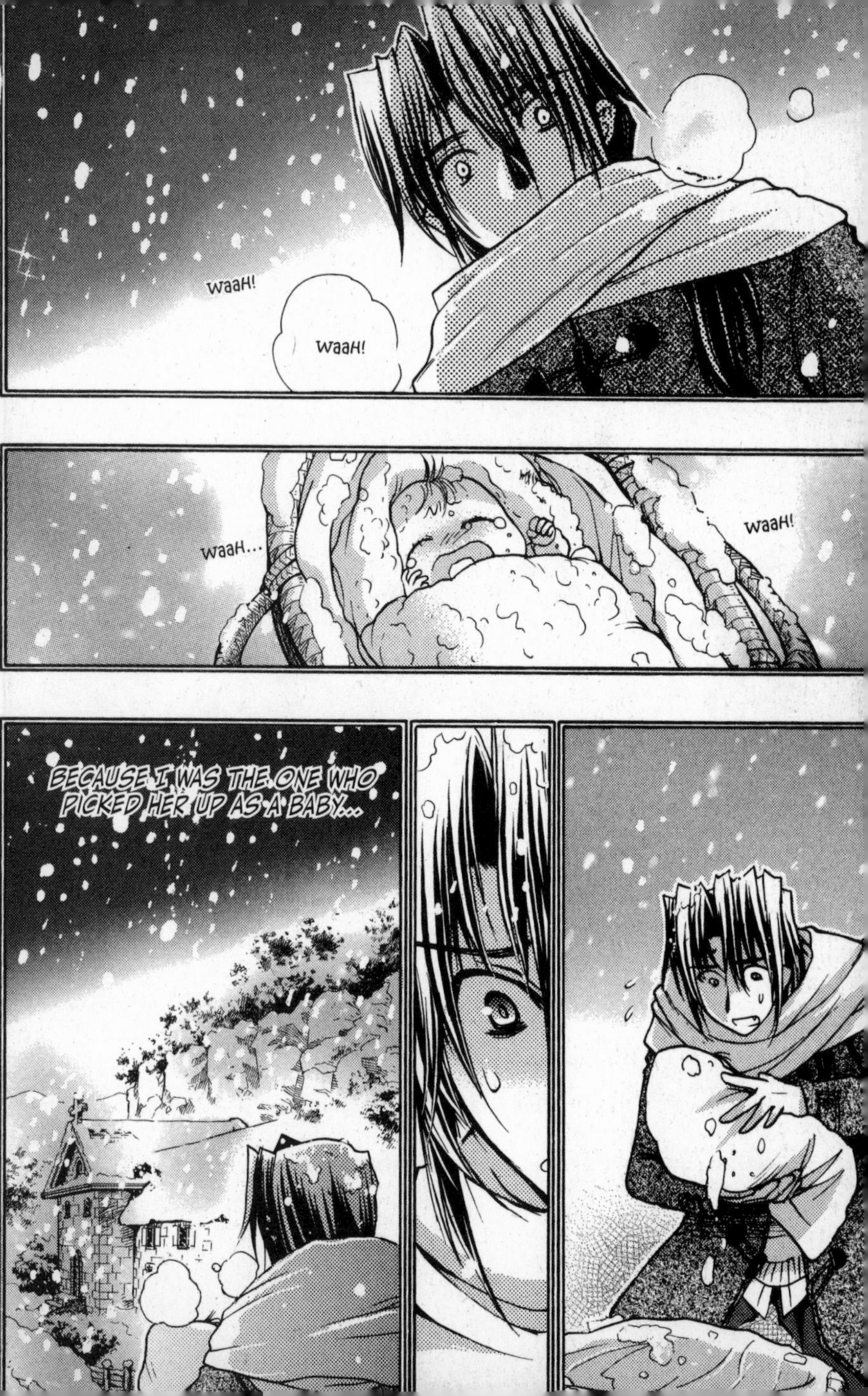
WAAH!
WAAH!
WAAH!
WAAH...
BECAUSE I WAS THE ONE WHO PICKED HER UP AS A BABY...

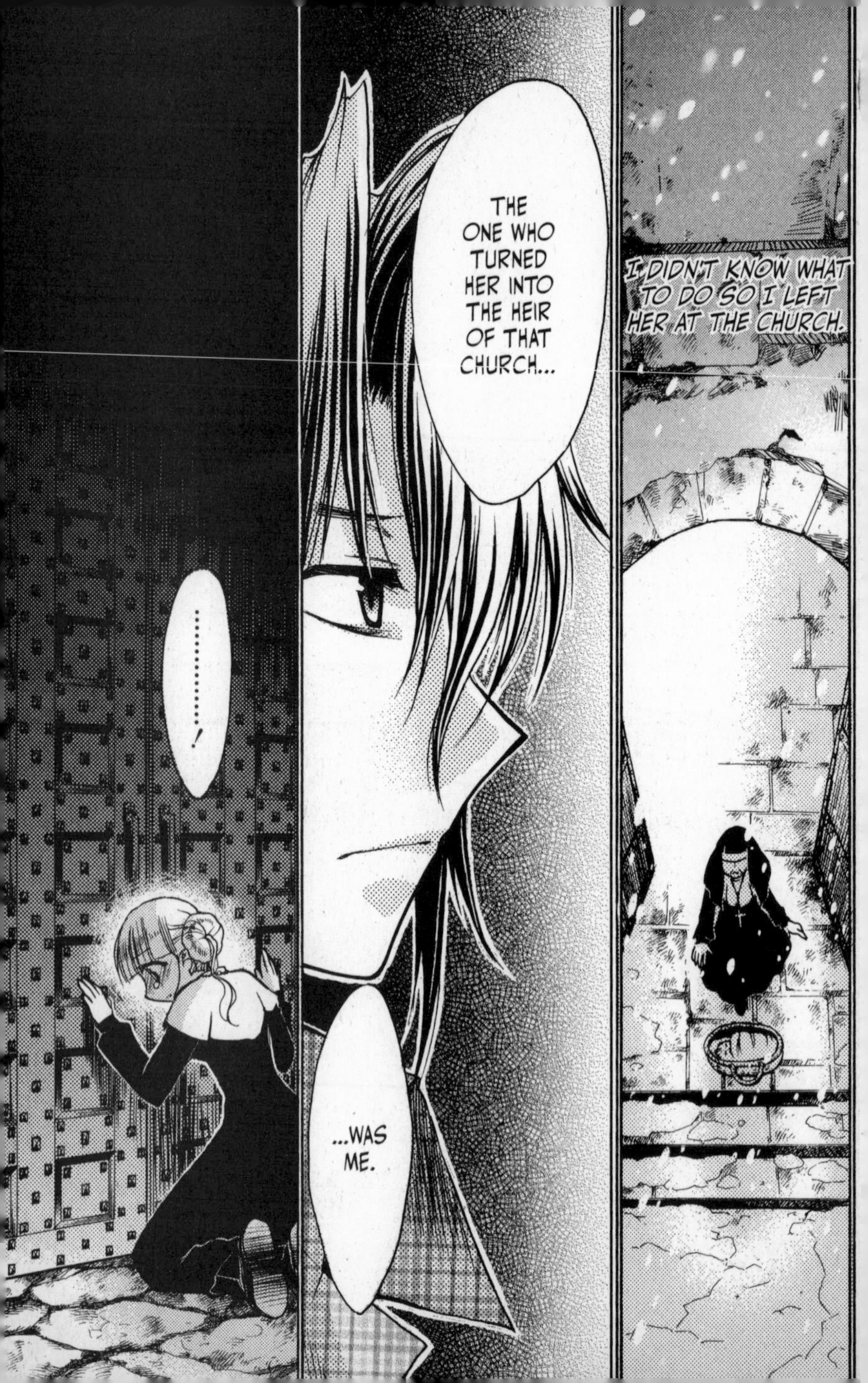
I DIDN'T KNOW WHAT TO DO SO I LEFT HER AT THE CHURCH.
THE ONE WHO TURNED HER INTO THE HEIR OF THAT CHURCH...
...WAS ME.
......!

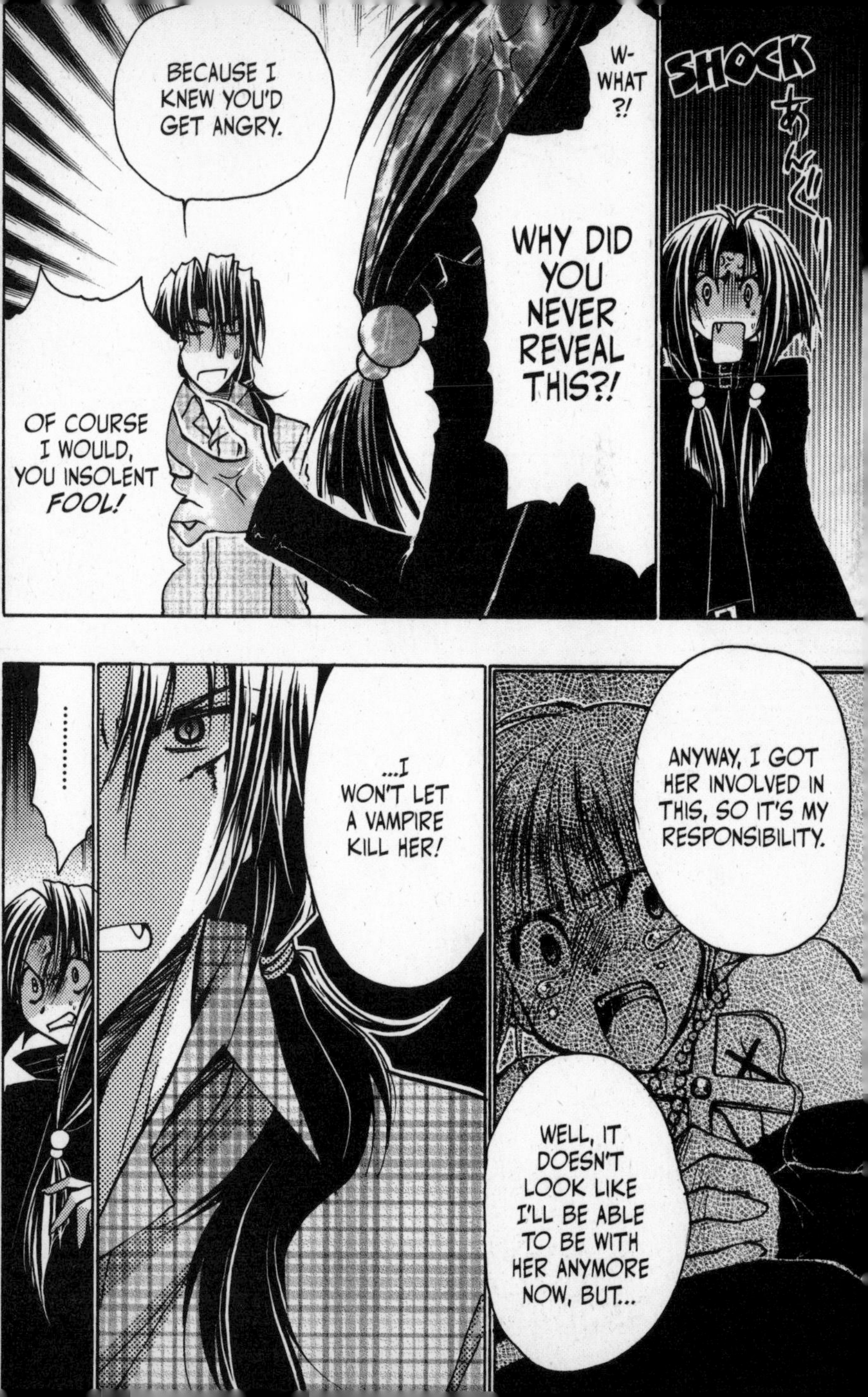
SHOCK
あんぐ!!
W-WHAT?!
WHY DID YOU NEVER REVEAL THIS?!
BECAUSE I KNEW YOU'D GET ANGRY.
OF COURSE I WOULD, YOU INSOLENT *FOOL!*
ANYWAY, I GOT HER INVOLVED IN THIS, SO IT'S MY RESPONSIBILITY.
WELL, IT DOESN'T LOOK LIKE I'LL BE ABLE TO BE WITH HER ANYMORE NOW, BUT...
...I WON'T LET A VAMPIRE KILL HER!
....

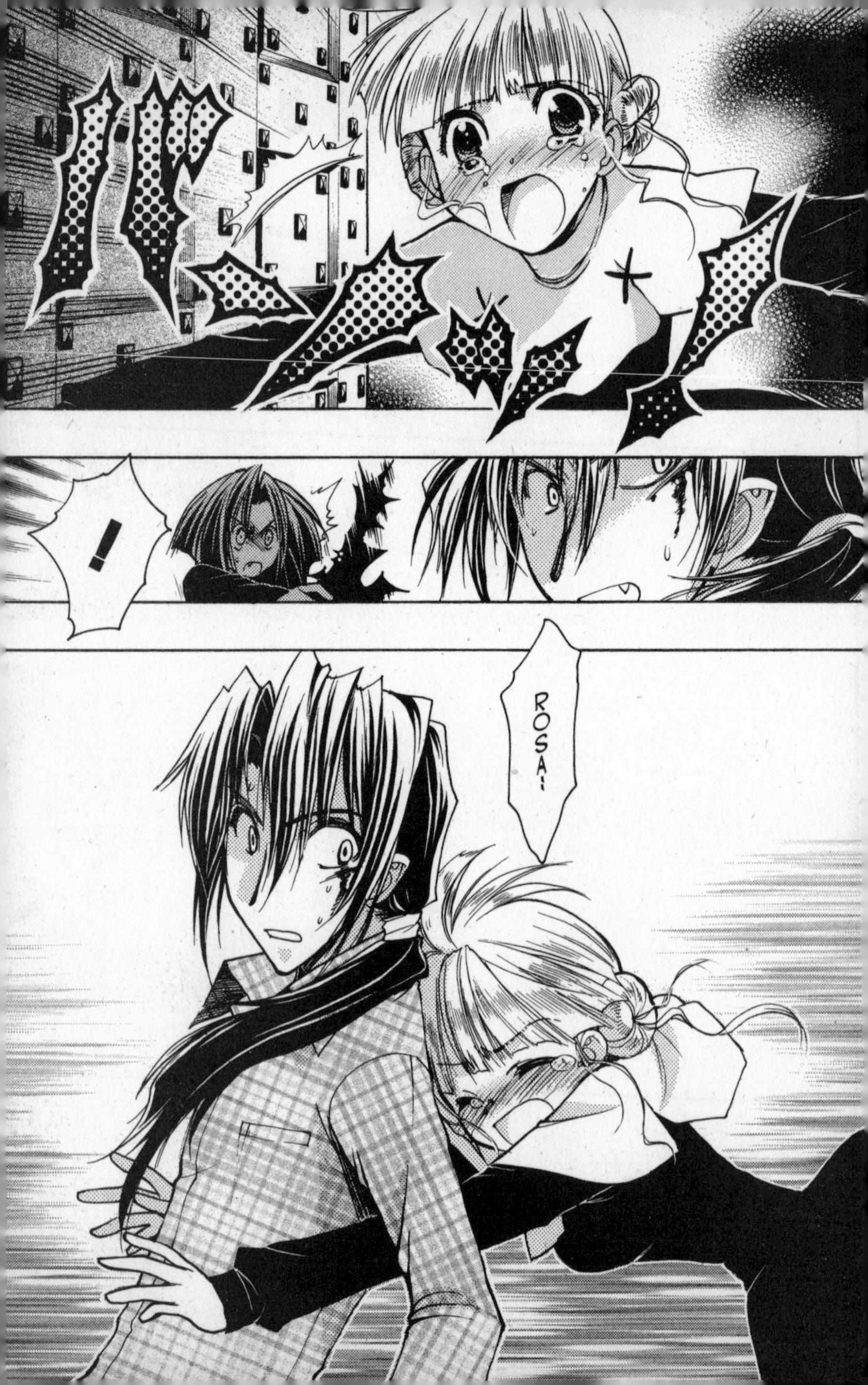
!
ROSA!

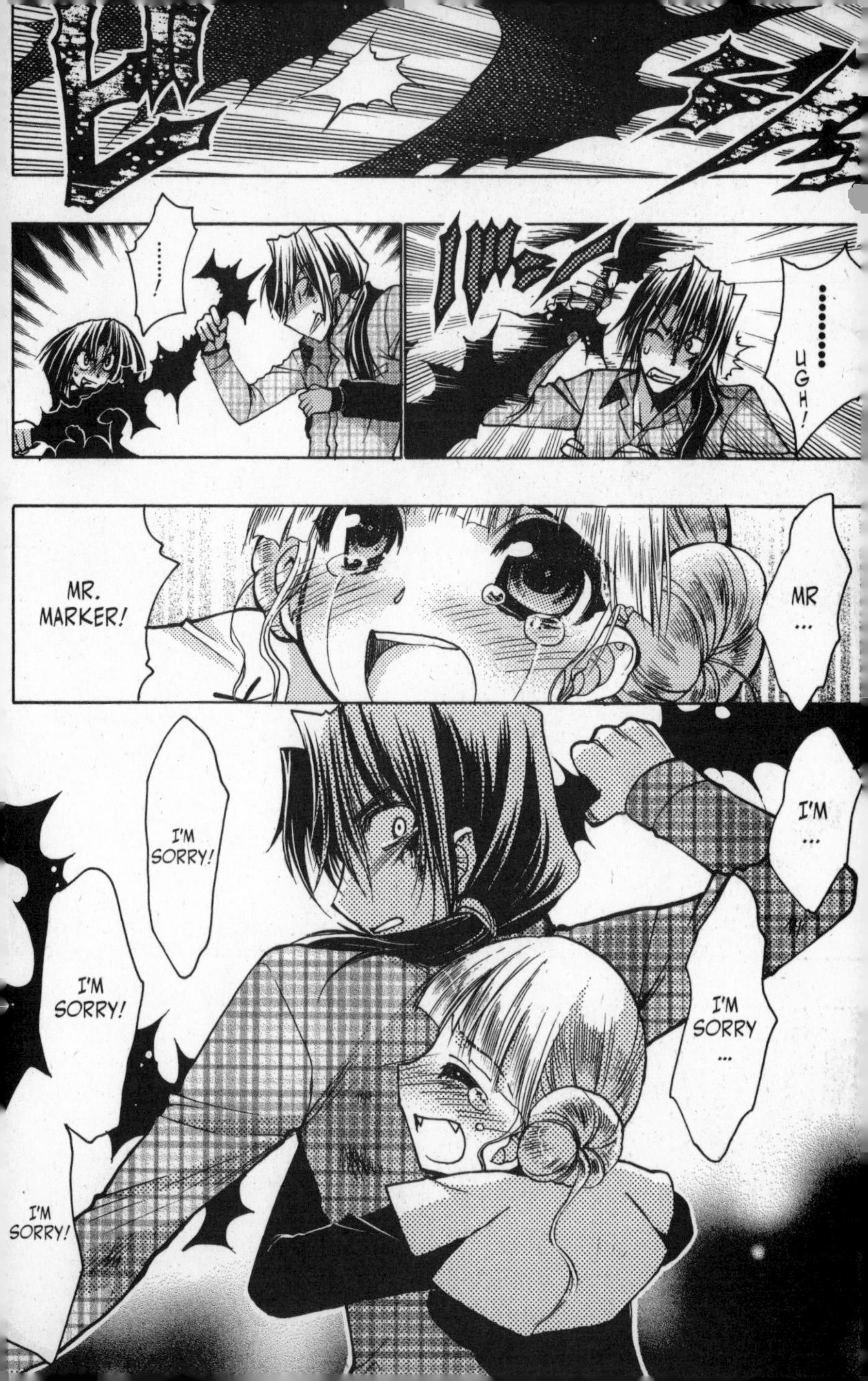

......
UGH!
......!
MR ...
MR. MARKER!
I'M ...
I'M SORRY!
I'M SORRY ...
I'M SORRY!
I'M SORRY!

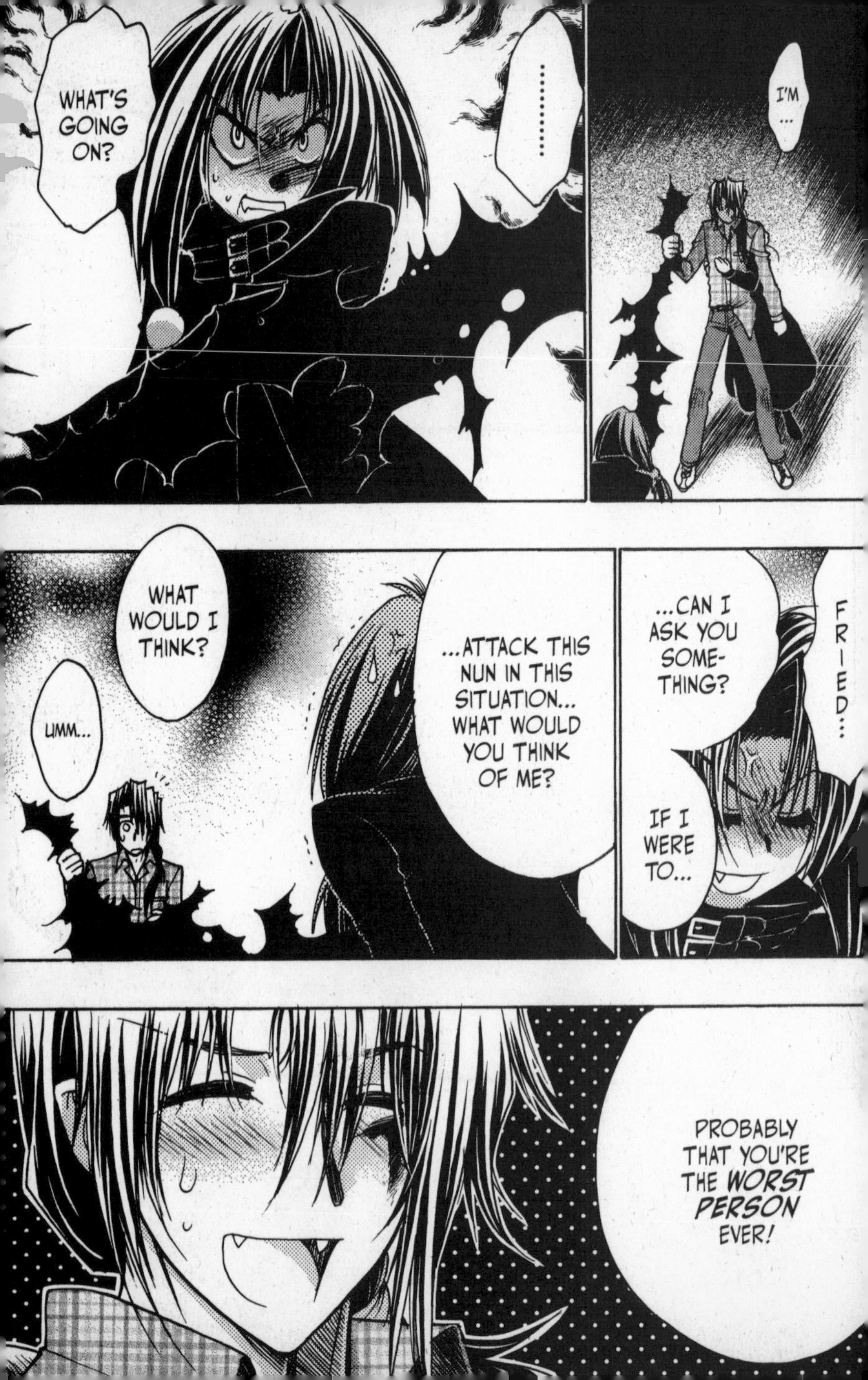
I'M ...
......
WHAT'S GOING ON?
FRIED...
...CAN I ASK YOU SOMETHING?
IF I WERE TO...
...ATTACK THIS NUN IN THIS SITUATION... WHAT WOULD YOU THINK OF ME?
WHAT WOULD I THINK?
UMM...
PROBABLY THAT YOU'RE THE WORST PERSON EVER!

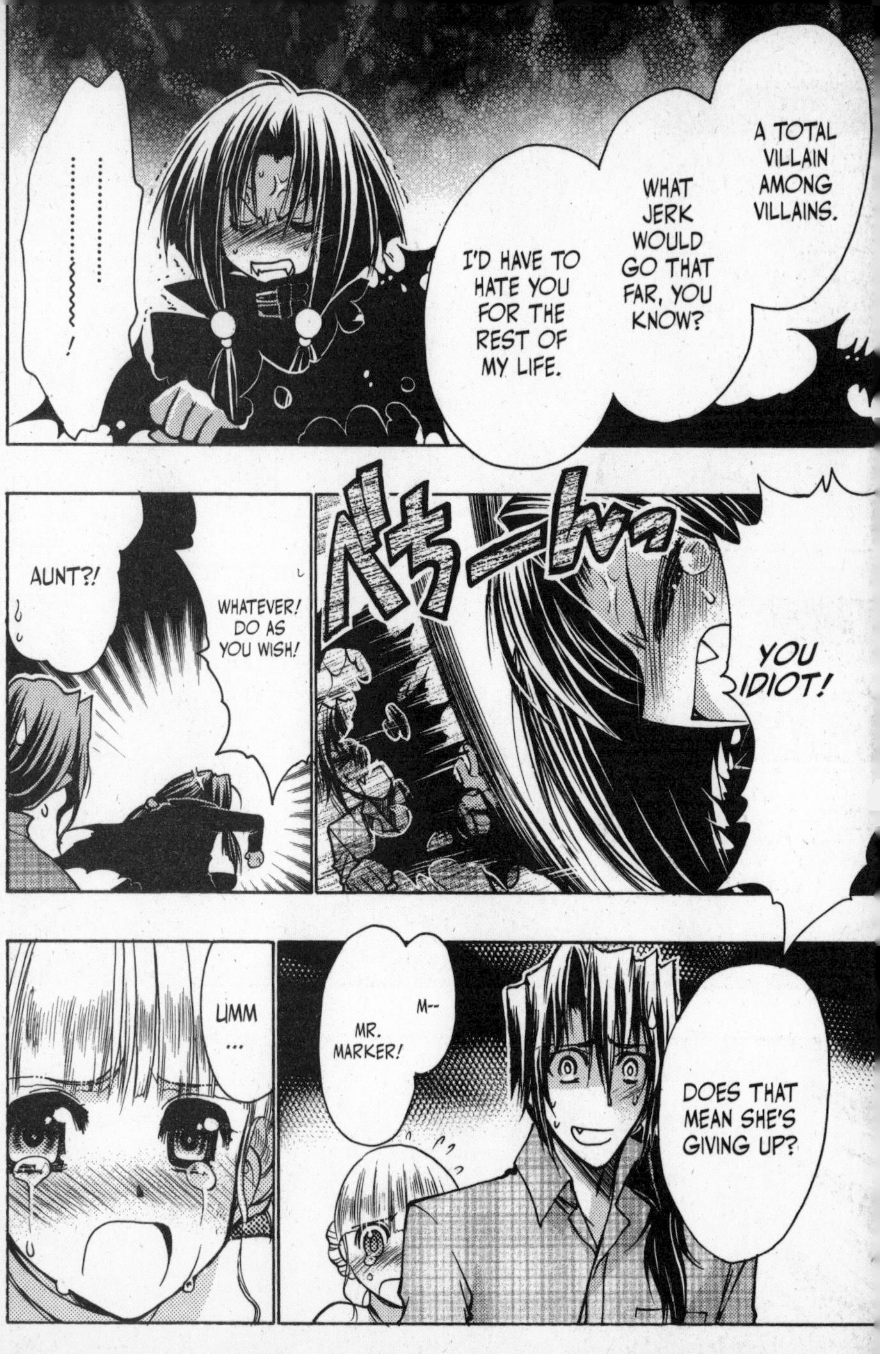
A TOTAL VILLAIN AMONG VILLAINS.
WHAT JERK WOULD GO THAT FAR, YOU KNOW?
I'D HAVE TO HATE YOU FOR THE REST OF MY LIFE.
......~!
べちーんっ
YOU IDIOT!
WHATEVER! DO AS YOU WISH!
AUNT?!
DOES THAT MEAN SHE'S GIVING UP?
M-- MR. MARKER!
UMM ...

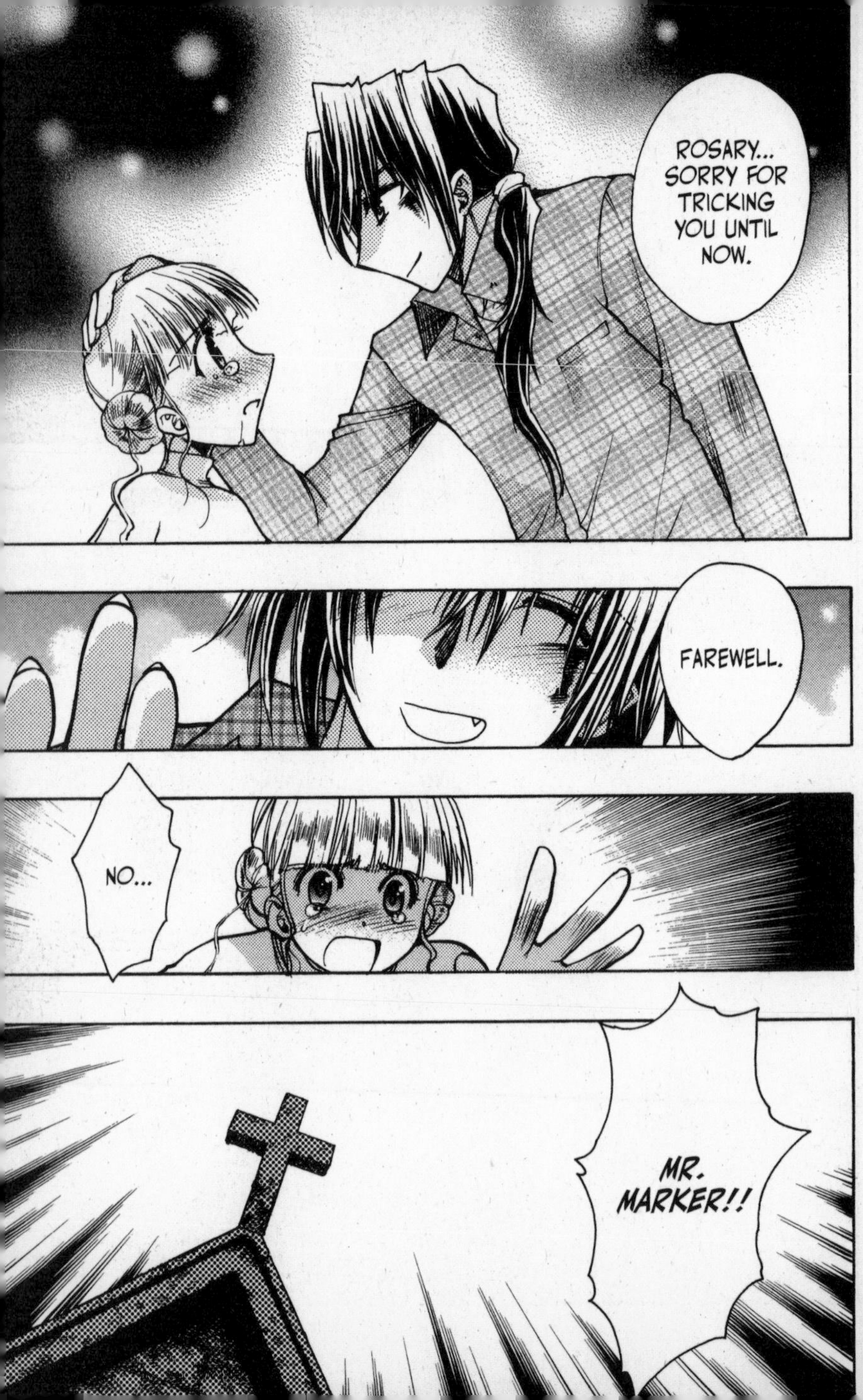
ROSARY... SORRY FOR TRICKING YOU UNTIL NOW.
FAREWELL.
NO...
MR. MARKER!!

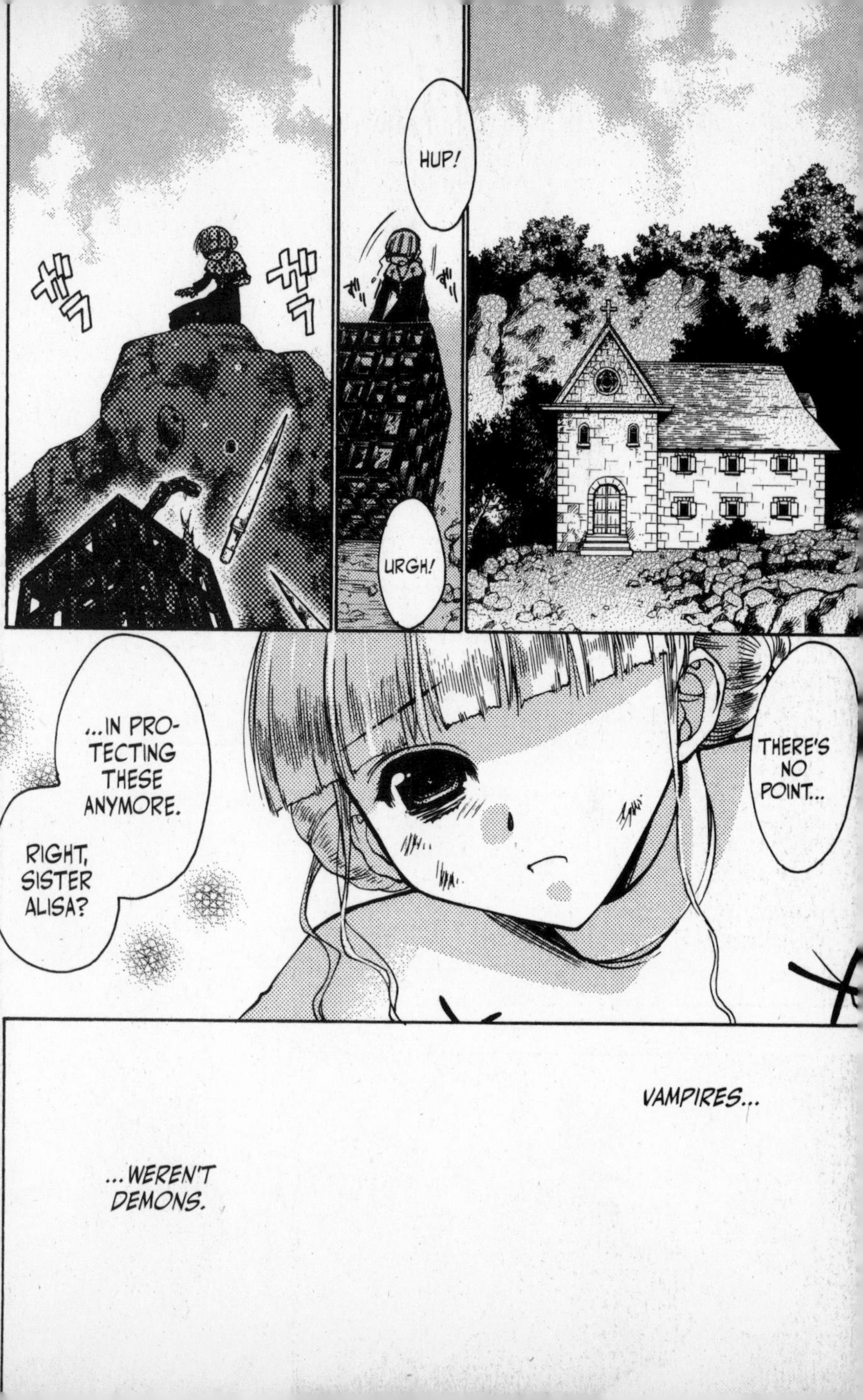
HUP!
URGH!
THERE'S NO POINT...
...IN PRO-TECTING THESE ANYMORE.
RIGHT, SISTER ALISA?
VAMPIRES...
...WEREN'T DEMONS.

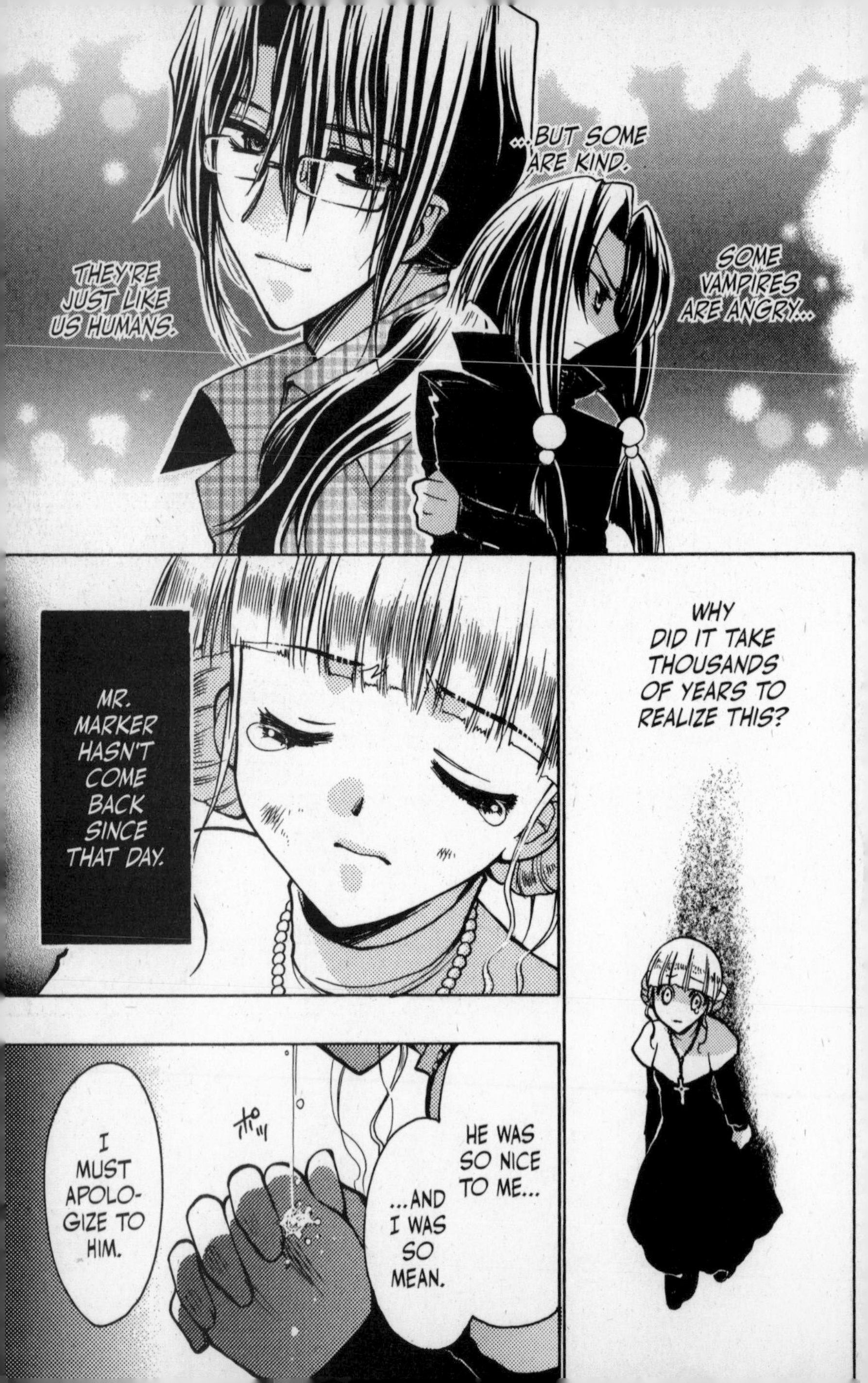
SOME VAMPIRES ARE ANGRY...
...BUT SOME ARE KIND.
THEY'RE JUST LIKE US HUMANS.
WHY DID IT TAKE THOUSANDS OF YEARS TO REALIZE THIS?
MR. MARKER HASN'T COME BACK SINCE THAT DAY.
HE WAS SO NICE TO ME...
...AND I WAS SO MEAN.
ポツ
I MUST APOLOGIZE TO HIM.

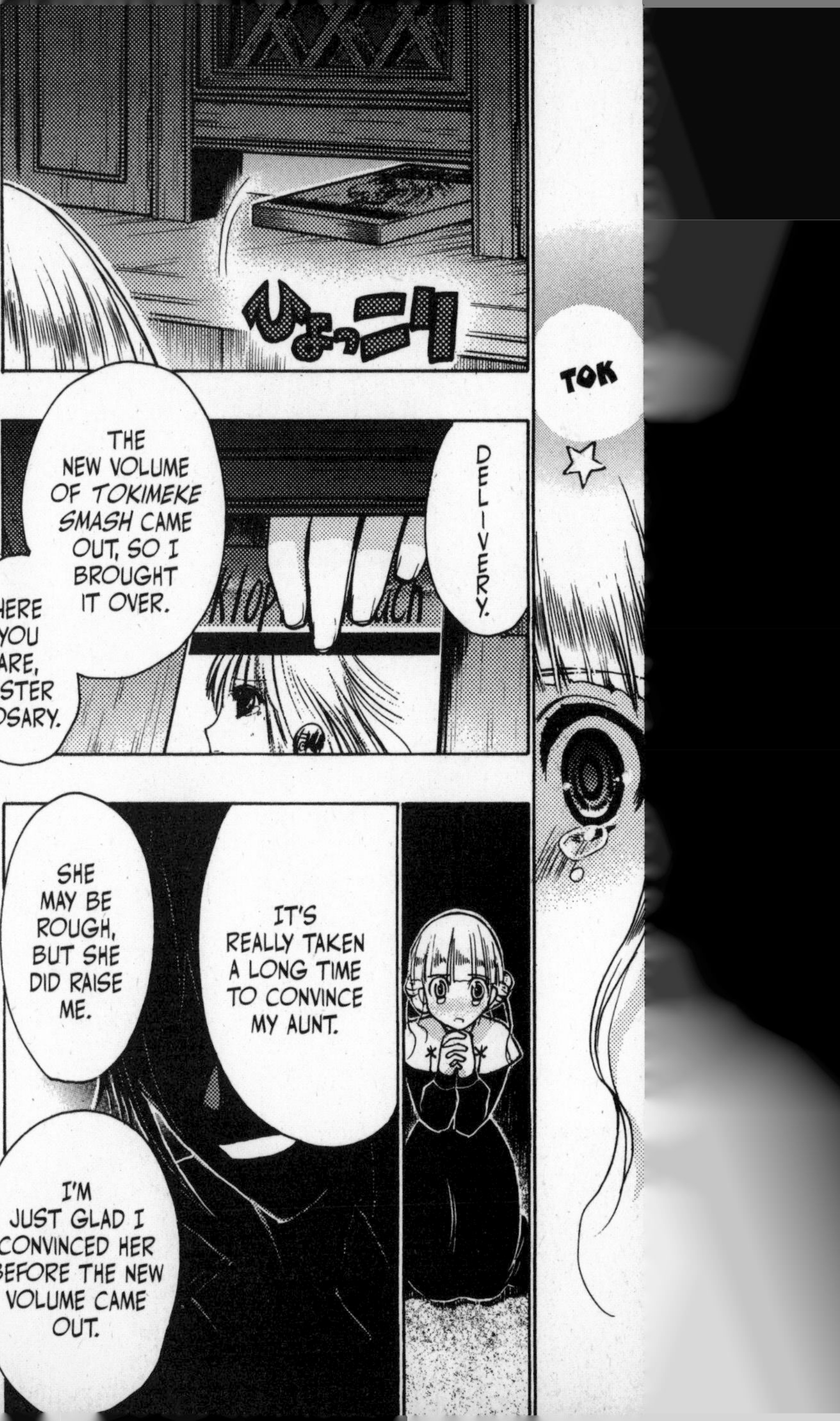
TOK
ひょっこり
DELIVERY.
THE NEW VOLUME OF *TOKIMEKE SMASH* CAME OUT, SO I BROUGHT IT OVER.
HERE YOU ARE, SISTER ROSARY.
IT'S REALLY TAKEN A LONG TIME TO CONVINCE MY AUNT.
SHE MAY BE ROUGH, BUT SHE DID RAISE ME.
I'M JUST GLAD I CONVINCED HER BEFORE THE NEW VOLUME CAME OUT.

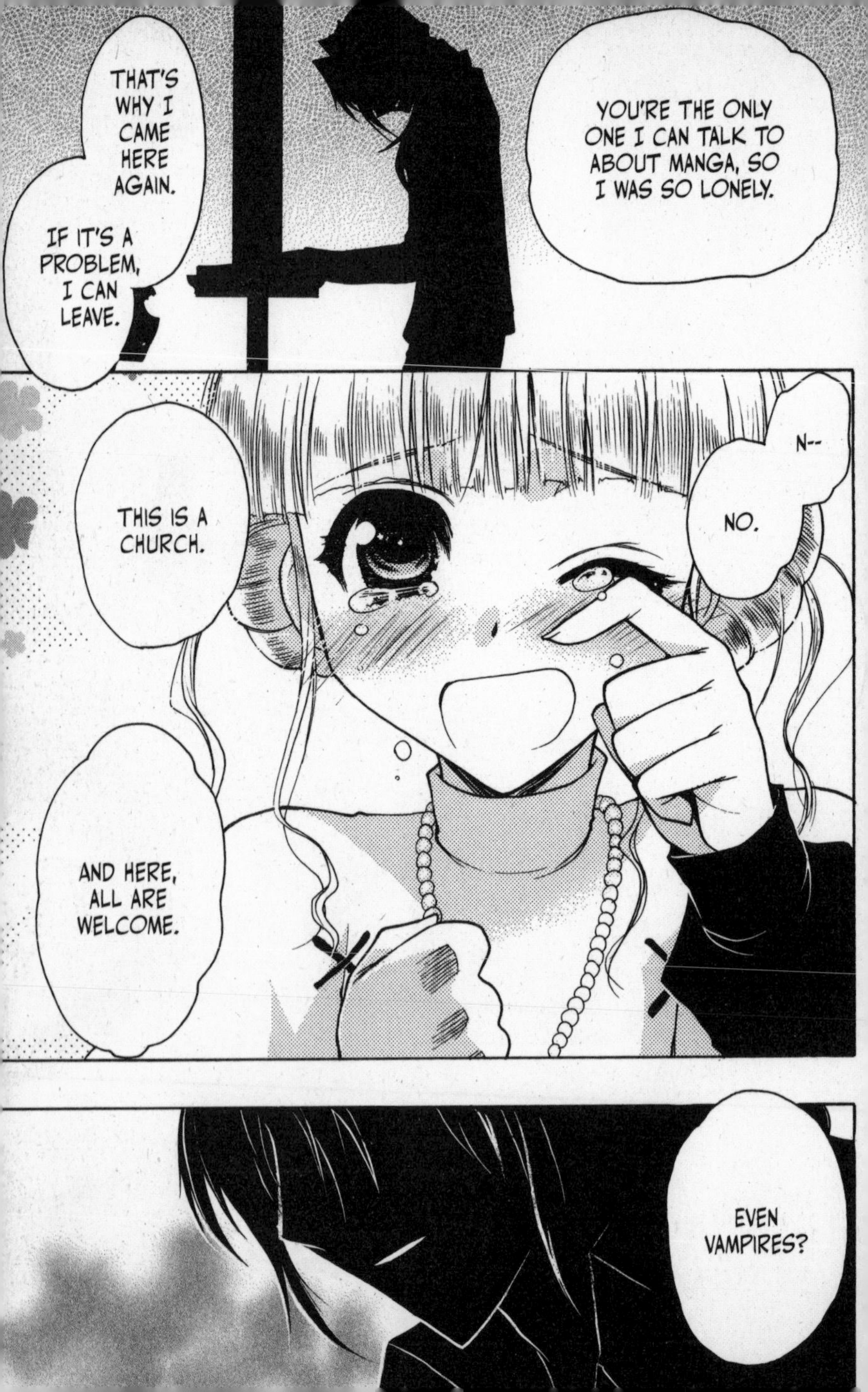
YOU'RE THE ONLY ONE I CAN TALK TO ABOUT MANGA, SO I WAS SO LONELY.
THAT'S WHY I CAME HERE AGAIN.
IF IT'S A PROBLEM, I CAN LEAVE.
N-- NO.
THIS IS A CHURCH.
AND HERE, ALL ARE WELCOME.
EVEN VAMPIRES?

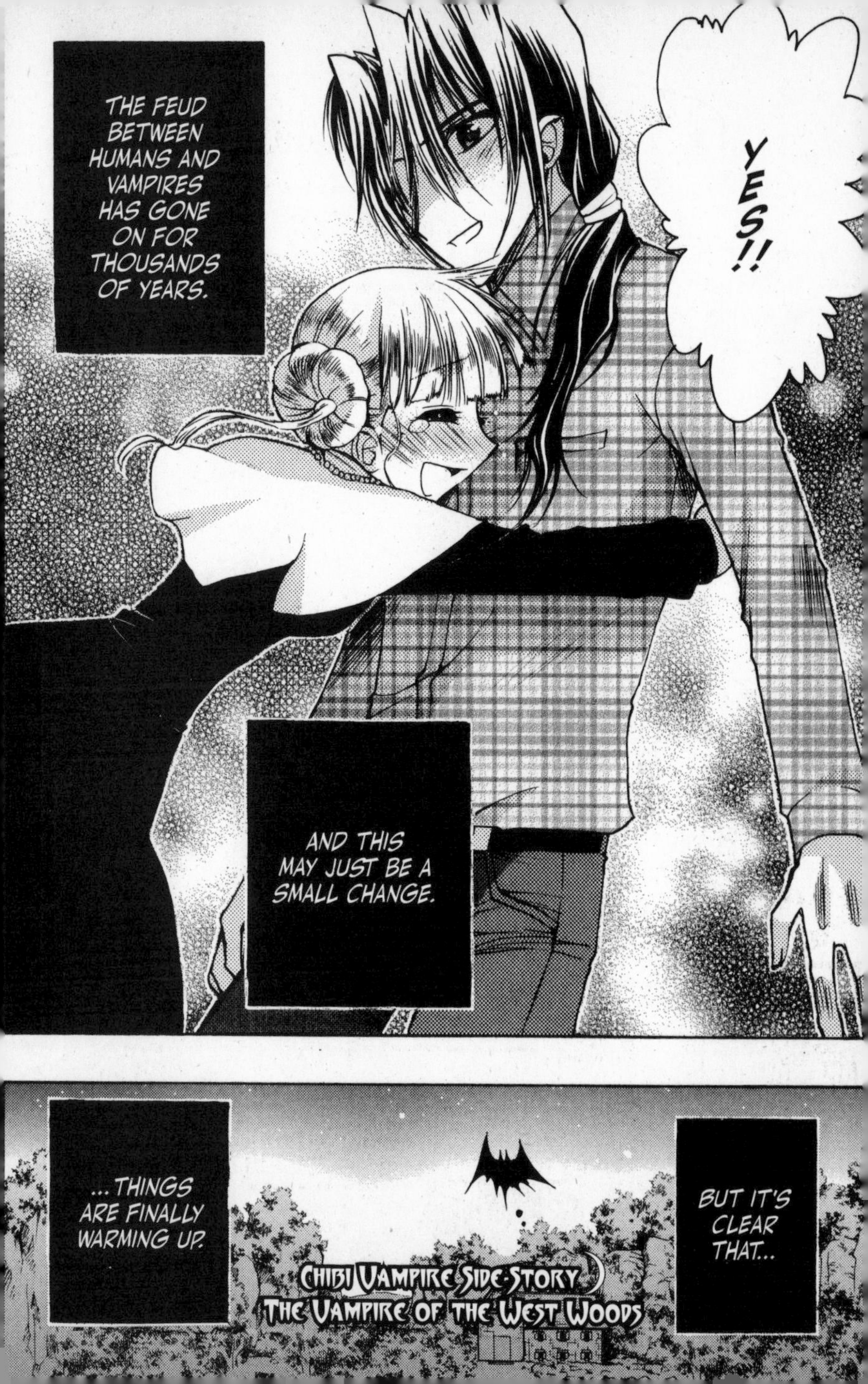
YES!!
THE FEUD BETWEEN HUMANS AND VAMPIRES HAS GONE ON FOR THOUSANDS OF YEARS.
AND THIS MAY JUST BE A SMALL CHANGE.
BUT IT'S CLEAR THAT...
...THINGS ARE FINALLY WARMING UP.
CHIBI VAMPIRE SIDE STORY
THE VAMPIRE OF THE WEST WOODS

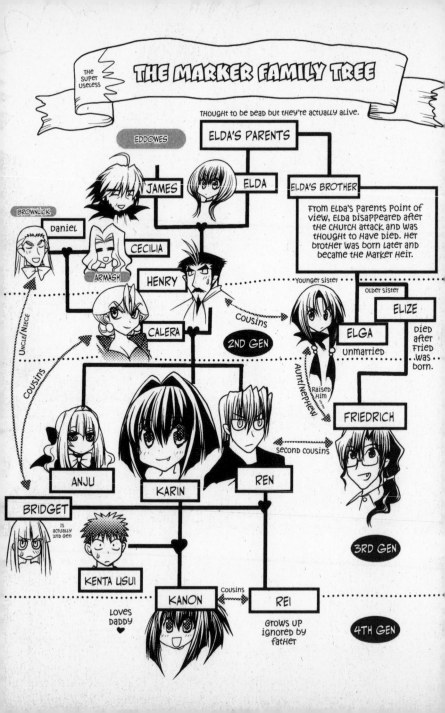

THE SUPER USELESS

THE MARKER FAMILY TREE

THOUGHT TO BE DEAD BUT THEY'RE ACTUALLY ALIVE.

EDDOWES

ELDA'S PARENTS

JAMES · ELDA — ELDA'S BROTHER

FROM ELDA'S PARENTS POINT OF VIEW, ELDA DISAPPEARED AFTER THE CHURCH ATTACK AND WAS THOUGHT TO HAVE DIED. HER BROTHER WAS BORN LATER AND BECAME THE MARKER HEIR.

BROWNLICK

DANIEL

CECILIA

ARMASH

HENRY

Younger sister · Older sister

ELGA · ELIZE

DIED AFTER FRIED WAS BORN.

Cousins

CALERA

2ND GEN

Unmarried

Uncle/Niece

Aunt/Nephew · Raised Him

Cousins

FRIEDRICH

ANJU · KARIN · REN

second cousins

3RD GEN

BRIDGET

IS ACTUALLY 2ND GEN

KENTA USUI

KANON · Cousins · REI

LOVES DADDY ♥

GROWS UP IGNORED BY FATHER

4TH GEN

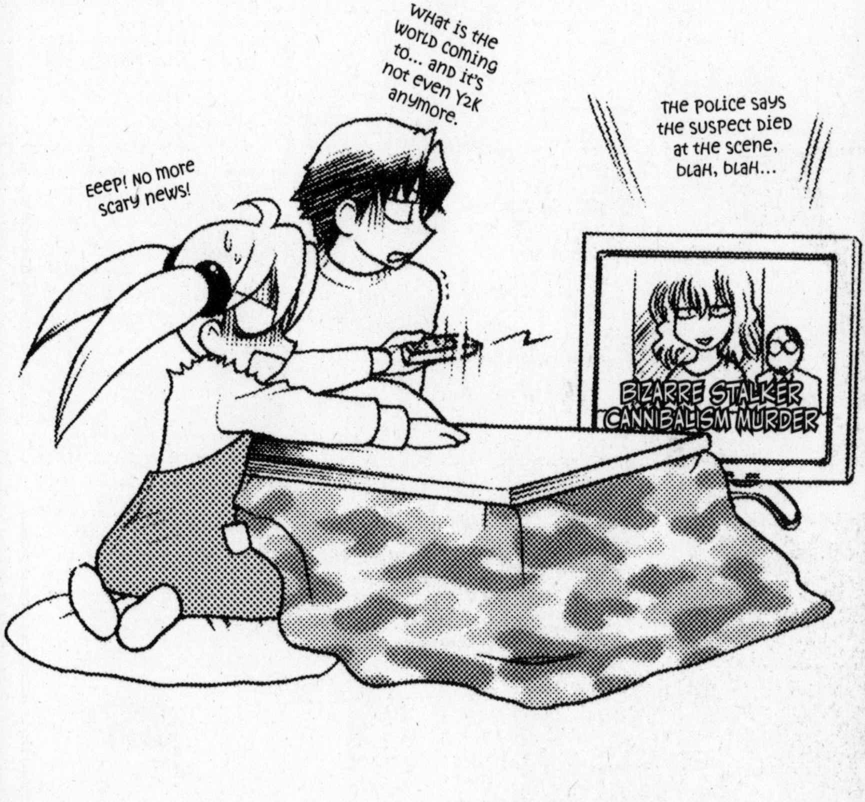
The police says the suspect died at the scene, blah, blah...
Bizarre Stalker Cannibalism Murder
What is the world coming to... and it's not even Y2K anymore.
Eeep! No more scary news!

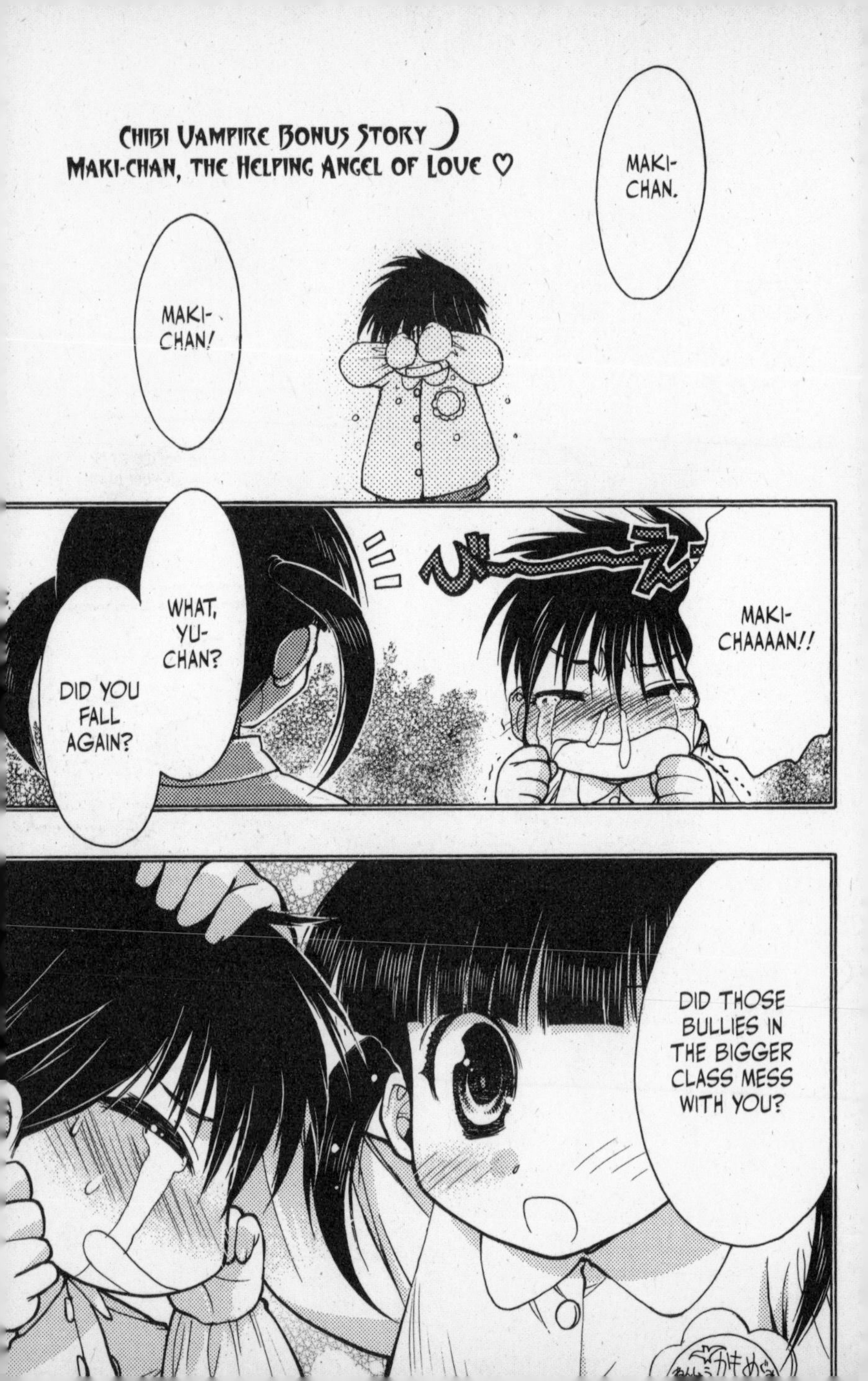
Chibi Vampire Bonus Story
Maki-chan, the Helping Angel of Love ♡
MAKI-CHAN.
MAKI-CHAN!
MAKI-CHAAAAN!!
WHAT, YU-CHAN?
DID YOU FALL AGAIN?
DID THOSE BULLIES IN THE BIGGER CLASS MESS WITH YOU?

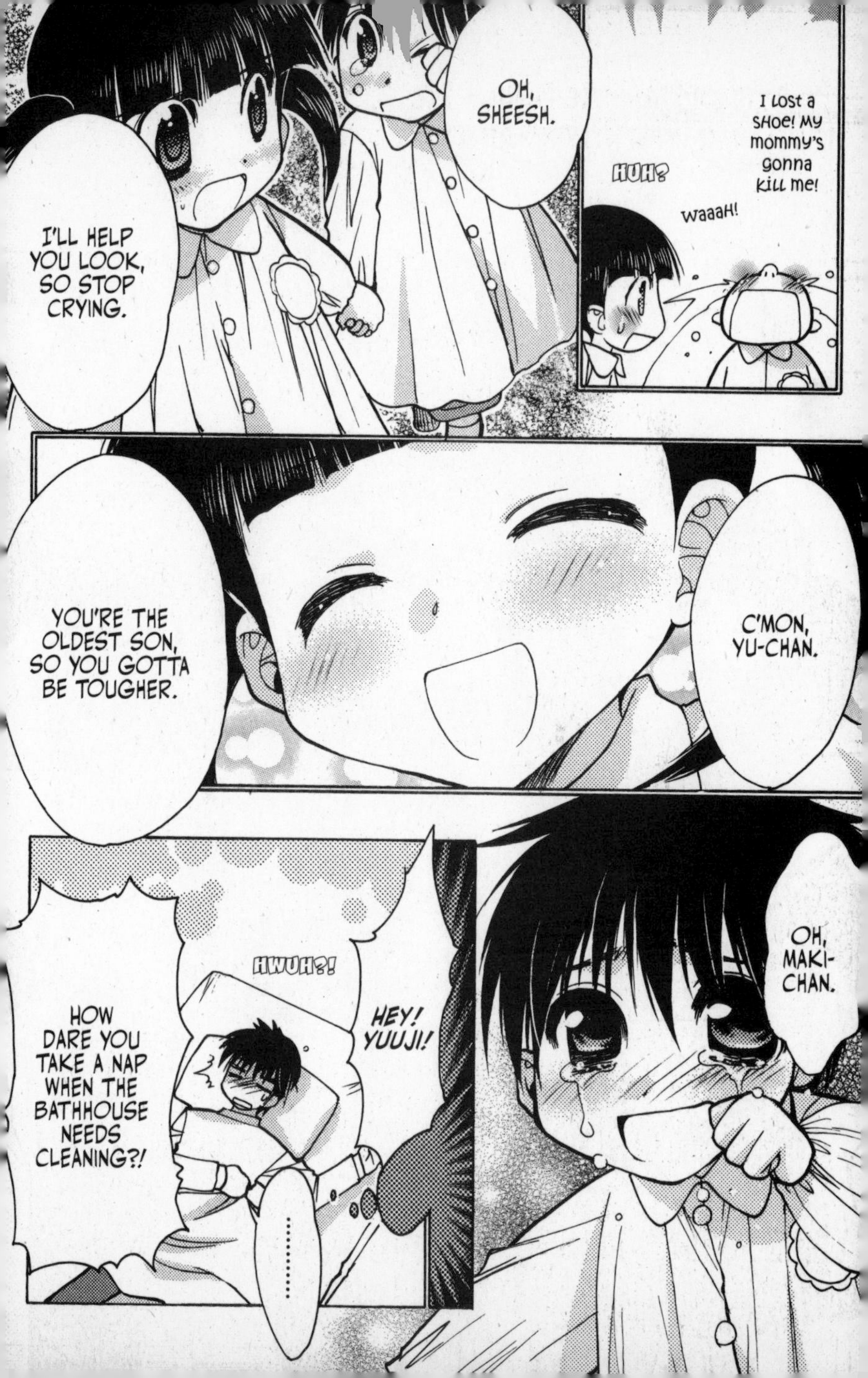
I lost a shoe! My mommy's gonna kill me!
Waaah!
HUH?
OH, SHEESH.
I'LL HELP YOU LOOK, SO STOP CRYING.
C'MON, YU-CHAN.
YOU'RE THE OLDEST SON, SO YOU GOTTA BE TOUGHER.
OH, MAKI-CHAN.
HEY! YUUJI!
HWUH?!
HOW DARE YOU TAKE A NAP WHEN THE BATHHOUSE NEEDS CLEANING?!
......

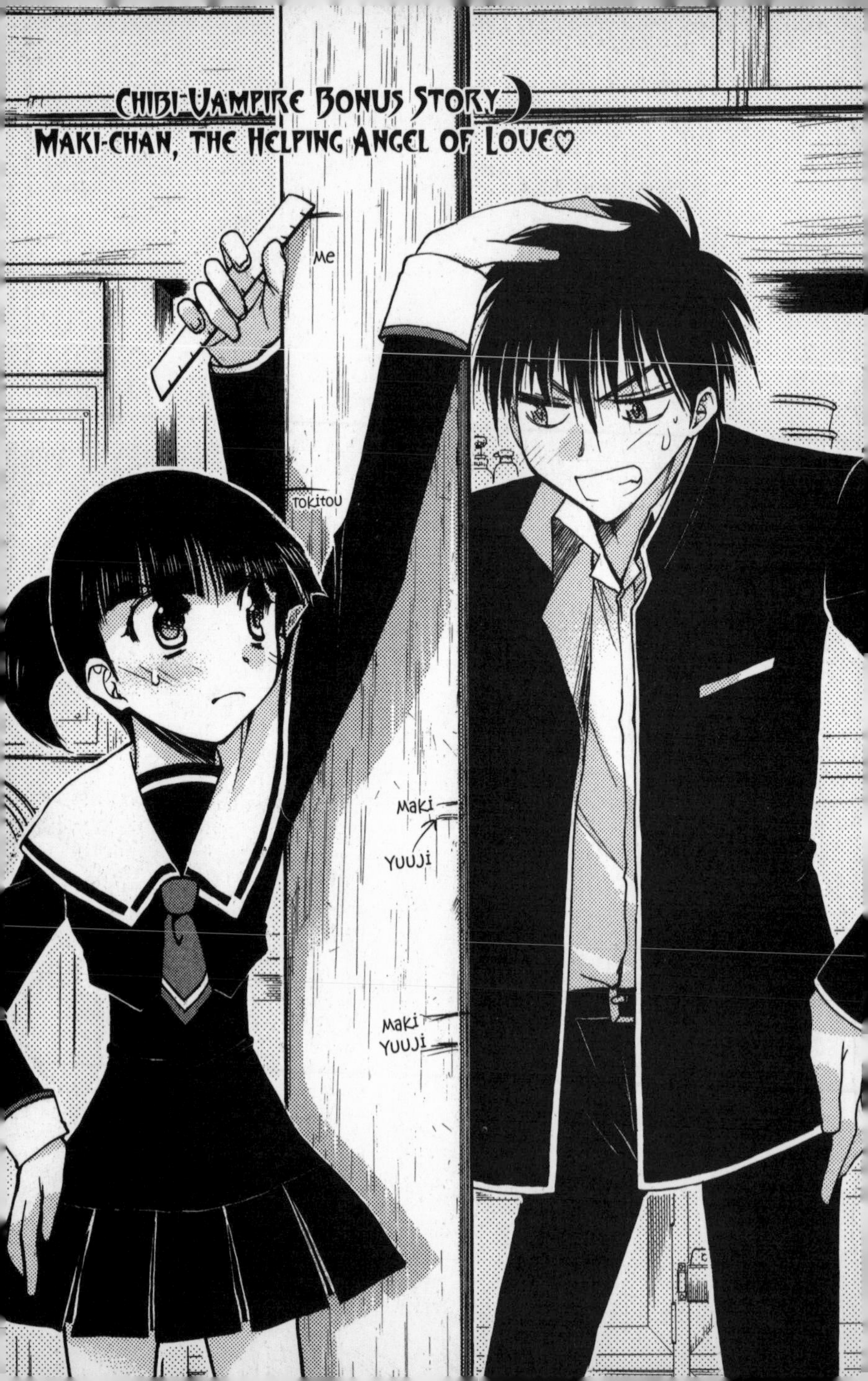
Chibi Vampire Bonus Story
Maki-chan, the Helping Angel of Love♡
Me
Tokitou
Maki
Yuuji
Maki
Yuuji

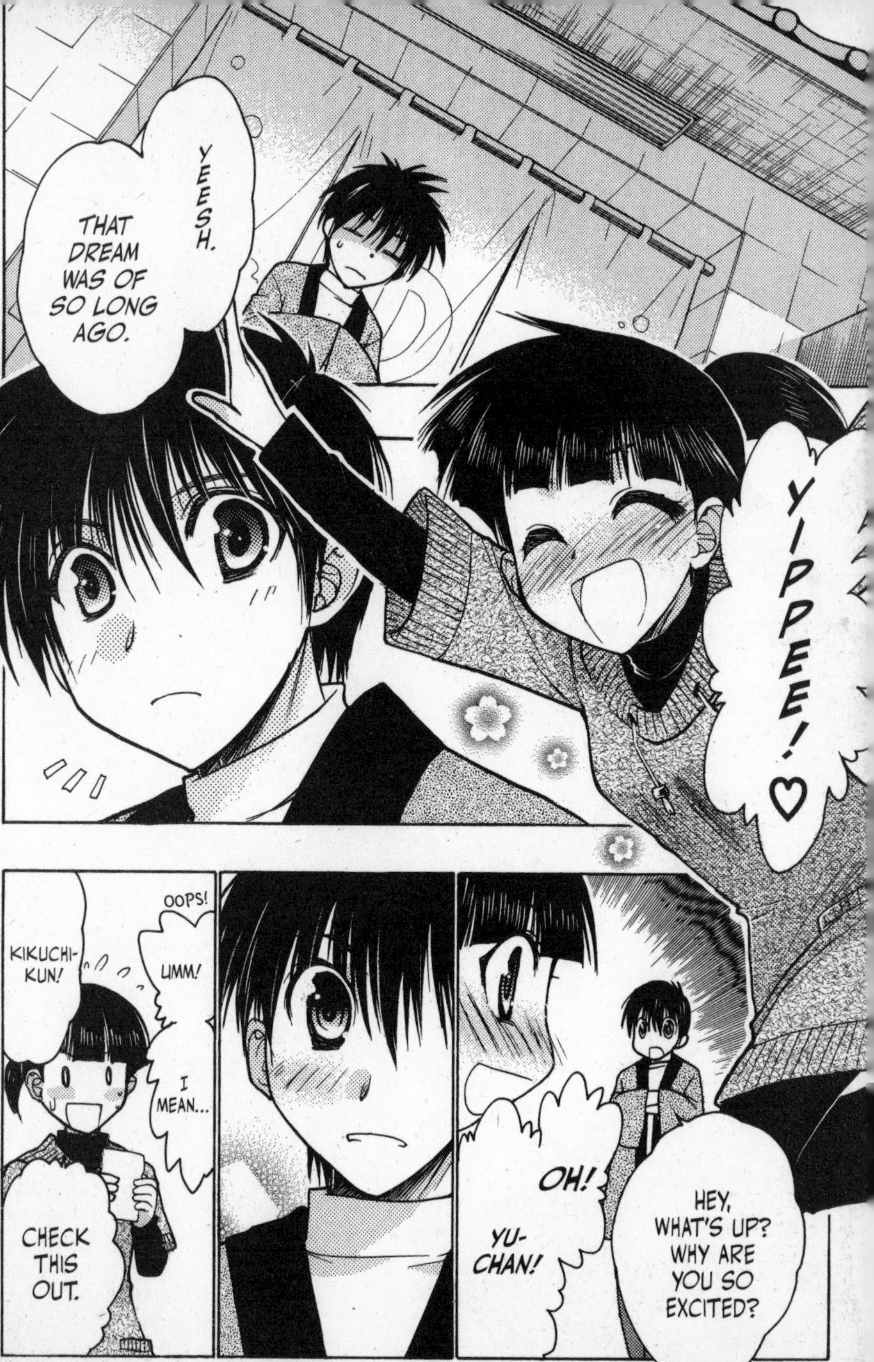
YEESH.
THAT DREAM WAS OF SO LONG AGO.
YIPPEE! ♡
HEY, WHAT'S UP? WHY ARE YOU SO EXCITED?
OH!
YU-CHAN!
OOPS!
UMM!
I MEAN...
KIKUCHI-KUN!
CHECK THIS OUT.

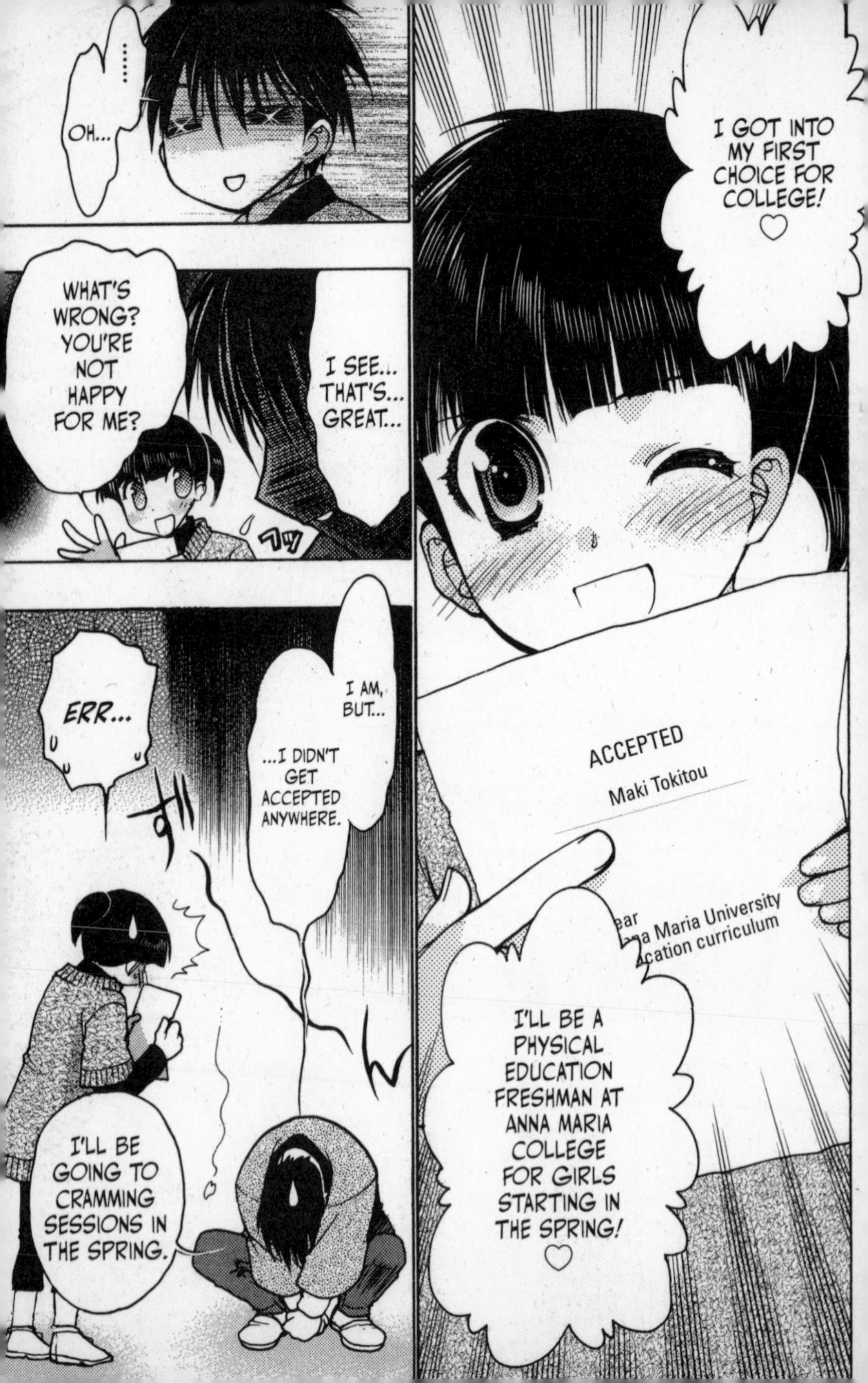
I GOT INTO MY FIRST CHOICE FOR COLLEGE! ♡
ACCEPTED
Maki Tokitou
I'LL BE A PHYSICAL EDUCATION FRESHMAN AT ANNA MARIA COLLEGE FOR GIRLS STARTING IN THE SPRING! ♡
......
OH...
I SEE... THAT'S... GREAT...
WHAT'S WRONG? YOU'RE NOT HAPPY FOR ME?
フッ
I AM, BUT...
...I DIDN'T GET ACCEPTED ANYWHERE.
ERR...
I'LL BE GOING TO CRAMMING SESSIONS IN THE SPRING.

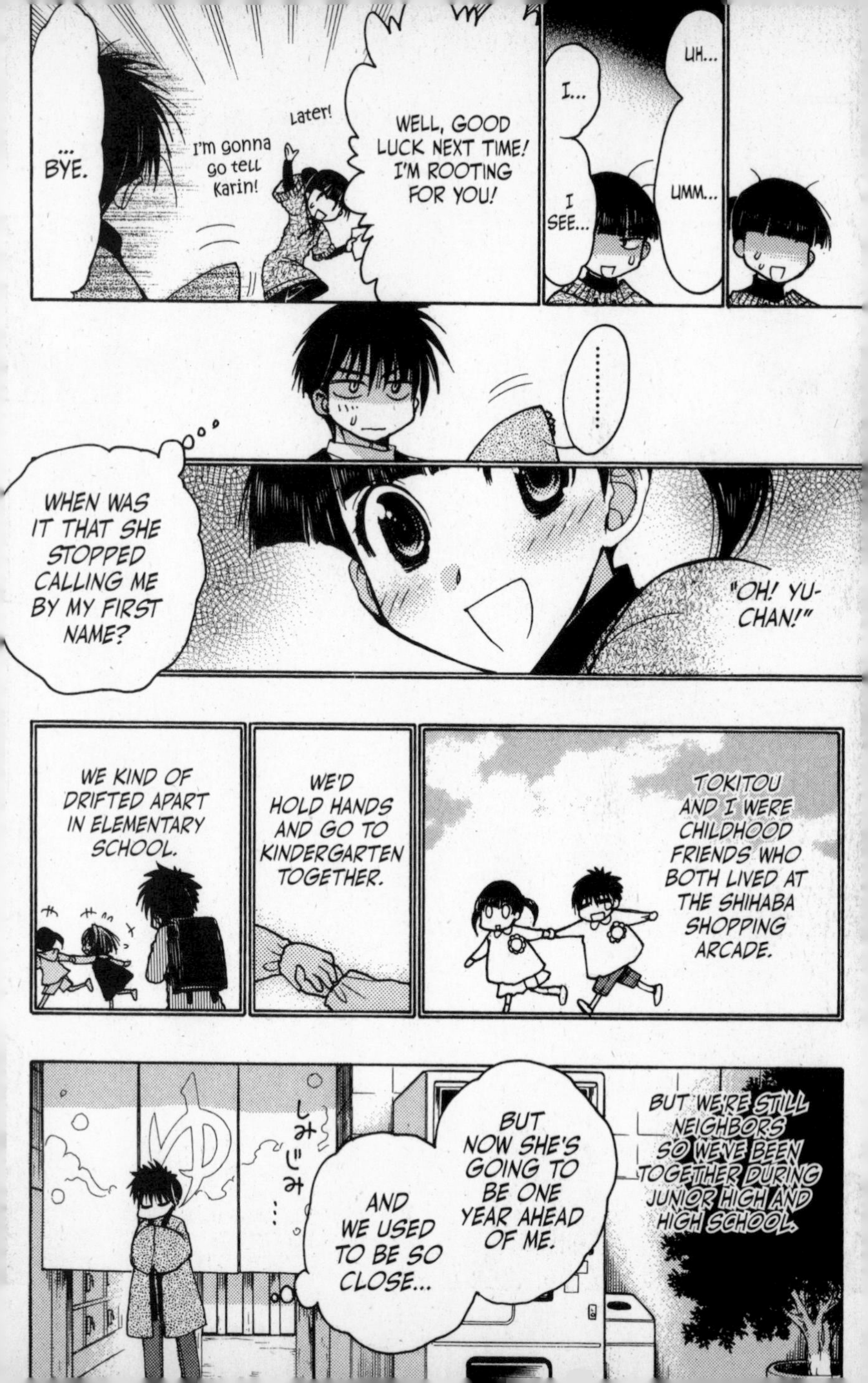
UH...
UMM...
I...
I SEE...
WELL, GOOD LUCK NEXT TIME! I'M ROOTING FOR YOU!
Later!
I'm gonna go tell Karin!
... BYE.
......
"OH! YU-CHAN!"
WHEN WAS IT THAT SHE STOPPED CALLING ME BY MY FIRST NAME?
TOKITOU AND I WERE CHILDHOOD FRIENDS WHO BOTH LIVED AT THE SHIHABA SHOPPING ARCADE.
WE'D HOLD HANDS AND GO TO KINDERGARTEN TOGETHER.
WE KIND OF DRIFTED APART IN ELEMENTARY SCHOOL.
BUT WE'RE STILL NEIGHBORS SO WE'VE BEEN TOGETHER DURING JUNIOR HIGH AND HIGH SCHOOL.
BUT NOW SHE'S GOING TO BE ONE YEAR AHEAD OF ME.
AND WE USED TO BE SO CLOSE...
しみじみ...

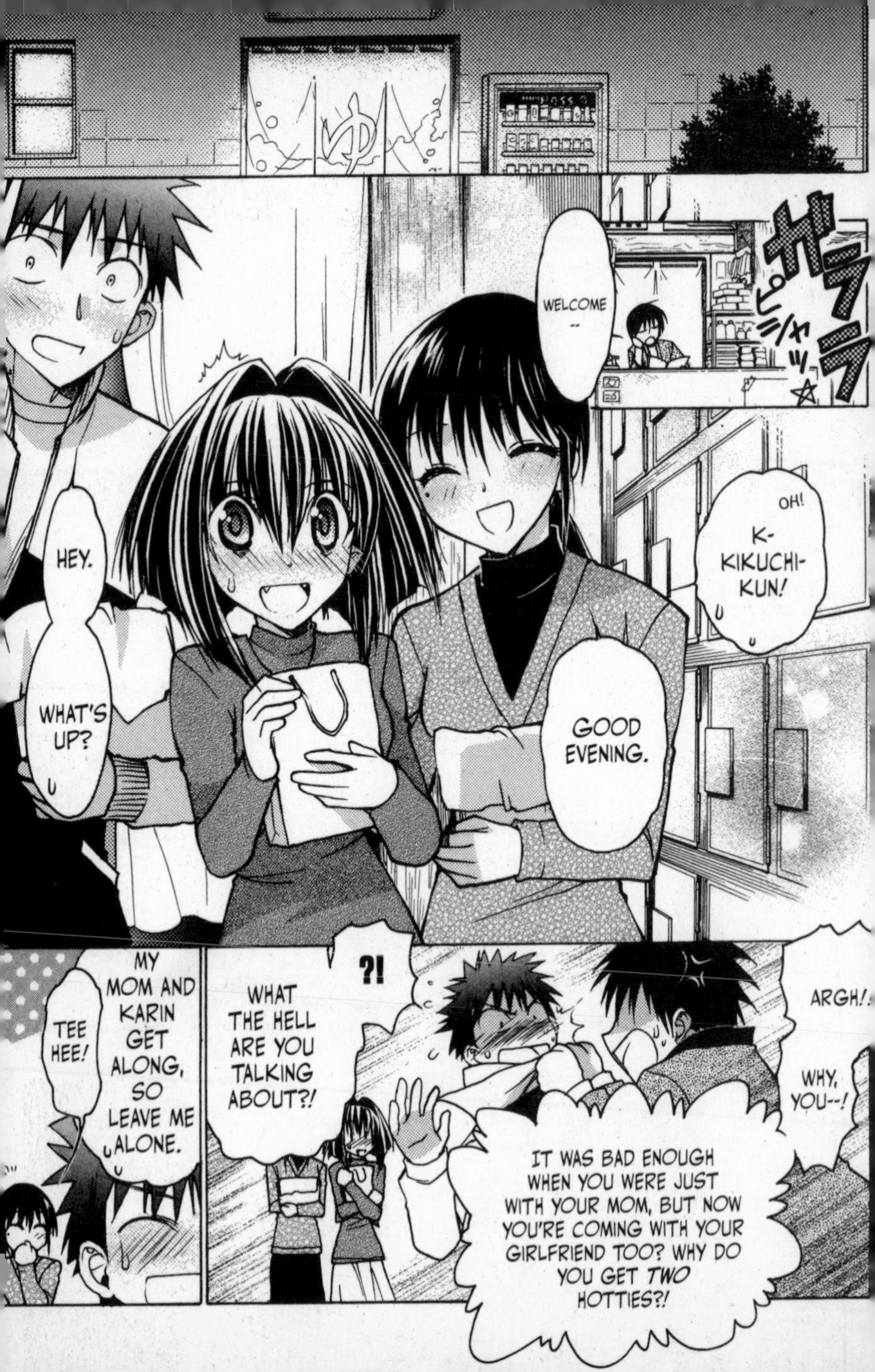

ガララ
ピシャッ
WELCOME --
OH! K-KIKUCHI-KUN!
GOOD EVENING.
HEY.
WHAT'S UP?
ARGH!
WHY, YOU--!
IT WAS BAD ENOUGH WHEN YOU WERE JUST WITH YOUR MOM, BUT NOW YOU'RE COMING WITH YOUR GIRLFRIEND TOO? WHY DO YOU GET *TWO* HOTTIES?!
?!
WHAT THE HELL ARE YOU TALKING ABOUT?!
MY MOM AND KARIN GET ALONG, SO LEAVE ME ALONE.
TEE HEE!

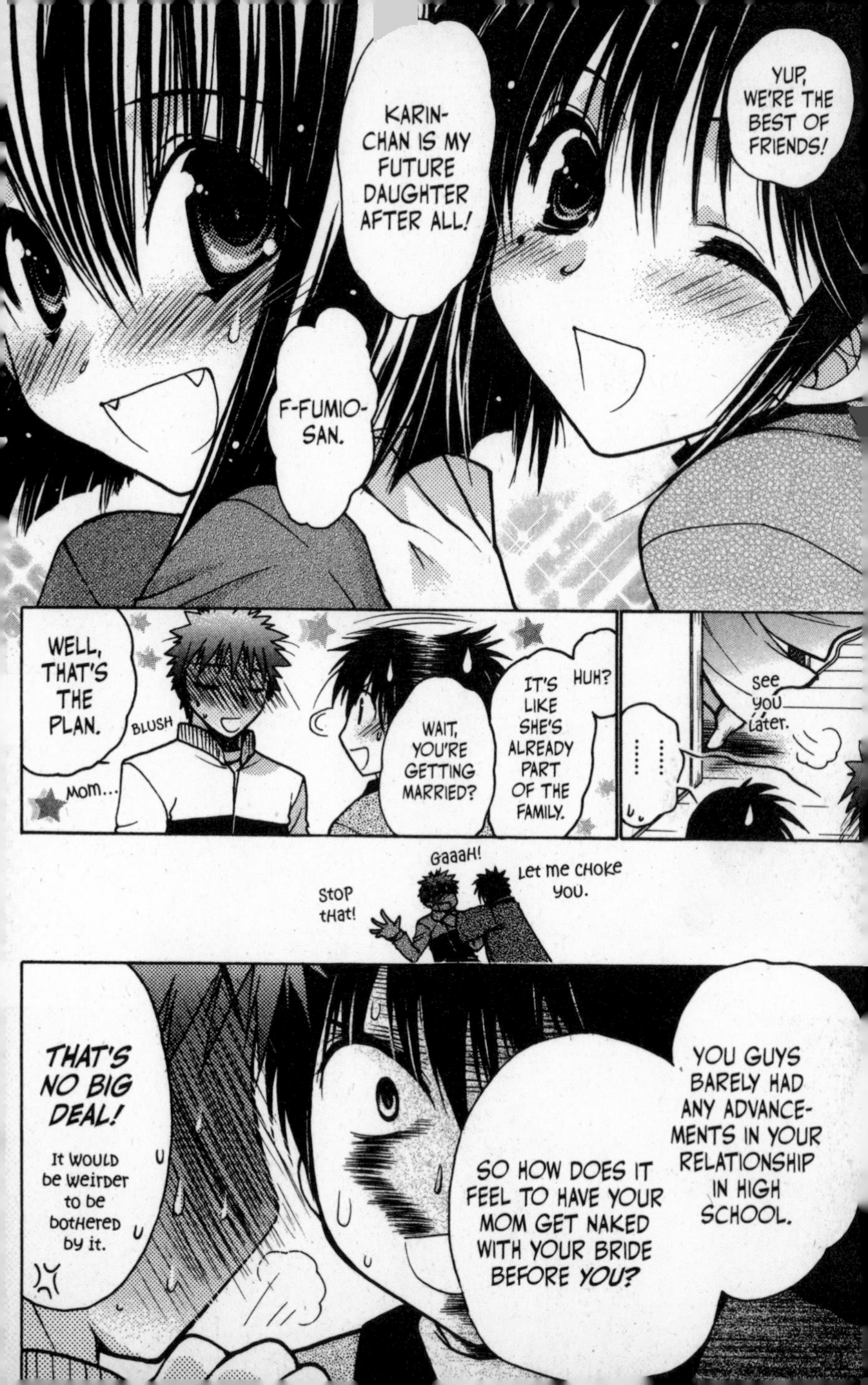
YUP, WE'RE THE BEST OF FRIENDS!
KARIN-CHAN IS MY FUTURE DAUGHTER AFTER ALL!
F-FUMIO-SAN.
see you later.
......
......
HUH?
IT'S LIKE SHE'S ALREADY PART OF THE FAMILY.
WAIT, YOU'RE GETTING MARRIED?
WELL, THAT'S THE PLAN.
BLUSH
mom...
Let me CHOKE you.
GaaaH!
StOP tHat!
YOU GUYS BARELY HAD ANY ADVANCE-MENTS IN YOUR RELATIONSHIP IN HIGH SCHOOL.
SO HOW DOES IT FEEL TO HAVE YOUR MOM GET NAKED WITH YOUR BRIDE BEFORE *YOU?*
THAT'S NO BIG DEAL!
It WOULD be weirder to be bothered by it.

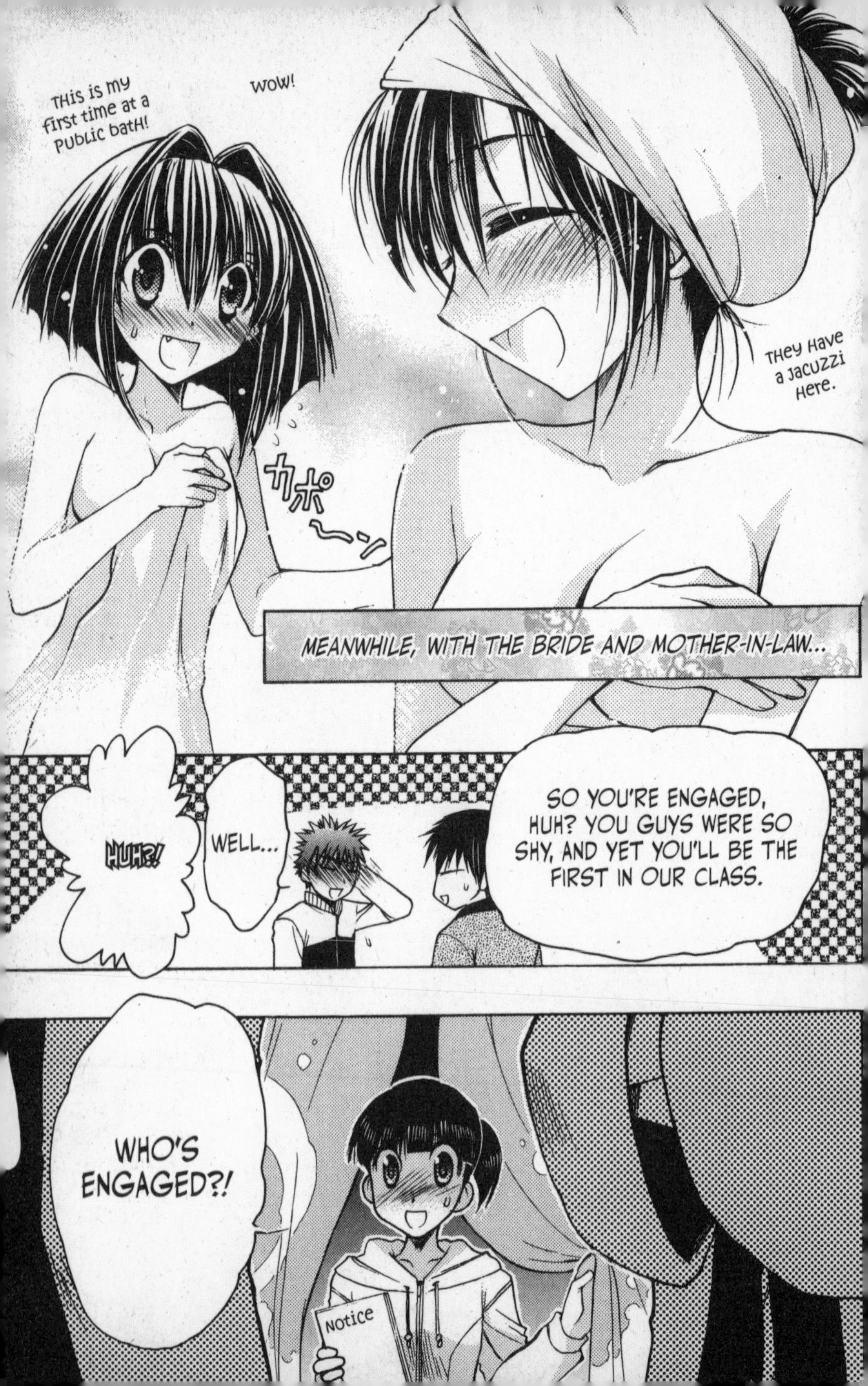
WOW!
THIS IS MY FIRST TIME AT A PUBLIC BATH!
THEY HAVE A JACUZZI HERE.
カポ〜ン
MEANWHILE, WITH THE BRIDE AND MOTHER-IN-LAW...
SO YOU'RE ENGAGED, HUH? YOU GUYS WERE SO SHY, AND YET YOU'LL BE THE FIRST IN OUR CLASS.
WELL...
HUH?!
WHO'S ENGAGED?!
Notice

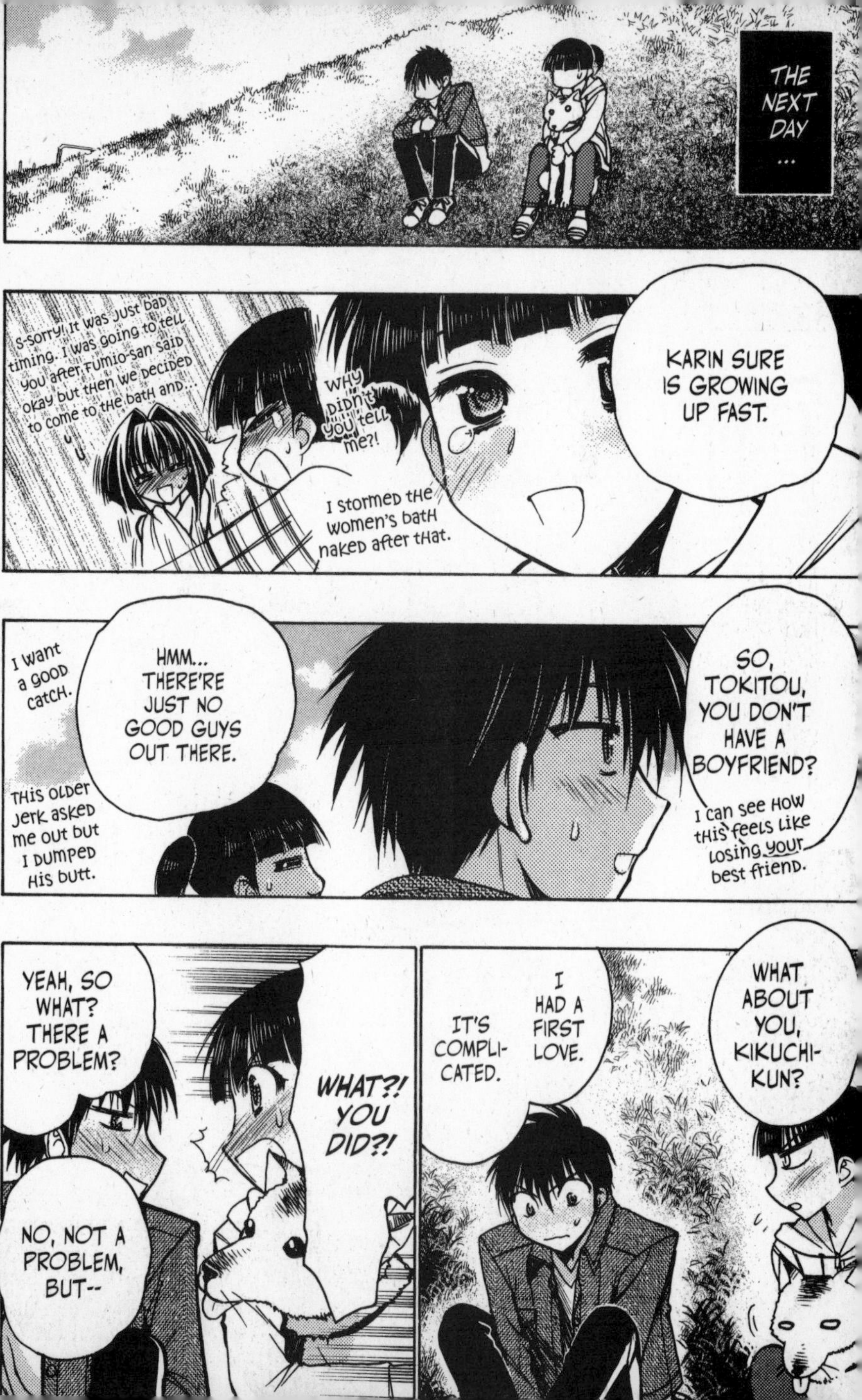
THE NEXT DAY ...
KARIN SURE IS GROWING UP FAST.
WHY DIDN'T YOU TELL ME?!
S-SORRY! IT WAS JUST BAD TIMING. I WAS GOING TO TELL YOU AFTER FUMIO-SAN SAID OKAY BUT THEN WE DECIDED TO COME TO THE BATH AND...
I STORMED THE WOMEN'S BATH NAKED AFTER THAT.
SO, TOKITOU, YOU DON'T HAVE A BOYFRIEND?
I CAN SEE HOW THIS FEELS LIKE LOSING YOUR BEST FRIEND.
HMM... THERE'RE JUST NO GOOD GUYS OUT THERE.
I WANT A GOOD CATCH.
THIS OLDER JERK ASKED ME OUT BUT I DUMPED HIS BUTT.
WHAT ABOUT YOU, KIKUCHI-KUN?
I HAD A FIRST LOVE.
IT'S COMPLI-CATED.
WHAT?! YOU DID?!
YEAH, SO WHAT? THERE A PROBLEM?
NO, NOT A PROBLEM, BUT--

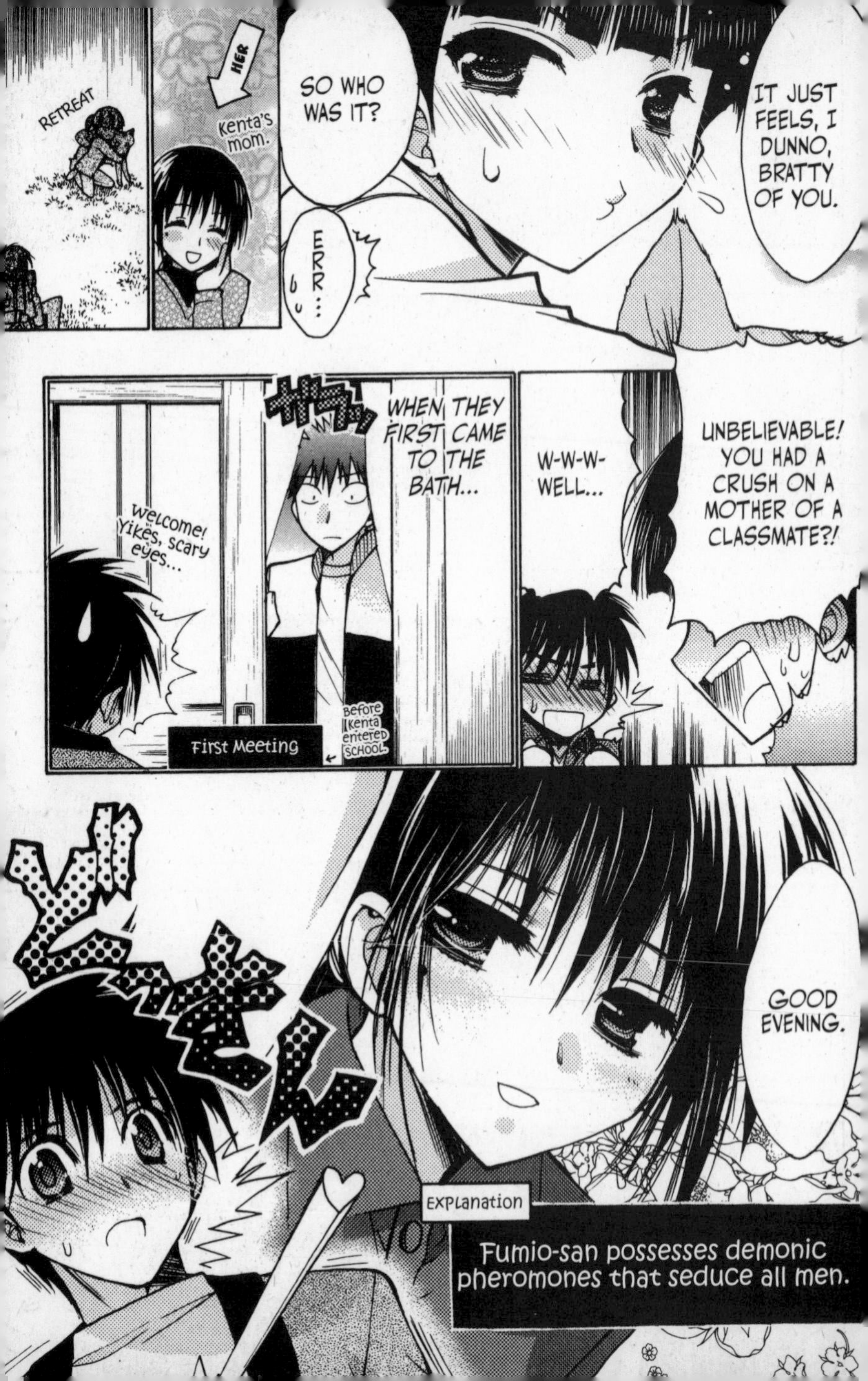
IT JUST FEELS, I DUNNO, BRATTY OF YOU.
SO WHO WAS IT?
ERR...
HER
Kenta's mom.
RETREAT
UNBELIEVABLE! YOU HAD A CRUSH ON A MOTHER OF A CLASSMATE?!
W-W-W-WELL...
WHEN THEY FIRST CAME TO THE BATH...
Welcome! Yikes, scary eyes...
Before Kenta entered SCHOOL.
First Meeting
GOOD EVENING.
Explanation
Fumio-san possesses demonic pheromones that seduce all men.

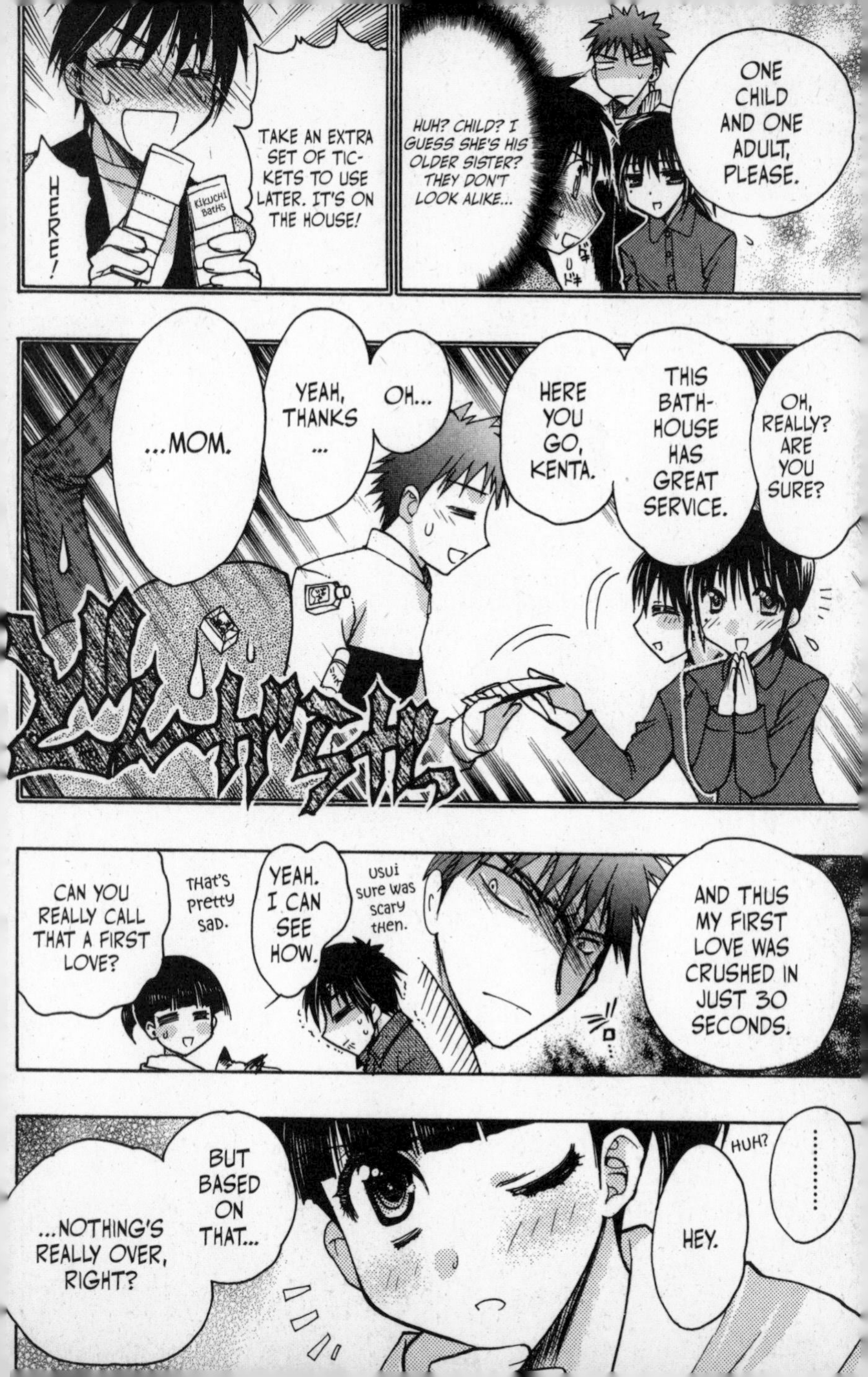
ONE CHILD AND ONE ADULT, PLEASE.
HUH? CHILD? I GUESS SHE'S HIS OLDER SISTER? THEY DON'T LOOK ALIKE...
TAKE AN EXTRA SET OF TIC-KETS TO USE LATER. IT'S ON THE HOUSE!
HERE!
KIKUCHI BATHS
OH, REALLY? ARE YOU SURE?
THIS BATH-HOUSE HAS GREAT SERVICE.
HERE YOU GO, KENTA.
OH...
YEAH, THANKS ...
...MOM.
AND THUS MY FIRST LOVE WAS CRUSHED IN JUST 30 SECONDS.
Usui sure was scary then.
YEAH. I CAN SEE HOW.
That's pretty sad.
CAN YOU REALLY CALL THAT A FIRST LOVE?
......
HUH?
HEY.
BUT BASED ON THAT...
...NOTHING'S REALLY OVER, RIGHT?

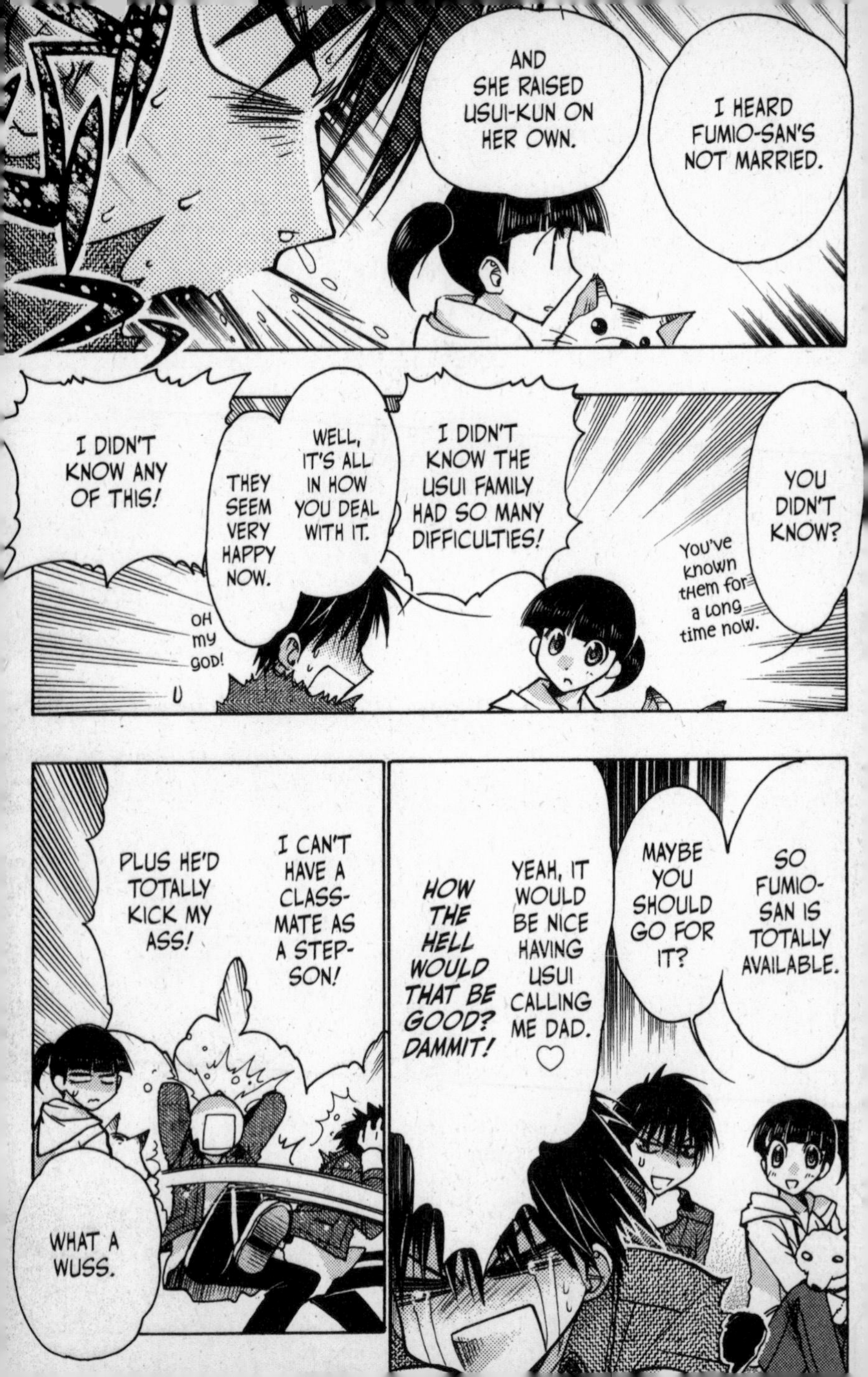
I HEARD FUMIO-SAN'S NOT MARRIED.
AND SHE RAISED USUI-KUN ON HER OWN.
YOU DIDN'T KNOW?
You've known them for a long time now.
I DIDN'T KNOW THE USUI FAMILY HAD SO MANY DIFFICULTIES!
WELL, IT'S ALL IN HOW YOU DEAL WITH IT.
THEY SEEM VERY HAPPY NOW.
I DIDN'T KNOW ANY OF THIS!
OH my GOD!
SO FUMIO-SAN IS TOTALLY AVAILABLE.
MAYBE YOU SHOULD GO FOR IT?
YEAH, IT WOULD BE NICE HAVING USUI CALLING ME DAD. ♡
HOW THE HELL WOULD THAT BE GOOD? DAMMIT!
I CAN'T HAVE A CLASSMATE AS A STEP-SON!
PLUS HE'D TOTALLY KICK MY ASS!
WHAT A WUSS.

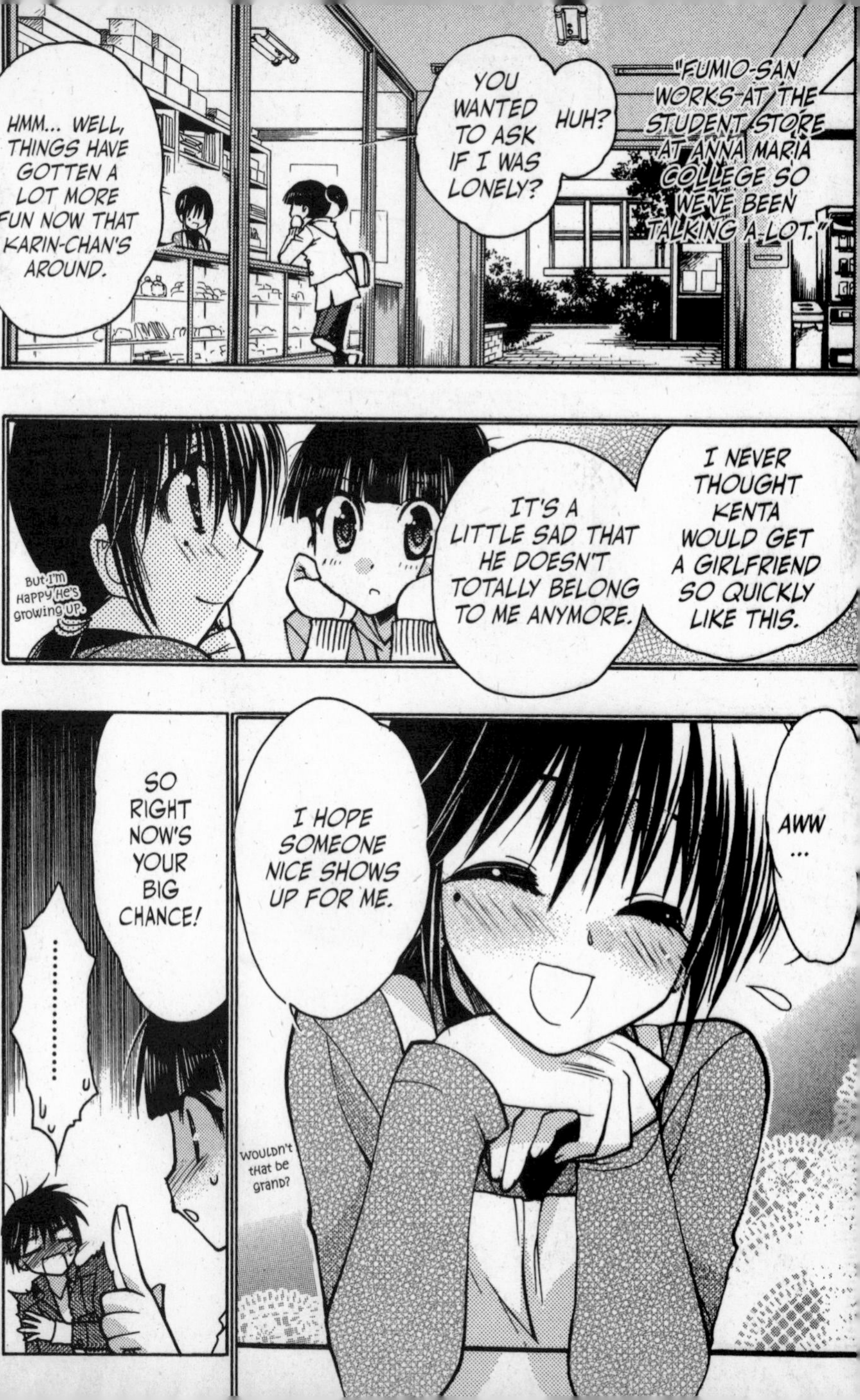
"FUMIO-SAN WORKS AT THE STUDENT STORE AT ANNA MARIA COLLEGE SO WE'VE BEEN TALKING A LOT."
HUH?
YOU WANTED TO ASK IF I WAS LONELY?
HMM... WELL, THINGS HAVE GOTTEN A LOT MORE FUN NOW THAT KARIN-CHAN'S AROUND.
I NEVER THOUGHT KENTA WOULD GET A GIRLFRIEND SO QUICKLY LIKE THIS.
IT'S A LITTLE SAD THAT HE DOESN'T TOTALLY BELONG TO ME ANYMORE.
But I'm happy he's growing up.
AWW ...
I HOPE SOMEONE NICE SHOWS UP FOR ME.
Wouldn't that be grand?
SO RIGHT NOW'S YOUR BIG CHANCE!
....

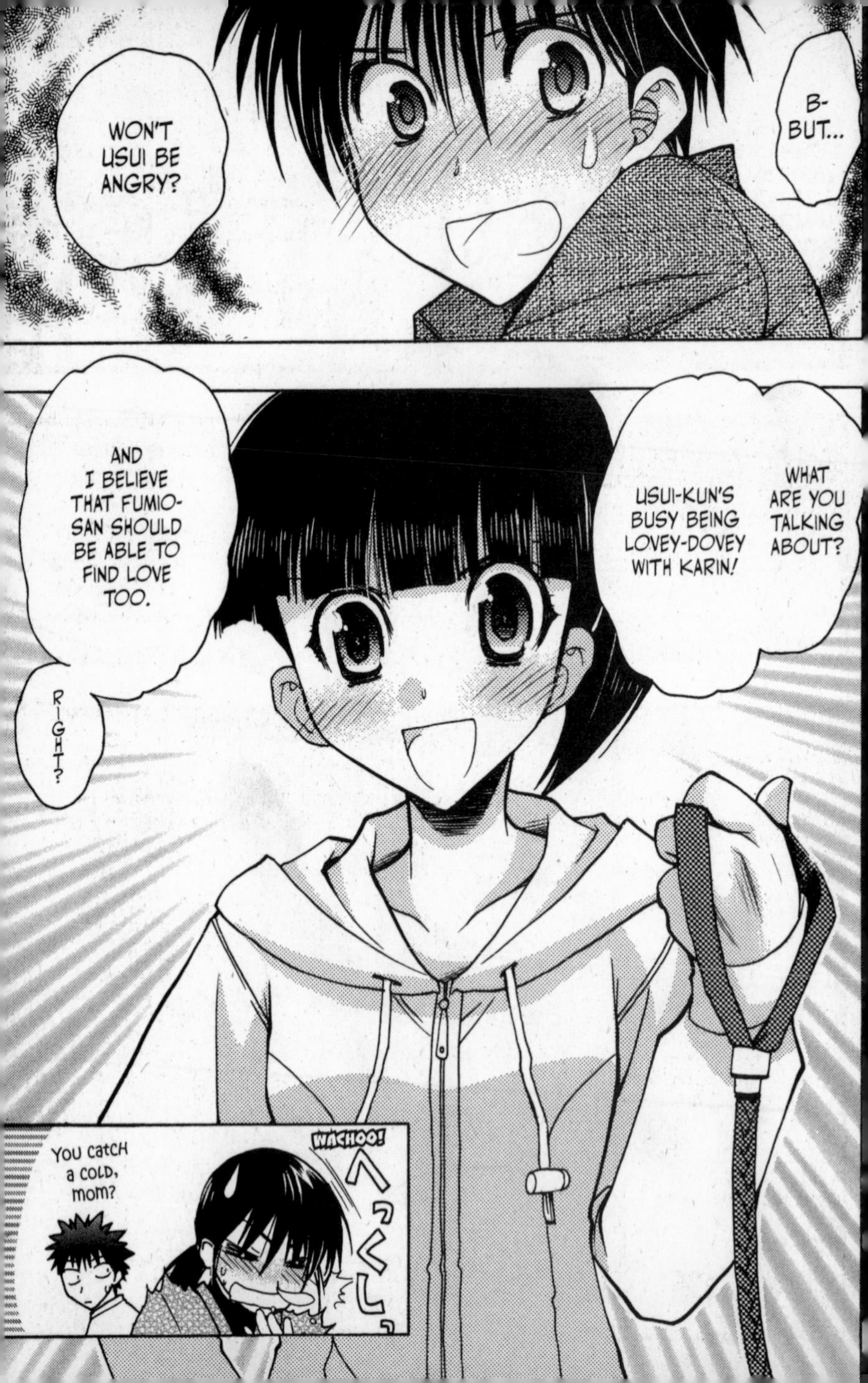
B-BUT...
WON'T USUI BE ANGRY?
WHAT ARE YOU TALKING ABOUT?
USUI-KUN'S BUSY BEING LOVEY-DOVEY WITH KARIN!
AND I BELIEVE THAT FUMIO-SAN SHOULD BE ABLE TO FIND LOVE TOO.
RIGHT?
WACHOO!
へっくしっ
You catch a cold, mom?

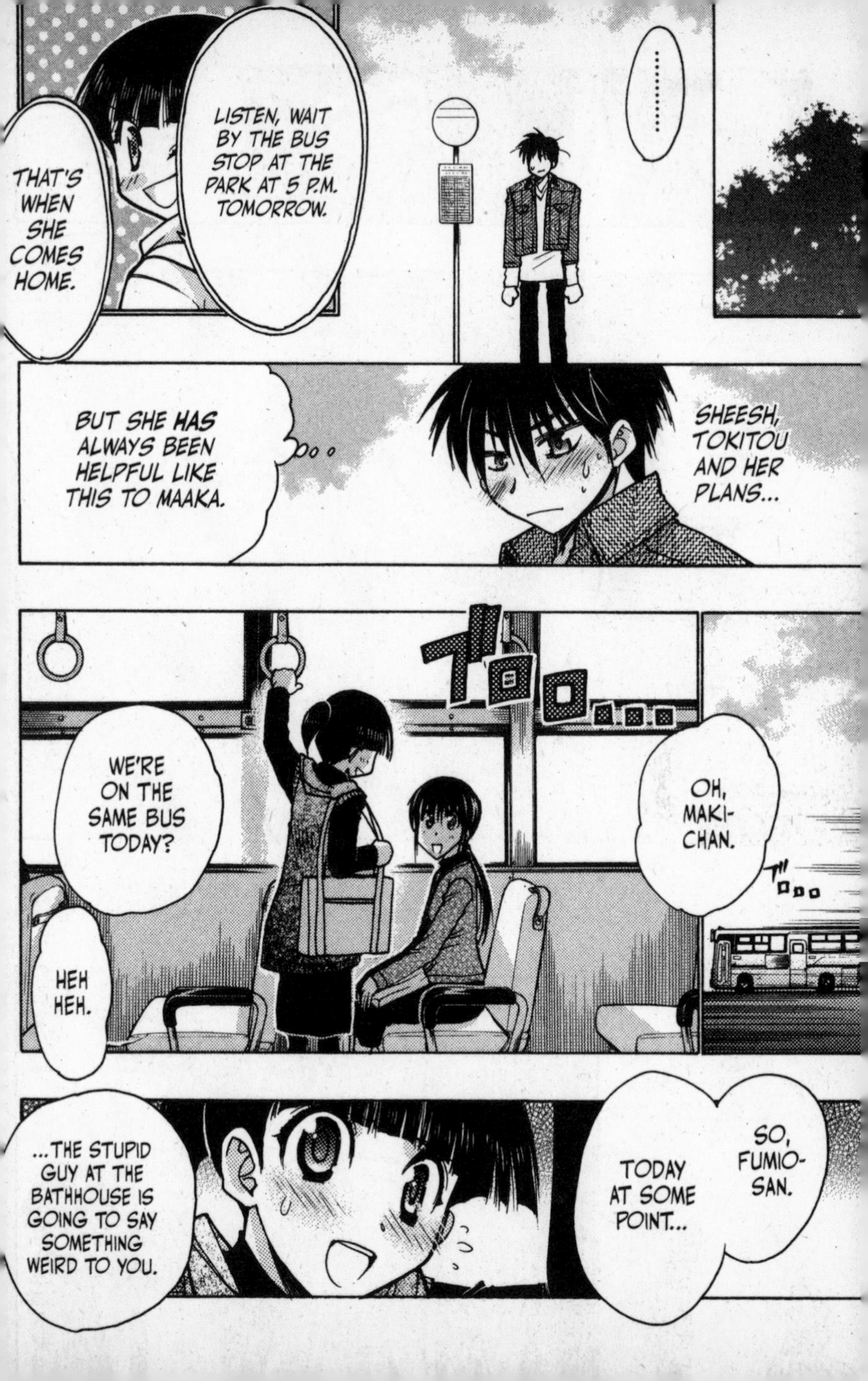
……
LISTEN, WAIT BY THE BUS STOP AT THE PARK AT 5 P.M. TOMORROW.
THAT'S WHEN SHE COMES HOME.
SHEESH, TOKITOU AND HER PLANS...
BUT SHE HAS ALWAYS BEEN HELPFUL LIKE THIS TO MAAKA.
ブロロ
ブロロ...
OH, MAKI-CHAN.
WE'RE ON THE SAME BUS TODAY?
HEH HEH.
SO, FUMIO-SAN.
TODAY AT SOME POINT...
...THE STUPID GUY AT THE BATHHOUSE IS GOING TO SAY SOMETHING WEIRD TO YOU.

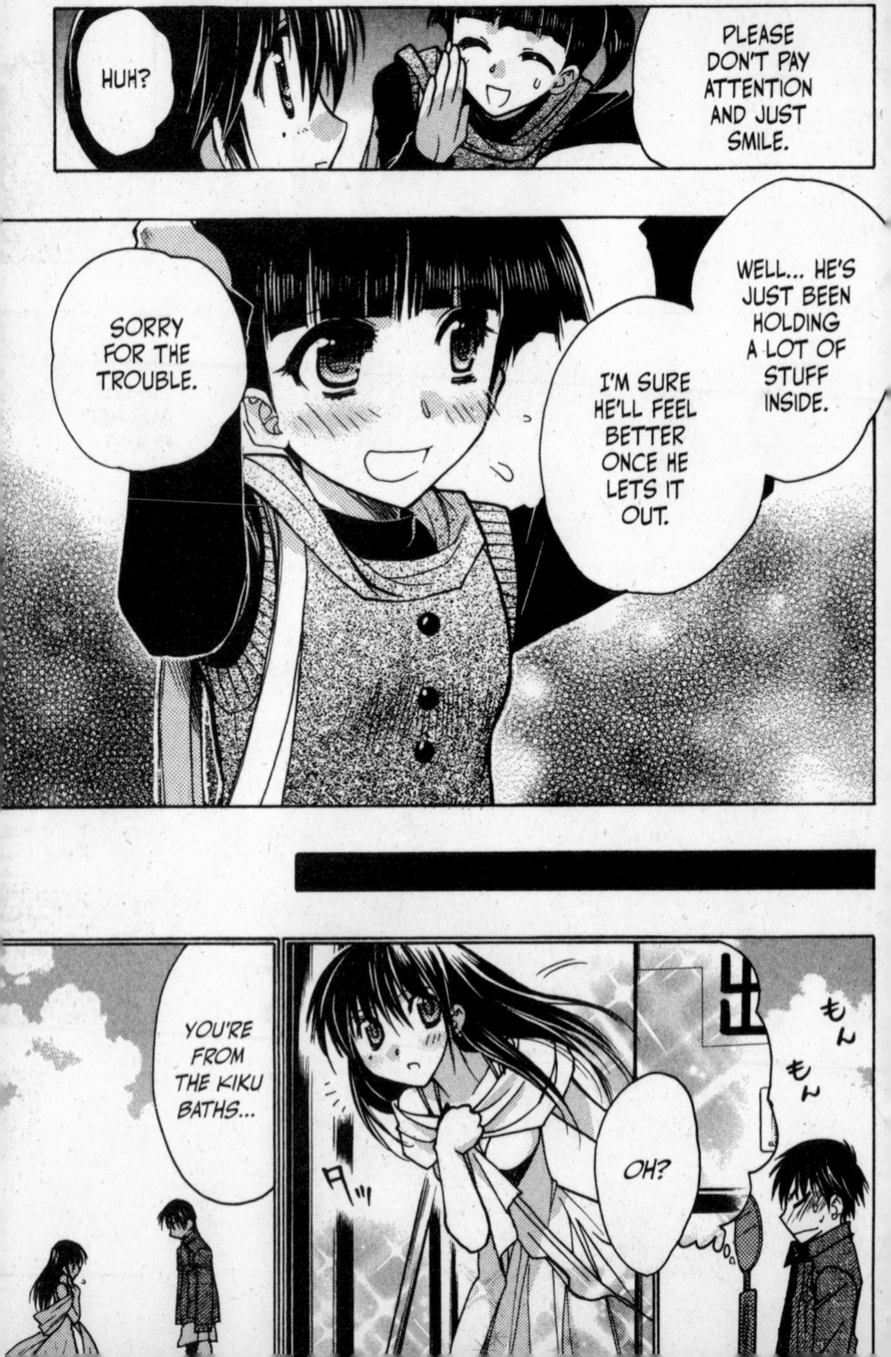
PLEASE DON'T PAY ATTENTION AND JUST SMILE.
HUH?
WELL... HE'S JUST BEEN HOLDING A LOT OF STUFF INSIDE.
I'M SURE HE'LL FEEL BETTER ONCE HE LETS IT OUT.
SORRY FOR THE TROUBLE.
もん
もん
OH?
タッ
YOU'RE FROM THE KIKU BATHS...

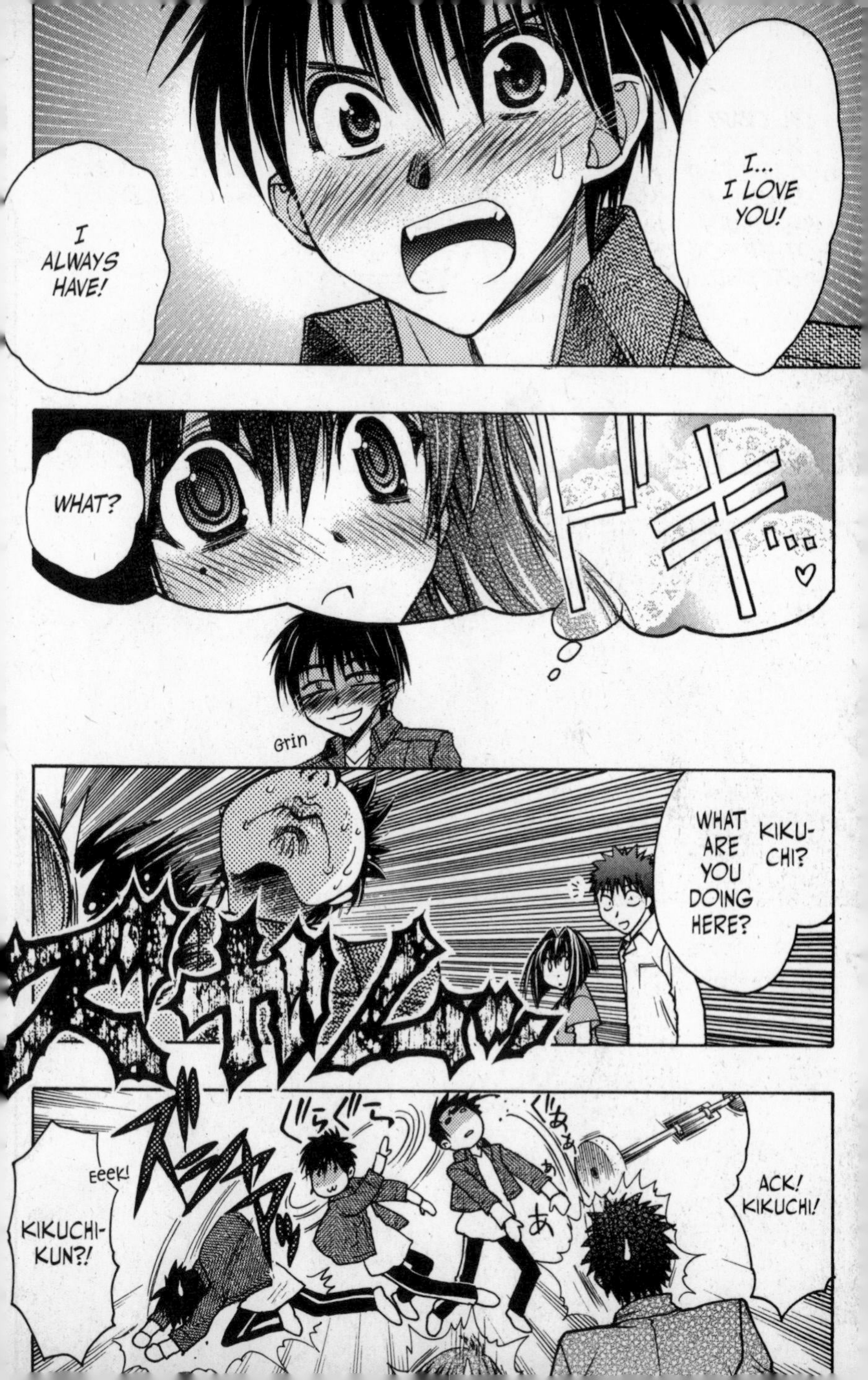
I... I LOVE YOU!
I ALWAYS HAVE!
WHAT?
Grin
KIKU-CHI? WHAT ARE YOU DOING HERE?
ACK! KIKUCHI!
Eeek!
KIKUCHI-KUN?!

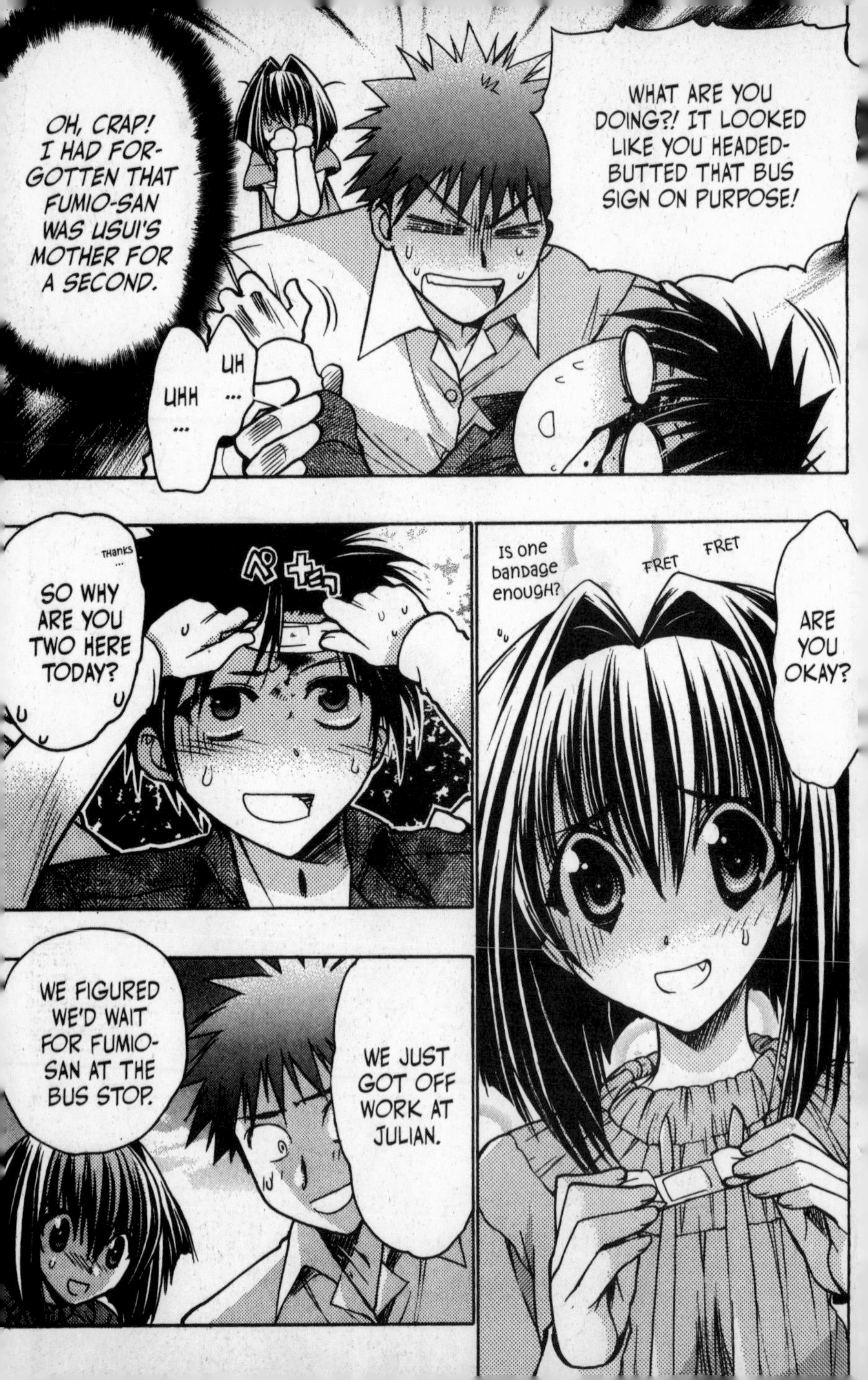
WHAT ARE YOU DOING?! IT LOOKED LIKE YOU HEADED-BUTTED THAT BUS SIGN ON PURPOSE!
OH, CRAP! I HAD FOR-GOTTEN THAT FUMIO-SAN WAS USUI'S MOTHER FOR A SECOND.
UH ...
UHH ...
ARE YOU OKAY?
FRET FRET
Is one bandage enough?
Thanks ...
SO WHY ARE YOU TWO HERE TODAY?
WE JUST GOT OFF WORK AT JULIAN.
WE FIGURED WE'D WAIT FOR FUMIO-SAN AT THE BUS STOP.

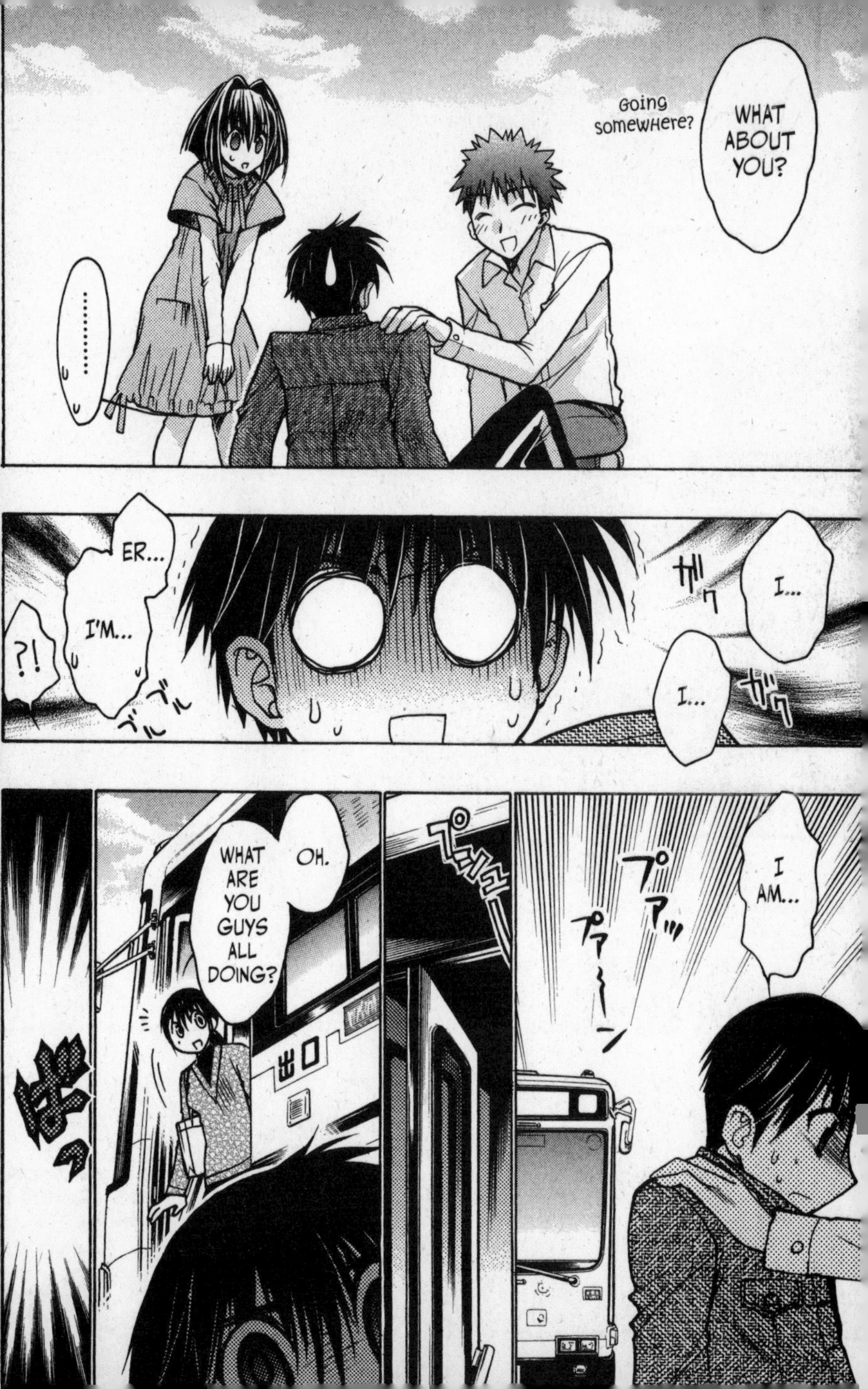
WHAT ABOUT YOU?
Going somewhere?
......
I...
I...
ER...
I'M...
?!
I AM...
OH.
WHAT ARE YOU GUYS ALL DOING?
出口

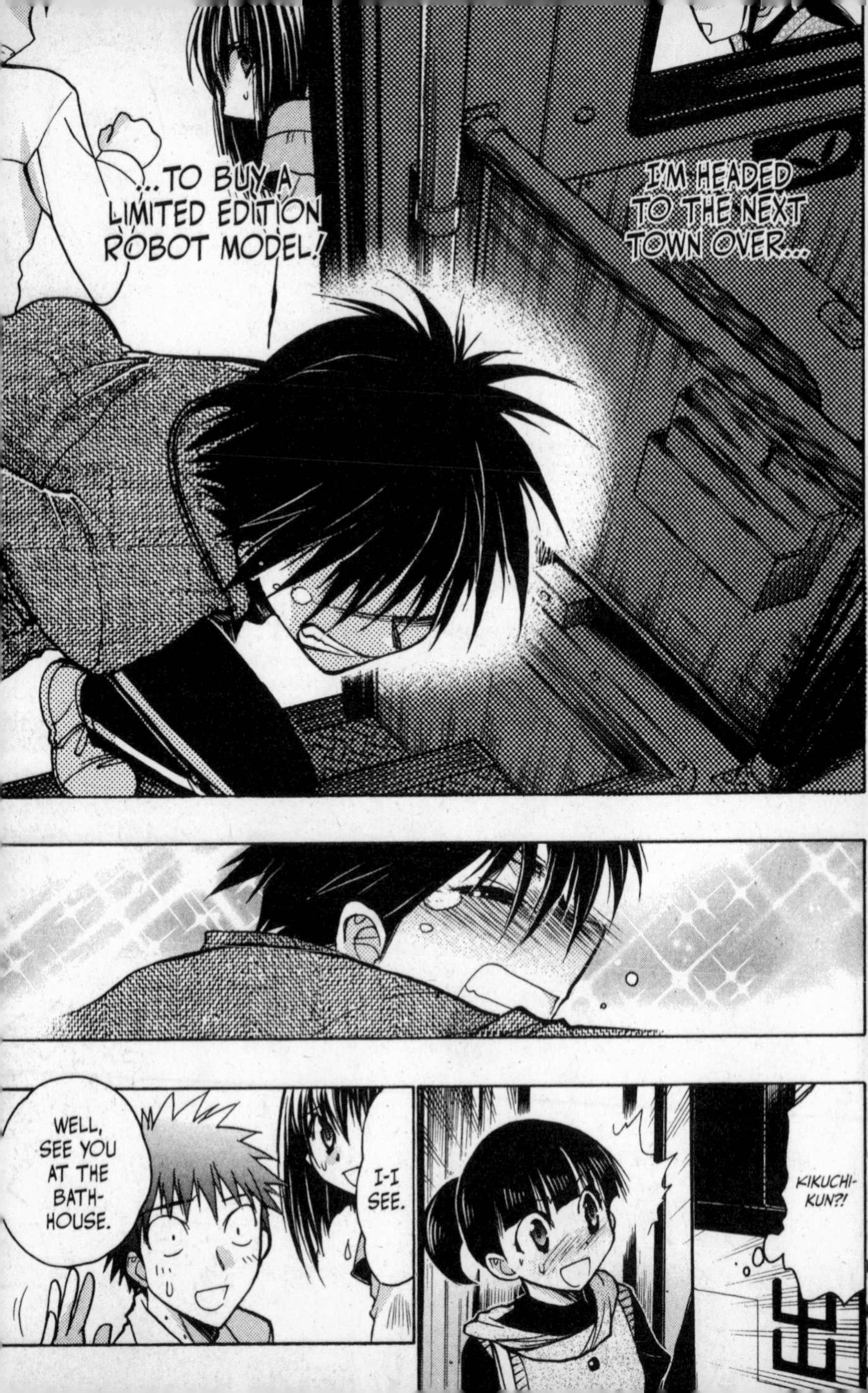
I'M HEADED TO THE NEXT TOWN OVER...
...TO BUY A LIMITED EDITION ROBOT MODEL!
KIKUCHI-KUN?!
I-I SEE.
WELL, SEE YOU AT THE BATH-HOUSE.

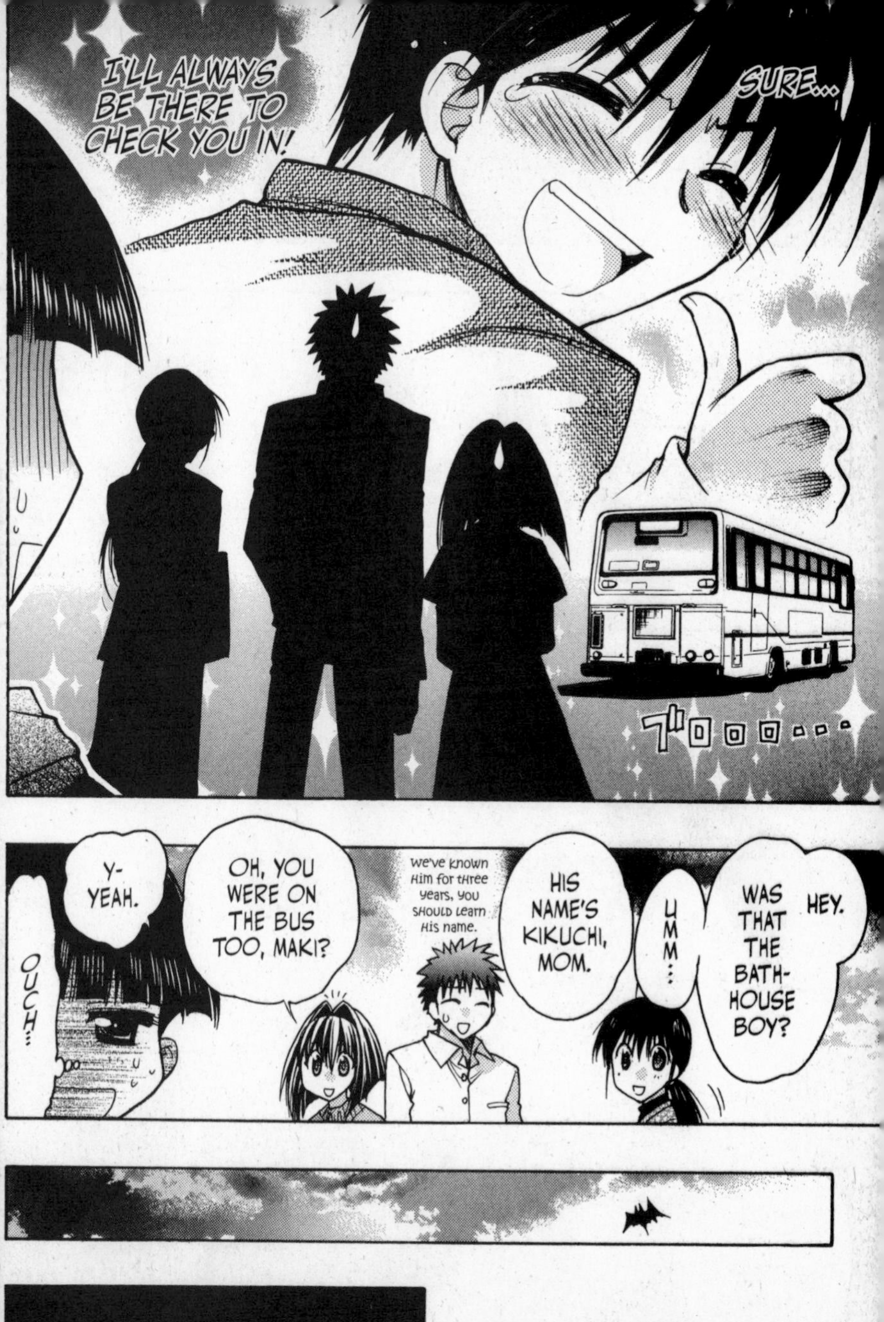

SURE...
I'LL ALWAYS BE THERE TO CHECK YOU IN!
ブロロロ...
HEY.
WAS THAT THE BATH-HOUSE BOY?
UMM...
HIS NAME'S KIKUCHI, MOM.
We've known him for three years, you should learn his name.
OH, YOU WERE ON THE BUS TOO, MAKI?
Y-YEAH.
OUCH...

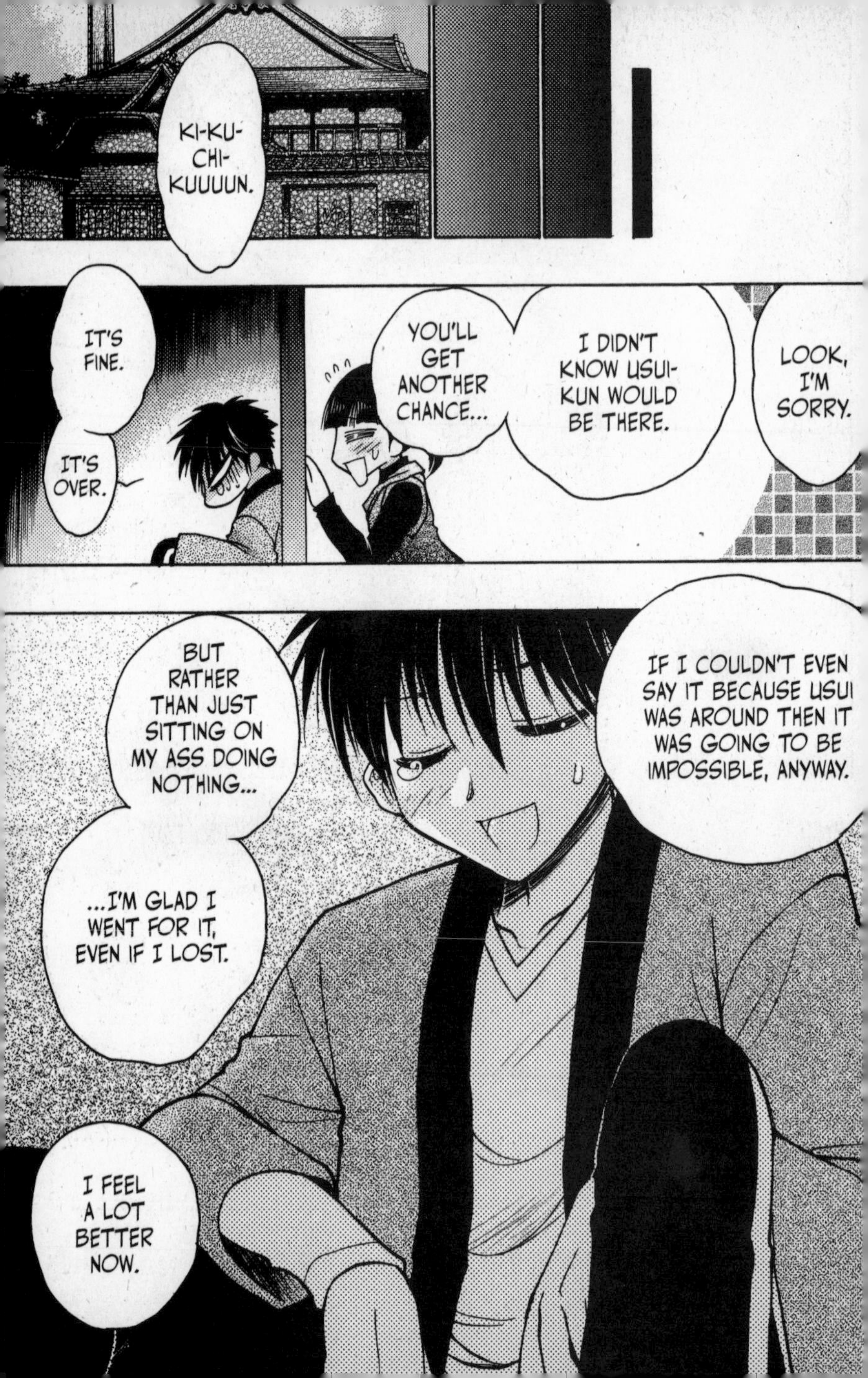
KI-KU-CHI-KUUUUN.
LOOK, I'M SORRY.
I DIDN'T KNOW USUI-KUN WOULD BE THERE.
YOU'LL GET ANOTHER CHANCE...
IT'S FINE.
IT'S OVER.
IF I COULDN'T EVEN SAY IT BECAUSE USUI WAS AROUND THEN IT WAS GOING TO BE IMPOSSIBLE, ANYWAY.
BUT RATHER THAN JUST SITTING ON MY ASS DOING NOTHING...
...I'M GLAD I WENT FOR IT, EVEN IF I LOST.
I FEEL A LOT BETTER NOW.

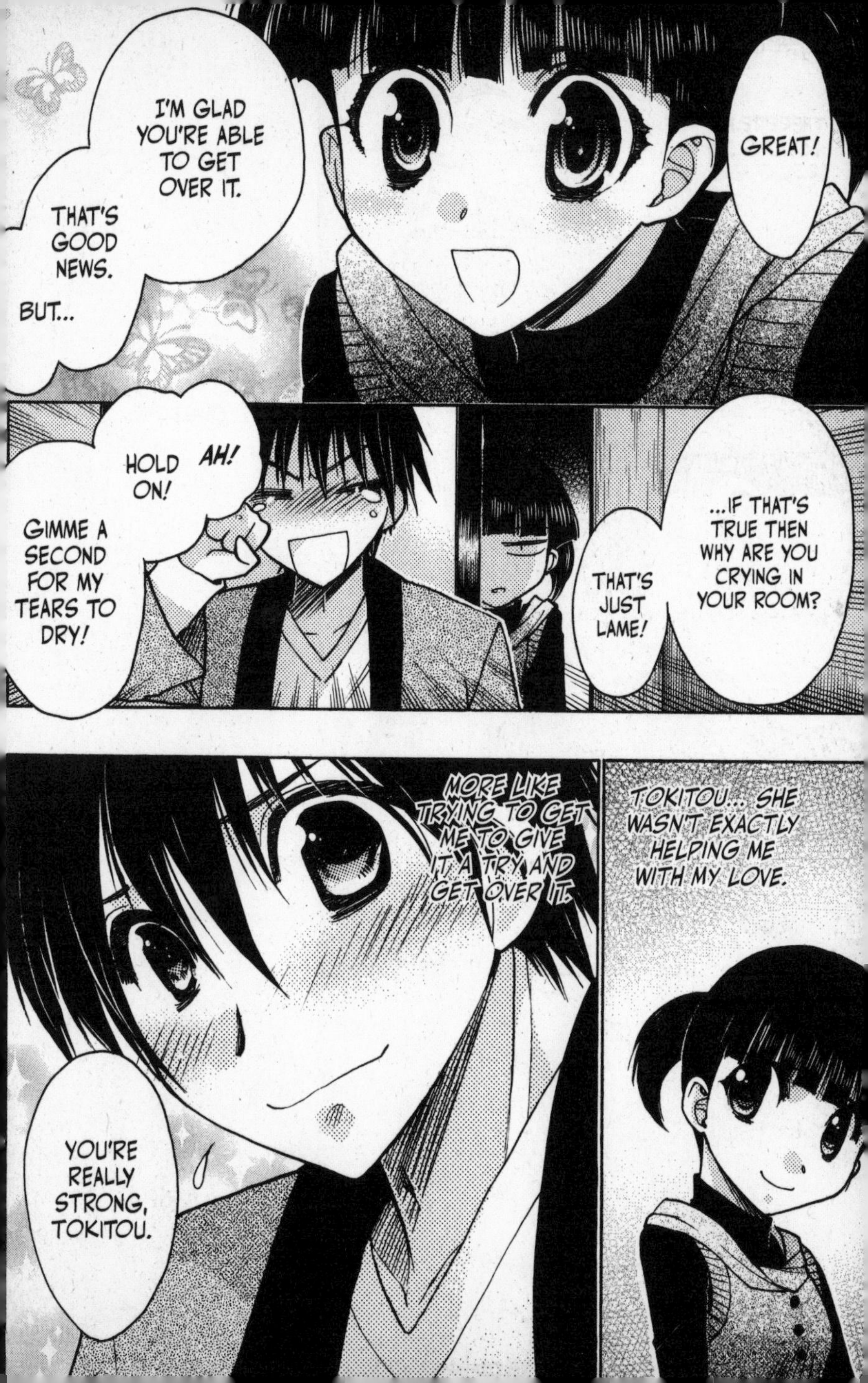
GREAT!
I'M GLAD YOU'RE ABLE TO GET OVER IT.
THAT'S GOOD NEWS.
BUT...
...IF THAT'S TRUE THEN WHY ARE YOU CRYING IN YOUR ROOM?
THAT'S JUST LAME!
AH!
HOLD ON!
GIMME A SECOND FOR MY TEARS TO DRY!
TOKITOU... SHE WASN'T EXACTLY HELPING ME WITH MY LOVE.
MORE LIKE TRYING TO GET ME TO GIVE IT A TRY AND GET OVER IT.
YOU'RE REALLY STRONG, TOKITOU.

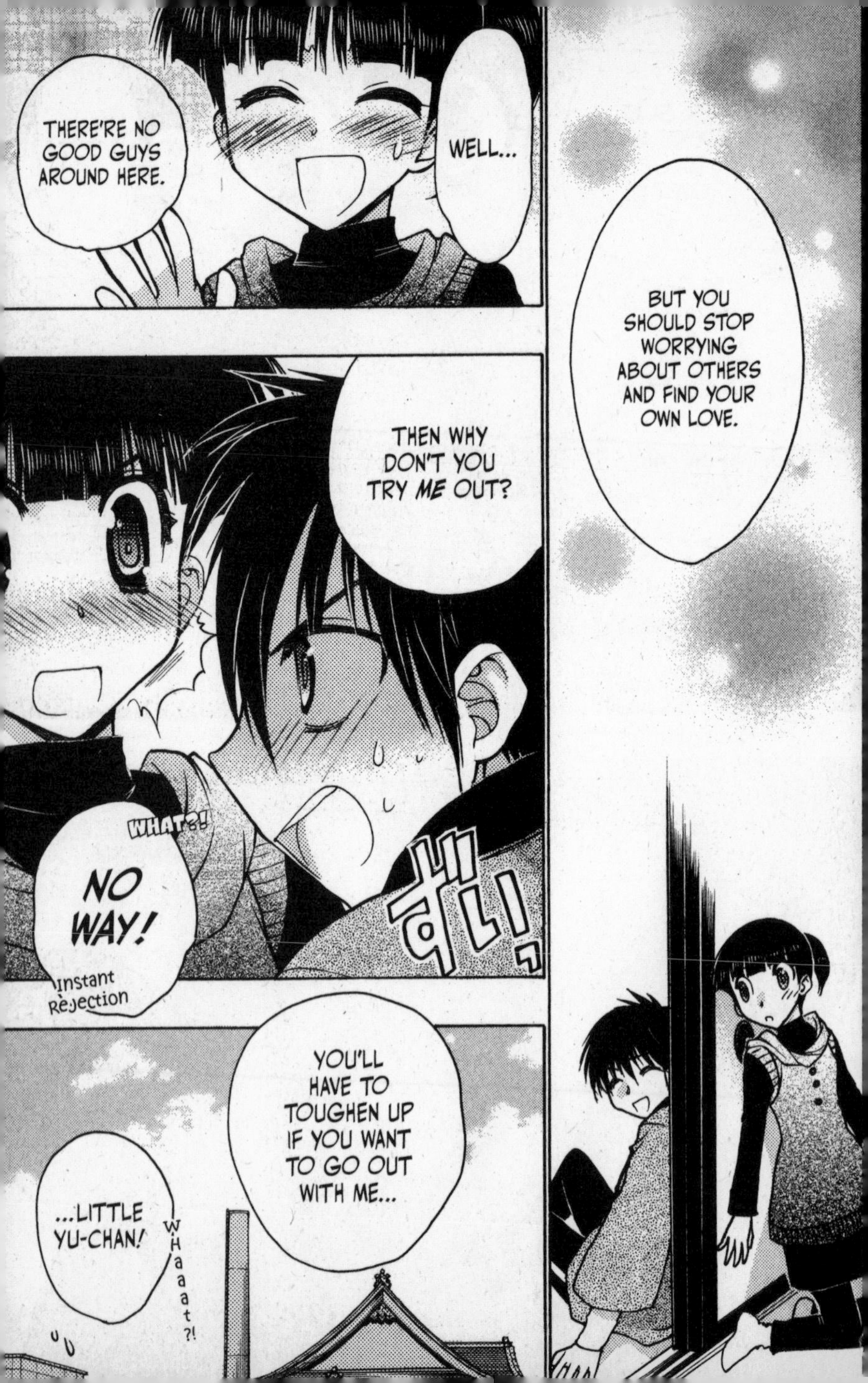
BUT YOU SHOULD STOP WORRYING ABOUT OTHERS AND FIND YOUR OWN LOVE.
WELL...
THERE'RE NO GOOD GUYS AROUND HERE.
THEN WHY DON'T YOU TRY *ME* OUT?
ずい
WHAT?!
NO WAY!
Instant Rejection
YOU'LL HAVE TO TOUGHEN UP IF YOU WANT TO GO OUT WITH ME...
...LITTLE YU-CHAN!
Whaaat?!

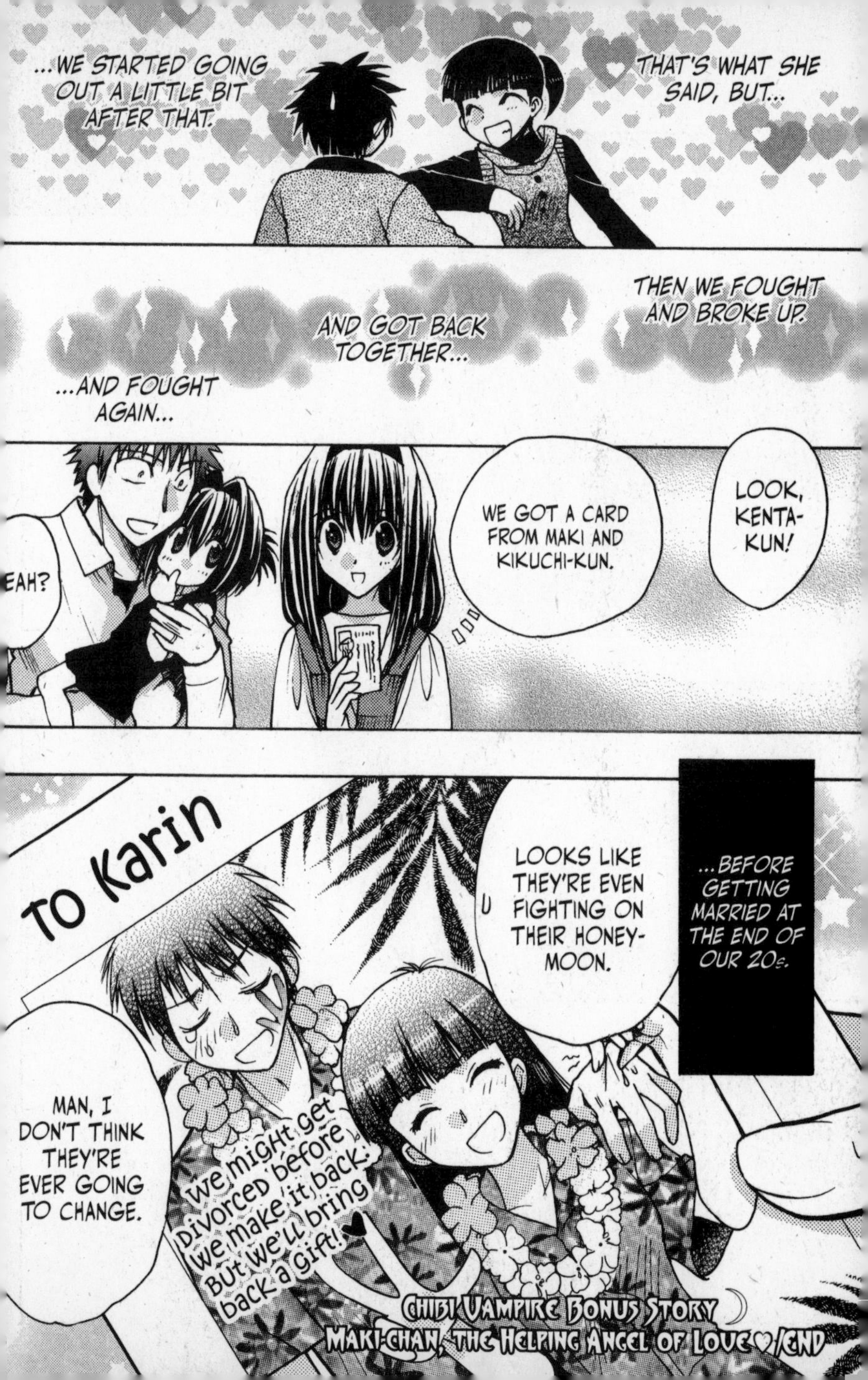
THAT'S WHAT SHE SAID, BUT...
...WE STARTED GOING OUT A LITTLE BIT AFTER THAT.
THEN WE FOUGHT AND BROKE UP.
AND GOT BACK TOGETHER...
...AND FOUGHT AGAIN...
LOOK, KENTA-KUN!
WE GOT A CARD FROM MAKI AND KIKUCHI-KUN.
EAH?
...BEFORE GETTING MARRIED AT THE END OF OUR 20s.
LOOKS LIKE THEY'RE EVEN FIGHTING ON THEIR HONEY-MOON.
To Karin
We might get divorced before we make it back. But we'll bring back a gift!
MAN, I DON'T THINK THEY'RE EVER GOING TO CHANGE.
CHIBI VAMPIRE BONUS STORY
MAKI-CHAN, THE HELPING ANGEL OF LOVE♡/END

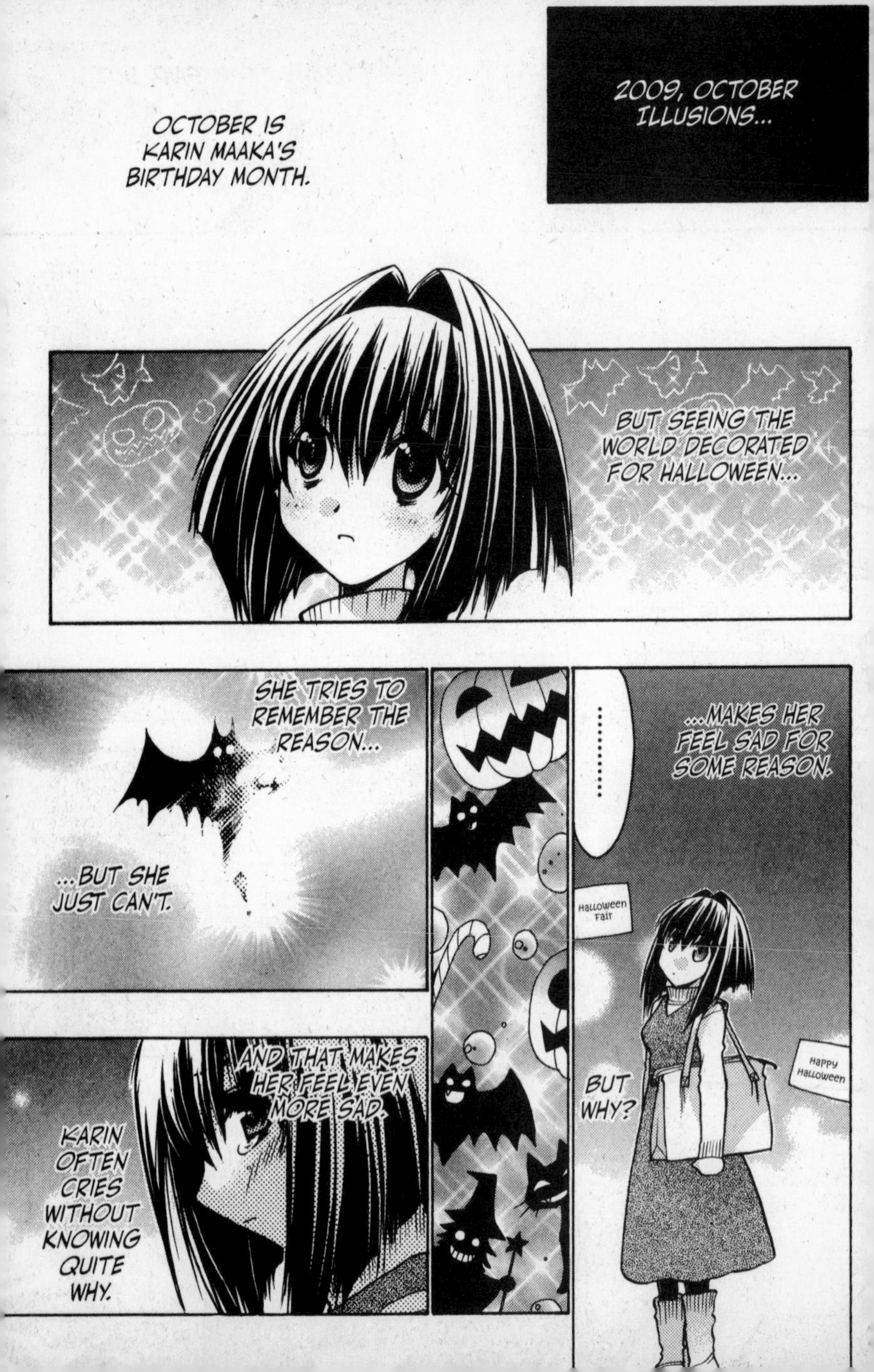
2009, OCTOBER ILLUSIONS...
OCTOBER IS KARIN MAAKA'S BIRTHDAY MONTH.
BUT SEEING THE WORLD DECORATED FOR HALLOWEEN...
......
...MAKES HER FEEL SAD FOR SOME REASON.
Halloween Fair
Happy Halloween
BUT WHY?
SHE TRIES TO REMEMBER THE REASON...
...BUT SHE JUST CAN'T.
AND THAT MAKES HER FEEL EVEN MORE SAD.
KARIN OFTEN CRIES WITHOUT KNOWING QUITE WHY.

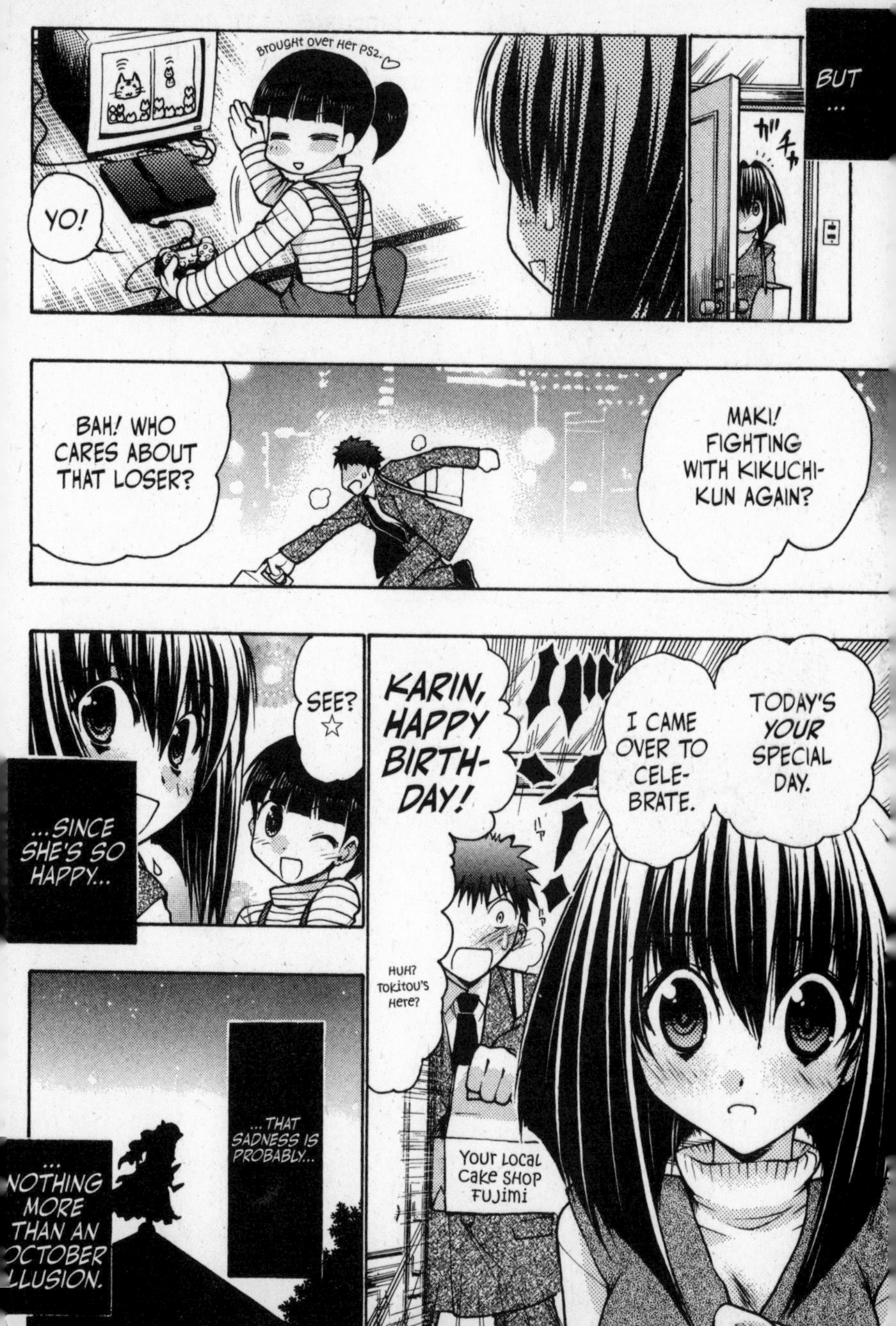
BUT ...
ガチャ
Brought over her PS2.♡
YO!
MAKI! FIGHTING WITH KIKUCHI-KUN AGAIN?
BAH! WHO CARES ABOUT THAT LOSER?
TODAY'S YOUR SPECIAL DAY.
I CAME OVER TO CELE-BRATE.
KARIN, HAPPY BIRTH-DAY!
HUH? Tokitou's here?
Your local Cake Shop Fujimi
SEE? ☆
...SINCE SHE'S SO HAPPY...
...THAT SADNESS IS PROBABLY...
...NOTHING MORE THAN AN OCTOBER ILLUSION.

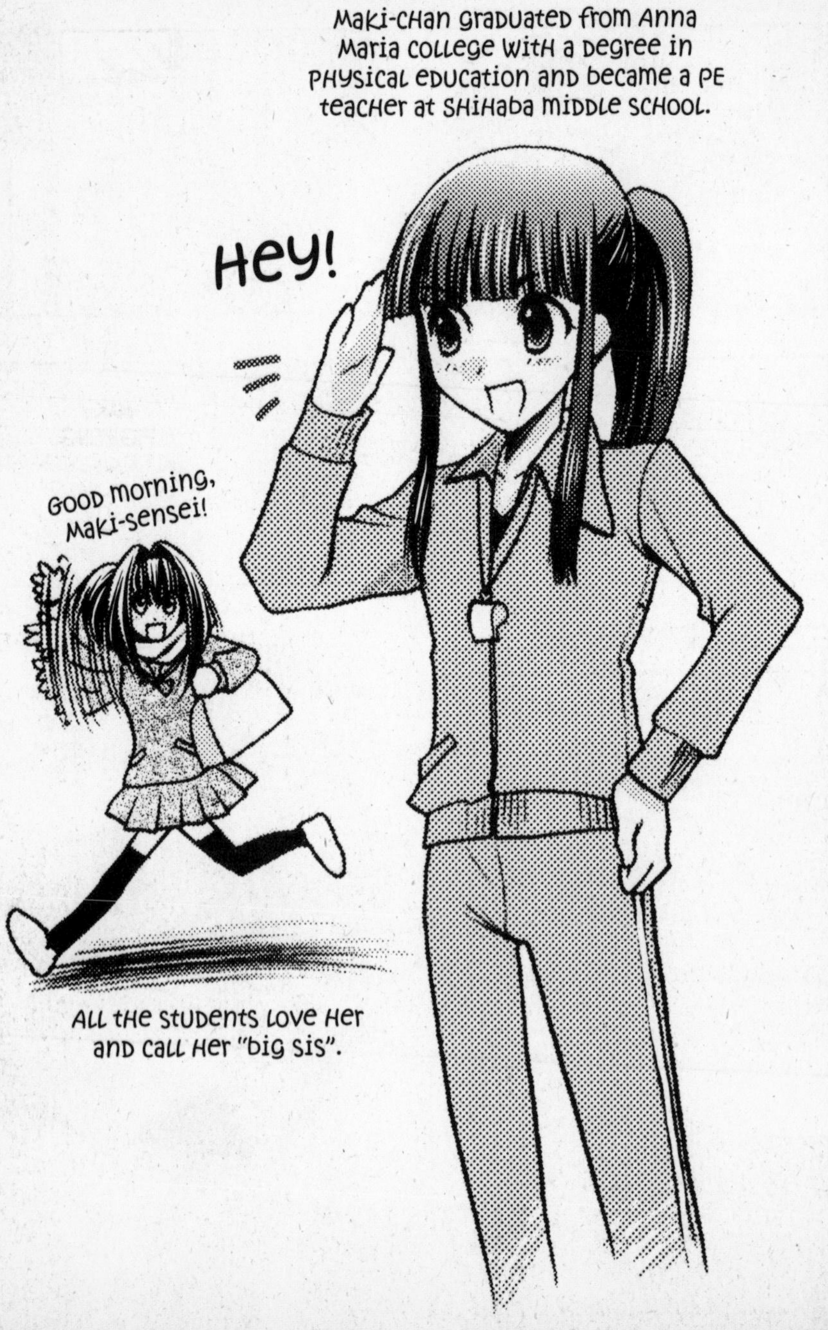
Maki-chan graduated from Anna Maria College with a degree in physical education and became a PE teacher at Shihaba Middle School.
Hey!
Good morning, Maki-sensei!
All the students love her and call her "big sis".

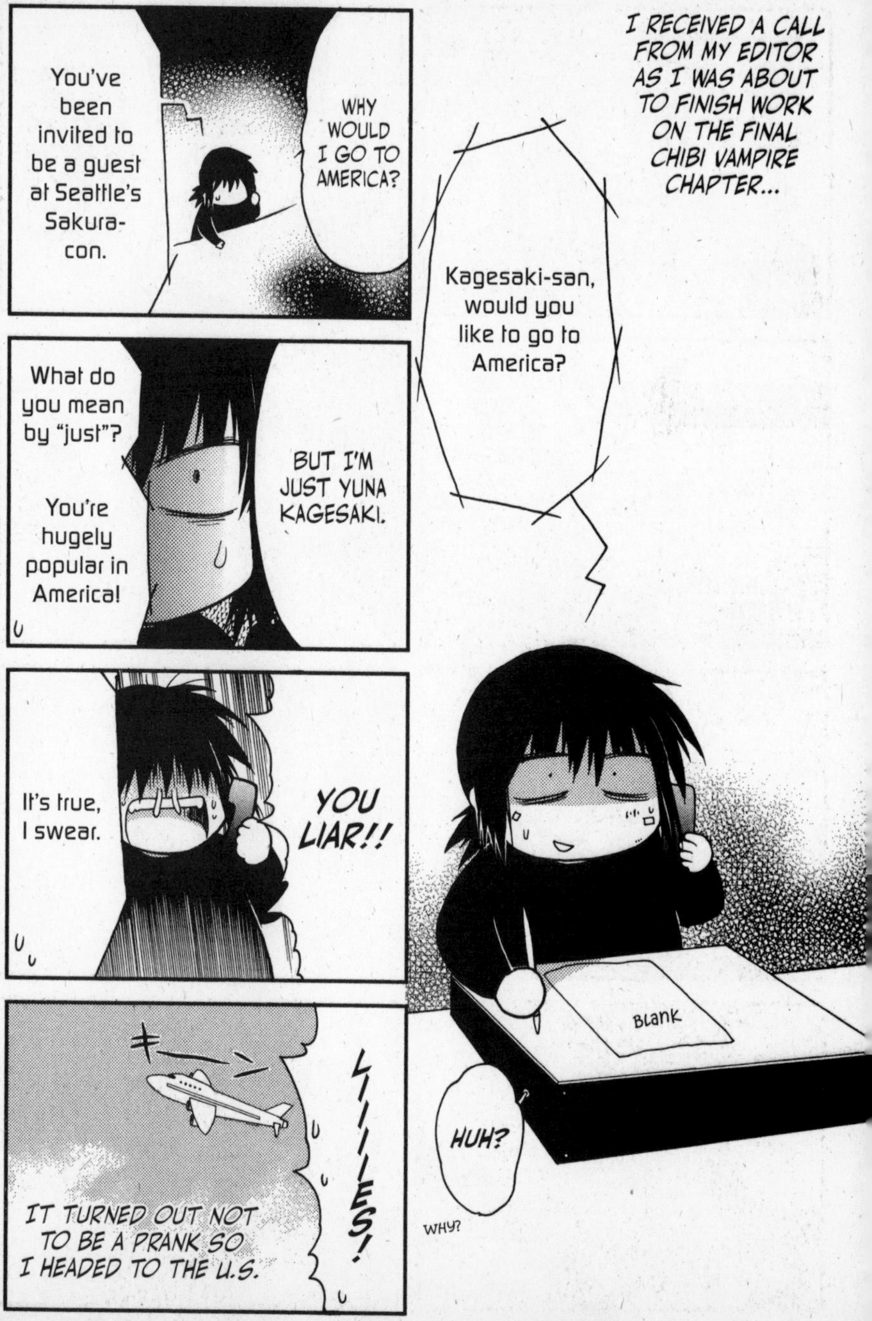
I RECEIVED A CALL FROM MY EDITOR AS I WAS ABOUT TO FINISH WORK ON THE FINAL CHIBI VAMPIRE CHAPTER...
Kagesaki-san, would you like to go to America?
Blank
HUH?
WHY?
WHY WOULD I GO TO AMERICA?
You've been invited to be a guest at Seattle's Sakura-con.
BUT I'M JUST YUNA KAGESAKI.
What do you mean by "just"?
You're hugely popular in America!
YOU LIAR!!
It's true, I swear.
LIIIIES!
IT TURNED OUT NOT TO BE A PRANK SO I HEADED TO THE U.S.

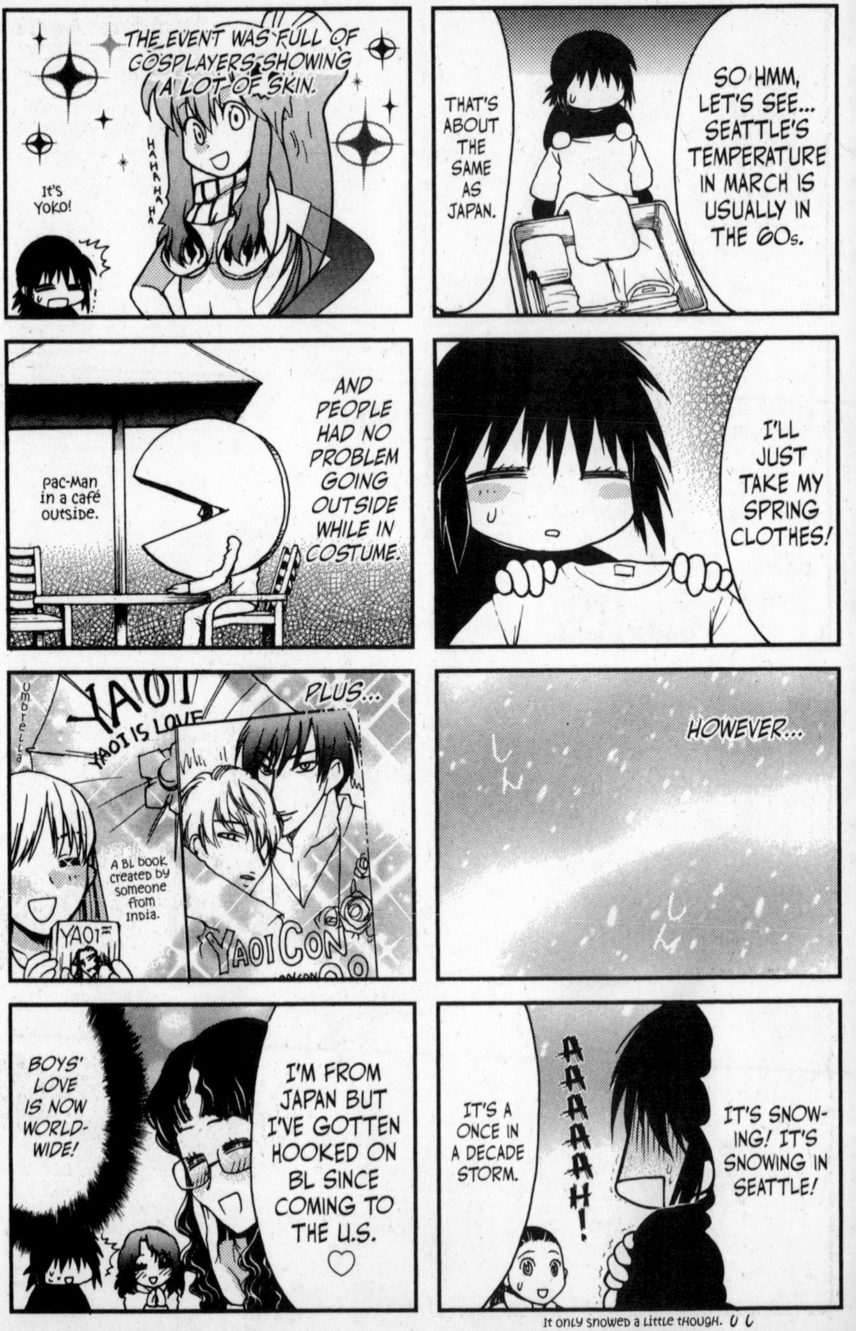
SO HMM, LET'S SEE... SEATTLE'S TEMPERATURE IN MARCH IS USUALLY IN THE 60s.
THAT'S ABOUT THE SAME AS JAPAN.
I'LL JUST TAKE MY SPRING CLOTHES!
HOWEVER...
IT'S SNOWING! IT'S SNOWING IN SEATTLE!
AAAAAH!
IT'S A ONCE IN A DECADE STORM.
THE EVENT WAS FULL OF COSPLAYERS SHOWING A LOT OF SKIN.
HAHAHAHA
It's YOKO!
AND PEOPLE HAD NO PROBLEM GOING OUTSIDE WHILE IN COSTUME.
Pac-Man in a café outside.
PLUS...
YAOI
YAOI IS LOVE
Umbrella
A BL book created by someone from India.
YAOI
YAOI CON
I'M FROM JAPAN BUT I'VE GOTTEN HOOKED ON BL SINCE COMING TO THE U.S. ♡
BOYS' LOVE IS NOW WORLD-WIDE!

It only snowed a little though.

CLUMSY BATTLE AMERICA

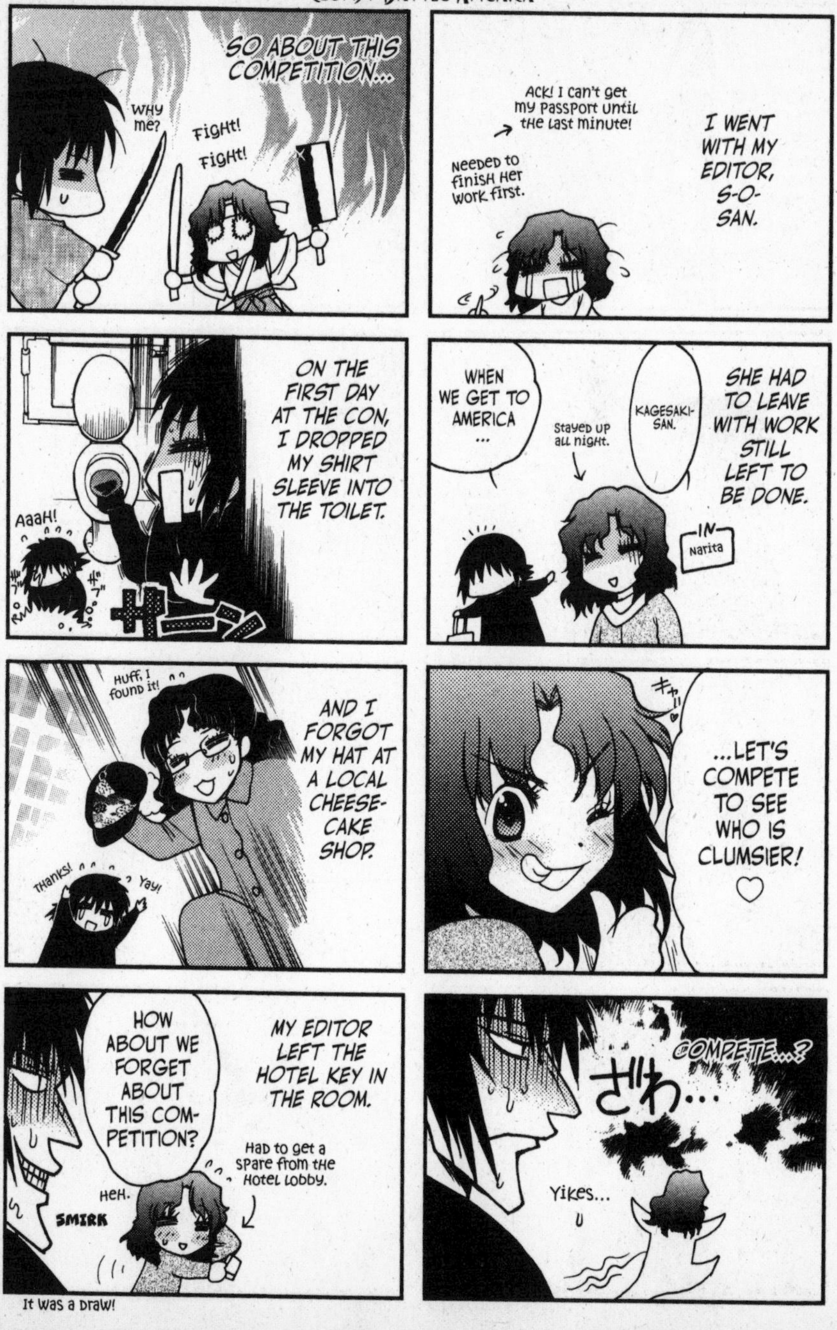

I WENT WITH MY EDITOR, S-O-SAN.
Ack! I can't get my passport until the last minute!
Needed to finish her work first.
SHE HAD TO LEAVE WITH WORK STILL LEFT TO BE DONE.
KAGESAKI-SAN.
WHEN WE GET TO AMERICA ...
Stayed up all night.
IN Narita
...LET'S COMPETE TO SEE WHO IS CLUMSIER! ♡
COMPETE...?
ざわ...
Yikes...
SO ABOUT THIS COMPETITION...
Why me?
Fight!
Fight!
ON THE FIRST DAY AT THE CON, I DROPPED MY SHIRT SLEEVE INTO THE TOILET.
AaaH!
AND I FORGOT MY HAT AT A LOCAL CHEESE-CAKE SHOP.
Huff, I found it!
Thanks!
Yay!
MY EDITOR LEFT THE HOTEL KEY IN THE ROOM.
Had to get a spare from the Hotel Lobby.
HOW ABOUT WE FORGET ABOUT THIS COMPETITION?
Heh.
SMIRK

It was a Draw!

Tomic Inspiration

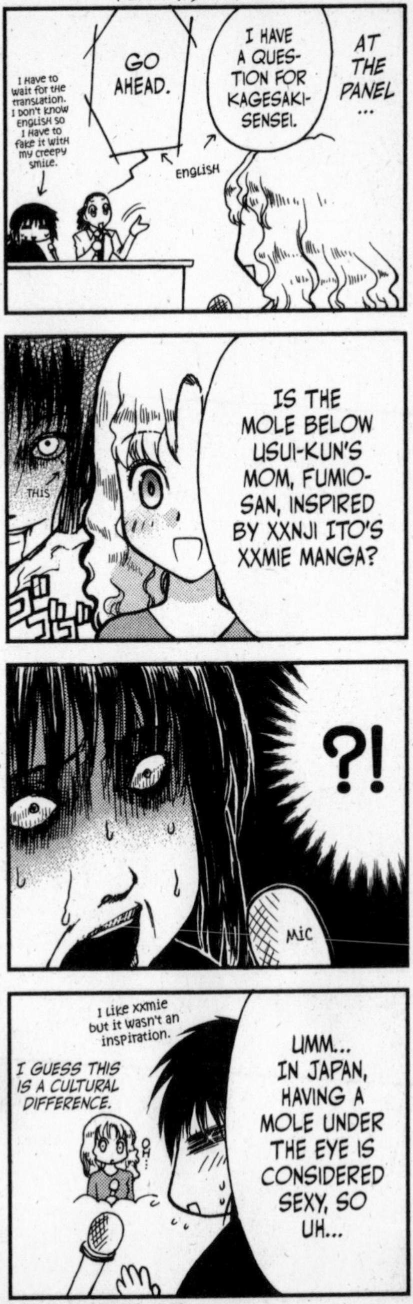
AT THE PANEL...
I HAVE A QUESTION FOR KAGESAKI-SENSEI.
ENGLISH
GO AHEAD.
I have to wait for the translation. I don't know English so I have to fake it with my creepy smile.
IS THE MOLE BELOW USUI-KUN'S MOM, FUMIO-SAN, INSPIRED BY XXNJI ITO'S XXMIE MANGA?
THIS
?!
MIC
UMM... IN JAPAN, HAVING A MOLE UNDER THE EYE IS CONSIDERED SEXY, SO UH...
I like xxmie but it wasn't an inspiration.
I GUESS THIS IS A CULTURAL DIFFERENCE.
OH...

Handmade Dolls

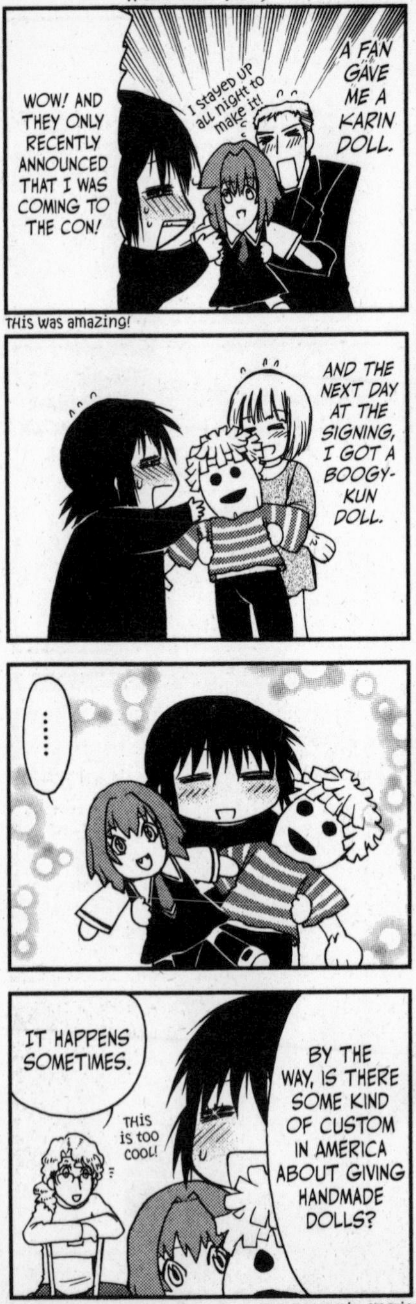
A FAN GAVE ME A KARIN DOLL.
I stayed up all night to make it!
WOW! AND THEY ONLY RECENTLY ANNOUNCED THAT I WAS COMING TO THE CON!
THIS was amazing!
AND THE NEXT DAY AT THE SIGNING, I GOT A BOOGY-KUN DOLL.
......
BY THE WAY, IS THERE SOME KIND OF CUSTOM IN AMERICA ABOUT GIVING HANDMADE DOLLS?
IT HAPPENS SOMETIMES.
THIS is too COOL!

To everyone in America, thank you so much!

Friedrich Has No Idea

うわーーんっ
Waaaaah!
Wha... What's going on, you two?!
Oh, Kenta-kun!
You'll never believe it!! This month's Tokemeke ☆ Smash ...
...is the story's grand finale!!
We've been following the story since junior high so we're soooo touched by the ending!!!!
I bet that's what's going on in Japan right now... chatting it up online about how great the ending was... you know?!
ヒュウウゥゥ
How depressing ...
I know... so jealous. We'll have to wait two years before we get our hands on it...

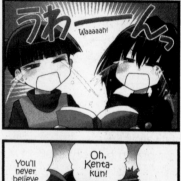

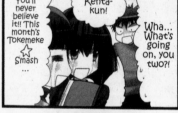

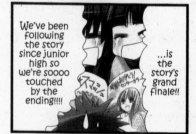

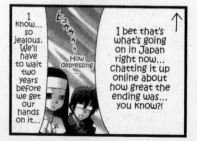

Fried has no idea that his second cousin is just as crazy about the very same manga...

Editor's Notes
Cindy Suzuki

It was yet another busy month here in the TOKYOPOP editorial department! There are many reasons why this month has been a bit crazier than the previous months. One reason being that we have a lot of big titles coming up! We've been plugging away trying to make these titles very special just for you.

Another reason why we're so busy is that it's intern rotation time. Meaning, our lovely interns Sarah and Noora have concluded their internship. Most editorial internships last for about three months, sometimes longer depending on whether the university is on a quarter or semester system. Anyhow, as we said sayonara to Sarah and Noora, we said konnichiwa to our new interns Tim and Joey. It's fantastic that we always get brilliant editorial interns, but training and re-training constantly keeps us on our toes.

Interested in the life of a TOKYOPOP editorial intern? Well, you can find out more by subscribing to our newsletter at www.TOKYOPOP.com or LIKING us on Facebook. Our interns write tons of neat articles that show off their incredible knowledge and love of manga, anime and Japanese culture. It's really inspiring to work with such a talented bunch. So, thanks all interns, current and past. We love ya <3

See you again next month!

Cindy Suzuki, Editor

For exclusive updates, be sure to find us here:

www.TOKYOPOP.com
www.Facebook.com/TOKYOPOP
www.Twitter.com/TOKYOPOP

A TOKYOPOP® Manga
E-mail: info@TOKYOPOP.com
Come visit us online at www.TOKYOPOP.com

THE SMALLEST HERO!?

RATMAN

Shuto Katsuragi is a superhero otaku. Only problem is, he's a shrimp always getting teased for his height...especially when he tries to emulate his favorite superhero! To make matters worse, Shuto suddenly gets abducted by his classmate and tricked into participating in some rather sketchy and super-villainous experiments! Why is it always one step forward and a hundred steps back for this little guy?

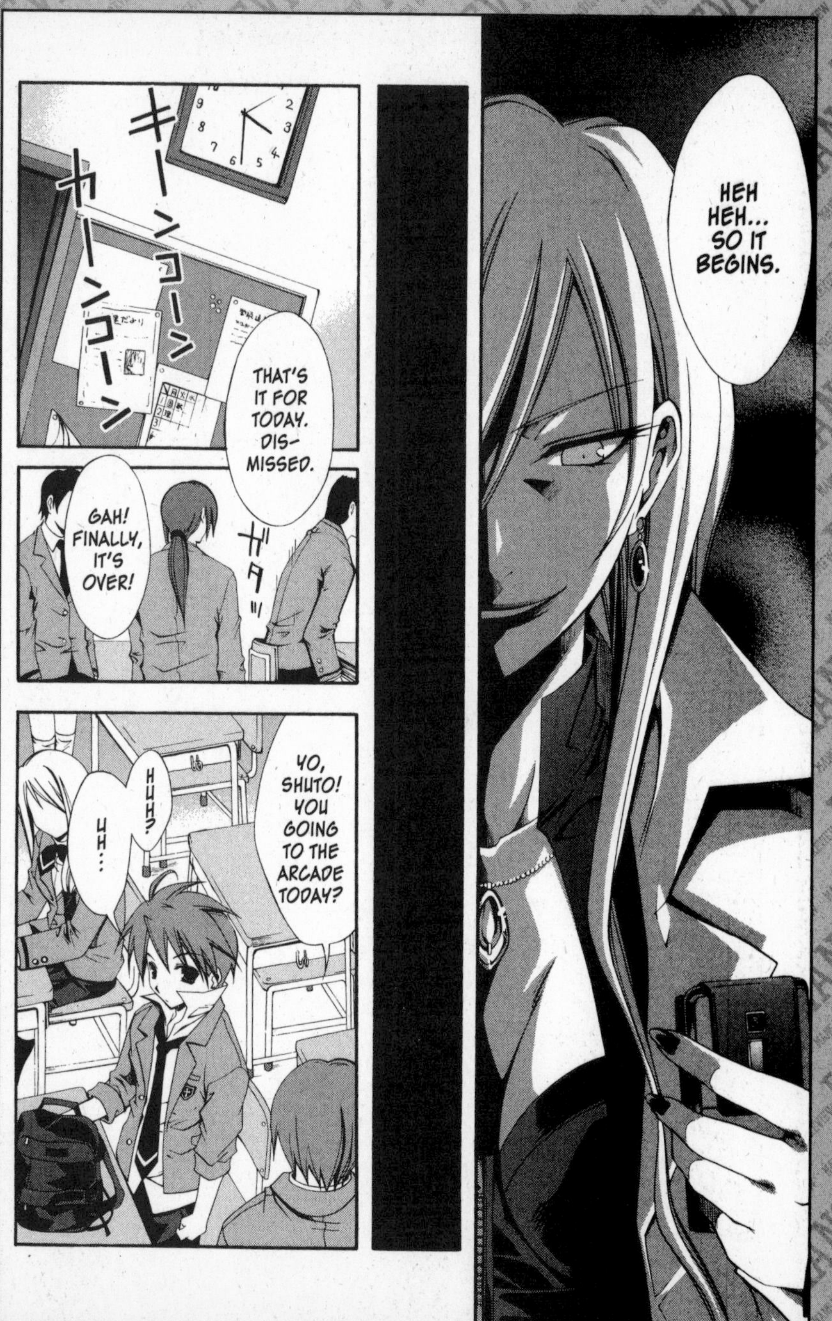
HEH HEH... SO IT BEGINS.
キーンコーン
カーンコーン
THAT'S IT FOR TODAY. DIS-MISSED.
ガタッ
GAH! FINALLY, IT'S OVER!
YO, SHUTO! YOU GOING TO THE ARCADE TODAY?
HUH?
UH...

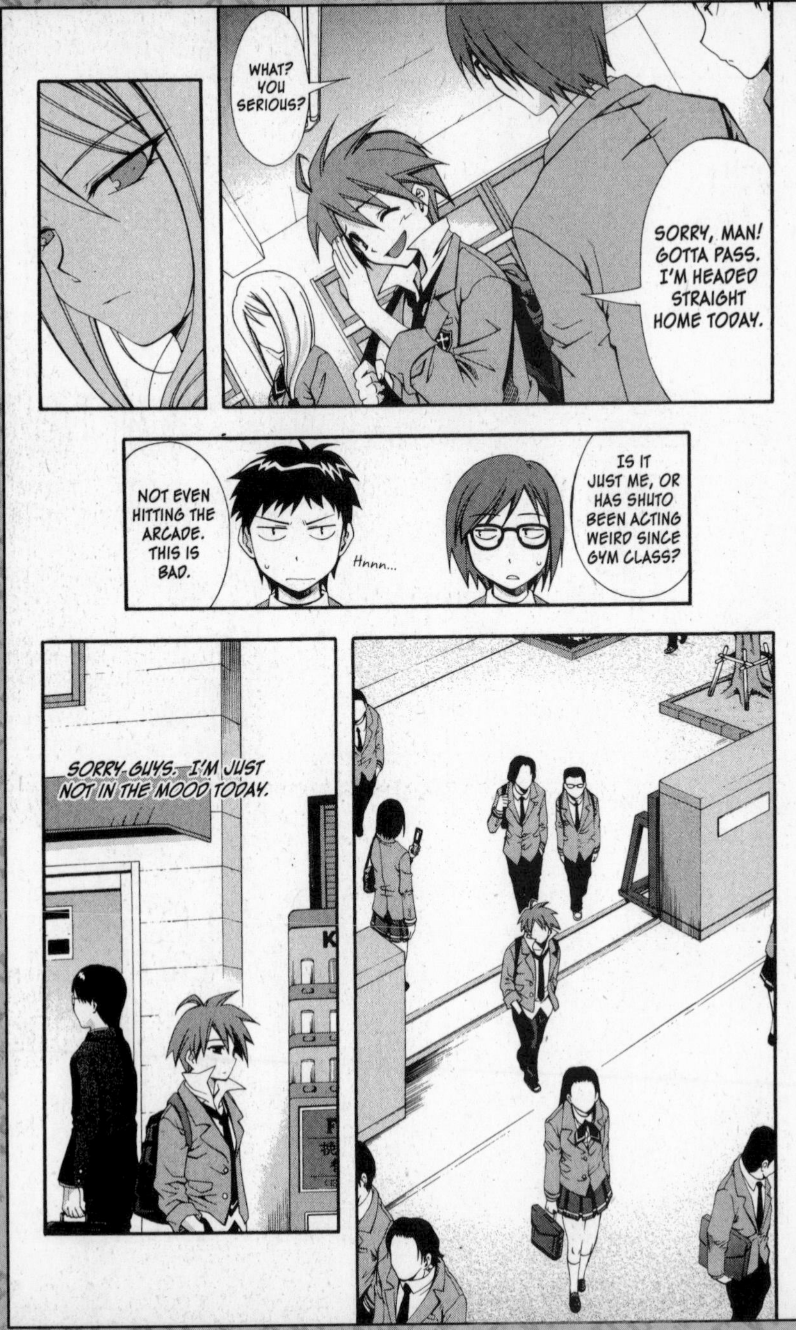
SORRY, MAN! GOTTA PASS. I'M HEADED STRAIGHT HOME TODAY.
WHAT? YOU SERIOUS?
IS IT JUST ME, OR HAS SHUTO BEEN ACTING WEIRD SINCE GYM CLASS?
Hmnn...
NOT EVEN HITTING THE ARCADE. THIS IS BAD.
SORRY GUYS. I'M JUST NOT IN THE MOOD TODAY.

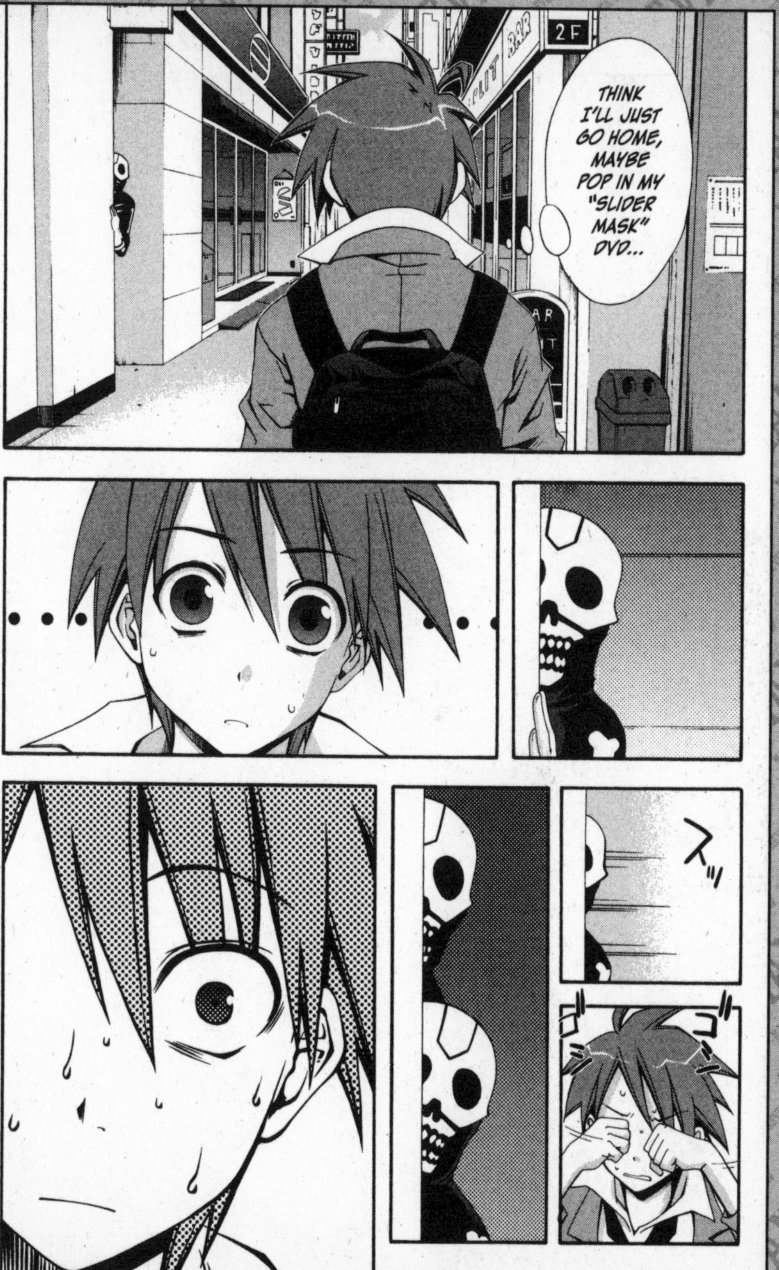
THINK I'LL JUST GO HOME, MAYBE POP IN MY "SLIDER MASK" DVD...
...
...
スッ

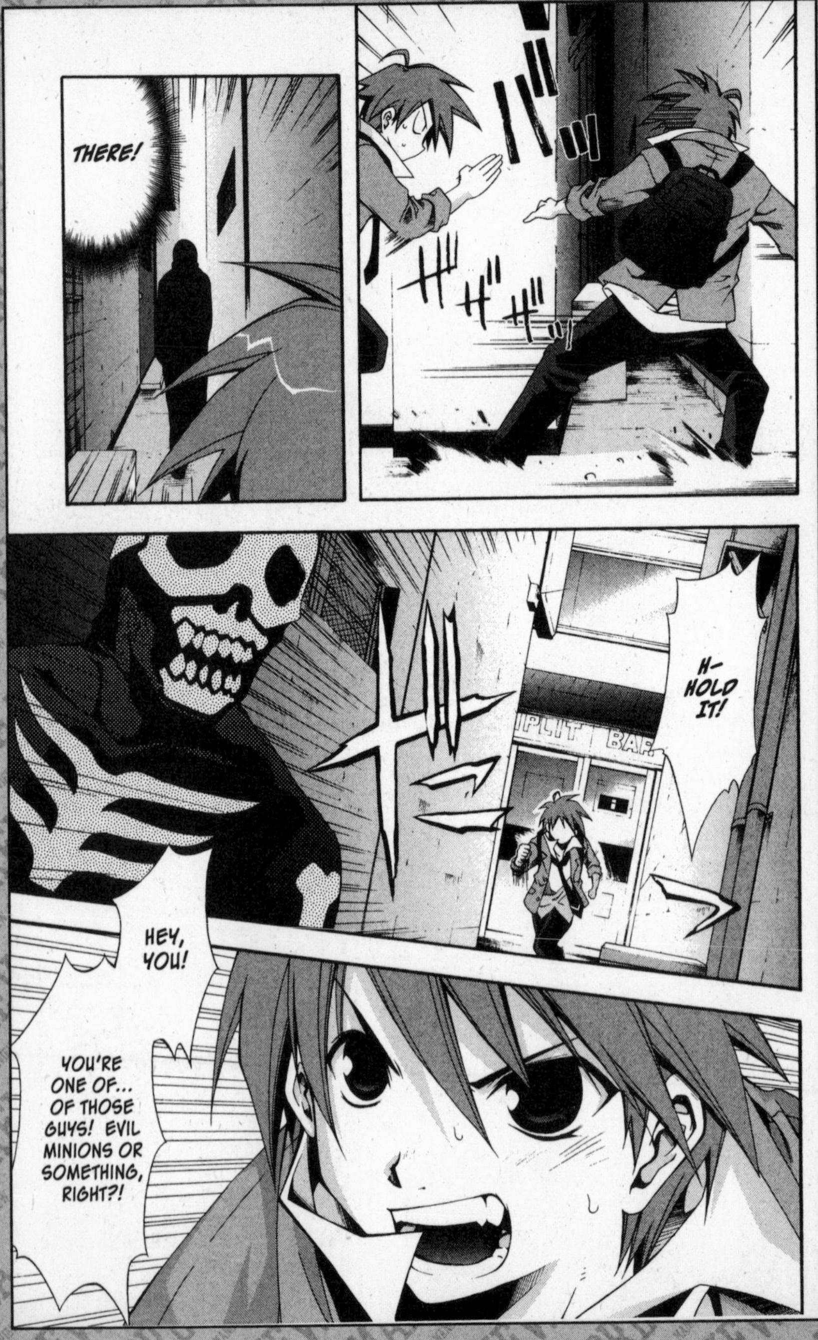
THERE!
H-HOLD IT!
HEY, YOU!
YOU'RE ONE OF... OF THOSE GUYS! EVIL MINIONS OR SOMETHING, RIGHT?!

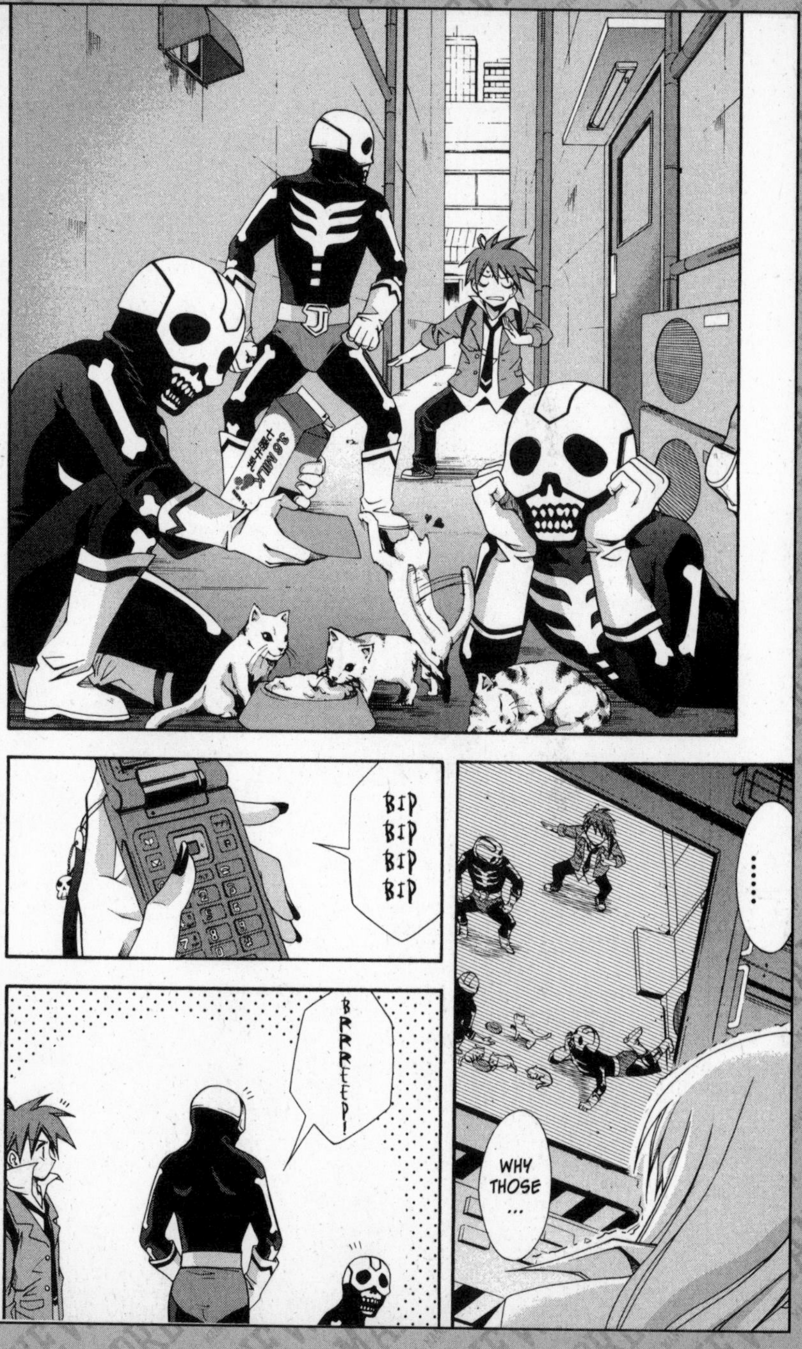
……
WHY THOSE ...
BIP BIP BIP BIP
BRRREEP!

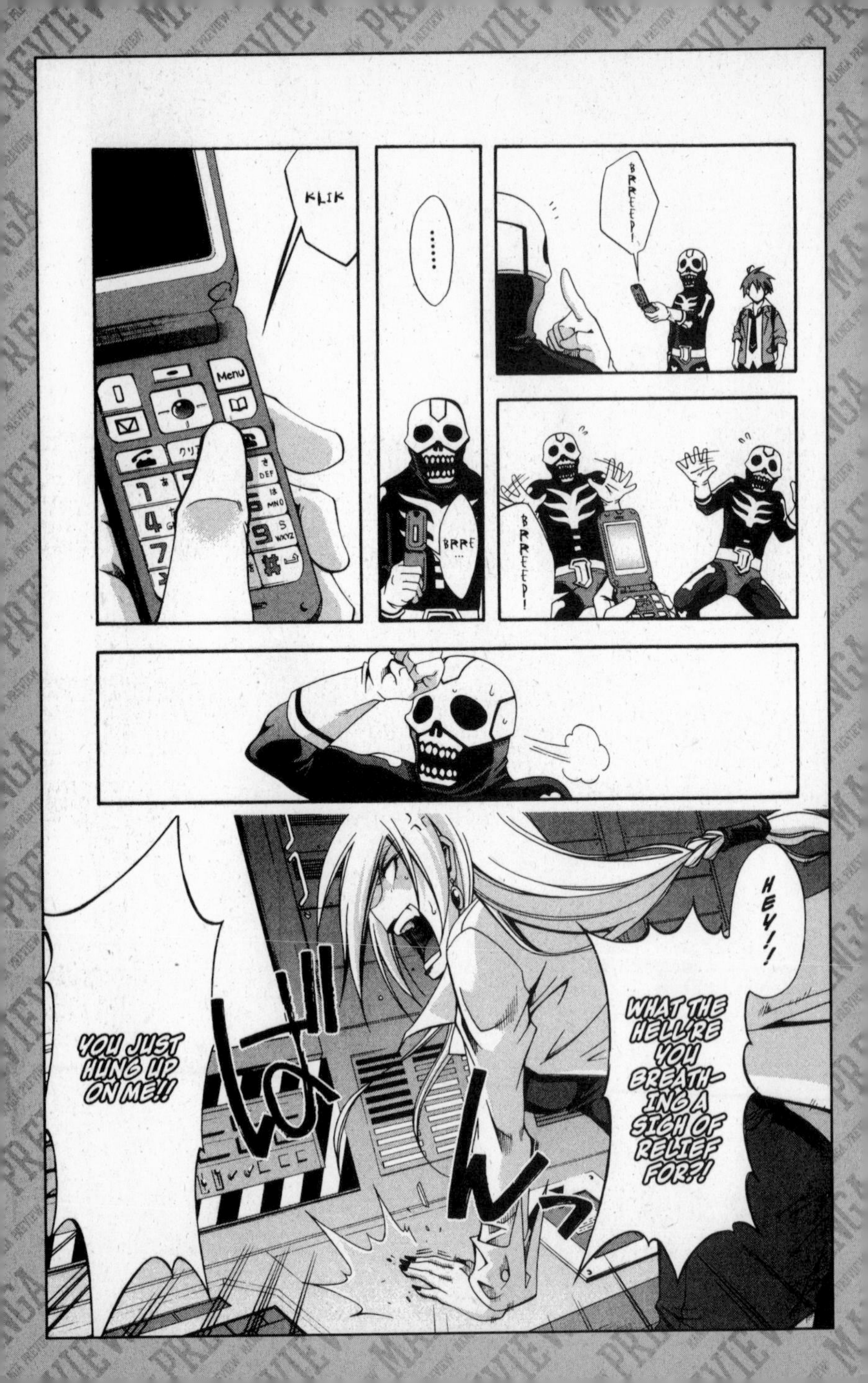
BRREEEP!
BRREEP!
……
BRRE…
KLIK
HEY!!
WHAT THE HELL'RE YOU BREATHING A SIGH OF RELIEF FOR?!
ばんっ
YOU JUST HUNG UP ON ME!!

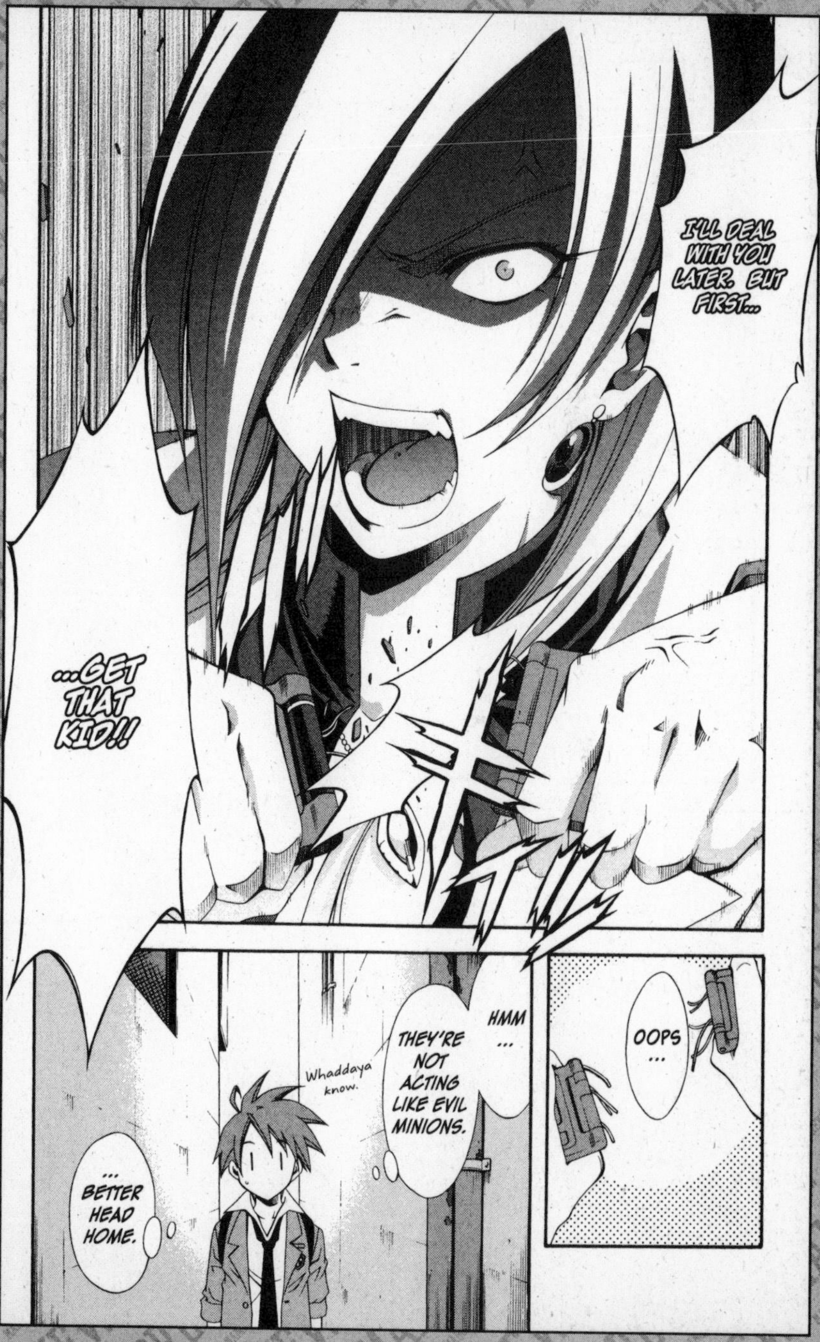
I'LL DEAL WITH YOU LATER. BUT FIRST...
...GET THAT KID!!
OOPS ...
HMM ...
THEY'RE NOT ACTING LIKE EVIL MINIONS.
Whaddaya know.
... BETTER HEAD HOME.

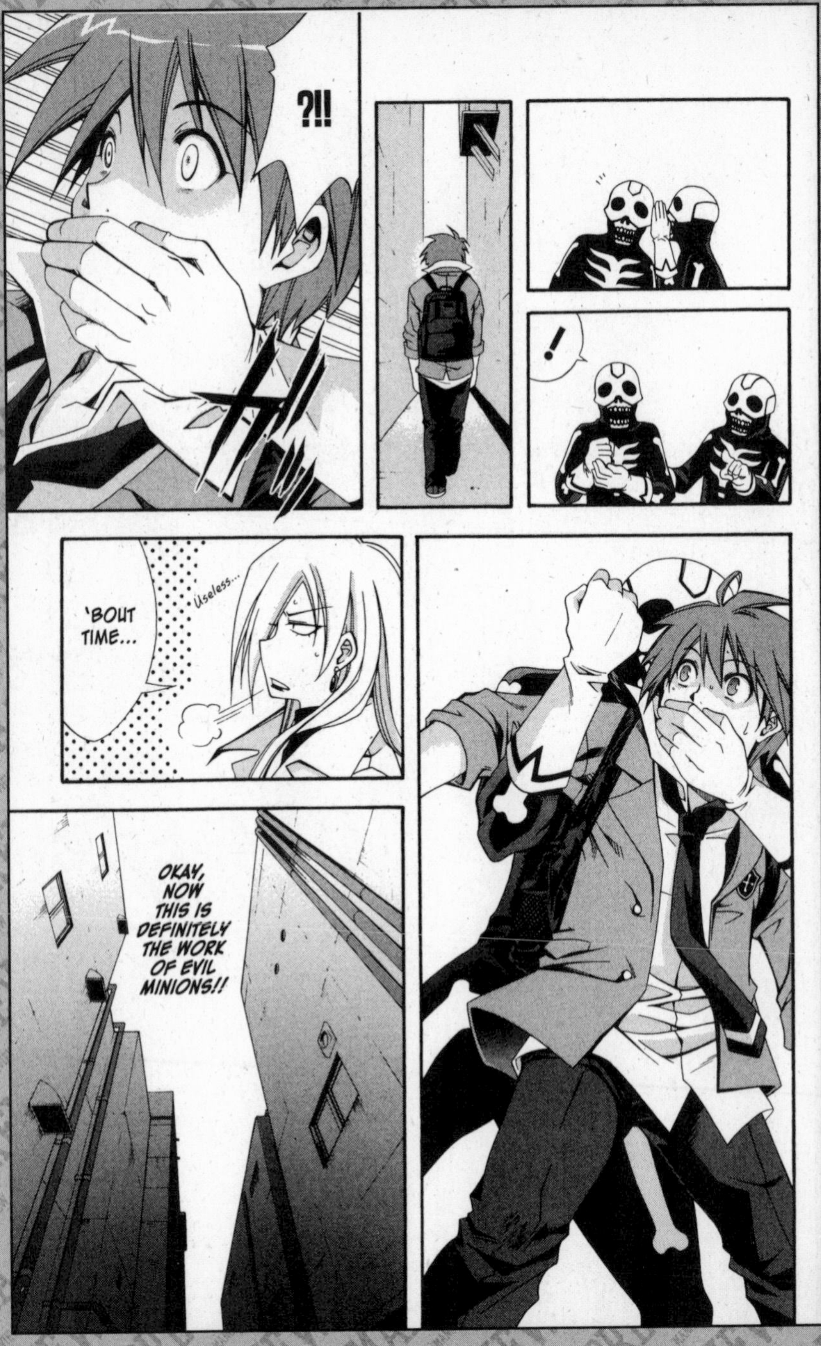
!
?!!
'BOUT TIME...
Useless...
OKAY, NOW THIS IS DEFINITELY THE WORK OF EVIL MINIONS!!

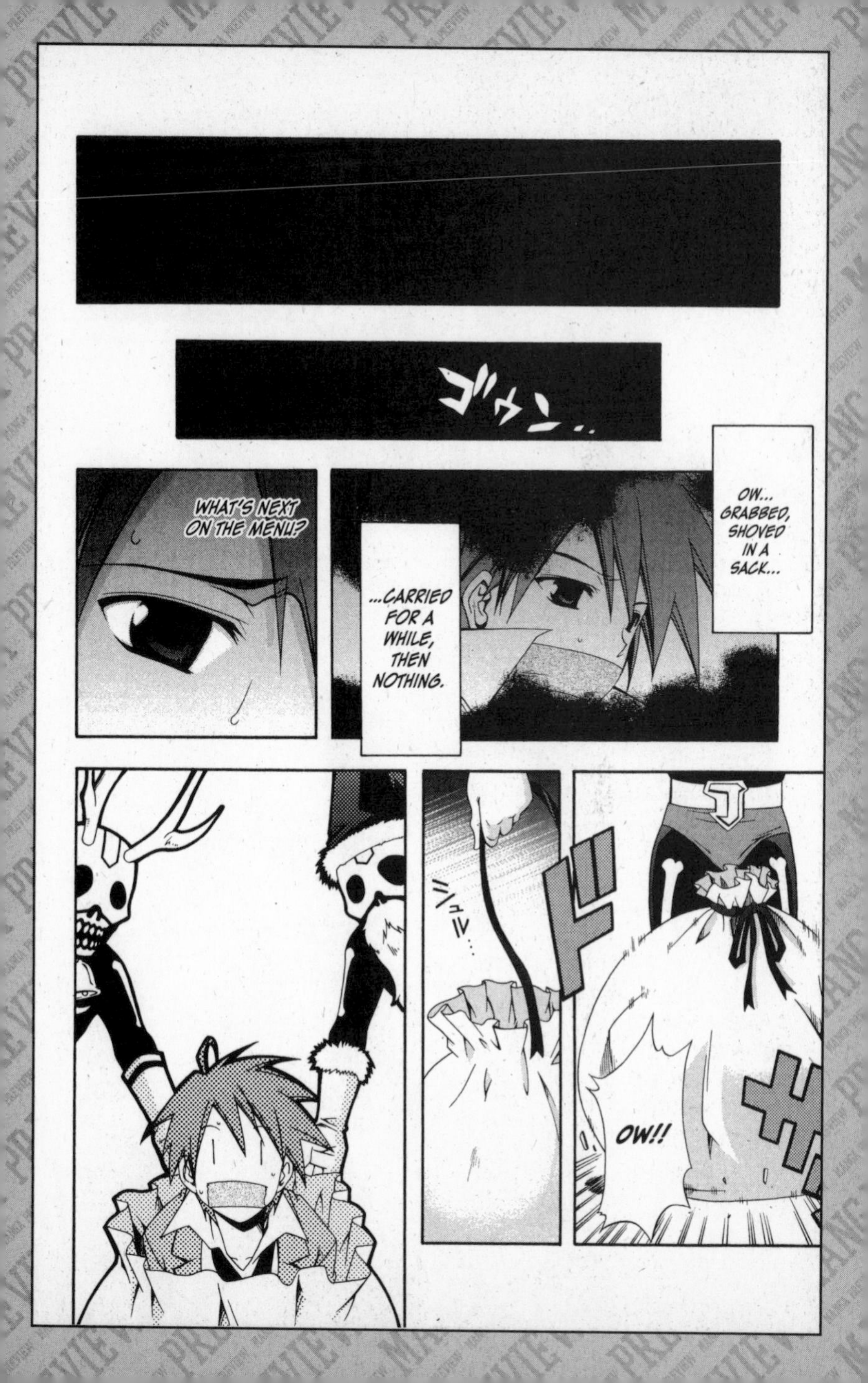
ゴゥン..
OW... GRABBED, SHOVED IN A SACK...
...CARRIED FOR A WHILE, THEN NOTHING.
WHAT'S NEXT ON THE MENU?
ド
OW!!
シュル…

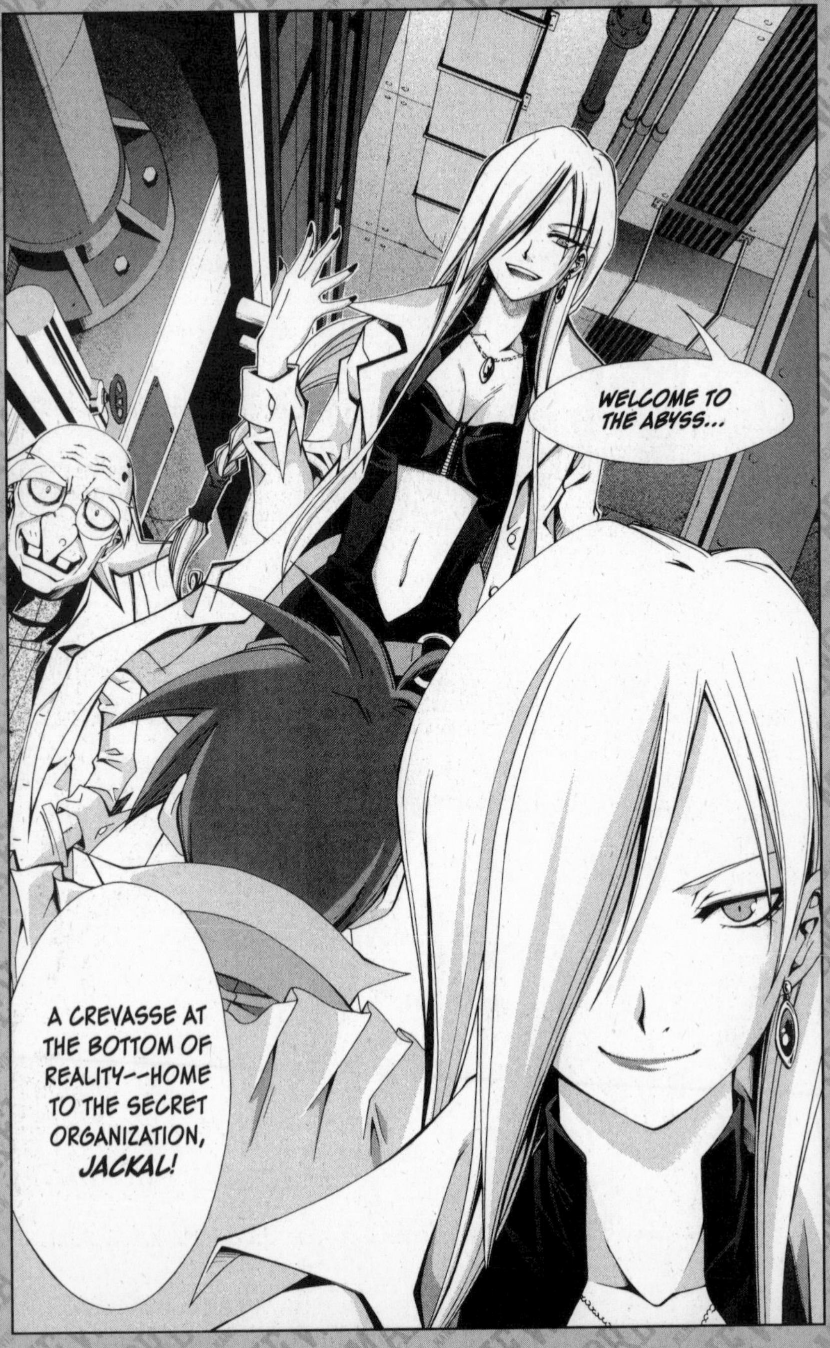
WELCOME TO THE ABYSS...
A CREVASSE AT THE BOTTOM OF REALITY--HOME TO THE SECRET ORGANIZATION, JACKAL!

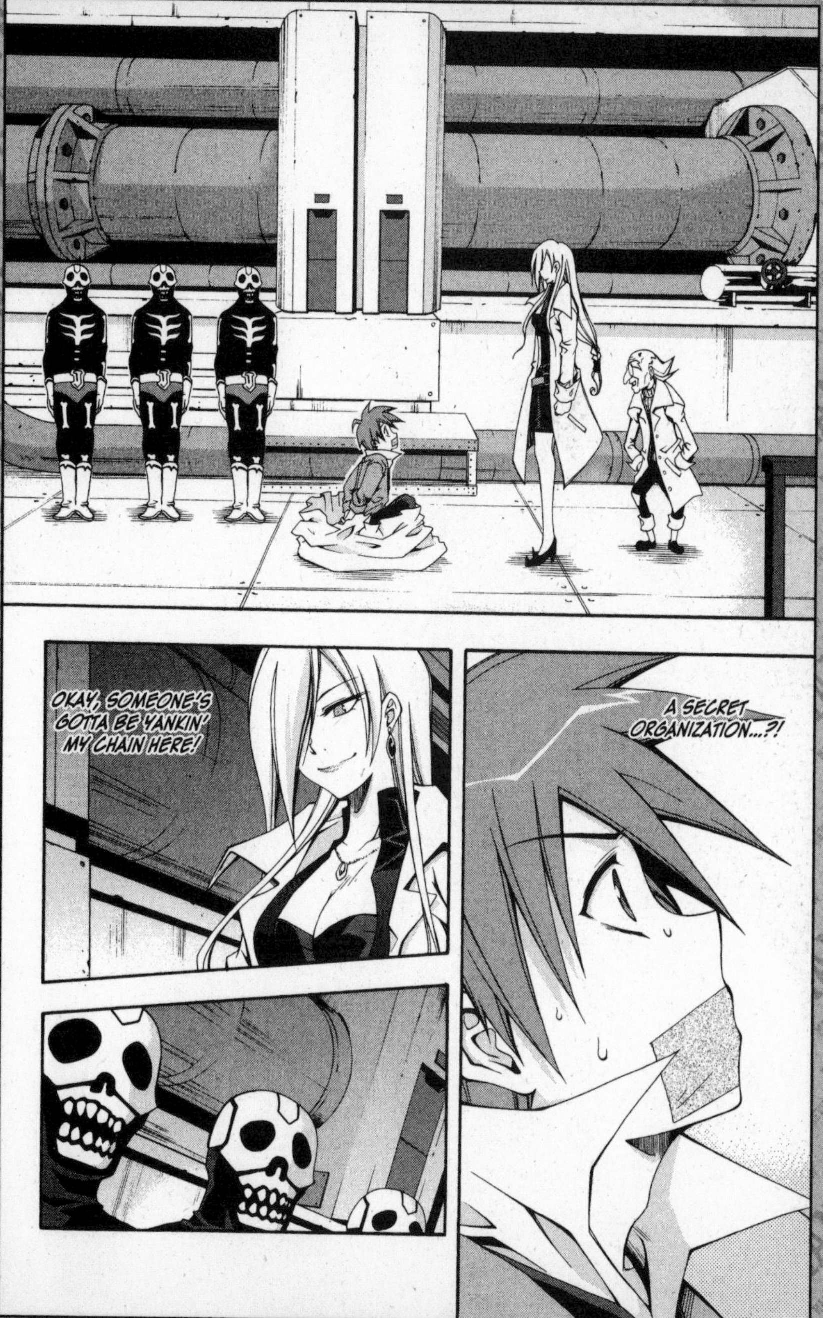
A SECRET ORGANIZATION...?!
OKAY, SOMEONE'S GOTTA BE YANKIN' MY CHAIN HERE!

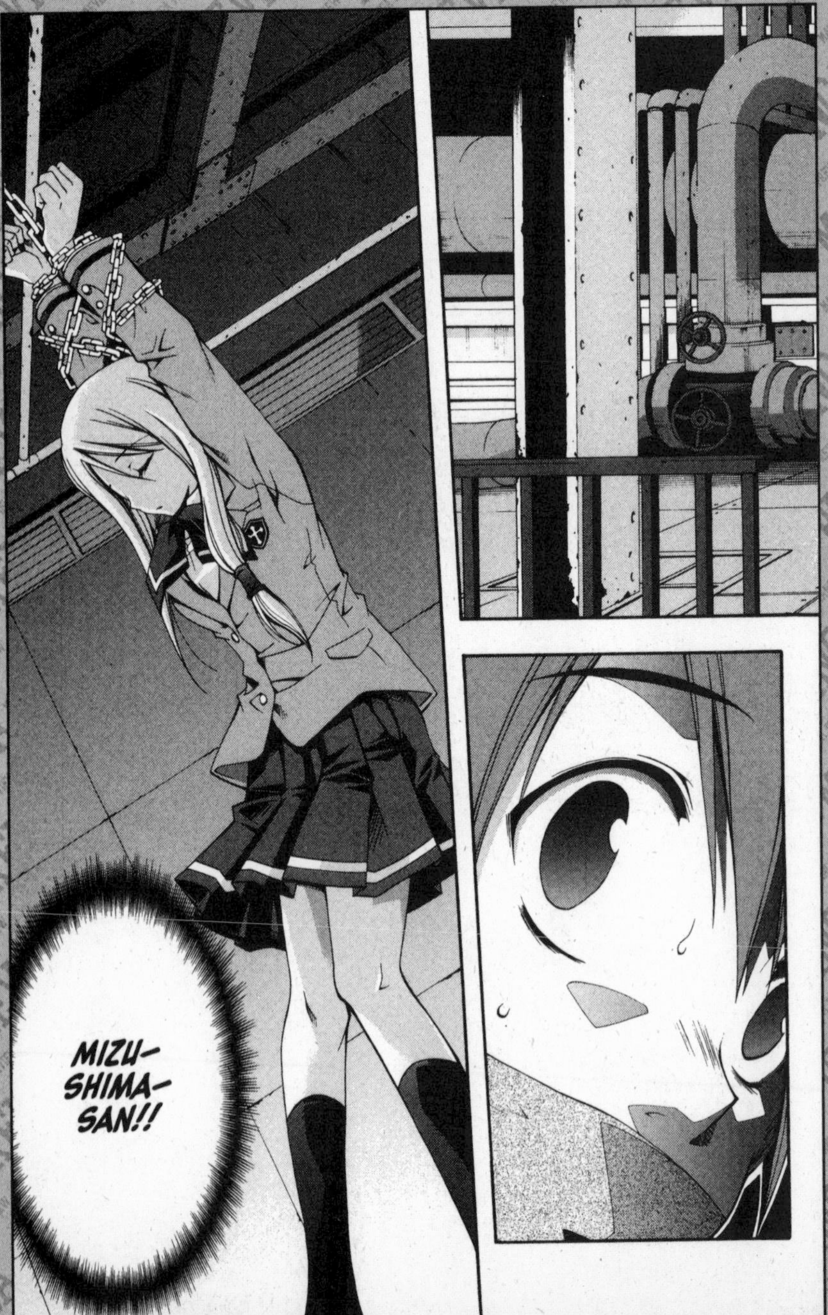
MIZU-
SHIMA-
SAN!!

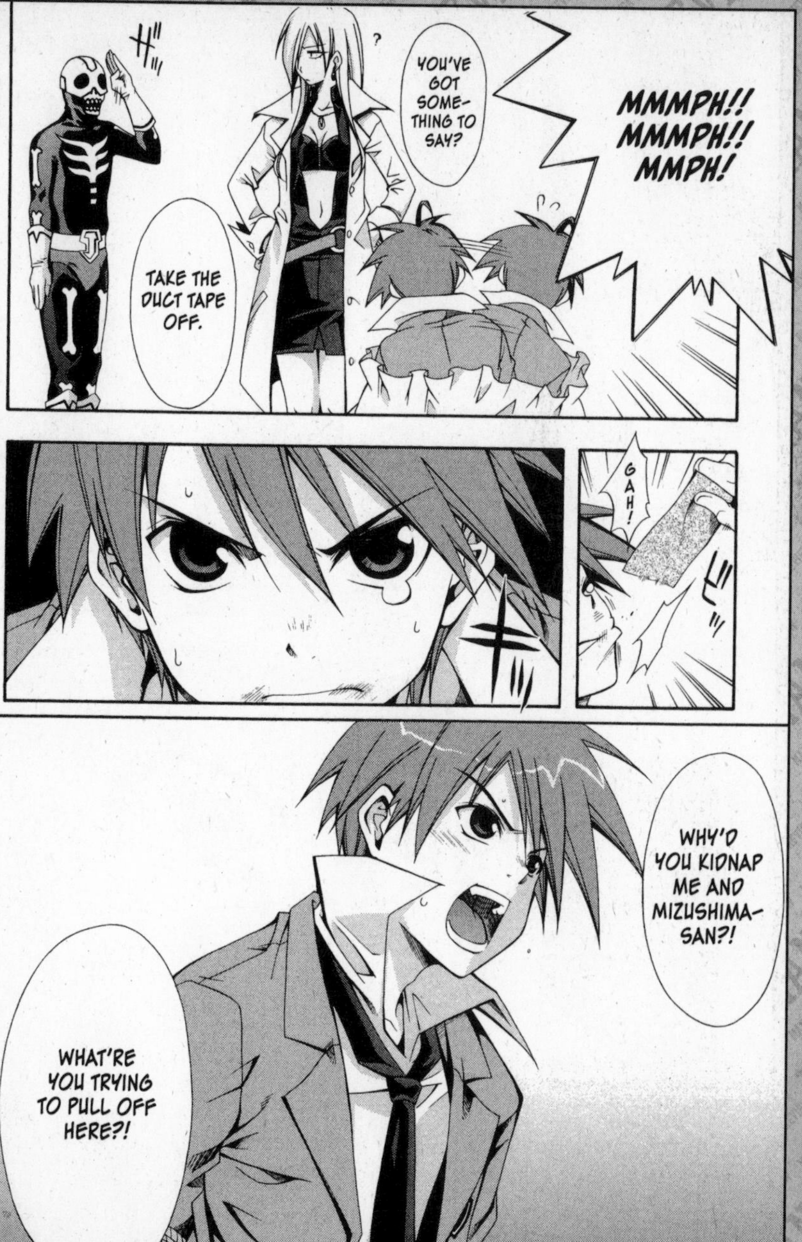
MMMPH!! MMMPH!! MMPH!
YOU'VE GOT SOME-THING TO SAY?
TAKE THE DUCT TAPE OFF.
GAH!
WHY'D YOU KIDNAP ME AND MIZUSHIMA-SAN?!
WHAT'RE YOU TRYING TO PULL OFF HERE?!

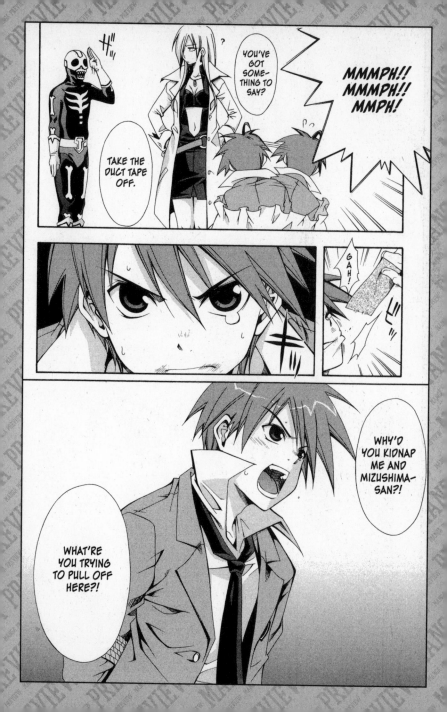

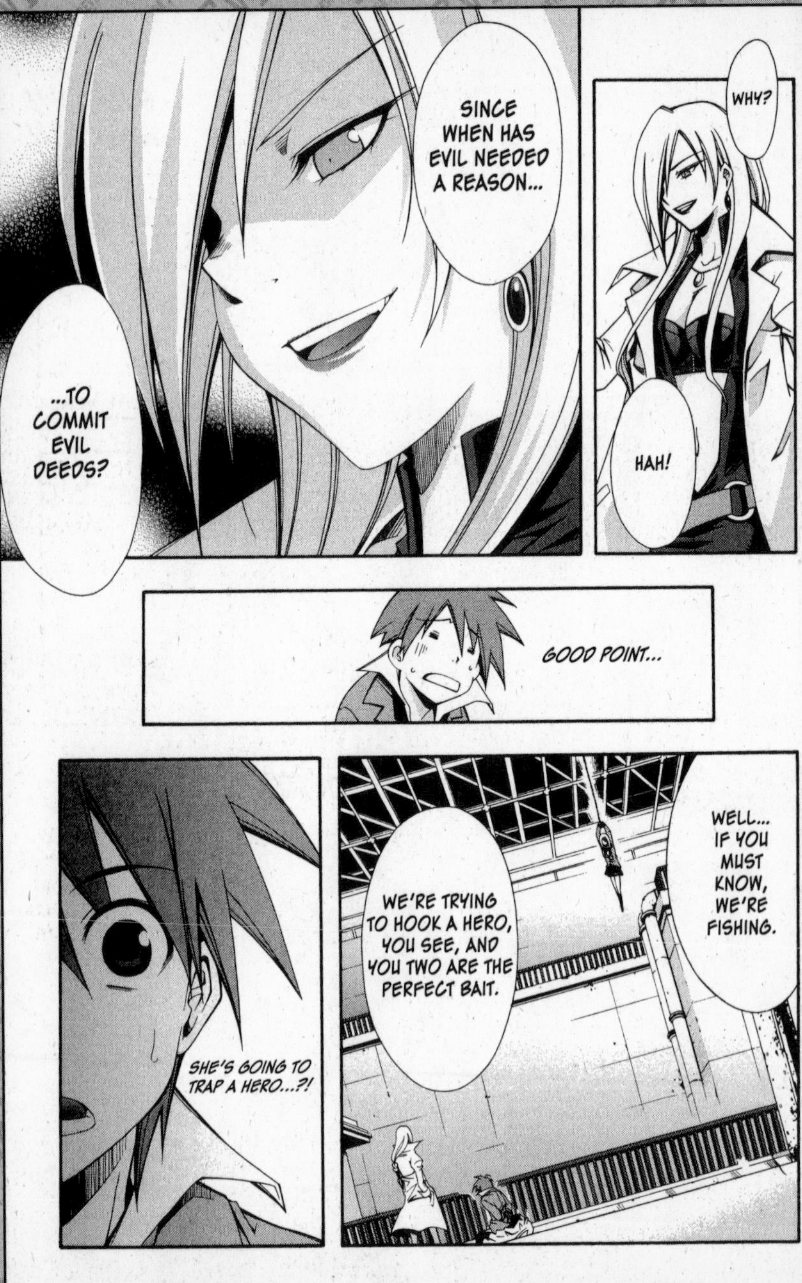
WHY?
HAH!
SINCE WHEN HAS EVIL NEEDED A REASON...
...TO COMMIT EVIL DEEDS?
GOOD POINT...
WELL... IF YOU MUST KNOW, WE'RE FISHING.
WE'RE TRYING TO HOOK A HERO, YOU SEE, AND YOU TWO ARE THE PERFECT BAIT.
SHE'S GOING TO TRAP A HERO...?!

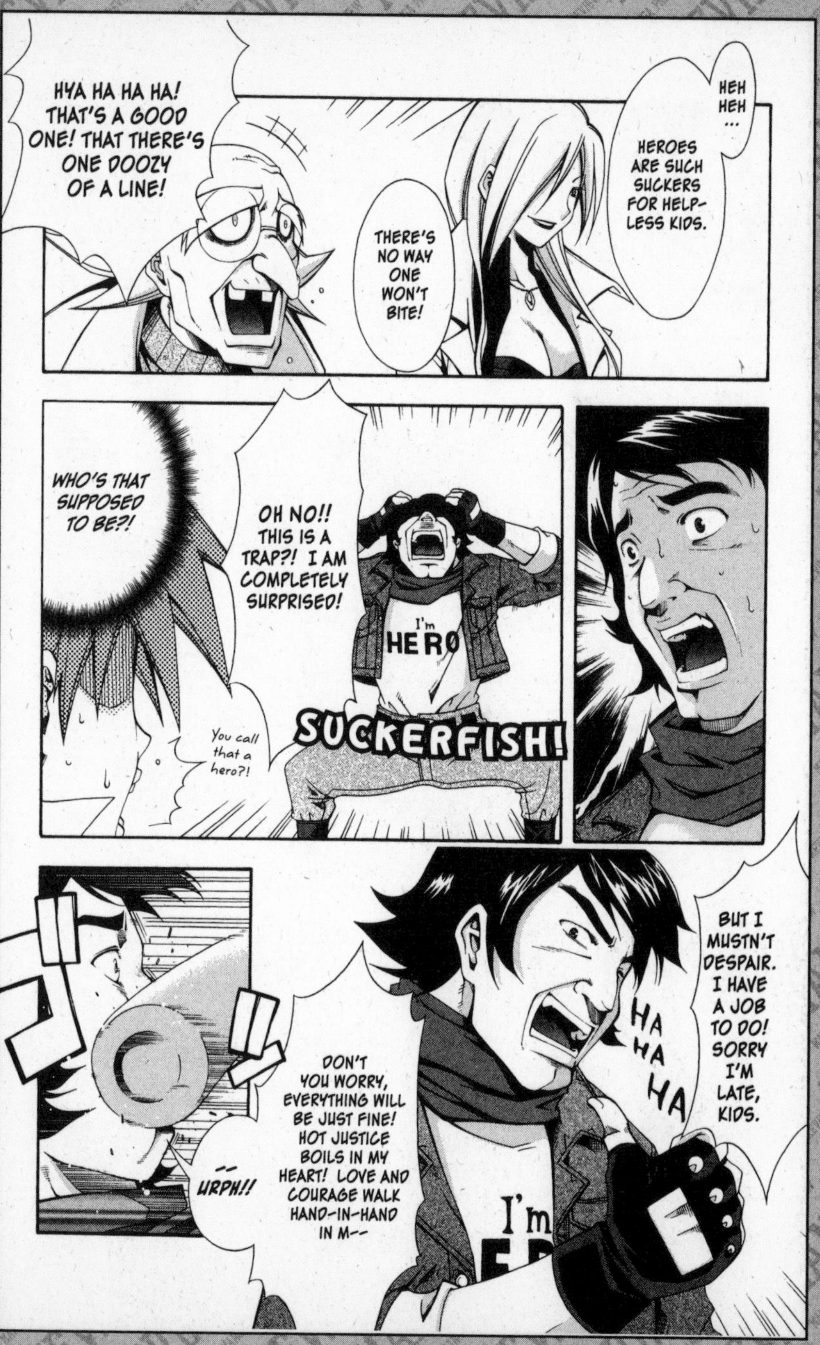
HEH HEH ...
HEROES ARE SUCH SUCKERS FOR HELP-LESS KIDS.
THERE'S NO WAY ONE WON'T BITE!
HYA HA HA HA! THAT'S A GOOD ONE! THAT THERE'S ONE DOOZY OF A LINE!
OH NO!! THIS IS A TRAP?! I AM COMPLETELY SURPRISED!
I'm HERO
WHO'S THAT SUPPOSED TO BE?!
SUCKERFISH!
You call that a hero?!
BUT I MUSTN'T DESPAIR. I HAVE A JOB TO DO! SORRY I'M LATE, KIDS.
HA HA HA
DON'T YOU WORRY, EVERYTHING WILL BE JUST FINE! HOT JUSTICE BOILS IN MY HEART! LOVE AND COURAGE WALK HAND-IN-HAND IN M--
I'm
-- URPH!!

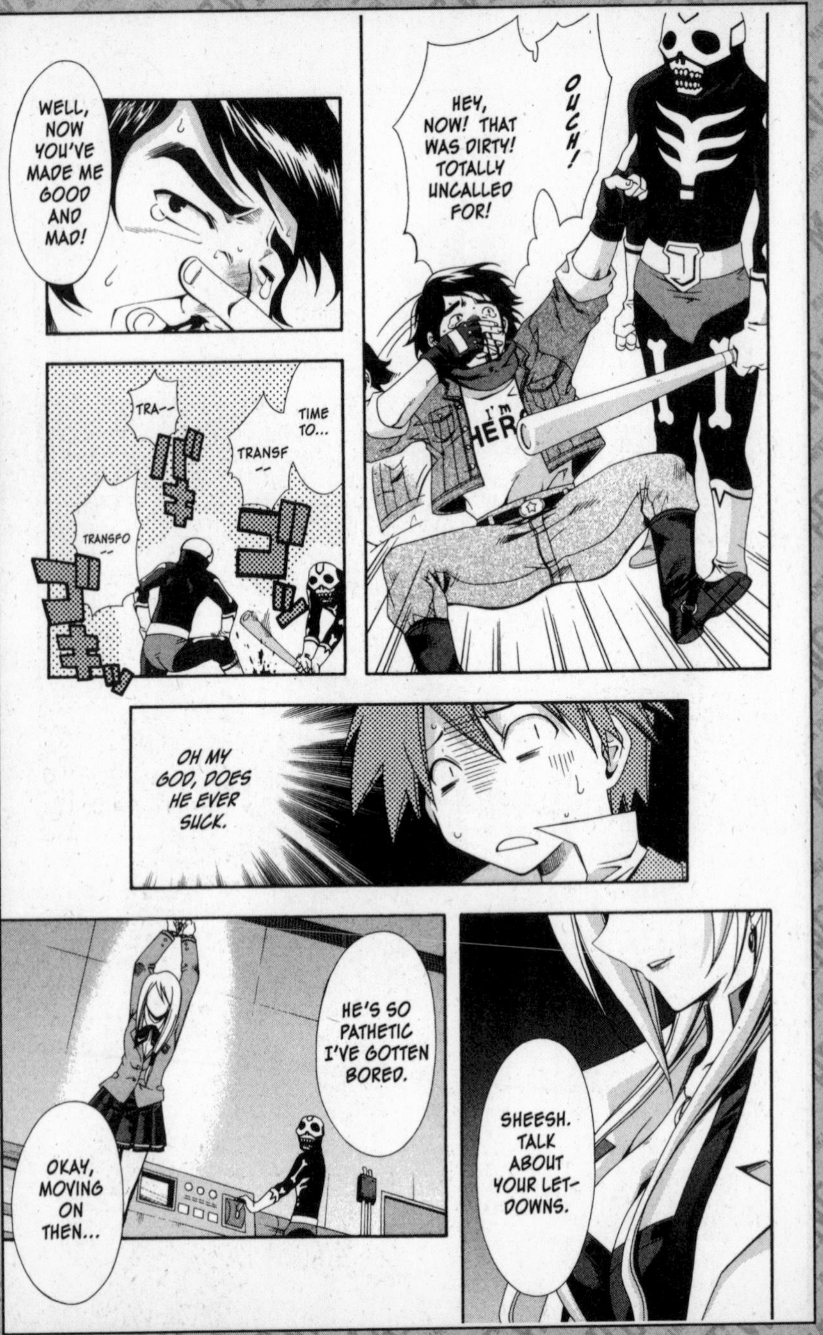
OUCH!
HEY, NOW! THAT WAS DIRTY! TOTALLY UNCALLED FOR!
WELL, NOW YOU'VE MADE ME GOOD AND MAD!
TIME TO...
TRA--
TRANSF --
TRANSFO --
OH MY GOD, DOES HE EVER SUCK.
SHEESH. TALK ABOUT YOUR LET-DOWNS.
HE'S SO PATHETIC I'VE GOTTEN BORED.
OKAY, MOVING ON THEN...

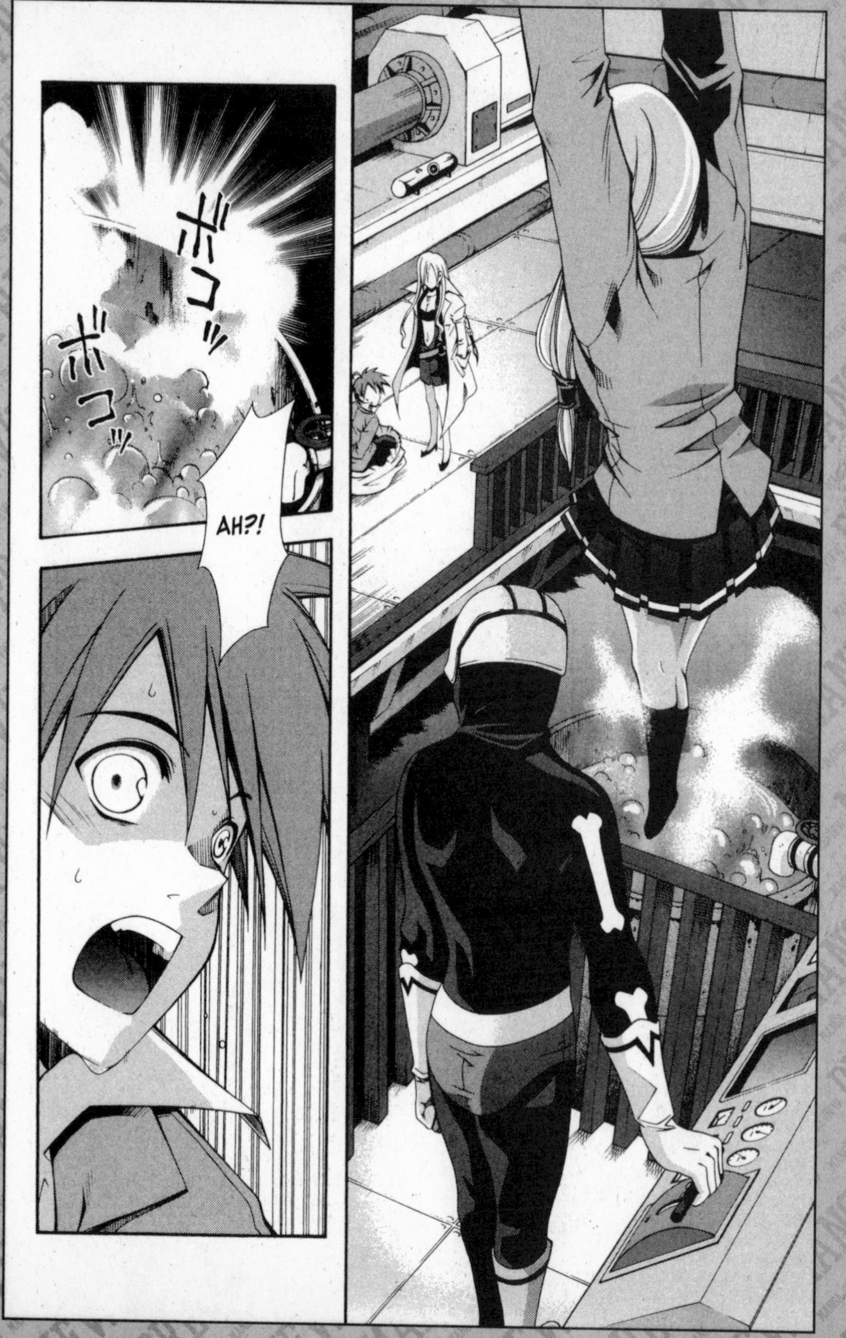
ボコッ
ボコッ
AH?!

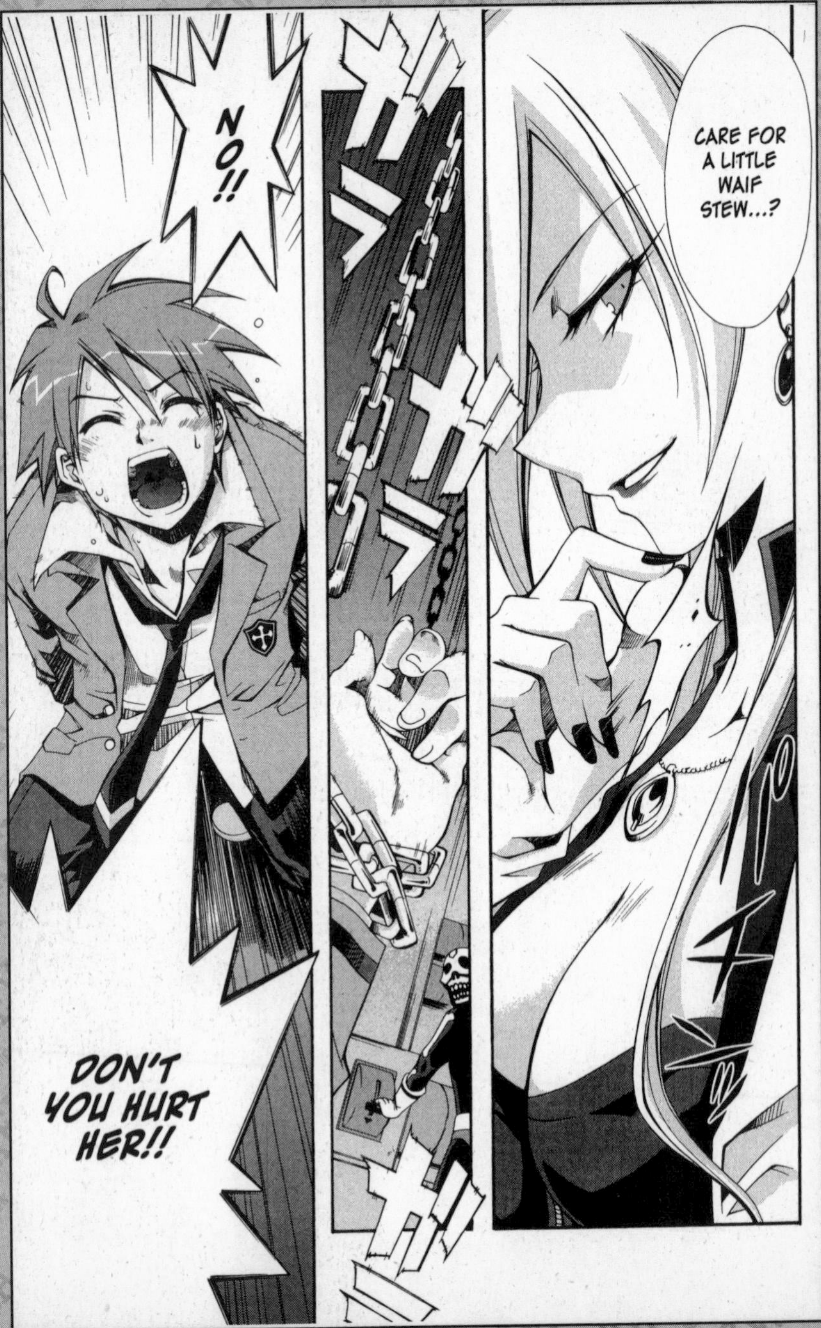
CARE FOR A LITTLE WAIF STEW...?
NO!!
DON'T YOU HURT HER!!

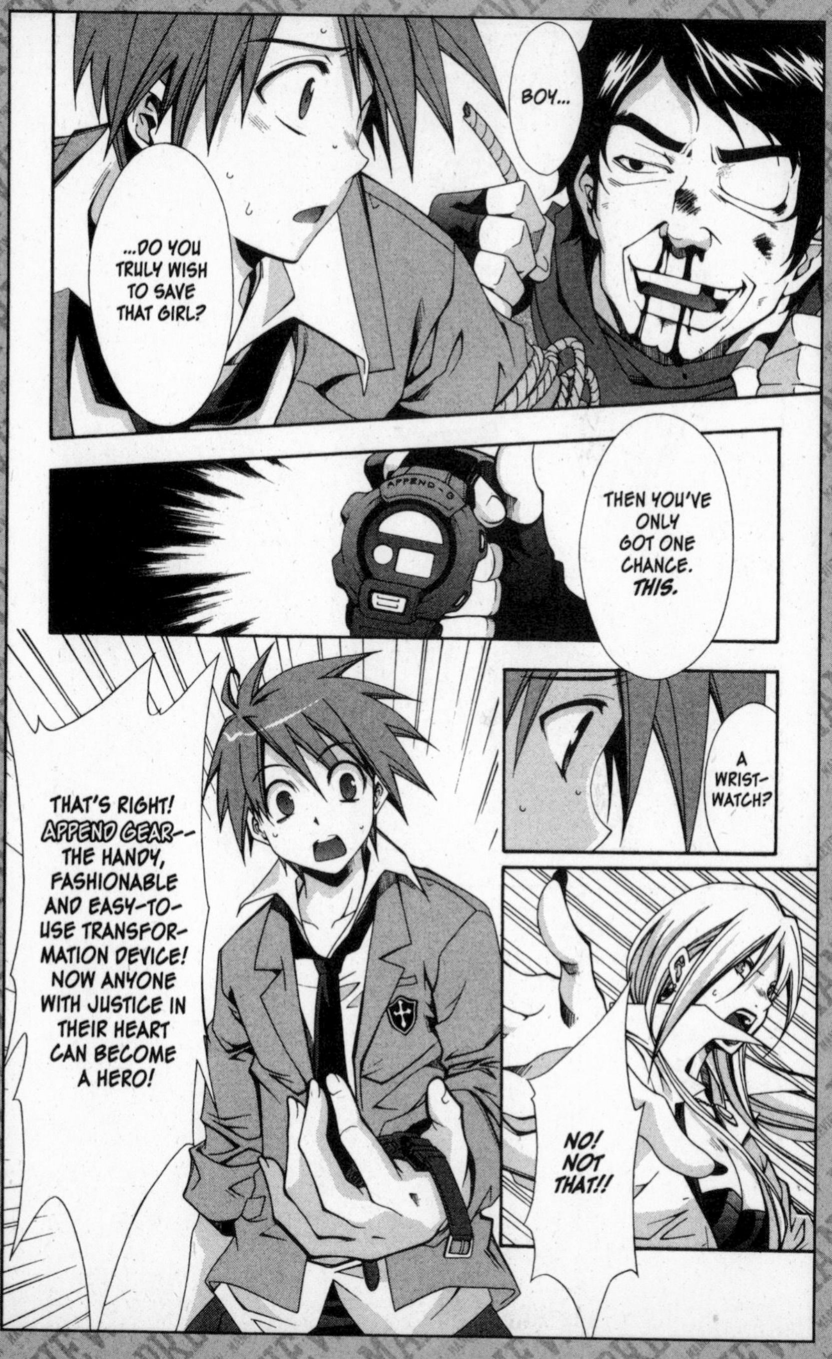
BOY...
...DO YOU TRULY WISH TO SAVE THAT GIRL?
APPEND-G
THEN YOU'VE ONLY GOT ONE CHANCE. *THIS.*
A WRIST-WATCH?
NO! NOT THAT!!
THAT'S RIGHT! APPEND GEAR--THE HANDY, FASHIONABLE AND EASY-TO-USE TRANSFORMATION DEVICE! NOW ANYONE WITH JUSTICE IN THEIR HEART CAN BECOME A HERO!

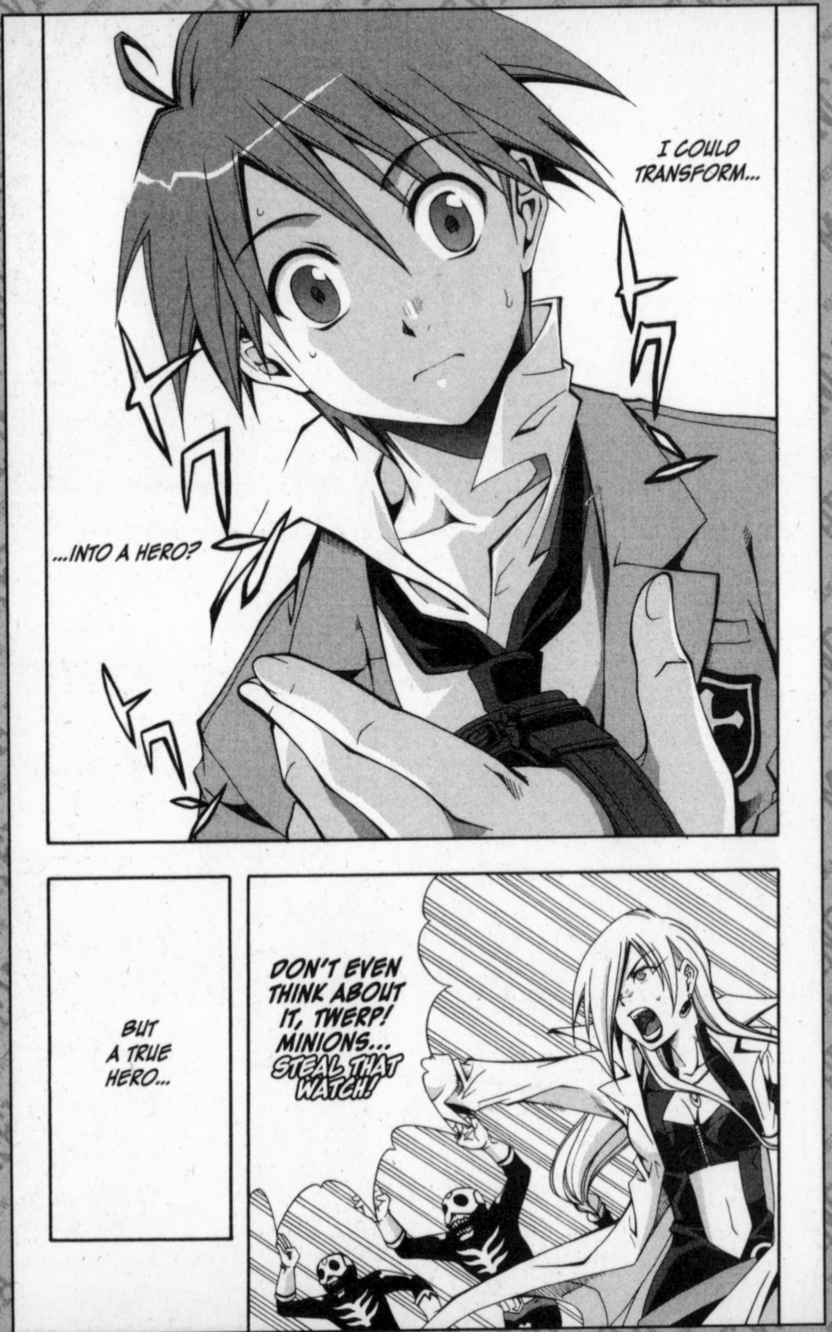
I COULD TRANSFORM...
...INTO A HERO?
DON'T EVEN THINK ABOUT IT, TWERP! MINIONS... STEAL THAT WATCH!
BUT A TRUE HERO...

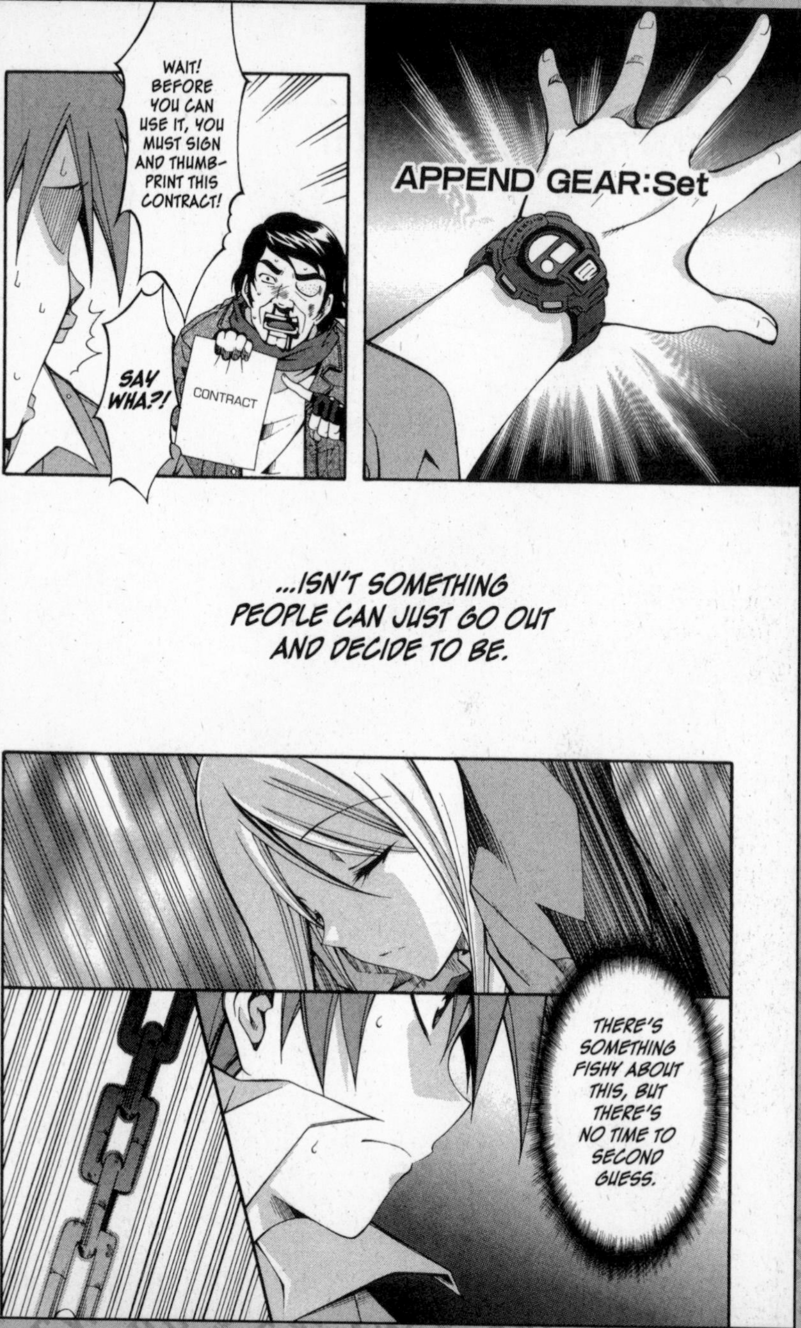
APPEND GEAR:Set
WAIT! BEFORE YOU CAN USE IT, YOU MUST SIGN AND THUMB-PRINT THIS CONTRACT!
CONTRACT
SAY WHA?!
...ISN'T SOMETHING PEOPLE CAN JUST GO OUT AND DECIDE TO BE.
THERE'S SOMETHING FISHY ABOUT THIS, BUT THERE'S NO TIME TO SECOND GUESS.

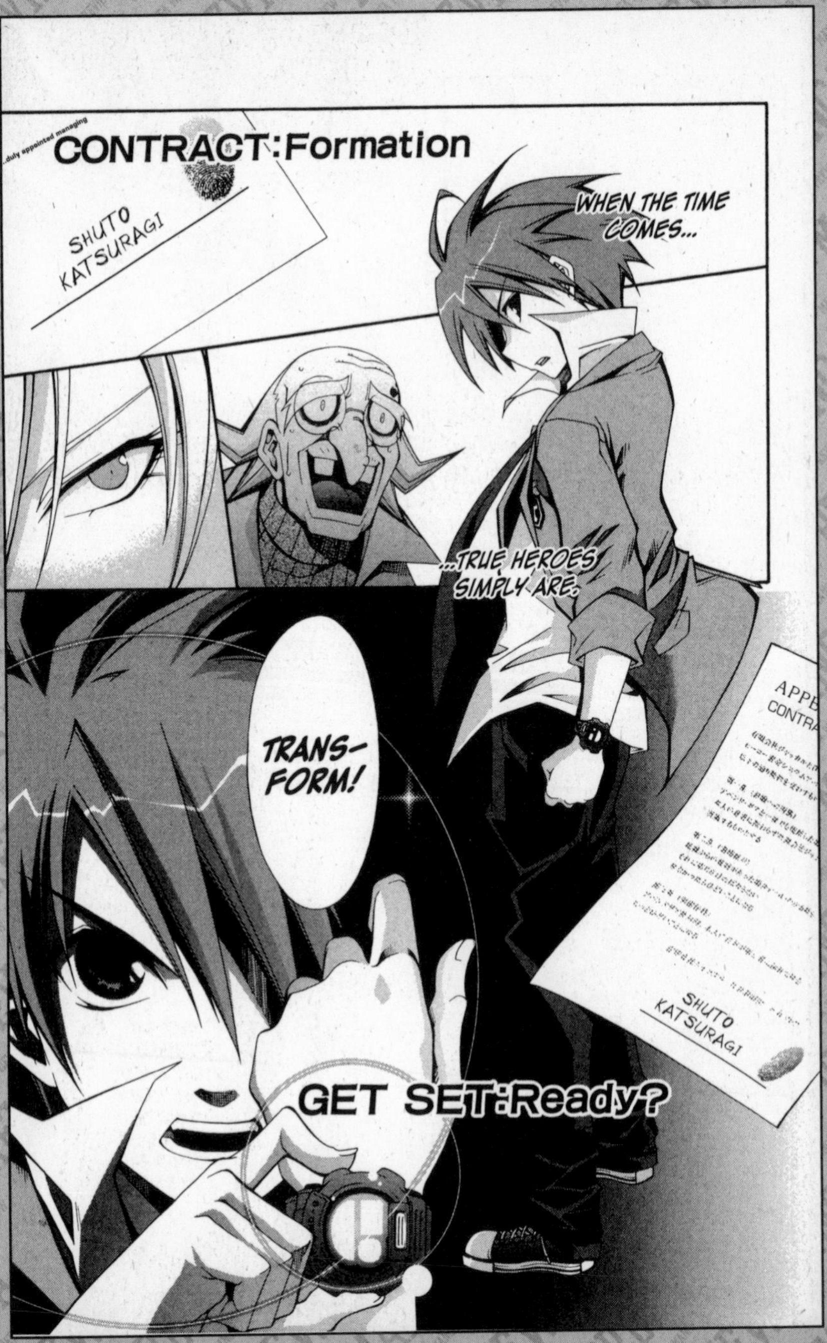
...duly appointed managing
CONTRACT:Formation
SHUTO KATSURAGI
WHEN THE TIME COMES...
...TRUE HEROES SIMPLY ARE.
TRANS-FORM!
SHUTO KATSURAGI
GET SET:Ready?

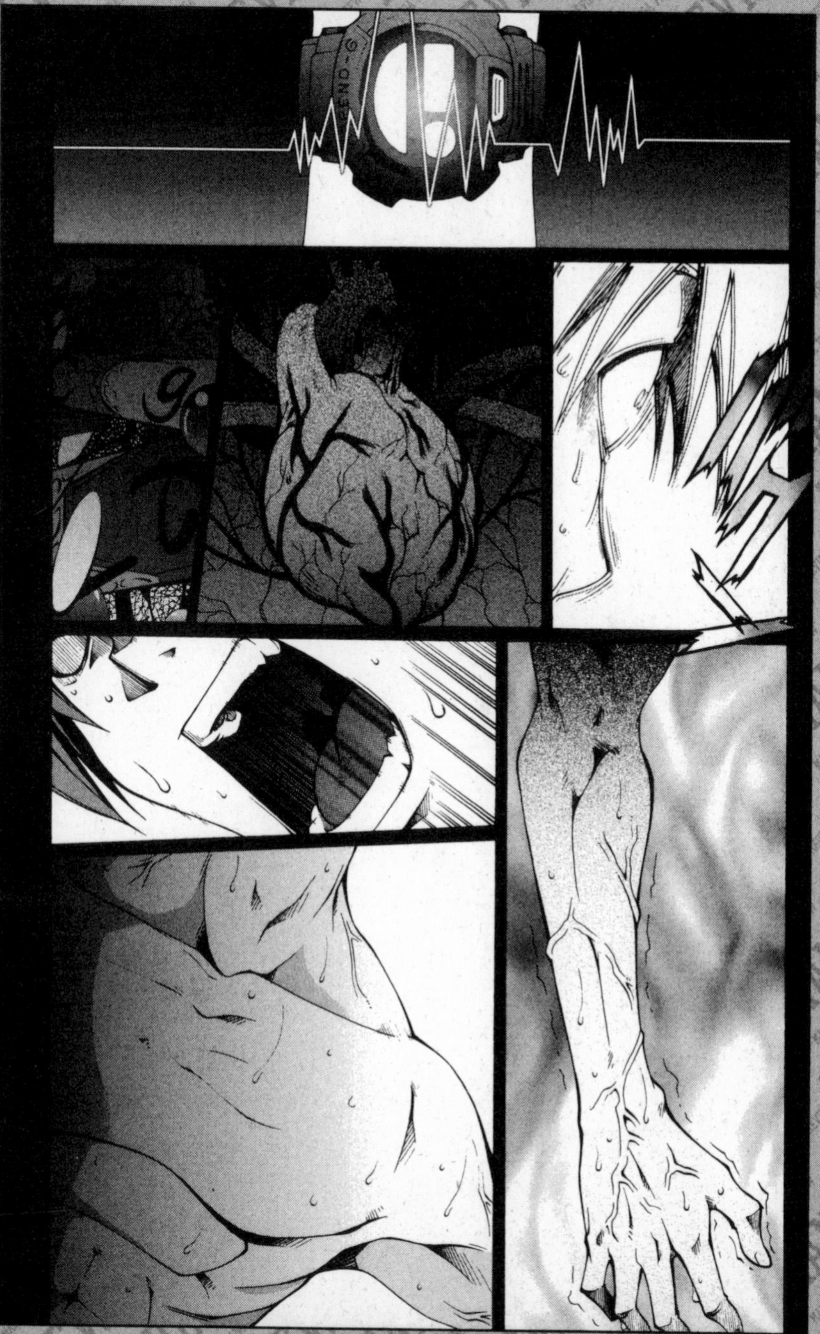
END-G

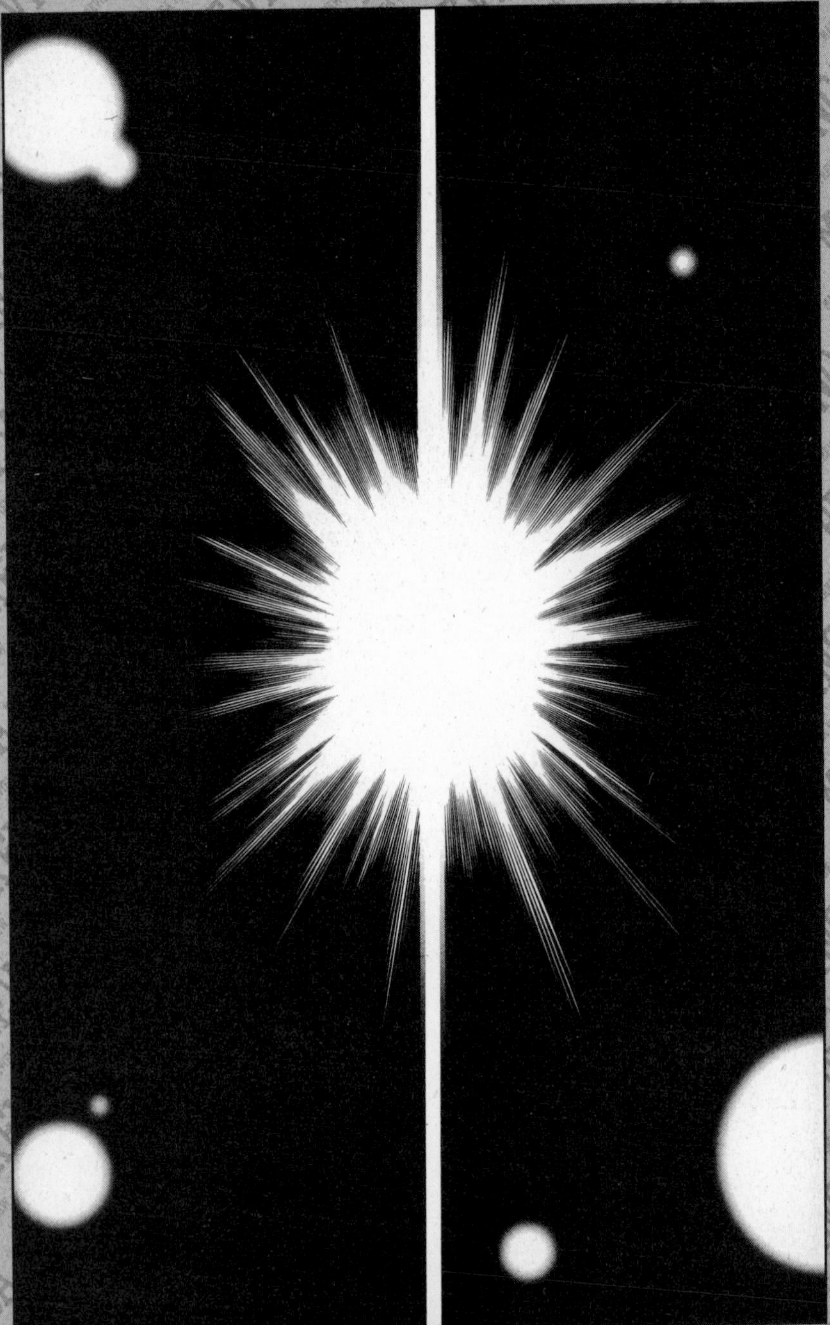

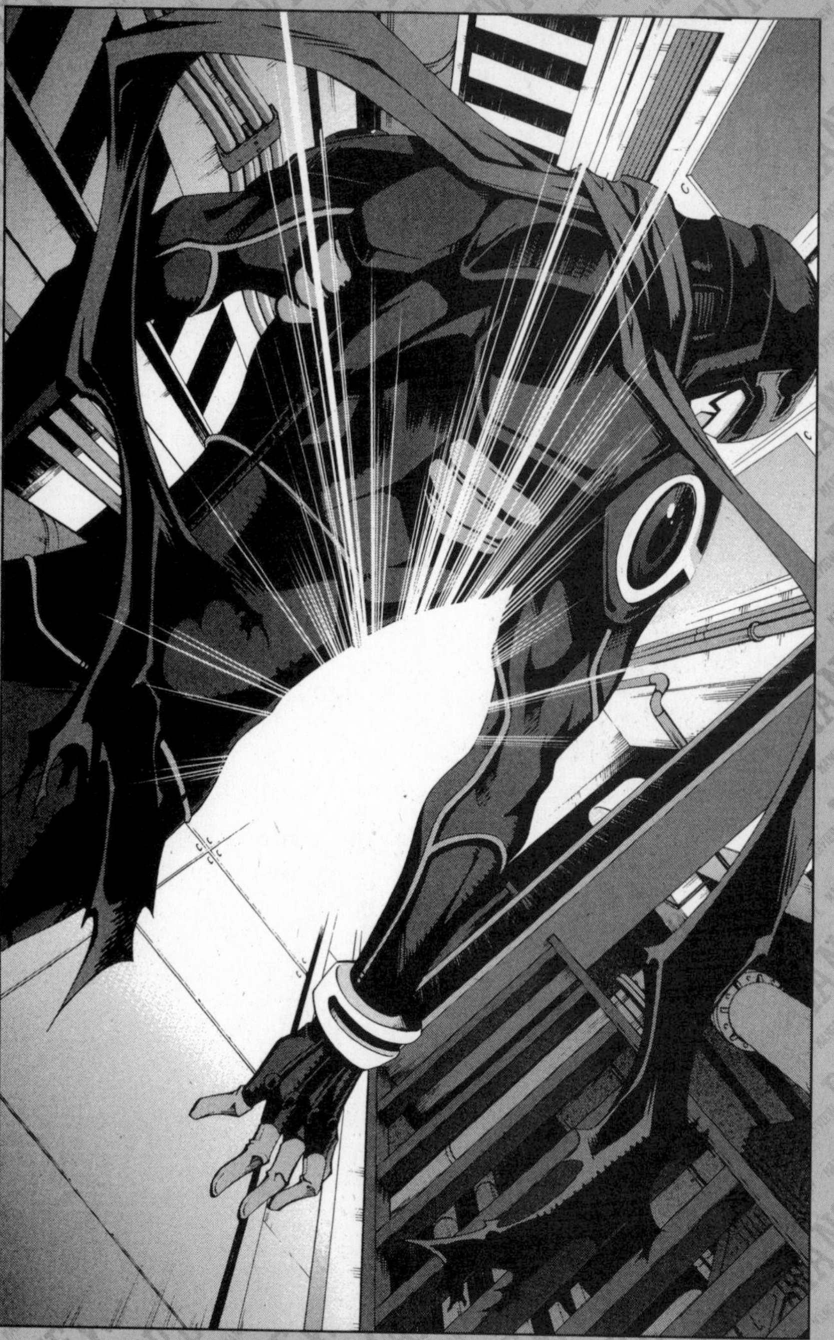

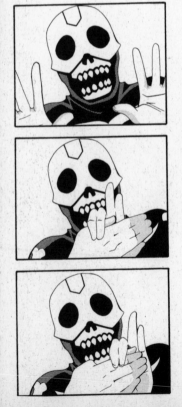

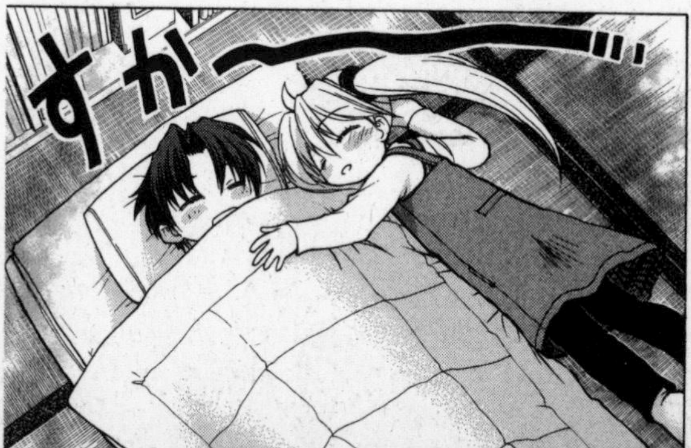
すか～～～～

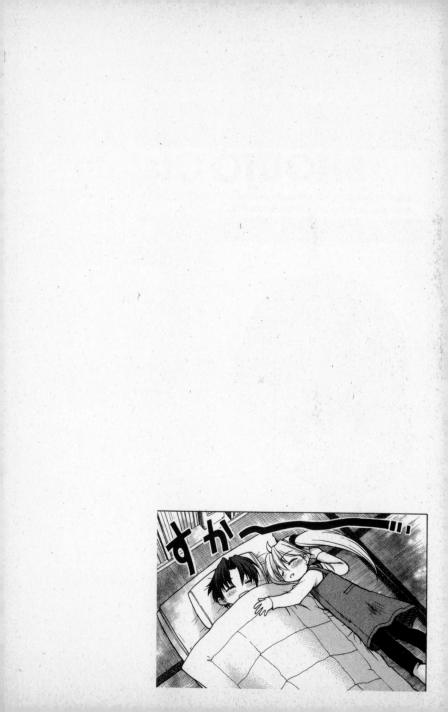

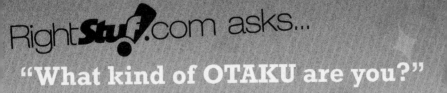

WHEN YOU CAN OWN ANY SERIES
FOR UNDER 30 BUCKS,
ONLY ONE QUESTION REMAINS UNANSWERED...

WHICH ONE DO I CHOOSE?!

THIS ONE?

OR... BOTH?

WALTER
Addictus Animemus

DISCOVER HOW IT ALL BEGAN

AN EVIL, ANCIENT AND HUNGRY, IS ROAMING THE
BADLANDS OF THE OLD WEST. IT SPARES NOT MAN,
WOMAN NOR CHILD, DEVOURING ALL THAT STAND
BEFORE IT. ONLY ONE MAN CAN STOP IT...A MYSTERIOUS
PRIEST WITH A CROSS CARVED INTO HIS HEAD. HIS NAME
IS IVAN ISAACS, AND HE WILL SMOTE ALL EVIL IN
A HAIL OF HOT LEAD. HALLELUJAH.

MIN-WOO HYUNG'S INTERNATIONAL MANWHA SENSATION RETURNS
WITH SPECIAL COLLECTOR'S EDITIONS FOR FANS OLD & NEW!

© MIN-WOO HYUNG, DAIWON C.I. INC.

Collect Them All!

The World Is Back, and It Will Surprise You!

Two years after the popular video game The World was shut down, Tokio Kuryuu cannot wait for The World R:X to come out. Unfortunately for him, he forgets to reserve a copy and finds himself without access. That is, until a beautiful new transfer student suddenly and mysteriously forces Tokio into the game and makes him her servant!

Preview at www.TOKYOPOP.com/hack_Link

STOP!

This is the back of the book.
You wouldn't want to spoil a great ending!

This book is printed "manga-style," in the authentic Japanese right-to-left format. Since none of the artwork has been flipped or altered, readers get to experience the story just as the creator intended. You've been asking for it, so TOKYOPOP® delivered: authentic, hot-off-the-press, and far more fun!

1
2
3
4
5
6
7
8
9
10

DIRECTIONS

If this is your first time reading manga-style, here's a quick guide to help you understand how it works.

It's easy... just start in the top right panel and follow the numbers. Have fun, and look for more 100% authentic manga from TOKYOPOP®!

THE MANGA REVOLUTION · LEADING THE MANGA REVOLUTION · LEADING
漫画革命